THE SMALL BUSI

THE Small Business GUIDE

SOURCES OF INFORMATION FOR NEW AND SMALL BUSINESSES

COLIN BARROW

BRITISH BROADCASTING CORPORATION

First published in conjunction with
the BBC Television series *Business Club*

The series is produced by John Twitchin

The illustration on the front cover of
the book is by Stuart Hughes

The author would like to thank the following people and
organisations for their help in compiling and checking material in
this guide:

Lucinda Dean, David Hibbs, Rosemarie McLavy, Thames
Polytechnic, The Thames Enterprise Agency Limited, Shell UK PLC
and the London Borough of Greenwich;

Chris Miller of Birmingham University for the use of her Local
Authority survey;

Peter Saunders of Thames Polytechnic for his bookkeeping survey;

Philip Beresford of *The Sunday Telegraph* for use of his Enterprise
Zone table;

The National Westminster Bank PLC for permission to reproduce
their business checklist.

First published 1982 Revised edition first published 1984
Published by the British Broadcasting Corporation
35 Marylebone High Street, London W1A 1AA
ISBN 0 563 21110 5

This book is set in Century
by Input Typesetting Limited, London
Printed and bound in England by
Pitman Press Limited, Bath

CONTENTS

5

SECTION 5   Finding out about your Market   **164**

SECTION 6   Raising the Money   **210**

SECTION 7 Business and the Law 263

SECTION 12 Indices 353

THE NEED FOR INFORMATION

Starting a new business is no longer a spectator sport. Nearly two million people are now working for themselves, with a record 140,000 new recruits in 1983. But to launch a small business or expand an existing one successfully is not a simple task. Good ideas, hard work, enthusiasm, skills, and knowledge about your product and how to make it, though essential, are not enough. Evidence for this is the ever-increasing volume of business failures and liquidations. In 1982, when the first edition of this guide was published, firms were folding at a record rate and that upward trend continued through 1983 and the opening months of 1984. Various estimates put the number of business 'deaths' last year at around 120,000, with some 40% of failures occurring within the first few years. These facts have made it increasingly clear that small businesses need special help, particularly in their formative period. For example, owners and managers often need help in acquiring business skills in such areas as basic book-keeping and accounting. Most failing businesses simply do not know their financial position. The order book is very often full when the cash runs out. Then they need information with which to make realistic assessments of the size and possibilities of their chosen market. Over-optimism about the size and ease with which a market can be reached is an all too common mistake.

Owners and managers also need to know what sorts of finance are available and how to put themselves in the best possible position to raise it. Surprisingly, there is no shortage of funds. Problems lie, rather, in the business proposition itself, or, more often, in the way in which the proposition is made to the financier. This calls for a 'business plan', a statement of business purpose, with the consequences spelt out in financial terms. For example, you must describe what you want your business to do, who its customers will be, how much they will spend, who will supply you, how much their supplies will cost. Then you must translate those plans and projections into cash; how much your business will need; how much you already have; how much you expect 'outsiders' to put in. For most people this calls for new knowledge. They have never prepared a business plan before, and they do not know how to start. Very often the same is true of the bank manager they are talking to, so they too may need help or education in this important area.

This plan will also help them to escape the 'pneumonia' of small businesses – underestimation of the amount of start-up capital they will need. It is difficult, if not impossible, to go back to a bank and ask for another 30% of funding six months after opening the doors, and retain any credibility at all. And yet this is what happens. New businesses consistently underestimate their capital requirements. Small businesses consistently underestimate how much they will need to finance growth. Both end up struggling where they need not have struggled, or failing where there was no 'market' reason for failure. Inventors and technologists have special problems of communication and security when they try to translate their ideas into businesses. All too often their inventions have been left for other countries to exploit, or else they feel unhappy about discussing ideas, believing that a patent is their only protection. But more often than not they simply do not know who to talk to, little realising that sophisticated help is often close at hand. Thus a path from the laboratory to the market-place has to be illuminated so that small firms and inventors can see a clear route. New technologies have to be made available to new business. The microcomputer that has revolutionised big business has now begun to knock on the doors of smaller businesses. For this reason these firms have to know how to exploit this technology and so remain competitive – or they may join the ranks of the failures.

New and revived business opportunities are springing up to meet the needs and aspirations of would-be 'entrepreneurs'. Franchising, workers' co-operatives and management buy-outs are just three such areas. These have grown from relative obscurity in the late 1970s to being major business opportunities in the 1980s. Grants and incentives to start up in rural areas, or in declining city areas are also a new feature of the small business scene.

There is inevitably a spate of paperwork, red tape and legislation surrounding every business venture. The registrations for VAT, pensions for the self-employed and employees' rights very often deter people either from launching into business or expanding in it. They believe, incorrectly, that it is possible to stand still and survive. They also over-estimate the problems and under-estimate the skills of the army of inexpensive professional advisers on hand to educate the novice.

All this implies that in order to keep out of the failure statistics it is vital for the owner or manager of a new or small business to be better informed.

There are now hundreds of organisations and even more publications that can provide the much-needed information for small business. Many of these organisations have only recently come into being. For example in 1979 there were only six active enterprise agencies, whilst in 1982 there were about 100, and this edition lists nearly 200. There has been a parallel growth in other organisations, some shaping their policies to recognise the needs of small ventures, and others being wholly new activities. So 'entrepreneurs' have plenty of help to turn to and evidence is beginning to emerge that those that take this advice improve their chances of survival significantly. They very often do not know where that help is, or just how much it can do for them. This book is a guide to these organisations and their services, and the important directories, books and periodicals that will provide up-to-date information on each main topic. Enough information is generally included to allow a choice of service organisation, or of publications to find and read. The decision to include or exclude an entry is based on two criteria. Does the organisation (or directory) provide either a service or information of specific help to a new or small business? Would the entry simply extend the reader's choice without necessarily extending the possible reward?

This is a reference book and is not intended to be read in its entirety. The reader will need to use the contents pages to focus attention on the areas of greatest interest (or importance) to him or her. The glossary explains any technical words in the text and there are two indices. The first is an index of enterprise agency sponsors, showing what support large organisations are providing to the small business sector. The second is a general index, which complements the contents page and extends the cross-referencing provided in the text.

SOURCES OF DIRECT HELP AND ADVICE

Last year over 500,000 people used the services of a small business advisory organisation. Most were simple telephone enquiries but others involved face to face counselling sessions – perhaps to help raise money or to cope with an in-depth tax problem. There are now over 300 organisations specifically concerned with providing help, advice and resources (including finance) for small businesses and those starting them. For the most part, these services are provided free or at a very low cost. In order to give a better understanding of their nature and purpose it will help to look at them in six groups: National Agencies, Local Enterprise Agencies, Local Councils, Property Services, Enterprise Zones and Business Associations.

NATIONAL AGENCIES

Although all the agencies and advisory services have their roots in the local community, the direct initiative for starting them often came from a central body. Five such bodies are in the forefront of these initiatives.

Small Firms Service
This service, which is provided by the Department of Trade and Industry, is an information and counselling service to help owners and managers of small businesses with their plans and problems. It is also an advisory service to those thinking of starting their own business. The service operates through a nationwide network of 12 Small Firms Centres backed up by over eighty Area Counselling Offices throughout Great Britain.

The service can help with almost any type of business enquiry and will provide information on such topics as raising finance, Government grants, sources of supply, industrial training, exporting, planning, industrial relations, new technology and marketing. It can also put you in touch with the right people in Government departments, local authorities, chambers of commerce, the professions or any other body that can help in solving your problems. As well as answering enquiries over the telephone the Small Firms Centre can arrange for a meeting with a Small Firms Business Counsellor who is himself an experienced businessman and who can offer impartial and confidential advice and guidance. Such meetings can either be at a local area counselling office or at the client's own premises. However, the decisions you make on the basis of advice given are your responsibility and yours alone. The information service is free. For counselling, the first three sessions are free; if further counselling is required a modest charge of about £30.00 is made for the fourth and subsequent sessions. To contact your regional Small Firms Centre dial 100 and ask the operator for Freefone 2444, or you can telephone direct or walk in and talk to them.

Small Firms Centres
Birmingham: 6th Floor, Ladywood House, Stephenson Street, Birmingham B2 4DT (021–643 3344)
Bristol: 5th Floor, The Pithay, Bristol BS1 2NB (0272 294546)
Cambridge: 24 Brooklands Avenue, Cambridge CB2 2BU (0223 63312)
Cardiff: 16 St David's House, Wood Street, Cardiff CF1 1ER (0222 396116)
Glasgow: 120 Bothwell Street, Glasgow G2 7JP (041-248 6014)
Leeds: 1 Park Row, City Square, Leeds LS1 5NR (0532 445151)
Liverpool: Graeme House, Derby Square, Liverpool L2 7UJ (051-236 5756)
London: Ebury Bridge House, 2–18 Ebury Bridge Road, London SW1W 8QD (01-730 8451)
Manchester: 3rd Floor, 320–325 Royal Exchange Buildings, St Ann's Square, Manchester M2 7AH (061-832 5282)
Newcastle: Centro House, 3 Cloth Market, Newcastle-upon-Tyne NE1 3EE (0632 325353)
Nottingham: Severns House, 20 Middle Pavement, Nottingham NG1 7DW (0602 581205)
Reading: Abbey Hall, Abbey Square, Reading RG1 3BE (0734 591733)

Centre Points outside England
The following agencies and organisations provide advisory services and assistance to new and small businesses, outside England.

SCOTLAND
The Scottish Development Agency, Small Business Division, Rosebery House, Haymarket Terrace, Edinburgh EH12 5EZ (031-337 9595). *Contact: Peter Carmichael – Director* They provide a free confidential information and advice centre, and a national counselling service available on Freefone 2444. The SDA publishes a comprehensive range of booklets and can advise on; finance, Government aid, marketing, market research, exporting, diversification, training, industrial relations, and of course high technology.

The agency is also the largest provider of industrial space in Scotland – factories, workshops and industrial estates. Sizes range from a couple of hundred square feet, to many thousands. The SDA can make finance available for certain small industrial and service enterprises, and has a strong interest in the craft field.

Small Firms Information Centre, 120 Bothwell Street, Glasgow (041-248 6014, Freefone 2444)

Centres:

Aberdeen: 16 Albert Street, Aberdeen AB1 1XQ (0224 641791/645705). *Contact: Philip Glendinning*

Dumfries: 16/18 Buccleuch Street, Dumfries DG1 2AH (03875 4444). *Contact: Brian McEnroy*

Dundee: The Nethergate Centre, Yeoman Shore, Dundee DD1 4BU (0382 29061). *Contact: George Galletly*

Edinburgh: Rosebery House, Haymarket Terrace, Edinburgh EH12 5EZ (031-337 9595). *Contact: Bernard Rutherford*

Fife: Fife and Central Region, Hillside, Balmullo, Fife KY16 0AW (033 4870 389). *Contact: Mr Norman Mitchell*

Galashiels: Borders Region, Greenwell, High Road, Galashiels, Selkirk (0896 3463). *Contact: Mr Gerry Thomson*

Glasgow: 120 Bothwell Street, Glasgow G2 7JP (041-248 2700). *Contact: Jerry Fisher*

Inverness: **The Highlands and Islands Development Board**, Bridge House, 27 Bank Street, Inverness, IV1 1QR (0463 234171). *Contact: Simon Armstrong* provides advice, assistance and counselling for new and existing businesses.

The Scottish Economic Planning Department, Alhambra House, 45 Waterloo Street, Glasgow G2 6AT (041-248 2855) the key organisation for companies in Scotland to turn to for extra grant assistance for investment and innovation. Their publication, the *Investment and Innovation Handbook* describes these services.

The Scottish Council, Development-and Industry Department, 23 Chester Street, Edinburgh EH3 7ET (031-225 7911) *Contact: Hamish Morrison* the council are involved in a number of important initiatives to promote new and small businesses in Scotland.

WALES

The Welsh Development Agency, Head Office, Treforest Industrial Estate, Pontypridd, Mid-Glamorgan CF37 5UT (044-385 2666). *Contact: A. A. Williams, Dep. Controller,* SBU particular assistance is afforded to small businesses by its Small Business Unit (SBU).

The SBU is the focal point for business advice in Wales and comprises some 60 full- and part-time staff who provide assistance to more than 3500 potential and existing businesses annually. The SBU is able to provide general and specific advice on all areas of business, eg general management, government legislation, technical advice, business counselling.

Specifically, the SBU has expert advisers on marketing, accountancy, engineering, production management, woodworking, pottery, wrought iron work. Additionally the SBU is responsible for administering the Counselling Service in Wales on behalf of the Department of Industry. This service utilises the expertise of retired and semi-retired successful businessmen who make their practical experience available to existing businesses and people hoping to start up in business.

Contacts
Gwent *Bob James (044385 2666)*
Mid/South Glamorgan *Peter Jones (044385 2666)*
West Glamorgan *Wyn Pryce (0792 586715)*
Dyfed *Andy Welsh (0267 235642)*
Gwynedd *Bryn Parry (0248 352606)*
Clwyd *Derek Jones*
     David Edwards   *(0978 61011)*

NORTHERN IRELAND

The Local Enterprise Development Unit (LEDU) Lamont House,
Purdy's Lane, Newtownbreda, Belfast BT8 4TB (0232 691031). *Contact:
George Mackey, Chief Executive* this Small Business Agency can help
manufacturing, craft or service businesses which employ up to 50
people. Their Product Ideas Licensing Library can help you to find
a start-up area, or their Research and Development Grant Scheme
can help you to bring your own product to market. They maintain a
register of private and public property and can provide technical
advice on a wide range of matters.

Their business centre in Linenhall Street has been specially
designed to hold trade shows, and are available for small businessmen to mount their own exhibition. They operate a counselling
service and have Local Area Offices keen to assist.
Area Offices:

East: 17/19 Linenhall Street, Belfast BT2 8AB (0232 242582) *Contact:
Mr David Eynon*

North: 17 The Diamond, Londonderry BT48 6HW (0504 67257)
Contact: Mr Joe Doherty

South: 12c Water Street, Newry BT34 1ES (0693 2955) *Contact: Mr
Tom Short*

West: 14e Mountjoy Road, Omagh BT79 7AD (0662 45763/4) *Contact:
James McBarron*

Council for Small Industries in Rural Areas (CoSIRA)

This is an agency of the Development Commission. Its objective
is to revitalise country areas in England by helping small rural
firms to become more prosperous. CoSIRA is Government-
financed but the staff in each rural county are backed up by
a voluntary committee of local people.

Enquiries and requests for assistance should be directed to
the nearest CoSIRA office. The CoSIRA Organiser, the local
representative, will arrange a meeting and should be able to
answer most questions on local matters, finding suitable
premises, assistance available from local authorities, how to
obtain planning permission, local sources of finance, etc. The
Organiser can also arrange a visit from one of CoSIRAs advisory
officers.

CoSIRA Services CoSIRA's team of professional and technical officers have all worked in industry and have a wide

range of skills and experience which is outlined below. Advice is normally given on a working visit to your factory or workshop.

Business Management Advice Accountancy, book-keeping, profit planning, cash flow forecasting, costing, applications for loans and overdraft facilities.

Marketing, market research, product planning, pricing and distribution, advertising and sales, export, exhibitions. Production Management, planning and control of production, buying and stock control, staff recruitment, employment legislation, statutory sick pay, supervisor training, use of microcomputers.

Technical Advice Building and estimating, structural engineering, joinery, building conversions, thatching, dry stone walling. Mechanical Engineering, electrical engineering, industrial safety, welding techniques, CNC machine tools, low-cost automation, jig and tool design, workshop layout, fibreglass lamination, thermo-plastics, clay products technology and pottery, abrasive wheels, vehicle electrics.

Furniture making, antique furniture restoration, upholstery, woodworking machinery, spraying and finishing. Sawmill management, timber technology, saw doctoring. Farriery, forgework, saddlery and leather work. Engineering projects and prototypes.

CoSIRA's own workshops can undertake the design and production of jigs, press tools and special-purpose machinery for small firms. They will also develop prototypes. This service is particularly valuable to non-engineering businesses.

Finance CoSIRA normally expects the major part of funding for small businesses to be arranged with a bank, ICFC or other commercial lending source. However, CoSIRA has its own limited loan fund which can be used in appropriate cases to finance part of the cost of a project, up to a maximum of £75,000. Repayment may be between two and 20 years according to the type of loan. CoSIRA Management Accountants are available to assist with the preparation of a case to support an application for a loan.

Grants In priority areas* only, grants are available towards the cost of converting buildings of all descriptions into workshops, including the cost of installing or upgrading mains services.

Training If you or one of your workers needs training or an extra skill, perhaps how to weld stainless steel, repair electronic ignition on a car, upholster an antique chair, or increase production from a spindle moulder, ask the Organiser. He can arrange either a visit from a technical officer or one of CoSIRA's intensive two- to five-day courses. These courses are planned to give practical skills with the minimum waste of working time.

New Entrant Training Scheme (NETS) CoSIRA provides longer periods of training for a limited number of young people, usually under 19 years of age. They must already be employed by a suitable firm. The training provided by CoSIRA is a series of one-week sessions over a period of from one to three years. NETS training is available in most of the skills mentioned above.

Other Services

Village shops At present assistance to shops is limited to villages with only one general retail outlet, eg the traditional village store/post office.

Tourism In the priority areas* CoSIRA extends its services to small tourism enterprises, guest houses, bed-and-breakfasts and small hotels.

Who can ask CoSIRA for help? If you live in the country or in a country town with less than 10,000 inhabitants CoSIRA is available to help you to start up, run, or expand your business. Normally CoSIRA helps manufacturing and service industries. Agriculture, horticulture and the professions are excluded. Any firm with less than 20 skilled employees can ask for CoSIRA help.

Charges No charge is made for the help and information given by the CoSIRA Organiser. The fees for Technical and Business Management Officers and Training Courses are very modest. For further information please get in touch with the CoSIRA Organiser for your county.

CoSIRA County Office Addresses

NORTH

Barnsley: Council Offices, York Street, Barnsley, S Yorkshire S70 1BD (0226 86141 ext 481)

Darlington: Morton Road, Darlington, Co. Durham DL1 4PT (0325 487123 for Durham, Tyne and Wear, Cleveland)

Howden: 14 Market Place, Howden Goole, N Humberside DN14 7BT (0430 31138)

Morpeth: Northumberland Business Centre, Southgate, Morpeth, NE61 2EH (0670 58807 or 514343, via Business Centre)

Priority areas In certain remoter country districts CoSIRA has priority areas, known as Rural Development Areas. In general these areas are in the North, on the East Coast, along the Welsh Border and in the West Country. Here several hundred small advance factories and workshops have been built by English Industrial Estates for the Development Commission for lease or sale to small firms.

Penrith: Ullswater Road, Penrith, Cumbria CA11 7EH (0768 65752/3)
Preston: 15 Victoria Road, Fulwood, Preston PR2 4PS (0772 713038)
York: The Lodge, 21 Front Street, Acomb, York YO2 3BW (0904 793228)

EAST

Bingham: Chancel House, East Street, Bingham, Notts NG13 8DR (0949 39222/3 for Nottingham, Leicester)
Cambridge: 24 Brooklands Avenue, Cambridge CB2 2BU (0223 354505)
Ipswich: 28a High Street, Hadleigh, Ipswich, Suffolk IP7 5AP (0473 827893)
Northampton: Hunsbury Hill Farm, Hunsbury Hill Farm Road, Northampton NN4 9QX (0604 65874)
Norwich: Augustine Stewart House, 14 Tombland, Norwich, Norfolk NR3 1HF (0603 24498)
Sleaford: Council Offices, Eastgate, Sleaford, Lincs (0529 303241)

SOUTH EAST

Bedford: Agriculture House, 55 Goldington Road, Bedford MK40 3LU (0234 61381 for Beds and Herts)
Braintree: Bees Small Business Centre, Hay Lane, Braintree, Essex CM7 6ST (0376 47623)
Guildford: 2 Jenner Road, Guildford, Surrey GU1 3PN (0483 38385)
Lewes: Sussex House, 212 High Street, Lewes, Sussex BN7 2NH (07916 71399)
Maidstone: 8 Romney Place, Maidstone, Kent ME15 6LE (0622 65222)
Newport: 6–7 Town Lane, Newport, Isle of Wight, Hants (0983 529019)
Wallingford: The Maltings, St John's Road, Wallingford, Oxon (0491 35523 for Oxford, Bucks and Berks)
Winchester: Northgate Place, Staple Gardens, Winchester, Hants SO23 8SR (0962 54747)

SOUTH WEST

Bristol: 209 Redland Road, Bristol, Avon BS6 6XU (0272 733433)
Dorchester: Room 12/13 Wing D Government Buildings, Prince of Wales Road, Dorchester, Dorset (0305 68558/69182)
Exeter: Matford Lane, Exeter, Devon EX2 4PS (0392 52616)
Salisbury: 141 Castle Street, Salisbury, Wilts SP1 3TP (0722 336255 ext 252)
Taunton: 1 The Crescent, Taunton, Somerset TA1 4EA (0823 76905)
Truro: 2nd Floor, Highshore House, New Bridge Street, Truro, Cornwall TR1 1AA (0872 73531/73281)

WEST

Malvern: 24 Belle Vue Terrace, Malvern, Worcs WR14 4PZ (06845 64506 for Gloucs, Herefordshire and Worcs)
Telford: Strickland House, The Lawns, Park Street, Wellington, Telford, Shropshire TF1 3BX (0952 47161/2/3 for Cheshire, Staffs and Shropshire)
Warwick: The Abbotsford, 10 Market Place, Warwick CV34 4SL (0926 499593)
Wirksworth: Agricola House, Church Street, Wirksworth, Derby DE4 4EY (062982 4848)

CoSIRA Headquarters, 141 Castle Street, Salisbury, Wiltshire SP1 3TP (0722 336255)

Action Resource Centre (ARC)

This was set up in 1973 by a group of businessmen to research and demonstrate how business skills could best be used for the community. Since 1976 ARC has concentrated on helping to create employment opportunities, using people seconded from industry and business to work on selected projects. Each ARC project is chosen with specific local needs and conditions in mind. For example, in the London Borough of Islington they run a Small Business Counselling Service; in Dundee, they assisted Goodwill Enterprises Ltd which takes in old furniture, refurbishes it and sells it to the public, thus creating work; in Nottingham ARC has introduced a financial advisory service (CAS Unit) for community organisations in the area. With financial and other support from several hundred major companies, and with 100 professional business advisers seconded from those companies working on projects up and down the country, their local impact is significant. To find out what ARC is doing near you, contact your nearest regional manager.

Action Resource Centre regional managers

Greater London: Henrietta House, 9 Henrietta Place, London WIM 9AG (01-629 3826) *Contact: Ceilia Allen*

Islington: Small Business Counselling Service, London Borough of Islington offices, 49/59 Old Broad Street, London EC1 (01-251 2752) *Contact: Norman Humphrey*

Leics: The Business Advice Centre, 30 New Walk, Leicester, LE1 6TF (0533 554464) *Contact: Ian Sothcott, Rachel Phipps*

Notts: 13/15 Bridlesmith Gate, Nottingham NG1 2GR (0602 51822/ 599741) *Contact: John Pyke, Anne Pollard*

South Wales: c/o ICI Fibres, Pontypool, Gwent NT4 8YD (04955 2420 ext 319) *Contact: Ron Norris*

South Yorks: c/o Sheffield City Polytechnic, Dyson House, Pond Street, Sheffield S1 1WB (0742 750036 direct line 0742 738261 ext 74) *Contact: John J Patton*

West Midlands: 1 Curzon Street, Birmingham B4 7XG (021-359 0384) *Contact: Mr Bob Lloyd*

West Yorks: c/o ICI Fibres, Hookstone Road, Harrogate HG2 8QN (0423 68021 ext 1295) *Contact: Mr Michael Kelly*

Scottish Action Resource Centre Director, Frank Bishop, 54 Shandwick Place, Edinburgh EH2 4RT (031-226 3669)

Clydeside: 4 Blythswood Square, Glasgow G2 4AB (041-226 3639) *Contact: Andy Cleland*

BSC (Industry) Ltd

This company, a subsidiary of British Steel Corporation, aims to help businesses in 17 locations in Scotland, England and Wales, with the objective of helping to put back sound jobs in those areas where the British Steel Corporation has discontinued or substantially reduced its activities.

In each of the 17 areas BSC Industry is associated with a local Business Opportunity Team, usually an Enterprise Agency but sometimes some other local organisation which exists to support businesses in the area. BSC Industry itself will provide financial assistance, where such assistance is necessary for a project to proceed. The assistance usually takes the form of an unsecured loan at below commercial rates of interest.

BSC Industry has also provided small industrial workshops in a number of its areas. These units range in size from a few hundred to a few thousand square feet, and are made available on a three-month rolling licence agreement with a minimum of formalities.

Contact points for further information

Corby: Corby Industrial Development Centre, Douglas House, Queen's Square, Corby, Northants NN17 1PL (05363 62571) *Contact: Fred McClenaghan*

Derwentside: Derwentside Industrial Development Agency Ltd, Berry Edge Road, Consett, County Durham DH8 5EU (0207 509124) *Contact: Laurie Haveron*

Dudley: Dudley Business Venture, Falcon House, The Minories, Dudley, West Midlands DY2 8PG (0384 231283) *Contact: John Standish*

Hartlepool: Hartlepool Enterprise Agency Limited, 5th Floor, Titan House, York Road, Hartlepool, Cleveland TS26 9HL (0429 221216) *Contact: Alan Humble*

London: BSC (Industry) Ltd, NLA Tower 12 Addiscombe Road, Croydon CR9 3JH (01-686 0366) *Contact: John Northcott*

Sheffield: Sheffield Business Venture, 317 Glossop Road, Sheffield, South Yorkshire S10 2HP (0742 755721) *Contact: Brian Perkins*

South Humber: South Humber Business Advice Centre Ltd, 7 Market Place, Brigg, South Humberside DN20 8HA (0652 57637/8) *Contact: Roger Thackery*

Teesside: Cleveland Enterprise Agency Limited, 52–60 Corporation Road, Middlesbrough, Cleveland TS1 2RN (0642 222836) *Contact: George Brown*

West Cumbria: Moss Bay Enterprise Trust Ltd, Mobet Trading Estate, Workington, Cumbria CA14 3YB (0900 65656) *Contact: Tony Winterbottom*

SCOTLAND

Cambuslang: Clyde Workshops, Fullarton Road, Tollcross, Glasgow G32 8YL (041-641 4972/3) *Contact: Stewart Morrison*

Garnock Valley: Garnock Valley Development Executive Ltd, 44 Main Street, Kilbirnie, Ayrshire KA25 7BY (0505 685455/685447/ 682439) *Contact: Bill Dunn*

Lanarkshire: Lanarkshire Industrial Field Executive (LIFE Ltd), 1–11 High Road, Motherwell, Lanarkshire ML1 3HU (0698 66622) *Contact: Peter Agnew*

WALES

Blaenau Gwent: Glaenau Gwent Business Advisory Committee, Blaenau Gwent Borough Council, Civic Centre, Ebbw Vale, Gwent NP3 6XB (0495 303401) *Contact: Preston Powell*

Deeside: Deeside Enterprise Trust Ltd, Park House, Deeside Industrial Park, Deeside, Clwyd CH5 2NZ (0244 815262/815783) *Contact: Peter Summers*

Llanelli: Llanelli Enterprise Company Ltd, 100 Trostre Road, Llanelli, Dyfed SA15 2EA (05542 2122) *Contact: David Williams*

South Glamorgan: Cardiff and Vale Enterprise, Mount Stuart Square, Cardiff CF1 6EE (0222 494411) *Contact: Adrian Atkinson*

South Gwent: Newport Enterprise Agency, Enterprise Way, Newport, Gwent NPT 2AQ (0633 54041) *Contact: John Crowley*

West Glamorgan: West Glamorgan Enterprise Trust, 12 St Mary Square, Swansea, West Glamorgan, SA1 3LP (0792 475345) *Contact: George Atkins*

BSC, Industry Workshops
ENGLAND

Consett Workshops, Berry Edge Road, Consett, County Durham DH8 5EU (0207 509124) *Contact: Eddie Hutchinson*

Corby Workshops, Central Works Site, Corby, Northants NN17 1YB (05363 64215) *Contact: Geoff Bent*

Hartlepool Workshops, Usworth Road Industrial Estate, Usworth Road, Hartlepool, Cleveland TS25 1PD (0429 65128) *Contact: Barbara Elsdon*

Normanby Park Workshops, Normanby Road, Scunthorpe, South Humberside DN15 8QZ (0724 843411) *Contact: Alan Henderson*

SCOTLAND

Clyde Workshops, Fullarton Road, Tollcross, Glasgow G32 8YL (041-641 4972) *Contact: Stewart Morrison*

WALES

Blaenau Gwent Workshops, Unit 6, Pond Road, Brynmawr, Gwent NP3 4BL (0495 311625) *Contact: Ray Davies*

Cardiff Workshops, Unit A, Lewis Road, East Moors, Cardiff, CF1 5EG (Cardiff 0222 486661) *Contact: Graham Blackburn*

Port Talbot Workshops, Addison Road, Port Talbot, West Glamorgan, SA12 6HZ (0639 887171) *Contact: Ivor Vincent*

URBED (Urban and Economic Development) Ltd

99 Southwark Street, London SE1 0JF (01-928 9515)

This non-profit-making company was established in 1976 with a grant from one of the Sainsbury Charitable Trusts in order to 'find practical solutions to the problems of regenerating run-down areas and creating new work'.

It has carried out a series of research studies in a cross-section of inner city areas, which have enabled URBED to develop a unique understanding of local economies, the needs of small firms, and the problems of under-utilised resources in inner city areas. Its surveys have formed the basis of a number of reports, including *Local Authorities and Economic Development* published in 1978, *Linking the College and Community* (1980) and *Promoting Economic Development in Urban Areas* (1983). A list of publications is available.

The company contributes to many conferences and working parties on employment and inner city regeneration, and has initiated or helped to popularise a number of basic ideas and solutions to the problems of local economic development. These include the establishment of workshops, working communities, small enterprise centres, industrial associations, small business clubs and local enterprise trusts. Through research into demand, case studies of successful conversions, feasibility studies and promotion material, the company has encouraged the conversion of redundant buildings into premises for small firms and has become involved in property finance.

It provides consultancy services for a range of clients, including local and public authorities and government departments. URBED's training initiatives include: 'Assessing Your Prospects' (a weekend course) and 'Getting Going' (a three-month course sponsored by the MSC). Their New Enterprise Network (NET) meets on the last Tuesday of each month. It is intended for anyone who has recently set up a business and is looking for support.

LOCAL ENTERPRISE AGENCIES

Local Enterprise Agencies or Trusts have been formed in about 200 places up and down the UK. Some have been in existence for a decade, but the great majority were formed in the last two or three years. They have in common the objectives of encouraging new and small businesses to start up in a particular area, and of helping businesses in their area to survive and prosper.

These agencies are usually run by a small staff (the largest has 21 people, but the average is two or three) who can call on the wealth of expertise within the organisations sponsoring the agency. It can be very useful to know in what particular field agencies' sponsors have experience and expertise. Many hundreds of organisations have sponsored one or more Enterprise Agencies. Sponsors include: local government; chambers of commerce; universities, polytechnics and colleges; industrial and commercial companies, both large and not so large; banks and merchant banks; accountancy firms; newspapers and television companies; insurance companies; and building societies. Moreover, organisations such as HM Dockyards, the Port of London Authority and the General and Municipal Workers' Union have played significant roles in the launching of Local Enterprise Agencies.

Many major organisations sponsor more than one agency. An index of sponsors and the agencies that they support is provided on page 355. The services provided by sponsoring bodies to the agencies include: financial support towards running costs; office and workshop space; secretarial and administrative services; management and commercial advice; training facilities and resources; literature production and dissemination (including the use of advertising media); desk or field research; board representation and help with forming and developing policy.

A rather smaller number of organisations second staff to help in the day-to-day running of the Enterprise Agency. These are very often specialists from banking or the property world, or experienced managers within big companies. There are even a few academics returning a step closer to the commercial world. These advisers are an important resource within the agency, but the sponsoring company is amply rewarded. For example, a secondee from a major clearing bank will see more new business proposals in a week at an Enterprise Agency than he may see in a year at a small local branch. At the end of his year's secondment he will be a seasoned campaigner and probably a better judge of a good proposal. Some organisations, such as BSC and ARC, who operate nationally, carry out much of their work through a local organisation similar to an Enterprise Agency in broad concept. Indeed, BSC Industry is currently converting its regional initiative into Enterprise Trusts, taking local councils, chambers of commerce and others into partnership to ensure the continuity of their initiative.

The scope of activities of each agency varies considerably. Some have focused their attention on providing small workshops and office premises; others run business advice clinics to help people to find money and other resources. Courses on marketing, on exporting, book-keeping, tax and employing people are run by some agencies, usually through their links with local colleges. Still others run 'marriage bureaux', putting people with ideas in touch with people with resources.

If you are actively considering starting up a business or are experiencing problems with your existing business then you would certainly be well advised to contact your nearest Enterprise Agency. If they cannot help or answer your questions they will almost certainly know who can.

The following chart is a guide to the agencies and their services:

(The figures in the 'Manage Property' column are a guide to rental prices in £s per square foot. The figure in the final column is the number of full-time advisory staff the agency has.)

ENGLAND

<table>
<tr><td></td><td>Advice Centre</td><td>Counselling Service</td><td>Education Service</td><td>Computer Advice</td><td>'Marriage' Bureau</td><td>Manage Property</td><td>Keep Prop. Reg.</td><td>Staff</td></tr>
</table>

ACCRINGTON: Hyndburn Enterprise Trust, c/o GEC, Blackburn Road, Clayton-le-Moors, Accrington, Lancashire BB5 5JW (0254 33241)
Contact: H. Patterson
Date founded: 1982

Advice Centre	Counselling Service	Education Service	Computer Advice	'Marriage' Bureau	Manage Property	Keep Prop. Reg.	Staff
●	●	●				●	1

ALDERSHOT: Blackwater Valley Enterprise Trust Ltd, The Old Town Hall, Grosvenor Road, Aldershot, Hants (0252 319272)
Contacts: Walter Oakey (Director) G. Vaux
Date founded: 1982

Advice Centre	Counselling Service	Education Service	Computer Advice	'Marriage' Bureau	Manage Property	Keep Prop. Reg.	Staff
●	●	●				●	1

ALTON: East Hampshire Enterprise Agency Ltd, c/o Bass Brewery (Alton) Ltd, Manor Park, Alton, Hants GU34 2PS (0420 87577)
Contact: Robert Dutton
Date founded: 1983

Advice Centre	Counselling Service	Education Service	Computer Advice	'Marriage' Bureau	Manage Property	Keep Prop. Reg.	Staff
●	●			●		●	1

ASHFORD: Enterprise Ashford Ltd, 28 North Street, Ashford, Kent TN24 8JR (0233 30307)
Contact: A. J. Duncan
Date founded: 1982

Advice Centre	Counselling Service	Education Service	Computer Advice	'Marriage' Bureau	Manage Property	Keep Prop. Reg.	Staff
●	●	●		●		●	1

ASHTON-UNDER-LYNE: Tameside Venture Trust, c/o Council Offices, Wellington Road, Ashton-under-Lyne, Greater Manchester OL6 6DL (061-344 3407)
Contact: Mrs Millman
Date founded: 1982
Organisations that second staff:
ICI plc BICC plc

Advice Centre	Counselling Service	Education Service	Computer Advice	'Marriage' Bureau	Manage Property	Keep Prop. Reg.	Staff
●	●		●	●		●	4

	Advice Centre	Counselling Service	Education	Computer Advice	Marriage Advice	Marriage Bureau	Manage Property	Keep Prop. Reg.	Staff
BARNSLEY: Barnsley Enterprise Centre, Pontefract Road, Barnsley s71 1AJ (0226 298091) *Contact: R. A. Brown Business Dev. Officer* Date founded: 1983	•	•		•	•		2.70 to 2.75	•	4
BARNSLEY: Employment Promotion & Development Unit, South Yorkshire County Council, County Hall, Barnsley s70 2TN South Yorkshire (0226 86141) *Contact: Mr R. L. Briant* Date founded: 1979 Organisations that second staff: Various departments of the County Council	•	•	•	•			1.40 to 2.50	•	16
BARNSTAPLE: North Devon Enterprise Group, Bridge Chambers, Barnstaple, N Devon EX31 1HE (Barnstaple 76365) *Contact: Mr J. Goodenough, Organiser* Date founded: 1982 Organisations that second staff: Small Firms Service, Dept of Industry CoSIRA Lloyds Bank	•	•	•	•	•			•	2
BARROW-IN-FURNESS: Furness Business Initiative Ltd, 111 Duke Street, Barrow-In-Furness, Cumbria LA14 1XA (0229 22132) *Contacts: P. Marsden, Mrs G. A. Clouter* Date founded: 1983	•	•	•						1
BASINGSTOKE: Basingstoke & Andover Enterprise Centre, 9 New Street, Basingstoke RG21 1DF (0256 54041) *Contact: Director, B. Affleck; Secretary, D. Pilkington* Date founded: 1983	•	•						•	1
BATH: Mendip & Wansdyke Local Enterprise Group, Ammerdown, Radstock,	•	•		•				•	1

Bath BA3 5SW (0761 35321)
Contact: Mr P. Whiting
Date founded: 1979

	Advice Centre	Counselling Service	Education	Computer Advice	'Marriage' Bureau	Manage Property	Keep Prop. Reg.	Staff
BIRMINGHAM: Birmingham Venture, Chamber of Commerce House, PO Box 360, 75 Harborne Road, Edgbaston, Birmingham B15 3DH (021-454 6171) *Contact: Mr D. Bullivant, Manager* Date founded: 1980 Organisations that second staff: Arthur Young McClelland Moores & Co Thornton Baker Lucas Industries	•	•	•	•	•	•	•	4
BIRMINGHAM: Small Business Centre, University of Aston, 200 Aston Brook Street, Birmingham B6 4SY (021-359 4647) *Contact: Mr D. Jones* Date founded: 1967	•	•	•	•	•	2.00		12
BLACKBURN: Blackburn & District Enterprise Trust, c/o Blackburn & District Chamber of Industry & Commerce, 14 Richmond Terrace, Blackburn BB1 7BH (0254 664747) *Contact: J. A. McKinstry* Date founded: 1982 Organisations that second staff: Midland Bank plc	•	•		•			•	2
BODMIN: Mid Cornwall Industrial Group, c/o Co-operative Retail Services Ltd, 2 Fore Street, Bodmin, Cornwall (0208 77512) *Contact: Mrs J. Thomson* Date founded: 1981	•	•	•		•			
BOLTON: Bolton Business Venture Ltd, 46 Lower Bridgeman Street, Bolton BL2 1DG (0204 391400)	•	•	•		•		•	1

Contact: Director, R. McMullan
Date founded: 1983
Organisations that second staff:
  Warburtons Ltd

	Advice Centre	Counselling Service	Education	Computer Advice	'Marriage' Bureau	Manage Property	Keep Prop. Reg.	Staff
BRAINTREE: Braintree Encourages Enterprise (BEES), Enterprise Office, Town Hall Centre, Market Square, Braintree, Essex CM7 6YG (0376 43140) *Adviser: Stuart Beckwith* Date founded: 1982	●	●	●	●	●	1.50 to 4.50	●	
BRIDGWATER: Small Industries Group Somerset, 68 Friarn St, Bridgwater, Somerset TA6 3LJ (0278 424456) *Contact: Fred Wedlake* Date founded: 1978	●	●	●	●	●	1.00 to 1.50	●	1
BRIGG: SOHBAC (South Humber Business Advice Centre Ltd), 7 Market Place, Brigg, South Humberside DN20 8HA (0652 57637/8) *Contact: Roger Thackery, Derek Marshall* Date founded: 1983	●	●	●		●		●	2
BRISTOL: Aid to Bristol Enterprises (ABE), 16 Clifton Park, Bristol, BS8 3BY (0272 741518) *Contact: Mike Mears, Colin Jones, Pat Cook* Date founded: 1979 Organisations that second staff: British Telecom Rolls Royce	●	●	●	●	●		●	2
BRISTOL: New Work Trust Company Ltd, Avondale Workshops, Woodland Way, Kingswood, Bristol BS15 1QH (0272 603871/575577) *Contact: Ms P. Underwood, Ms R. Wagstaffe, Mr M. Pope* Date founded: 1981	●	●		●	●	5.00 to 8.00	●	30

	Advice Centre	Counselling Service	Education	Computer Advice	Marriage' Bureau	Manage Property	Keep Prop. Reg.	Staff
BURTON-ON-TRENT: Burton Enterprise Agency, The Grain Warehouse, Derby Street, Burton on Trent (0283 37151/2) *Contact: Peter Harris, Ms C. Heathcote* Date founded: 1983 Organisations that second staff: Ind Coope Burton Brewery Limited (sponsor the Director for two years)	●	●	●	●		●		1
BURY: Bury Enterprise Centre, 12 Tithebarn Street, Bury, Lancs BL9 0JR (061-797 5864) *Contact: D. Gough* Date founded: 1982	●	●	●	●			●	1
CAMBOURNE: West Cornwall Enterprise Trust Ltd, Wesley Street, Camborne, Cornwall TR14 8DR (0209 714914) *Contact: Philip Staton, Mrs G. Beeching* Date founded: 1982	●	●					●	2
CARLISLE: Business Initiatives Carlisle, Tower Buildings, Scotch Street, Carlisle CA3 8RB (0228 34120) *Contact: A. W. Dickinson* Date founded: 1983	●	●		●	●		●	
CHATHAM: Medway Enterprise Agency, Railway Street, Chatham, Kent ME4 4RR (0634 400301) *Contact: Guy Sibley, Director* Date founded: 1982	●	●	●	●			●	4
CHESTER: Employment Promotion Group, Cheshire County Council, Commerce House, Hunter Street, Chester, CH1 1SN (0244 603155) *Contact: Mr M. Cordwell, Mrs F. Southorn,*	●	●	●		●		●	2

Mr I. Lawrence
Date founded: 1979

	Advice Centre	Counselling Service	Education	Computer Advice	'Marriage' Bureau	Manage Property	Keep Prop. Reg.	Staff
CHESTERFIELD: Chesterfield Business Advice Centre, 34 Beetwell Street, Chesterfield, Derbyshire s40 1sh (0246 208743) *Contact: Robert Taylor, Manager* Date founded: 1982 Organisations that second staff: clearing banks nationalised industries	•	•					•	2
CLEVELEYS: Wyre Business Agency Ltd, Colchester House, Burnhall Industrial Estate, Fleetwood Road, Fleetwood fy7 8js Lancs (0253 864014) *Contact: Director Michael Burton* Date founded: 1983	•	•	•	•	•		•	1
COLCHESTER: Colchester Business Enterprise Agency, Gate House, High Street, Colchester, Essex (0206 48833) *Contact: Director Mr Tom Ford* Date founded: 1983 Organisations that second staff: Royal London Mutual Insurance Society	•	•		•				2
CONSETT: Derwentside Industrial Development Agency, Derwentside Industrial Centre, Berry Edge Road, Consett, Co. Durham dh8 5eu (0207 509124) *Contact: L. Haveron* Date founded: 1982 Organisations that second staff: Barclays Bank BSC (Industry) Ltd	•	•		•	•		•	4
CORBY: Corby Business Advisory Bureau, Douglas House, 37 Queen's Square, Corby, Northants, nn17 1pl (05363 62571)	•	•			•	1.75 to 2.50	•	2

Contact: L. C. Howard, Mrs M. Hunter
Date founded: 1978
Organisations that second staff:
Thornton Baker, Chartered Accountants

COVENTRY: Coventry Business Centre Ltd, Ground Floor, Spire House, New Union Street, Coventry CV1 2PW (0203 552781)
Contact: Mrs C. A. Jarvis
Date founded: 1982
Organisations that second staff:
Barclays Bank plc

CRANFIELD: Interwork Business Development Centre, Cranfield, Bedford MK43 0AL (0234 752767)
Contact: Prof. B. Wilson, Paul Stait, Gilbert Jenkins, Eileen Williams
Date founded: 1981
Organisations that second staff:
BP (current), ICI (previously)

CROYDON: Croydon Business Venture Ltd, 26 Barclay Road, Croydon, Surrey CR0 1JN (01-681 8339)
Contact: Mrs N. Chessum
Date founded: 1983
Organisations that second staff:
Barclays Bank plc
Deloitte, Haskins & Sells

DARLINGTON: Darlington & S W Durham Business Venture, Imperial Centre, Grange Road, Darlington, Co. Durham DL1 5NQ (0325 480891)
Contact: Cyril Beere, Keith Ormrod
Date founded: 1983
Organisations that second staff:
ICI
Carreras Rothman

	Advice Centre	Counselling Service	Education	Computer Advice	'Marriage' Bureau	Manage Property	Keep Prop. Reg.	Staff
COVENTRY	•	•	•	•			•	2
CRANFIELD	•	•			•			3
CROYDON	•	•	•				•	2
DARLINGTON	•	•		•	•		•	1

	Advice Centre	Counselling Service	Education	Computer Advice	'Marriage' Bureau	Manage Property	Keep Prop. Reg.	Staff
DERBY: Derby & Derbyshire Business Venture, Saxon House, Heritage Gate, Friary Street, Derby DE1 1NL (0332 360345) *Contact: Ex. Director M. C. Powell, Lynn Green, Secretary/PA* Date founded: 1983 Organisations that second staff: British Rail (Research & Development Div.) – full-time executive director on secondment	•	•		•			•	1
DUDLEY: Dudley Business Venture, Falcon Hse, The Minories, Dudley DY2 8PG, West Midlands (0384 231283) *Contact: Mr John Standish, Mr David Needham* Date founded: 1983	•	•	•	•	•		•	2
DURHAM: Enterprise North, Durham University Business School, Mill Hill Lane, Durham DH1 3LD (0385 41919) *Contact: Derek Craven, Margaret Robertson* Date founded: 1973/74	•	•	•	•				2
FLEETWOOD, Lancashire Enterprises Ltd, 6 Fish Trades Building, Fleetwood, Lancs FY7 6PP (0772 735821) *Contact: Mr Banford* Date founded: 1982	•	•	•			•		N/A
GLOUCESTER, Gloucestershire Enterprise Agency, 90 Westgate Street, Gloucester GL1 2NZ (0452 501411) *Contact: Director, Jack Tester; Brian Hurley* Date founded: 1982 Organisations that second staff: Rank Xerox Whitbread	•	•	•				•	4

	Advice Centre	Counselling Service	Education	Computer Advice	Marriage' Bureau	Manage Property	Keep Prop. Reg.	Staff
GRAVESEND: Gravesham Industry Enterprise Agency, 8 Parrock Street, Gravesend, Kent DA12 1ET (0474 27118) *Contact: Paul Beard, Mrs H. Gray* Date founded: 1983 Organisations that second staff: Blue Circle Industries plc	•	•	•				•	2
GRAVESEND: Gravesham Industry Ltd, Gravesham Borough Council, Civic Centre, Windmill St, Gravesend, Kent DA12 1AU (0474 64422) ext 274/5 *Contact: Mr R. Dewar* Date founded: 1983	•	•	•	•			•	1
GREAT YARMOUTH: Great Yarmouth Business Advisory Service, 165a King Street, Great Yarmouth, Norfolk, NR30 2PA (0493 58157) *Contact: John Norton, Roy Northcott* Date founded: 1983	•	•	•			0.90 to 2.25	•	1
GRIMSBY: Great Grimsby Small Firms Advisory Bureau, Devonshire House, Grimsby (0472 59161) *Contact: John Robertson* Date founded: 1979	•	•				•	•	2
HALIFAX: Calderdale Small Business Advice Centre, 4 Clare Road, Halifax (0422 69487) *Contact: Director, Ron Chandler* Date founded: 1982 Organisations that second staff: Halifax Building Society	•	•	•	•			•	2
HALIFAX (CALDIS) Calderdale Information Service for Business & Industry, Library Centre, Percival Whitely College of F.E., Francis Street, Halifax, W Yorkshire HX1 3UZ (0422 58221) *Contact: D. Manley* Date founded: 1966	•		•	•	•			1

	Advice Centre	Counselling Service	Education	Computer Advice	'Marriage' Advice	Manage Property	Keep Prop. Reg.	Staff
HARLOW: Harlow Enterprise Agency	•	•	•				•	2
HARROW: Enterprise Agency	•	•	•	•			•	1
HARTLEPOOL: Hartlepool Enterprise Agency Ltd	•	•			•		•	2
HARTLEPOOL: Hartlepool New Development Sup. (HANDS)	•	•	•		•	•	•	2
HASTINGS: Hastings Business Ventures	•	•		•	•		•	1

HARLOW: Harlow Enterprise Agency, 19 The Rows, The High, Harlow, Essex. (0279 38077)
Contact: Dennis Williams
Date founded: 1983
Organisations that second staff:
  Tesco Stores plc

HARROW: Enterprise Agency, Brush House, Rosslyn Crescent, Harrow, Middlesex HA1 2SE (01-427 6188)
Contact: Ex. Dir. Richard Robinson
Date founded: 1983
Organisations that second staff:
  Barclays Bank plc

HARTLEPOOL: Hartlepool Enterprise Agency Ltd, 5th Floor, Titan House, York Road, Hartlepool, Cleveland TS26 9HL (0429 221216)
Contact: Director, Alan Humble; Geoff Coates
Date founded 1982
Organisations that second staff:
  BSC (Industry) Ltd
  Barclays Bank plc
  GEC (Telecommunications) Ltd

HARTLEPOOL: Hartlepool New Development Sup. (HANDS), Old Municipal Buildings, Upper Church St, Hartlepool, Cleveland (0429 66522 ext 374)
Contact: Mrs B. Morley, C. C. Doram, R. Preece

HASTINGS: Hastings Business Ventures, 6 Havelock Road, Hastings, East Sussex TN34 1BP (0424 433333)
Contact: Victoria John   Date founded: 1983

	Advice Centre	Counselling Service	Education	Computer Advice	Marriage Bureau	Manage Property	Keep Prop. Reg.	Staff
HEBDEN BRIDGE: Penine Heritage Ltd, The Birchcliffe Centre, Hebden Bridge, W Yorkshire HX7 8DG (0422 845100) *Contact: Bill Breakell, General Manager* Date founded: 1979						1.00 to 4.00		2
HONITON: East Devon Small Industries Group, 115 Border Road, Heath Park, Honiton, Devon EX14 8BT (0404 41806) *Contact: A. D. Johnson (Development Officer)* Date founded: 1981	●	●		●	●		●	1
HULL: Business Advice Centre, 24 Anlaby Road, Hull HU1 2PA (0482 27266) *Contact: A. G. Spice* Date founded: 1983 Organisations that second staff: seconded assistance available	●	●						2
IPSWICH: Enterprise Trust (IPSENTA), 30a Lower Brooke Street, Ipswich, Suffolk (0473 59832) *Contact: Director, David Rolfe* Date founded: 1983	●	●						NIL
LANCASTER: Business for Lancaster, St Leonards House (Room B32), St Leonards Gate, Lancaster LA1 1NN (0524 66222) *Contact: Peter Stiles, Mrs A. Morris* Date founded: 1982	●	●					●	1
LANCASTER: Enterprise Lancaster, Town Hall, Lancaster LA1 1PH (0524 65272) *Contact: R. H. Kelsall* Date founded: 1968	●		●	●		0.17 to 2.90	●	N/A
LEEDS: LCVS Enterprises Ltd, 31–35 Aire Street, Leeds LS1 4HT (0532 435897) *Contact: W. Shutt* Date founded: 1980	●					2.00 to 3.00		1

Organisations that second staff:
ARC

	Advice Centre	Counselling Service	Education	Computer Advice	Marriage Bureau	Manage Property	Keep Prop. Reg.	Staff
LEEDS: Leeds Business Venture, 4th floor, Merrion House, The Merrion Centre, Leeds LS2 8LY (0532 446474 & 457583)	•	•	•		•			3
LEICESTER: Leicestershire Business Advice Centre, 30 New Walk, Leicester LE1 6TF (0533 554464)	•	•		•	•			2
LEICESTER: Leicestershire Small Firms Centre, 8 St Martins, Leicester LE1 5DD (0533 29684)	•	•					•	7
LETCHWORTH: Letchworth Garden City Business Centre, Works Road, Letchworth Garden City, Hertfordshire SG6 1LB (94626 78272)	•	•				2.00 to 3.95	•	1

LEEDS: Leeds Business Venture, 4th floor, Merrion House, The Merrion Centre, Leeds LS2 8LY (0532 446474 & 457583)
Contact: Mike Riley
Date founded: 1980
Organisations that second staff:
previously Marks & Spencer plc and Lloyds Bank plc; currently Halifax Building Society

---

LEICESTER: Leicestershire Business Advice Centre, 30 New Walk, Leicester LE1 6TF (0533 554464)
Contact: Mrs Jane Burgess, PA to Director
Date founded: 1981
Organisations that second staff:
Lloyds Bank plc, one Business Advisory Manager may be used by us one day per week if required

(above centre is for information and advice)

LEICESTER: Leicestershire Small Firms Centre, 8 St Martins, Leicester LE1 5DD (0533 29684)
Contact: Mr C. M. Britt, Director; Mrs J. A. Dewhurst, Consultancy Administrator
Date founded: 1979
Organisations that second staff:
Leicester Polytechnic

(above centre is for consultancy service)

LETCHWORTH: Letchworth Garden City Business Centre, Works Road, Letchworth Garden City, Hertfordshire SG6 1LB (94626 78272)
Contact: Colin Fricker
Date founded: 1983

	Advice Centre	Counselling Service	Education	Computer Advice	'Marriage' Bureau	Manage Property	Keep Prop. Reg.	Staff
LIVERPOOL: Business in Liverpool Ltd, The Innovation Centre, 131 Mount Pleasant, Liverpool L3 5TF (051-709 1231) *Contact: Director, L. T. Williams* Date founded: 1982 Organisations that second staff: Barclays Bank plc United Biscuits Ltd	•	•					•	1
LONDON: Business Advice & Consultance Service (London Borough of Newham), Town Hall, Barking Road, East Ham, London E6 2RP (01-552 5324) *Contact: Tom Brandon (Ind. Co-ord. Officer)*	•	•					•	N/A
LONDON: Camden Enterprise, 57 Pratt Street, Camden Town, London NW1 0DP (01-482 2128) *Contact: Laurie Ewins, Manager* Date founded: 1983 Organisations that second staff: Prudential Assurance Camden Council	•	•	•	•			•	3
LONDON: The Fashion Centre, 46 Great Eastern Street, London EC2A 3LE (01-729 0962) *Contact: Director, David Jones; Ann Priest* Date founded: 1982	•	•	•	•	•		•	7
LONDON: Hackney Business Promotions Centre, 46 Great Eastern Street, London EC2A 3EP (01-739 9606) *Contact: Mr A. G. Wood for Business Advice, Mr D. Griffin for property* Date founded: 1978	•	•				5.50 to 6.50	•	3
LONDON: Hammersmith & Fulham Business Resources Ltd, c/o Ind. Development Unit, PO Box 501, Hammersmith Town Hall, King St, London W6 9JU (01-741 7248)	•	•	•				•	2

Contact: Executive Director, Michael Smith
Date founded: 1981
Organisations that second staff:
  Midland Bank plc

LONDON: Kensington & Chelsea Resources Centre, 9 Thorpe Close, London W10 5XL (01-969 9455)
Contact: M. Lewthwaite
Date founded: 1978

LONDON: Lambeth Industrial Enterprises, 62 Tritton Road, London SE21 8DE (01-670 4411)
Contact: John Morris
Date founded: 1978

LONDON: Lambeth Business Advisory Service, Directorate of Town Planning and Economic Dev., Courtenay Hse, 9–15 New Park Rd, London SW2 4DU (01-674 9844)
Contact: Richard Boulter
Date founded: 1982
Organisations that second staff:
  National Westminister Bank plc
  British Petroleum

LONDON: London Enterprise Agency (LENTA), London Chamber of Commerce & Industry, 69 Cannon Street, London EC4N 5AB (01-236 2676 or 01-248 4444)
Contact: Brian Wright, Director
Date founded: 1979
Organisations that second staff:
  Shell UK, IBM UK, Barclays Bank plc, Midland Bank plc, Arthur Andersen, Arthur Young McClelland Moore, Unilever, National Westminster Bank plc, Lloyds Bank plc, Dept of Environment, BP, Whitbreads, Citibank, Marks and Spencer plc

Organisation	Advice Centre	Counselling Service	Education	Computer Advice	Marriage Advice	Manage Property	Keep Prop. Reg.	Staff
Kensington & Chelsea Resources Centre	•	•	•	•			•	4
Lambeth Industrial Enterprises	•	•				2.00 to 4.50		1
Lambeth Business Advisory Service	•	•	•	•			•	9
London Enterprise Agency (LENTA)	•	•	•	•	•	3.00 to 6.00	•	21

40

	Advice Centre	Counselling Service	Education	Computer Advice	'Marriage' Bureau	Manage Property	Keep Prop. Reg.	Staff
LONDON: Park Royal Enterprise Trust, Waxlow Road, London NW10 7NU (01-961 2717) *Contact: Chairman, R. L. T. Jones* Date founded: 1980	•						•	
LONDON: Spitalfields Small Business Association Ltd, 170 Brick Lane, London E1 (01-247 1892) *Contact: Kay Jordan, co-ordinator* Date founded: 1981	•	•			•		•	3
LONDON: Tower Hamlets Centre for Small Businesses Ltd, 99 Leman Street, London E1 8EY (01-481 0512) *Contact: B. Kennon* Date founded: 1978 Organisations that second staff: Barclays Bank plc British Petroleum plc Peat, Marwick, Mitchell & Co	•	•	•				•	4
LONDON: Wandsworth Business Resource Service, 140 Battersea Park Road, London SW11 4NB (01-720 7053/7097) *Contact: Clare Nesbit, Manager* Date founded: 1980	•	•					•	4
LOUGHTON: Forest Enterprise Agency Trust (FEAT), c/o Central Library, Traps Hill, Loughton, Essex IG10 1SZ (01-508 7435) *Contact: Peter Scarlett* Date founded: 1983 Organisations that second staff: Bank of England Printing Works	•	•	•	•			•	1
LOWESTOFT: Lowestoft Enterprise Trust, 1 All Saints Road, Pakefield, Lowestoft, Suffolk NR33 0LJ (0502 63286) *Contact: Chris Barnes, Manager* Date founded: 1981	•	•	•			1.25 to 1.75	•	2

	Advice Centre	Counselling Service	Education	Computer Advice	'Marriage' Bureau	Manage Property	Keep Prop. Reg.	Staff
LUTON: Bedfordshire & Chiltern Enterprise Agency (BECENTA), Enterprise House, 7 Gordon Street, Luton LU1 2QP (0582 452288) *Contact: D. J. Upcott, E. R. Pearce* Date founded: 1981	•	•	•		•		•	
MACCLESFIELD: Macclesfield Business Venture, c/o Josolyne & Co., Silk House, Park Green, Macclesfield, Cheshire (0625 615113) *Contact: John Rosthorn, Anita Crawshaw* Date founded: 1983 Organisations that second staff: ICI, Pharmaceuticals Division	•	•		•			•	1
MAIDSTONE: Maidstone Enterprise Agency Ltd, 25a Pudding Lane, Maidstone, Kent ME14 1PA (0622 675547) *Contact: John Lee, Director* Date founded: 1982 Organisations that second staff: National Westminster Bank plc Kimberly-Clark Ltd	•	•						1
MALDON: Colchester and Maldon Business Enterprise Agency, Maldon District Council, Market Hill, Maldon, Essex CM9 7QN (0621 54477) *Contact: Anna Cronin* Date founded: 1983	•	•			•	•		
MANCHESTER: Greater Manchester Enterprise, Gt Man. Economic Development Agency, Bernard House, Piccadilly Gardens, Manchester M1 4DD (061-236 4412) *Contact: M. E. E. Morton* Date founded: 1979	•				•		•	7

	Advice Centre	Counselling Service	Education	Computer Advice	'Marriage' Bureau	Manage Property	Keep Prop. Reg.	Staff
MANCHESTER: Manchester Business Venture, c/o Tootal Group PLC, 56 Oxford Street, Manchester M60 1HJ (061-228 1144) *Contact: Brian Bawden, Director* Date founded: 1982 Organisations that second staff: National Westminster Bank plc	•	•			•		•	1
MANCHESTER: North West Industrial Development Association, Brazennose House, Brazennose Street, Manchester M2 5AZ (061-834 6778) *Contact: John Timperley, Information Officer* Date founded: 1931	•						•	13
MIDDLESBROUGH: Cleveland Enterprise Agency, 52 Corporation Road, Middlesbrough, Cleveland, TS1 2RN (0642 222836) *Contact: Director, George Brown; Ken Anderson, John Hufton, Alan Pounder, Alan Sykes, Marilyn Twidale* Date founded: 1982 Organisations that second staff: ICI, National Westminster Bank plc; GEC	•	•			•		•	6
MIDDLESBROUGH: New Enterprise Centre, Silver Street, St Hildas, Middlesbrough TS2 1NF (0642 224839) *Contact: Mr J. E. Corbett, Manager* Date founded: 1981	•	•				0.40 to 0.80		4
MILTON KEYNES: Milton Keynes Business Venture, Sentry House, 500 Avebury Boulevard, Saxon Gate West, Milton Keynes (0908 660044) *Contact: John Carpenter, Doug Strachan* Date founded: 1983	•	•			•	1.50 to 8.00	•	2
MITCHAM: Merton Enterprise Agency, Vestry Hall Annex, London Road, Mitcham, Surrey CR4 3UD (01-640 5182) *Contact: Richard Pook, Manager*	•	•						1

	Advice Centre	Counselling Service	Education	Computer Advice	'Marriage' Bureau	Manage Property	Keep Prop. Reg.	Staff
MORPETH: Northumberland Business Centre, Southgate, Morpeth, Northumberland NE61 2EH (0670 514343) *Contact: John Hamilton, Manager* Date founded: 1982	•	•	•			0.90 to 2.00	•	6
NEWCASTLE-UPON-TYNE: Project North-East, 5 Saville Place, Newcastle-Upon-Tyne NE1 8DQ (0632 617856) *Contact: David Grayson, David Irwin* Date founded: 1980	•	•	•	•				2
NEWCASTLE-UPON-TYNE: Tyne & Wear Enterprise Trust Ltd (ENTRUST), SWS House, Stoddart Street, Newcastle-upon-Tyne NE2 1AN (0632 619122) *Contact: John Eversley, Director; Tim Atterton* Date founded: 1981 Organisations that second staff: Prudential Assurance Northern Rock Building Society North Eastern Electricity Board	•	•	•	•			•	14
NEWPORT: Isle of Wight Enterprise Agency, 6/7 Town Lane, Newport, Isle of Wight PO30 1NR (0983 529120) *Contact: Christopher Young, Director* Date founded: 1981	•	•	•	•	•			4
NORTHAMPTON: Northamptonshire Enterprise Agency Ltd, 67 The Avenue, Cliftonville, Northampton NN1 5BT (0604 37401) *Contact: David Mann, Managing Director* Date founded: 1983 Organisations that second staff: Express Lift Company Ltd	•	•	•	•	•		•	3

	Advice Centre	Counselling Service	Education	Computer Advice	Marriage Bureau	Manage Property	Keep Prop. Reg.	Staff
NORTHWICH: Vale Royal Small Firms Ltd (Business back-up), Mid-Cheshire Business Centre, Winnington Avenue, Winnington, Northwich, Cheshire CW8 4EE (0606 77711) *Contact: John Bone, General Manager* Date founded: 1982 Organisations that second staff: ICI plc; Trustee Savings Bank	•	•					•	1
NORWICH: Norwich Enterprise Agency Trust (NEAT), Norwich Chamber of Commerce & Ind., 112 Barrack Street, Norwich NR3 1TX (0603 613023) *Contact: Director* Date founded: 1981 Organisations that second staff: Barclays Bank plc	•	•		•				2
NOTTINGHAM: Nottinghamshire Business Venture, c/o John Players, Nottingham NG7 5PY (0602 787711) *Contact: Gordon Mackenzie, Director* Date founded: 1982	•	•	•				•	1
NOTTINGHAM: Nottingham Community Project, Baker Gate House, Belward Street, Nottingham NG1 1JZ (0602 581933) *Contact: P. Teague* Date founded: 1980						•		3
NOTTINGHAM, Nottinghamshire County Council Economic Development Unit, County Hall, West Bridgford, Nottingham NG2 7QP (0602 023823) *Contact: L. D. Harker, G. B. Anderton* Date founded: 1975	•	•		•		1.60 to 2.20	•	2
NOTTINGHAM, East Midlands Initiatives, Lyndhurst House, Malvern Road, Mapperley, Nottingham NG3 5GZ (0602 626089)	•	•		•			•	1

Contact: *Brian Hopewell, Director*
Date founded: 1983
Organisations that second staff:
  Nottingham Community Project (part of
  the Community Projects Foundation)

	Advice Centre	Counselling Service	Education	Computer Advice	'Marriage' Bureau	Manage Property	Keep Prop. Reg.	Staff
NOTTINGHAM, Hyson Green Workshops Limited, Lindsey Street, Radford Road, Nottingham (0602 708779)	•	•				4.00	•	1
OLDHAM: Business in Oldham, Orme Mill, Greenacres Road, Waterhead, Oldham OL4 3JA (061-665 1225)	•	•	•	•	•		•	1
OXFORD: Oxford, Enterprise Trust, c/o Taylor & Co., 125 London Road, Headington, Oxford (0865 63092)	•	•		•		•		
PENRITH: East Fellside & Alston Moor Project, c/o Eden District Council, Mansion House, Penrith, Cumbria CA11 7YG (0768 64671)	•							1
PETERBOROUGH: Peterborough Enterprise Programme, Broadway Court, Broadway, Peterborough PE1 1RP (0733 310159)	•	•	•		•		•	2

NOTTINGHAM, Hyson Green Workshops Limited, Lindsey Street, Radford Road, Nottingham (0602 708779)
Contact: *Brian Stanley, Manager*
Date founded: 1981
Organisations that second staff:
  Nottingham Community Project (part of
  the Community Projects Foundation)

OLDHAM: Business in Oldham, Orme Mill, Greenacres Road, Waterhead, Oldham OL4 3JA (061-665 1225)
Contact: *Roy Newton, Manager*
Date founded: 1982
Organisations that second staff:
  ICI, Ferranti, Information Technology

OXFORD: Oxford, Enterprise Trust, c/o Taylor & Co., 125 London Road, Headington, Oxford (0865 63092)
Contact: *J. C. W. Burrough*
Date founded: 1978

PENRITH: East Fellside & Alston Moor Project, c/o Eden District Council, Mansion House, Penrith, Cumbria CA11 7YG (0768 64671)
Contact: *A. Berlin*
Date founded: 1979

PETERBOROUGH: Peterborough Enterprise Programme, Broadway Court, Broadway, Peterborough PE1 1RP (0733 310159)
Contact: *John Duckworth, Director*

Date founded: 1982
Organisations that second staff:
  clearing banks

	Advice Centre	Counselling Service	Education	Computer Advice	'Marriage' Bureau	Manage Property	Keep Prop. Reg.	Staff
PLYMOUTH: South Hams Small Industries, The Croft, Brixton, Plymouth, Devon (0752 880210) *Contact: Alan Lovering* Date founded: 1979	•	•	•	•	•			
PORTSMOUTH: Portsmouth Area Enterprise, First Floor Offices, 27 Guildhall Walk, Portsmouth, PO1 2RY (0705 833321) *Contact: Bill Summer, Jim Pryer, Alex Addison* Date founded: 1982 Organisations that second staff: Whitbread & Co.	•	•			•		•	2
READING: Berkshire Enterprise Agency, The Old Shire Hall, The Forbury, Reading, Berks RG1 3EJ (0734 585715) *Contact: R. D. Hale* Date founded: 1982 Organisations that second staff: Marks & Spencer plc	•	•	•		•		•	2
ROCHDALE: Metropolitan Enterprise Trust Rochdale Area (METRA), c/o TBA Industrial Products Ltd, PO Box 40, Rochdale OL12 7EQ (0706 356250) *Contact: Mr Islwyn M. Jones* Date founded: 1982	•	•			•		•	1
ROSSENDALE: Rossendale Enterprise Trust, 29 Kay Street, Rawtenstall, Rossendale, Lancashire, BB4 7LS (0706 229838) *Contact: Mr Bruce Harris* Date founded: 1981	•	•	•	•	•	1.00 to 2.50	•	2

	Advice Centre	Counselling Service	Education	Computer Advice	'Marriage' Bureau	Manage Property	Keep Prop. Reg.	Staff
ROTHERHAM: Rotherham Enterprise Agency Ltd, Guardian Centre, Rotherham, South Yorks s65 1DD (0709 2121) *Contact: George Linney, Geoffrey Morris* Date founded: 1983 Organisations that second staff: BSC	•	•					•	2
RUNCORN: Business Link Ltd, 62 Church Street, Runcorn, Cheshire WA7 1LD (09285 63037/73549) *Contact: B. W. Burton, General Manager; A. G. Griffiths, J. Forrester* Date founded: 1979 Organisations that second staff: ICI (Mond Division) Spicer and Pegler	•	•	•	•	2.50 to 4.25		•	3
SAFFRON WALDEN: Small Business Advisory Service, 18 St John's Close, Saffron Walden, Essex CB11 4AR (0799 27853) *Contact: John Martin* Date founded: 1977	•	•	•	•				N/A
SCUNTHORPE: Industrial Development Enterprise Agency, Civic Centre, Ashby Road, Scunthorpe, South Humberside DN16 1AB (0724 869494) *Contact: Mr R. I. Robertson, Mr I. Hutchison, Mrs J. C. Knox* Date founded: 1978	•	•		•	1.20 to 2.60		•	5
SHEFFIELD: Sheffield Business Venture, 317 Glossop Road, Sheffield s10 2HP (0742 755721) *Contact: Brian Perkins, Director; John Dickson, Adviser* Date founded: 1982	•	•		•			•	1

Organisations that second staff:
National Westminster Bank plc
Whitbread & Company, East Pennines &
Scotland

	Advice Centre	Counselling Service	Education	Computer Advice	Marriage Bureau	Manage Property	Keep Prop. Reg.	Staff
SHREWSBURY: Shropshire Employment Promotion Association, Shirehall, Abbey Foregate, Shrewsbury, Shropshire SY2 6ND (0743 222379) *Contact: Stuart Morris, Ron Shone, Ruth Mochrie* Date founded: 1978	●	●	●	●	●	2.00	●	4
SITTINGBOURNE: SWIM/SWAP Swale Workshop Action Project, Newington Enterprise Centre, Wardwell Lane, Newington, Sittingbourne, Kent ME9 7BS (0795 843802) *Contact: W. A. Penney* Date founded: 1982	●	●		●		1.80 to 4.00		1
SOUTHAMPTON: Southampton Enterprise Agency, Solent Business Centre, Millbrook Road West, Southampton SO1 0HW (0703 788088) *Contact: John Townesend, Director* Date founded: 1981 Organisations that second staff: National Westminster Bank plc	●	●	●	●	●		●	3
SOUTHPORT: Southport Enterprise, 54 West Street, Southport, Lancashire (0704 44173) *Contact: B. E. Cresswell, Secretary* Date founded: 1981	●	●		●			●	1
ST AUSTELL: Restormel Local Enterprise Trust Ltd, Lower Penarwyn, St Blazey, Par, Nr St Austell, Cornwall PL24 2D (072 681 3079)	●	●				1.20 to 3.60	●	3

Contact: A. G. Tourell, Honorary Director
Date founded: 1981

	Advice Centre	Counselling Service	Education	Computer Advice	'Marriage' Bureau	Manage Property	Keep Prop. Reg.	Staff
ST HELENS: Community of St Helens Trust Ltd, PO Box 36, St Helens, Merseyside (0744 692570)	•	•	•		•	1.65 to 2.16	•	8
STAFFORD: Staffordshire Development Assoc., Staff. Business Adv. Centre, 3 Martin Street, Stafford ST16 2LH (0785 3121 ext 7370)	•	•	•	•			•	5
STEVENAGE: Stevenage Initiative, Business and Technology Centre, Bessemer Drive, Stevenage, Herts, SG1 2DX (0438 315733)	•	•	•		•	4.00 to 6.50	•	2
STOCKPORT: High Peak Business Centre Ltd, Shudehill House, Hayfield, via Stockport SK12 5EP (0663 42701)	•	•	•	•				1
STOKE-ON-TRENT: Business Initiative, North Staffs & District, Gordon Chambers, 36 Cheapside, Hanley, Stoke-on-Trent ST1 1HE (0782 279013)	•	•						2

ST HELENS: Community of St Helens Trust Ltd, PO Box 36, St Helens, Merseyside (0744 692570)
Contact: Mr D. Boult, Dr R. Halford, G. White
Date founded: 1979
Organisations that second staff:
  all high street banks
  Coopers & Lybrand
  Peat Marwick

STAFFORD: Staffordshire Development Assoc., Staff. Business Adv. Centre, 3 Martin Street, Stafford ST16 2LH (0785 3121 ext 7370)
Contact: Mr A. F. Davidson, Mr M. S. Cox, Mr P. Wilson
Date founded: 1974

STEVENAGE: Stevenage Initiative, Business and Technology Centre, Bessemer Drive, Stevenage, Herts, SG1 2DX (0438 315733)
Contact: R. M. Hamill, F. E. Tippler
Date founded: 1982
Organisations that second staff:
  Imperial Chemical Industries plc
  British Aerospace plc, Lloyds Bank

STOCKPORT: High Peak Business Centre Ltd, Shudehill House, Hayfield, via Stockport SK12 5EP (0663 42701)
Contact: Edwin A. Whiting
Date founded: 1979

STOKE-ON-TRENT: Business Initiative, North Staffs & District, Gordon Chambers, 36 Cheapside, Hanley, Stoke-on-Trent ST1 1HE (0782 279013)

Contact: David Gage, Carol Probyn
Date founded: 1981
Organisations that second staff:
  National Westminster Bank plc

	Advice Centre	Counselling Service	Education	Computer Advice	'Marriage' Bureau	Manage Property	Keep Prop. Reg.	Staff
SUNDERLAND: New Enterprise Advisory Service, Citizens Advice Bureau, 48 John Street, Sunderland, Tyne & Wear SR1 1QH (0783 44027) *Contact: Ivor Saville* Date founded: 1978	•	•	•				•	1
SWINDON: Swindon Enterprise Trust Ltd, 1 Commercial Road, Swindon, Wilts SN1 5NE (0793 487793) *Contact: R. H. D. Hardy* Date founded: 1982 Organisations that second staff: Burmah Oil Trading	•	•	•	•	•	2.50 to 3.50	•	1
TELFORD: Industrial Development Unit, Telford Industrial Centre, Stafford Park 4, Telford, Shropshire TF3 3BA (0952 610329) *Contact: A. E. Johnson, D. Chiva* Date founded: 1980	•	•		•	•		•	3
TELFORD: Shropshire Enterprise Trust, Nat. West. Bank Chambers, The Green, Church Street, Wellington, Telford, Shropshire TF1 1DN (0952 56624) *Contact: Mr R. B. Williams, Mr R. C. Jebb* Date founded: 1982 Organisations that second staff: National Westminster Bank plc (full-time) Thomson McLintock (part-time)	•	•	•					1
WAKEFIELD: Kirklees & Wakefield Venture Trust, Walker House, 12 Rishworth Street, Wakefield WF1 3BY (0924 381343 & 0484 31352)	•	•	•	•	•		•	2

51

Contact: *L. Mullins, Director*
Date founded: 1981

	Advice Centre	Counselling Service	Education	Computer Advice	'Marriage' Bureau	Manage Property	Keep Prop. Reg.	Staff
WALSALL: Walsall Small Firm Advice Unit, Jerome Chambers, Bridge Street, Walsall WS1 1EX (0922 646614) *Contact: Jeff Hughes* Date founded: 1981 Organisations that second staff: Thomson McLintock & Co	•	•	•					2
WARRINGTON: Warrington Business Promotion Bureau, Barbauld House, Barbauld Street, Warrington WA1 2QY (0925 33309) *Contact: Brian Rick* Date founded: 1982	•	•		•	•		•	2
WARWICK: Warwickshire Enterprise Agency, Northgate South, Northgate Street, Warwick CV34 4JH (0926 495685) *Contact: C. D. Edwards, Director; Mrs C. M. Heath* Date founded: 1983	•	•		•	•		•	2
WASHINGTON: Tyne & Wear Small Business Club, Usworth Hall, Stephenson District 12, Washington, Tyne & Wear NE37 3HS (09141 75555) *Contact: Mrs G. M. Wright, General Manager; Mr B. L. Wilson, Chairman* Date founded: 1978	•	•	•		•			1
WATFORD: Watford Enterprise Agency, 7 Clarendon Road, Watford, Herts (0923 47373) *Contact: K. W. Hards* Date founded: 1983	•	•					•	1

	Advice Centre	Counselling Service	Education	Computer Advice	'Marriage' Bureau	Manage Property	Keep Prop. Reg.	Staff
WEMBLEY: Brent Business Venture Ltd	•	•	•		•	2.50 to 6.50	•	1
WEST MIDLANDS: Sandwell Enterprise	•	•	•	•	•		•	2
WIGAN: Wigan New Enterprise Ltd	•	•	•	•	•		•	7
WIRRAL SOUTH: ENTEP Trust Ltd	•	•	•				•	1
WIRRAL: In Business Ltd	•	•	•		•	•	•	2

WEMBLEY: Brent Business Venture Ltd,
12 Park Lane (off High Road), Wembley,
Middlesex HA9 7RP (01-903 7300/7329)
Contact: A. C. Nicholls
Date founded: 1983
Organisations that second staff:
United Biscuits plc

WEST MIDLANDS: Sandwell Enterprise,
22 Lombard Street, West Bromwich, West
Midlands B70 8RT (021-569 2231)
Contact: E. P. Tiltman
Date founded: 1983
Organisations that second staff:
Thornton Baker, Chartered Accountants

WIGAN: Wigan New Enterprise Ltd,
11 Bridgeman Terrace, Wigan, WN1 1SZ
(0942 496591)
Contact: P. Davidson
Date founded: 1982
Organisations that second staff:
Wigan College of Technology
Dept of Industry

WIRRAL SOUTH: ENTEP Trust Ltd,
118 Whitby Road, Ellesmere Port, South
Wirral L65 6TF (051-356 3555)
Contact: C. D. Leatherbarrow
Date founded: 1982
Organisations that second staff:
Shell UK Ltd

WIRRAL: In Business Ltd, Small Business
Centre, Claughton Road, Birkenhead,
Wirral L41 6ES, Merseyside (051-647 7574)
Contact: Paul Farrow
Date founded: 1980

	Advice Centre	Counselling Service	Education	Computer Advice	'Marriage' Bureau	Manage Property	Keep Prop. Reg.	Staff
WISBECH: Fens Business Enterprise Trust, 2 York Row, Wisbech, Cambridgeshire PE13 1EB (0945 587084) *Contact: Ron Wheeler, Director* Date founded: 1982	•	•		•			•	2
WOLVERHAMPTON: Wolverhampton Enterprise Ltd, Business Advice Centre, Lich Chambers, 44 Queen's Sq, Lich Gate, Wolverhampton WV1 1TS (0902 713737) *Contact: Mr R. P. Thompson, Director* Date founded: 1982	•	•	•	•			•	2
WOLVERHAMPTON: Wolverhampton's Small Business Consortium, Marston Road, Wolverhampton WV2 4LU (0902 714582) *Contact: John B. Thomas, Manager* Date founded: 1980	•	•	•	•	•	•	•	2
WORCESTER: Business Promotion Centre, Hereford & Worcester County Council, Taylors Lane, Worcester WR1 1PN (0905 21312) *Contact: John Chidlow*	•	•	•					N/A
WORKINGTON: Moss Bay Enterprise Trust (MOBET), Mobet Trading Estate, Workington, Cumbria CA14 3YB (0900 65656) *Contact: T. Winterbottom, Manager; R. McNeil, Financial Adviser; J. Leighton, Workshop Manager* Date founded: 1981 Organisations that second staff: National Westminster Bank plc NCR Copeland and Allerdale Councils	•	•			•	0.75 to 2.50	•	6

	Advice Centre	Counselling Service	Education	Computer Advice	Marriage Bureau	Manage Property	Keep Prop. Reg.	Staff
YORK: Vale of York Small Business Assoc, Lower Friargate, York YO1 1SL (0904 641401) *Contact: Gil Elliott, Director* Date founded: 1982 Organisations that second staff: ICI Fibres	•	•			•		•	1

SCOTLAND

	Advice Centre	Counselling Service	Education	Computer Advice	Marriage Bureau	Manage Property	Keep Prop. Reg.	Staff
AIRDRIE: Monklands Enterprise Trust, Unit 2, 17 Upper Mill Street, Mill St Ind. Estate, Airdrie ML6 6JJ (023 64 69255) *Contact: Mr M. M. Martin* Date founded: 1984	•	•			•		•	1
AYR: Ayr Local Enterprise Resources Trust (ALERT), ALERT Office, 88 Green Street, Ayr (0292 264181) *Contact: Mr Hugh Frew* Date founded: 1983 Organisations that second staff: Digital, Long John International Scottish Express International, Barr Construction, Kyle & Carrick District Council	•	•		•	•			2
BATHGATE: Bathgate Area Support for Enterprise (BASE), 19 North Bridge Street, Bathgate (0506 634024) *Contact: Mr M. J. Fass, Director* Date founded: 1983 Organisations that second staff: Lothian Regional Council	•	•	•		•	0.50 to 2.70	•	5
DUNDEE: Dundee Industrial Association, Blackness Trading Precinct, West Hendersons Wynd, Dundee DD1 5BY (0382 26001/2)	•	•			•	1.12 to 2.90	•	2

Contact: Mr Ron Bear, Mrs G. Doyle
Date founded: 1983

	Advice Centre	Counselling Service	Education	Computer Advice	Marriage Bureau	Manage Property	Keep Prop. Reg.	Staff
EDINBURGH: Edinburgh Venture Enterprise Trust (EVENT), 9 Hanover Buildings, Rose Street, Edinburgh EH2 2YQ (031-226 5783) *Contact: Mr J. MacMillan, Chairman; N. K. Campbell, PR & Research; J. F. Jacobs, Asst Director* Date founded: 1983 Organisations that second staff: Trustee Savings Bank, Peat Marwick & Mitchell, Coopers & Lybrand, John Menzies plc, Hewlett Packard	•	•	•	•		2.50 to 4.50	•	3
EDINBURGH: Leith Enterprise Trust (LET), 25 Maritime Street, Leith, Edinburgh EH6 5PW (031-553 5566) *Contact: Mr J. Prettyman* Date founded: 1983 Organisations that second staff: SDA, Sponsors from Private Sector, LRC EDC	•	•			•		•	2
FALKIRK: Falkirk Enterprise Action Trust (FEAT), Suite A Haypark, Marchmont Avenue, Polmont, Stirlingshire FK2 0NZ (0324 716868) *Contact: Mr J. M. Jackson, Director* Date founded: 1983	•	•	•	•	•	3.00 to 5.00	•	1
GLASGOW: McPhail Street Properties Ltd, Greenhead Bridgeton Factors, 23 McPhail St, Glasgow G40 1EL (041- 556 2433) *Contact: Mr W. Hibberd, Mrs B. G. Ogston* Date founded: 1964	•					0.50 to 1.50	•	3

	Advice Centre	Counselling Service	Education	Computer Advice	Marriage Bureau	Manage Property	Keep Prop. Reg.	Staff
GLASGOW: Strathclyde Regional Council Industrial Development Unit, Strathclyde House 4, 3 India Street, Glasgow G2 4PF (041-227 3866) *Contact: Garrath Le Sueur, Ind. Dev. Manager*	•	•			•	0.80 to 2.50	•	9
GLASGOW: Glasgow Opportunities Enterprise Agency (GO), 7 West George Street, Glasgow (041-221 0955) *Contact: Mr George Paterson, Director; Jim Andrew, Tony Deeley, John Whitehead* Date founded: 1983	•	•	•					4
GLENROTHES: Glenrothes Enterprise Trust (GET), North House, North Street, Glenrothes, Fife KY7 5NA (0592 757903) *Contact: Mr Brian Turnbull, Director* Date founded: 1983	•	•		•	•	1.25 to 3.50	•	1
GREENOCK: Inverclyde Enterprise Trust, 26 Clyde Square, Greenock PA15 1LY (0475 86240) *Contact: P. Hingston* Date founded: 1984	•	•		•				2
INVERNESS: Highland Craftpoint, Beauly, Inverness IV4 7EH (0463 782578) *Contact: Donald McFall, Head of Development Services* Date founded: 1979	•	•	•					N/A
KILMARNOCK: Kilmarnock Venture, Clydesdale Bank, 30 The Foregate, Kilmarnock (0563 44602) *Contact: Director, A Ferguson; G. Rutherford, Project Manager; Liz Graham, Secretary* Date founded: 1983 Organisations that second staff: United Biscuits	•	•		•	•	1.71 to 3.14	•	3

	Advice Centre	Counselling Service	Education	Computer Advice	'Marriage' Bureau	Manage Property	Keep Prop. Reg.	Staff
MOTHERWELL: Lanarkshire Industrial Field Executive (LIFE), 1–11 High Road, Motherwell ML1 3HU (0698 66622) *Contact: Terry Currie, Ian Long, David Hawkes* Date founded: 1983	•	•	•		•		•	10
MOTHERWELL: Motherwell Enterprise Trust (MET), 54 Brandon Parade, Motherwell ML1 1UJ (0698 69333) *Contact: Mr Andrew Christie, Mrs C. Abraham* Date founded: 1983 Organisations that second staff: Scottish & Newcastle Breweries plc	•	•	•		•		•	2
PAISLEY: Local Enterprise Advisory Project, Westfield Annex, Paisley College, Paisley (041-887 1241) Ext 286 *Contacts: John Pearce, Duncan McTavish* Date founded: 1978	•	•	•					4
SALTCOATS: Ardrossan-Saltcoats-Stevenson Enterprise Trust (ASSET), 21 Green Street, Saltcoats, Ayrshire (0294 602515) *Contact: Mr Douglas Martyn, Director; G. Weir, Project Officer; W. S. McArthur, Enterprise Fund* Date founded: 1981 Organisations that second staff: Clydesdale Bank (support one member of staff)	•	•	•		•	0.30 to 1.50	•	5
STIRLING, Business Park, c/o Ind. Dev. Dept. Central Regional Council, Viewforth, Stirling FK8 2ET (0786 3111 ext 216) *Contact: B. Nicholson* Date founded: 1984	•	•				1.00 to 2.50	•	4

WALES

	Advice Centre	Counselling Service	Education	Computer Advice	'Marriage' Bureau	Manage Property	Keep Prop. Reg.	Staff
CARDIFF: Cardiff & Vale Enterprise, 5 Mount Stuart Square, Cardiff CF1 6EE (0222 494411) *Contact: A. Atkinson, Managing Executive* Date founded: 1983 Organisations that second staff: Marks & Spencer plc, National Westminster Bank plc, Cardiff City Council, South Glamorgan County Council, Welsh Development Agency	•	•	•	•	•	•	•	7
CARDIFF: Mid-Glamorgan County Council, Industrial Dev. & Promotion Unit, Greyfriars Road, Cardiff CF1 3LG (0222 28033 ext 143) *Contact: Mr D. Griffin, Ind. Dev. Officer*	•	•		•	•		•	7
DEESIDE: Deeside Enterprise Trust Ltd, Park House, Deeside Industrial Park, Deeside, Clwyd CH5 2NZ (0244 815262) *Contact: Peter Summers, Director; Norman Sturt, Felicity Agar* Date founded: 1982	•	•		•			•	3
HAVERFORDWEST: Pembrokeshire Business Initiative, Lombard Chambers, 14 High St, Haverfordwest, Dyfed SA61 2LD (0437 67655/6) *Contact: P. L. M. Davies OBE, Managing Director; J. E. Lloyd* Date founded: 1983	•	•	•	•	•		•	3
LLANDRINDOD WELLS, Powys Self Help, Old Town Hall, Temple Street, Llandrindod Wells, Powys (0597 4576) *Contact: Mrs S. Bailey, Roger Palmer* Date founded: 1983	•	•	•	•	•		•	2

	Advice Centre	Counselling Service	Education	Computer Advice	Marriage' Bureau	Manage Property	Keep Prop. Reg.	Staff
LLANELLI: Llanelli Enterprise Company, 100 Trostre Road, Llanelli, Dyfed (055 42 2122) *Contact: Mr A. W. G. Giles, D. C. Williams, Mrs J. M. Mactavish* Date founded: 1983 Organisations that second staff: Llanelli Radiators Subuter Automotive Components	•	•	•			1.00 to 1.50	•	2
MERTHYR TYDFIL: Merthyr Agency for the Development of Enterprise Ltd, The Enterprise Centre, Merthyr Ind. Park, Pentrebach Mid-Glamorgan CF48 4DR (0443 692233) *Contact: Mr J. Pride, Director* Date founded: 1983	•	•	•	•	•	3.00	•	1
NEATH: The Neath Partnership, 7 Water Street, Neath, West Glamorgan SA11 3EP (0639 54111) *Contact: J. A. Filmer-Bennett, Chairman; E. A. J. Carr, Business Development Director; Ellen Pierce, Tourism Dev. Manager* Date founded: 1982 Organisations that second staff: International Thomson Organisation plc Metal Box plc	•	•	•	•	•	1.75 to 2.25	•	4
NEWCASTLE EMLYN: Antur Teifi Ltd, Swyddfair Graig, Castell Newydd Emlyn, Dyfed SA38 9BH (0239 710238) *Contact: Wynfford James, Development Officer* Date founded: 1981	•	•	•	•	•		•	1
NEWPORT: Newport Enterprise Agency, Enterprise Way, off Bolt Street, Newport, Gwent NPT 2AQ (0633 54041)	•	•	•	•		1.40 to 2.30		5

Contact: John Crowley, General Manager
Date founded: 1983
Organisations that second staff:
  Lloyds Bank plc
  Central Electricity Generating Board
  British Alcan Sheet Ltd
  Fibreglass Limited

	Advice Centre	Counselling Service	Education	Computer Advice	'Marriage' Bureau	Manage Property	Keep Prop. Reg.	Staff
NEWTOWN: Development Board for Rural Wales, Business Advisory Service, Ladywell House, Newtown, Powys SY16 1JB (0686 26956/27168/27518) Contact: Mr Jackson Date founded: 1977	●	●	●	●	●	0.95 to 1.35	●	1
PONTYPRIDD: Industrial Resource Centre, Treforest Industrial Estate, Pontypridd, Mid Glamorgan CF37 5YL (0443 85 4133/4/5/6) Contact: Mr Peter Davies, Mr Ray Howorth Date founded: 1983	●	●		●	●	●		15
SWANSEA: Swansea Centre for Trade and Industry, Singleton Street, Swansea SA1 3QH (0792 476666) Contact: J. R. W. Evans, Director; D. R. Nutt, Business Services Manager; M. E. Burns, Assistant Director Date founded: 1979	●	●	●		●	1.50 to 2.50	●	6
SWANSEA: West Glamorgan Enterprise Trust, 12a St Mary's Square, Swansea, West Glamorgan SA1 3LP (0792 475345) Contact: George Atkins, Director Date founded: 1983	●	●		●			●	3

NORTHERN IRELAND

	Advice Centre	Counselling Service	Education	Computer Advice	'Marriage' Bureau	Manage Property	Keep Prop. Reg.	Staff
BANGOR: North Down Economic Development, Town Hall, The Castle, Bangor BT20 4BT (0247 54371)	●	●	●	●	●	1.50 to 2.50	●	1

Contact: Mr T. Boal
Date founded: 1984

Organisation	Advice Centre	Counselling Service	Education	Computer Advice	'Marriage' Bureau	Manage Property	Keep Prop. Reg.	Staff
BELFAST: Belfast Development Agency, 2nd floor, Canada House, 22 North Street, Belfast BT1 1LA (0232 249655) *Contact: Mr T. G. Crawford* Date founded: 1981 Organisations that second staff: Belfast City Council, Belfast Chamber of Trade, NI Chamber of Commerce and Industry, Irish Congress of Trade Unions, CBI, Belfast Harbour Commissioners (Whilst these organisations nominate representatives to sit on the Agency's Board of Directors, these representatives are not in the true sense 'seconded staff'. However, several provide large amounts of time for direct assistance)	•	•		•		1.00 to 4.00	•	2
CARRICKFERGUS: Enterprise Carrickfergus, c/o Courtaulds Industry Centre, 75 Belfast Road, Carrickfergus, Co. Antrim BT38 8PH (09603 68005) *Contact: P. J. Conway, Chairman* Date founded: 1982	•	•	•	•	•		•	3
CRAIGAVON: Craigavon New Ind. Council, Civic Centre, Lake View Road, Craigavon, N. Ireland (0762 41199) *Contact: M. Graham* Date founded: 1981	•	•	•	•		1 to 1.25	•	1
ENNISKILLEN: Fermanagh Enterprise, Project House, Regal Pass, Enniskillen, Co. Fermanagh (0365 25050) *Contact: Mr G. Burns* Date founded: 1984	•	•	•	•	•	•	•	2

	Advice Centre	Counselling Service	Education	Computer Advice	'Marriage' Bureau	Manage Property	Keep Prop. Reg.	Staff
LISBURN: Economic Development Organisation, Town Hall, Castle Street, Lisburn BT27 4ST (084-62 2259) *Contact: H. Anderson* Date founded: 1981	•	•	•	•	•			2
LONDONDERRY: Enterprise House, Little James Street, Londonderry (0504 264015) *Contact: Con McAlister* Date founded: 1982	•	•				0.05	•	2
LONDONDERRY: North West Ulster Enterprise Development Agency, 1/3 Clarendon Street, Londonderry BT48 7EP (0504 265817) *Contact: Dr V. Furness, Director* Date founded: 1983	•	•			•			1
NEWRY: Newry & Mourne Co-operative Ltd, 71 Hill Street, Newry BT34 1DG (0693 67011) *Contact: Mr F. Dolaghan* Date founded: 1972	•	•	•		•	•	•	3
STRABANE: Strabane Industrial Development Co Ltd, c/o 3/4 Abercorn Square, Strabane, N Ireland (0504 882505) *Contact: D. McLaughlin* Date founded: 1976	•	•						N/A

You may not have a local Enterprise Agency but feel that there are local problems that such an agency could help solve. In this case to make contact with your local council's Industrial Development Officer or the chamber of commerce would be a good starting point. Recently a private initiative called 'Business in the Community' has been formed to encourage and help industry and commerce with local economic and social development. It will give advice on setting up local Enterprise Agencies:

Business in the Community, 227a City Road, London EC1V 1JU (01-253 3716)

SCOTBIC, Eagle Star House, 23 St Andrew Square, Edinburgh EH2 1AF (031-556 9761) *Contact: Mr Graham Ross*

Business in the Community, Welsh Regional Director, Aubrey Jones, The Enterprise Centre, Merthyr Industrial Park, Pentrebach, Merthyr Tydfil, Mid Glamorgan (0443 692233)

From April 1982 contributions to approved Enterprise Agencies, in cash or kind, from companies, partnerships and sale traders, should be eligible for tax relief. The essential requirement for approval is that the agency is not a profit-making body.

The Department of the Environment and the Department of Industry, through their regional offices (listed below) will offer advice to individuals or firms who are thinking about establishing an agency.

Department of the Environment and Department of Industry Regional Offices

NORTH WEST
DoE, Room 1122 Sunley Building, Piccadilly Plaza, Manchester M1 4BA (061-832 9111) *Contact: Mr D. J. Morrison*

DI, Sunley Building, Piccadilly Plaza, Manchester M1 4BA (061-236 2171)

NORTH
DoE, Room 704, Wellbar House, Gallowgate, Newcastle-upon-Tyne NE1 4TX (0632 327575 ext 307) *Contact: Mr R. Bell*

DI, Stanegate House, 2 Groat Market, Newcastle-upon-Tyne NE1 1YN (0632 324722)

YORKSHIRE & HUMBERSIDE
DoE, Room 1108, City House, New Station Street, Leeds LS1 4JH (0532 438232 ext 402) *Contact: Mr K. Beaumont*

DI, Priestley House, Park Row, Leeds LS1 5LF (0532 443171)

WEST MIDLANDS
DoE, Room 815, Five Ways Tower, Frederick Road, Edgbaston, Birmingham B15 1SJ (021-643 8191 ext 2542) *Contact: Mr N. H. Perry*

DI, Ladywood House, Stephenson Street, Birmingham B2 4DT (021-632 4111)

EAST MIDLANDS
DoE, Room 609, Cranbrook House, Cranbrook Street, Nottingham NG1
1EY (0602 46121 ext 261)
DI, Severns House, 20 Middle Pavement, Nottingham NG1 7DW (0602
506181)

EASTERN
DoE, Room 402, Charles House, 375 Kensington High Street, London
W14 8QH (01-603 3444 ext 413) *Contact: Miss K. B. Pailling*
DI, Charles House, 375 Kensington High Street, London W14 8QH (01-
603 2060)

SOUTH EASTERN
DoE, Room 535, Charles House, 375 Kensington High Street, London
W14 8QH (01-603 3444 ext 4) *Contact: Mr N. Thompson*
DI, Charles House, 375 Kensington High Street, London W14 8QH (01-
603 2060) *Contact: Mr B. Raiment (ext 302) for Enterprise Agency
Enquiries, Mr R. Dennis (ext 376) for other advice*

LONDON
DoE, Room C8/10, 2 Marsham Street, London SW1P 3EB (01-212 3186)
Contact: Mr R. Williams

SOUTH WEST
DoE, Room 10A/03 Froomsgate House, Rupert Street, Bristol BS1 2QB
(0272 297201 ext 342)
DI, The Pithay, Bristol BS1 2PB (0272 291071)

LOCAL COUNCILS

During 1983 and the opening months of 1984 local authorities
have continued their enthusiastic support for the small business sector. Some useful facts have emerged from a recent study
by Chris Miller of Birmingham University's Centre for Urban
and Regional Studies. This shows that some local authorities
are doing much more than others. The only way to check what
is happening in your area is to talk to your council's Industrial
Development Officer. The following facts might be useful as
background information when talking with him. Chris Miller's
stratified survey of 86 local authorities in England and Wales
showed that only three were not providing some kind of specific
assistance to small firms. The main ways in which local authorities seem to be helping are described below.

Policies Complaints that past policies had frequently harmed
or restricted the development of many small businesses have
been taken seriously. For example 75 of the local authorities in
this sample were making provision for small enterprise developments. They were, for example, identifying disused buildings
and converting them into 'nursery units' for use by small firms;

66 were relaxing controls on industry and for example, allowing light industry into residential areas; 64 were giving priority to industrial and commercial planning applications; and 41 of the authorities were operating a policy of local 'bias' in their own purchasing of goods and services. A smaller number were trying to link this policy with their efforts to encourage small firms by themselves providing a ready market for some products. Others run local business-to-business exhibitions so that people can see what is available locally.

Advice and Information   Local authorities are also aware of the difficulties experienced by many small businessmen in dealing with the 'Bureaucracy'. Many have tried to improve the co-ordination and administration of their services that relate to business. This is often through the employment of an Industrial Development Officer (72% of the sample had one) or through a small firms advice/information service (67%).

Here are some examples of local authority activities in this area. Northamptonshire County Council has set up INPUT to encourage the development of new firms. It runs small business exhibitions; it is establishing small marketing clubs with the aim of encouraging more inter-trade amongst local companies (these consist of six one-hour sessions when the principal of five small industries will discuss small industry problems); and it has also held 'Search for the Entrepreneur' campaigns.

Berkshire County Council runs a Business Advisory Service, a joint public/private-sector service providing general management advice to small firms.

The GLC runs training courses for would-be as well as existing small businessmen throughout the year in conjunction with the London Enterprise Agency. The London Borough of Bexley operate a Small Business Development Centre providing information on premises and advice and counselling for would-be and existing small businessmen. Similarly, Brent runs a Business Information Centre; Hackney a Business Promotions Centre; and Tower Hamlets, a Small Business Centre.

Tamworth District Council runs a small business workshops approximately every 12 months, and these provide advice on how to set up and/or develop new enterprises.

Rhymney Valley District Council runs seminar forums to discuss problems experienced by local industrialists.

St Helen's Metropolitan District Council has set up, in conjunction with other local bodies such as banks, firms and unions, the St Helen's Trust to help small businesses. It is an Enterprise Trust which acts as a kind of switchboard, helping new businesses to make contact with local sources of facilities available in the major firms and institutions. It also provides advice on how to raise funds commercially, and in some cases provides 'seed capital'. It works alongside new businesses through all the formative stages, providing information or advice on such matters, as business management, opportunities and markets.

Norwich City Council, Wakefield Metropolitan District Council, and Bedfordshire County Council have also been involved in setting up Enterprise or Venture Trusts to Assist small businesses through activities similar to those of the St Helen's Trust. Kensington Council runs a Resource Centre, providing advice on setting up a business and has run local education workshops on 'How to Start a Business'. It has also provided a workshop/retail project, where people can work during the week and open the units up as shops at the weekends.

Somerset County Council's Economic Development unit published a 71-page booklet entitled *Help for the Small Firm*, a guide to sources of assistance for the small firm. As well as giving information on local authorities, the guide gives a good overview of national resources and sources of finance.

Loans and Grants Some local authorities also provide loans and grants to certain types of new and small businesses. This activity tends to be limited to metropolitan, county, district councils and London boroughs, although a few shire county councils do provide some financial assistance (see table overleaf).

Many of the local authorities offered their loans and/or grants specifically for small firms.* There are also some new initiatives being developed. For example, Scunthorpe District Council considers the financing of business development plans for small companies and the payment of grants to cover part of a small firm's bank loan interest. North Yorkshire County Council launched a Small Business Grant Scheme in April 1982, under which companies employing fewer than 20 skilled workers will be eligible for grants up to £1000 per annum for three years. In exceptional circumstances this could be raised to £2000.

In June 1982 the West Yorkshire Metropolitan County Council and the Midland Bank formed a partnership to invest within the County boundaries. Up to £10 million a year will be available for joint equity investments in unquoted companies.

*Merseyside County Council has run a number of schemes to assist small firms – eg CHASE (County Help for Active Small Enterprises), which provides interest-relief grants for construction works, plant and machinery, and working capital.

This is the first link of this nature between a British clearing bank and a county council. A further extension of this concept is to be for councils to consider setting up their own Business Expansion Schemes (see Finance Section, pages 222, 238). Lancaster County Council, using ratepayers money owns Lancashire Enterprise Ltd., which has invested £6.6 million in local business ventures.

Loans and Grants by Local authorities (%)

Contributions	Metropolitan counties	Metropolitan districts	Shire counties	Shire districts	London boroughs	% of total authorities surveyed
Land acquisition	100	58	9	24	18	27
Construction of industrial premises	100	75	27	18	45	34
Purchase of industrial buildings	100	75	18	13	36	28
Provision or improvement of services to industrial land	100	67	18	13	27	26
Provision or improvement of services to industrial buildings	100	67	18	13	27	26
Plant and machinery	100	67	27	11	27	27
Relocation from outside authority's area	33	33	5	5	18	12
Relocation within authority's area	33	67	5	5	18	16
Provision of rent-free periods for new or relocated firms on council land property	–	75	23	53	45	30

Finance for Co-operatives   A more recent area of local authority activity is the provision of finance for co-operatives. Of the authorities surveyed 28% were providing financial assistance to co-operatives (all the metropolitan counties, 58% of metropolitan districts, 5% of shire counties, 21% of shire districts, and 45% of London boroughs). Cleveland County Council and the London Borough of Greenwich have set up Co-operative Development Agencies to encourage the development of co-operatives (see section on Co-operatives for more information on CDAs, p. 91).

Analysis Studies   A number of local authorities now under-take analyses of particular relevance to small firms. Of the authorities surveyed 74% had carried out studies of the particular needs of small firms; and 23% of authorities had instigated investigations of gaps in the market for certain products. (This latter activity is mainly undertaken by the county councils – 67% of the metropolitan counties and 41% of the shire counties.) As examples, Leicester City investigates new product availability such as through the availability of licences or franchises. Sunderland Metropolitan District has a Business Opportunities Research Unit which provides technical and market research support to small firms. The London Borough of Hackney runs the City Technology Centre, which offers information and advice on developments in new technology.

Enterprise Competitions   Many local authorities have sponsored or co-sponsored competitions for new or existing small businesses with substantial prizes in cash or kind.

You may find it profitable, therefore, to get in touch with your local council's Chief Executive's department. Ask to speak to the Industrial Development Officer, and find out what your local authority can do to help you. (See also p. 240.)

More Information
A useful book and two information services, on economic activities in local authorities are listed below.
Business Location Handbook, published by Beacon Publishing, Jubilee House, Weston Favel, Northampton NW3 4WW (0604 407288) gives details of local authority officers responsible for industrial and economic development. Also gives details of local professional advisers. Price: £9.95 + 95p p&p

Financial Resources for Economic Development (FRED) is a service for those who need immediate, reliable and up-to-date information on the help available to develop new enterprises and to maintain and expand those that exist. A loose-leaf reference manual brings together full details of the wide range of financial and other assistance available for business development. It is available from the Institute of Local Government, University of Birmingham, PO Box 363, Birmingham B15 2TT.

Local Economic Development Information Service (LEDIS) was launched in April 1982 to provide concise and factual information on local economic employment initiatives being implemented throughout the UK. The service sets out to show how much each initiative costs, how long it took to develop, what the aim of the initiative was and, finally, how successful it was. The Planning Exchange, 186 Bath St, Glasgow G2 4HL (041-332 8541) can provide further details of the service.

PROPERTY SERVICES

Finding suitable premises is one of the main problems that many people starting up a new business encounter. However, apart from the Enterprise Agencies and local councils, a growing number of organisations are helping to provide suitable premises for new and small businesses.

The Government has recently made a number of important tax provisions with the aim of encouraging developers and others to build or renovate small industrial premises. For example, until April 1985, small workshops of less than 1250 sq ft will be eligible for 100% accelerated tax allowance, an extremely attractive proposition to most businesses. A property development company to be called Inner City Enterprises (ICE), blessed by the Government and backed by the financial institutions, is under active consideration. This company (if it is formed) will take the initiative in finding suitable sites to be developed for new firms in the cities. (See also Premises, pages 274–9.)

Government or National Property Services There are a number of government or national organisations which can help and advise on the availability of premises:

English Estates, St George's House, Team Valley Trading Estate, King's Way, Gateshead, Tyne and Wear NE11 0NA (0632 878941)

CoSIRA, 141 Castle Street, Salisbury SP1 3TP (0722 336255)

Beehive Workshops Ltd are developing small workshops of 500–1000 sq ft in many parts of the country. The rents, which start from £30.00 per week, cover all structural and external repairs and normal user insurance. All mains services – electricity, water, telephone and gas (where available) are provided and brought to the unit. A toilet, hand basin and electric water heater are also provided in each unit. Tenancy agreements can be terminated at three months' notice. Larger units of 1500–2500 sq. ft are also available on some locations on leases from six to 12 years. Contact the Estate Manager at:

Salterbeck Industrial Estate, Workington, Cumbria CA14 5DX (0946 830469)

53 Fore Street, Bodmin, Cornwall PL31 2JB (0208 3631)

Sandon House, 157 Regent Road, Liverpool L5 9TF (051-933 2020)

Forster House, Allensway, Thornaby-on-Tees, Cleveland TS17 9HA (0642 604911)

Hallgate House, 19 Hallgate, Doncaster, South Yorkshire DN1 3NN (0302 66865)

Methven House, Kingswear, Team Valley, Gateshead, Tyne and Wear NE11 0LN (0632 874711)

The Department of Industry has sections responsible for helping business people to find small industrial and office premises. Some maintain registers, and will certainly be able to put you in contact with estate agents and local authorities who are concerned with industrial/office premises in their region.

ENGLAND
South Eastern Region, Charles House, 375 Kensington High Street, London W14 8QH (01-603 2060)
East Midlands Region, Severns House, 20 Middle Pavement, Nottingham NG1 7DW (0602 56181)
West Midlands Region, Ladywood House, Stephenson Street, Birmingham B2 4DT (021-632 4111)
North Eastern Region, Stangate House, 2 Groat Market, Newcastle-upon-Tyne NC1 1YN (0632 324722)
North Western Region, Sunley Building, Piccadilly Plaza, Manchester M1 4BA (061-236 2171)
South Western Region, The Pithay, Bristol BS1 2PB (0272 291071); Phoenix House, Notte Street, Plymouth (0752 21891)
Yorkshire & Humberside, Priestly House, 1 Park Row, Leeds LS1 5LF (0532 443171)

NORTHERN IRELAND
Department of Commerce, Chichester House, 64 Chichester Street, Belfast BT1 4JX (0232 34488)
Local Enterprise Development Unit, Lamont House, Purdy's Lane, Newtownbreda, Belfast BT8 4TB (0232 691 031)

SCOTLAND
Scottish Office, Alhambra House, 45 Waterloo Street, Glasgow G2 6AT (041-248 2855)
Scottish Development Agency, Small Business Division, Rosebury House, Haymarket Terrace, Edinburgh EH12 SE2 (031-337 9595)
Highlands and Islands Development Board, Bridge House, 26 Bank Street, Inverness IV1 1QR (0463 34171)

WALES
Welsh Office Industry Department, Government Buildings, Gabilfa, Cardiff CF4 4YL (0222 62131)
British Steel (Industries) Ltd, NLA Tower, 12 Addiscombe Road, Croydon, CR9 3JH (01-686 0366) – they have small industrial and office premises available in the areas in which they operate (see pages 22, 23)

Some Local Property Services A growing number of organisations specialise in providing small office and workshop facilities at modest prices.
Some of these are listed below:

ENGLAND
BIRMINGHAM: Birmingham New Enterprise Workshop, 99 Clifton Road, Balsall Heath, Birmingham (021-449 8125) *Contact: Mr Isherwood*
BRISTOL: Avondale Workshops, Woodland Way, Kingswood, Bristol BS15 1QH (0272 603871) *Contact: Mr Michael Winwood*

COUNTY DURHAM: British Steel Corporation (Industry) Ltd, Berry Edge Road, Consett, Co Durham (0207 509124) *Contact: E. Hutchinson*

CUMBRIA: Moss Bay Enterprise Trust, Mobet Trading Estate, Workington, Cumbria (0900 2197) *Contact: Max de Redder*

HARTLEPOOL: Hartlepool Workshops, Sandgate Industrial Estate, Mainsforth Terrace, Hartlepool, Cleveland TS25 1UB

LONDON: Aladdin Workspace, London Borough of Ealing, Industrial Information Unit, 24 Uxbridge Road, London W5 2BP

Barley Mow Workspace Ltd, 10 Barley Mow Passage, Chiswick, London W4 (01-994 6477) *Contact: P. G. Shearmur*

Clerkenwell Workshops, 31 Clerkenwell Close, London EC1 (01-251 4821) *Contact: T. Haynes*

Great Eastern Workspace Ltd, Coldharbour Works, 245a Coldharbour Lane, London SW9 8RR (01-274 7700) *Contact: Mr Bob Gunning*

Kirkaldy's, 99 Southwark Street, London SE1 0JF (01-928 9515) *Contact: Vivian Church*

Old Loom House, Black Church Lane, London E1 1LU (01-488 0144)

The Old Nichol, 19 Old Nichol Street, Shoreditch E2 7HR (01-729 4243)

Omnibus Workspace, 41 North Road, London N7 (01-607 7021) *Contact: Gillian Harwood*

Panther House, 38 Mount Pleasant, London WC1X 0AP (01-278 8011) *Contact: A. S. Perloff*

The Portobello Green Centre, North Kensington Ammenity Trust, 1 Thorpe Close, London W10 5XL (01-969 7511)

Rotherithe Workshop, Hope Sufferance Wharf, 61 St Mary Church Street, London SE16 4GE (01-237 5299) *Contact: Ron Perfield*

LIVERPOOL: New Enterprise Workshops, South West Brunswick Dock, Liverpool L3 4AR (051-708 0952)

NEWCASTLE-UPON-TYNE: Newcastle-upon-Tyne New Enterprise Workshop, Albion Row, Byker, Newcastle-upon-Tyne NE6 1LQ (0632 764244) *Contact: R. Dolman*

NOTTINGHAM: Hyson Green Workshops, Lindsay Street, Hyson Green, Nottingham NG7 6AP (0602 708779) *Contact: Mr Brian Sweet*

Sharespace, 13/15 Bridlesmith Gate, Nottingham NG1 2GR (0602 583851) *Contact: Virginia Stunt, Andrew James*

SHIPLEY: Saltaire Workshops, Ashley Lane, Shipley (0274 596746) *Contact: Mr Frank Khune*

TYNE AND WEAR: Tyne and Wear Innovation and Development Co. Ltd, Green Lane Industrial Estate, Pelaw, Tyne and Wear NE10 0UW (0632 382468) *Contact: Dr J. A. Hedley*

WEST MIDLANDS: Waterfall Lane, c/o A & J Mucklow, Halesowen Road, Cradley Heath, Warley B64 7JB (021–550 1841)

WEST YORKSHIRE: Pennine Heritage Ltd, The Birchplace Centre, Hebden Bridge, West Yorkshire HX7 8GD (042-284 3626) *Contact: Jennifer Holt*

SCOTLAND

DENNY: The Denny Bonnybridge Project, 42 Stirling Street, Denny, FK6 6DJ (0324 825574)

DUNDEE: Dundee Enterprise Workshop, Logie Avenue, Dundee DD2 2ER (0382 67951) *Contact: Mr Finan*

GLASGOW: Clyde Workshops, Fullarton Road, Tollcross, Glasgow G32 8YL (041-641 4972) *Contact: S. Morrison*
Govan Workspace, 6 Harmony Row, Glasgow G51 3BA (041-445 2340) *Contact: Pat Cassidy*
HAMILTON: Hamilton New Enterprise Workshops, Dept of Strathclyde Regional Council, Portland Place (behind Brown's Car Wash), Hamilton (0698 283082) *Contact: Mr Tom Clark*
PAISLEY: Paisley New Enterprise Workshop, Storey Street, Paisley (041-889 0688) *Contact: Mr R. Wright*
FORT WILLIAM: Enterprise Workshops, Locgaber, Annat Point, Corpach, Fort William, Inverness-shire (0397 7391)

WALES
SWANSEA: The Swansea Business Centre, Alexandra House, Alexandra Rd, Swansea SA1 1ED (0792 476076)

Other Initiatives

These are recorded in part because they are new and important and also as they may be indicative of trends elsewhere in the country.

The IBA Register, 12 Scott Road, Hove BN3 5HN (0273 720836) *Contact: Mary Hoskins* If you want to construct your own small workshop and take advantage of the generous 100% capital allowance, you could invest £10.00 for a subscription to this register. It is a list of properties that qualify for the industrial building allowance tax shelter, and is updated each month. The service was launched in December 1983.

London Property Register, Greater London Council, Island Block, County Hall, London SE1 7PB (01-633 7494). This provides a wide range of free advisory services to help businessmen to locate, re-locate and expand in London. These include:

- a register of available sites and buildings for rent or sale throughout Greater London, whether in public or private ownership;
- advice on administrative and statutory requirements, such as building, planning and fire regulations, aimed at saving time and cutting through all unnecessary red tape, so that delays and frustrations in implementing development plans are minimised;
- assistance and advice on all matters concerned directly or indirectly with the development or redevelopment of industrial/commercial land and buildings, whether privately or publicly owned;
- help with the recruitment of staff by operating a scheme to find homes for essential workers;
- immediate access to a network of contacts in industry, the

73

London boroughs, and government departments concerned with trade, and industry and land use;

- contacts with banks and finance houses to help firms resolve their financial problems;
- information on eligibility for grants or loans in support of schemes to protect and create jobs in certain designated areas of London under the Inner Urban Areas Act, 1978.

(Other major cities probably have similar centres; ring your town hall for details.)

Lenta Properties Ltd, 69 Cannon Street, London EC4 5AB (01-248 9383) Formed in 1981 to act as a catalyst in the supply of premises and an adviser to those looking for premises in and around London. It has also bought and developed property itself. One site completed in 1982 has 45 small workshops and stores ranging from 200 to 1300 sq. ft.

The London Small Business Property Trust, 2/3 Robert Street, London WC2N 6BH. Set up in 1982 to invest in small business property in the Greater London area. Using some £7 million of local authority pension fund money, it can provide finance to help the development of suitable premises for small firms. The Trust is promoted by an associate company of the Chartered Institute of Public Finance and Accountancy, Granby Hunter and URBED (Urban & Economic Development Ltd).

Conventional Methods

Do not forget the more obvious ways of finding premises. These still account for the great majority of satisfied customers.

Dalton's Weekly specialises in a wide range of business areas, including both vacant property and going concerns.

Local newspapers often have a special day each week for business premises (see Section 3, page 88, for more details).

Business transfer agents are analogous to estate agents and are listed in the Yellow Pages.

Local authorities frequently have lists; contact your Industrial Development Officer for advice on local agencies.

Estate agents specialising in business premises are listed in the Yearbook of the Royal Institute of British Architects, available in the commercial section of larger public libraries.

A Guide to Office and Industrial Rental Trends in England and Wales is published free every six months by Jones Lang Wootton, Research Library, 103 Mount Street, London W1Y6 AS (01-493 6040) This will give you some idea of the level of rents in 50 major towns in England and Wales.

ENTERPRISE ZONES

Twenty-five Enterprise Zones have been defined within some inner cities and other neglected urban black spots. The zones can give new businesses substantial financial benefits as well as freedom from control. In this way business both inside and on the perimeter of the zones will be strengthened. The zones are not aimed exclusively at small or new firms, but nevertheless they provide an attractive commercial inducement to locate in them. The first zone to become operational was in the lower Swansea Valley in June 1981. The facilities, grants and other assistance available within each zone are comprehensively described in Zoning in on Enterprise by David Rodrigues and Pete Bruinvels (Kogan Page Ltd, 120 Pentonville Road, London N1). Monitoring Enterprise Zones, by Roger Tym and Partners, 26 Craven Street, London WC2 Price: £14.00. This report was prepared on performances of the first 11 Enterprise Zones, for the government, by these consultants (January 1984). The Zones are:

Belfast Enterprise Zone Office, Clarendon House, 9/21 Adelaide Street, Belfast BT2 8DJ (0232 248449) *Contact: D. Myles*

Clydebank Enterprise Zone, Clydebank District Council, Clydebank District Council Offices, Clydebank G81 1PG (041-941 1331) *Contact: Mr D. Wilson*

Corby Enterprise Zone, Douglas House, 34 Queen's Square, Corby (053-63 62571) *Contact: Mr McClenaghan*

Delyn Enterprise Zone, Enterprise House, Aberpark Place, Clwyd CH6 5AY (0352 64004) *Contact: M. Gibson*

Dudley Enterprise Zone, Industrial Development Unit, Dudley Metropolitan Borough, Council House, Dudley, West Midlands DY1 1HF (0384 55433) *Contact: Mr Roger Lathan*

Glanford (Flixborough) Enterprise Zone, Glanford Borough Council, Station Road, Brigg St, Humberside (0652 52441) *Contact: Mr D. D. H. Cameron*

Hartlepool Enterprise Zone, Hartlepool Borough Council, Civic Centre, Hartlepool, Cleveland FS24 8AY (0429 665522) *Contact: Mr E. Morley, Industrial Development Officer*

Invergordon Enterprise Zone, 62 High Street, Invergordon IV18 0DH (0349 853666) *Contact: C. Rennie, A. McCreevey*

London Enterprise Zone, London Docklands Development Corporation, West India House, Millwall Dock, London E14 (01-515 3000) *Contact: Sue Hepburn*

Londonderry Enterprise Zone, 3 Water Street, Londonderry BT48 6BQ (0504 263992) *Contact: E. Cartin*

Middlesbrough: Britannia Enterprise Zone, Middlesbrough (0642 222279) *Contact: D. Brydon*

Milford Haven Waterways Enterprise Zone, Preseli District Council, Cumbria House, Haverfordwest, Dyfed (0437 4551) *Contact: I. W. R. David*

Newcastle City Council, Econ. Development Unit Policy Service Department, Civic Centre, Newcastle NE1 8QN (0632 328520 ext 5046) *Contact: C. Hammer*

N E Lancashire Enterprise Zone, Stephen House, Bethesda St, Burnley, Lancs BB11 1PR (0282 37411) *Contact: I. W. Brodhurst*

N W Kent Enterprise Zone, Medway Development Offices, Mountbatten House, 88 Military Road, Chatham, Kent ME4 4TE *Contact: D. Homewood*

Rotherham Enterprise Zone, Ind. Development Unit, Norfolk House, Walker Place, Rotherham S60 1QT (0709 72099) *Contact: P. Fairholm*

Scunthorpe Enterprise Zone, Ind. Dev. and Enterprise Agency, Scunthorpe Borough Council, Civic Centre, Ashby Road, Scunthorpe, S Humberside *Contact: J. Knox*

Speke Enterprise Zone, Liverpool Development Agency, 11 Dale Street, Municipal Buildings, Liverpool L2 2ER (051-227 3296) *Contact: Tom Miller*

Swansea Enterprise Zone, 63–75 Samlet Road, Llanlet, Swansea SA7 9AG *Contact: the Manager*

Tayside Enterprise Zone, Industrial Development Office, Angus District Council, Market Street, Forfar (0307 65101 or 0382 29122) *Contact: W. Ferguson*

Telford Enterprise Zone, Hasledene House, Central Square, Telford Centre, Telford TF3 4TL (0952 502277) *Contact: M. Morgan*

Trafford Park Enterprise Zone, Borough Council, Birch House, Talbot Road, Old Trafford, Lancashire (061-872 6133) *Contact: R. M. C. Shields, Chief Executive*

Tyneside Enterprise Zone, Gateshead MBC, Town Hall, West Street, Gateshead MA8 1B (0632 771011) *Contact: Mr C. Smith*

Wakefield Enterprise Zone, City of Wakefield MDC, Newton Bar, Wakefield (0924 370211) *Contact: Mr Williams or Mr Clay (ext 535)*

Wellingborough Enterprise Zone, Director of Development, Borough Council of Wellingborough Council Offices, Tithebarn Road, Wellingborough, Northants NN8 1BN (0933 229777) *Contact: R. H. Entwistle*

Workington (Allerdale) Enterprise Zone, Mobet Trading Estate, Workington CA14 3YB (0900 65656) *Contact: D. G. Thomas*

OTHER BUSINESS ASSOCIATIONS

Alliance of Small Firms and Self-employed People Ltd, 42 Vine Road, East Molesey, Surrey KT8 9LF (01-979 2293) The alliance aims to represent and publicise the interests of its members at both national and local level. Membership costs £15.00 per annum (subscription of newsletter for non-members costs £9.00), and a legal expenses insurance cover is available for a further £15.00. Members can use the Alliance's Enquiry

Services, which give advice and information on a wide range of tax, legal and employment matters. If they cannot give you an answer they will put you in touch with a consultant who can. The first consultation is free, and thereafter you agree a price with the consultant direct.

Association of Independent Businesses, Trowbray House, 108 Weston Street, London SE1 3QB (01-403 4066). This was established in 1968 to promote the cause of the smaller business. The aim of the association is to remove discrimination against independent businesses in existing and proposed legislation, and so it maintains close contact with both Whitehall and Westminster. Its small national office staff has a limited capacity to answer members' queries on typical problems that face independent businesses. They can also signpost enquirers to other useful sources of advice.

Association of British Chambers of Commerce, Sovereign House, 212a Shaftesbury Avenue, London WC2H 8EW (01-240 5832/6). A co-ordinating body for Chambers of Commerce (see Chambers of Industry and Commerce below)

Association of Industrial Liaison Officers, c/o David Shepherd, Cambridge College of Arts and Technology, Collier Road, Cambridge CB1 2AJ (0223 63271). Formed in 1979 to promote better understanding and collaboration between education establishments and industry.

Black Business Development Unit, Polytechnic of the South Bank, Manor House, 58 Clapham Common Northside, London SW4 9RZ (01-223 8977/8)

Centre for Employment Initiatives, 140a Gloucester Mansions, Cambridge Circus, London WC2H 8PA (01-240 8901) Established in 1982 to provide practical assistance to organisations who are trying to deal with unemployment problems. They are independent and non-profit orientated. Their quarterly journal *Initiatives* has articles on new local economic development activities.

Chambers of Industry and Commerce, Sovereign House, 212a Shaftesbury Avenue, London WC2H 8EW (01-240 5831/6) Apart from playing an important role in providing information and help for existing businesses, chambers of commerce have been a major force in the launching of many of the most prominent and effective Enterprise Agencies. They have also sponsored many local new business competitions. They are a very important source of information, advice and help for new and small businesses. (They should be listed in your telephone directory.)

Confederation of British Industry (CBI), Centre Point, 103 New Oxford Street, London WC1A 1DU (01-379 7400). Their Smaller Firms Council carries out research and publishes papers concerning the needs of smaller firms. Through this work they set out to influence government policy towards small business and government-sponsored activity in this field.

Ethnic Minority Small Business Centre, The Queens College, Glasgow, 1 Park Drive, Glasgow G3 6LP (041-334 8141) *Contact: Dr G. Richardson.* This is to be set up in the autumn of 1984 with the following objectives:

- to provide appropriate business training facilities;
- to provide an information centre;
- to undertake research designed to increase knowledge about small business activity in ethnic minority groups;
- to provide a consultancy service to new and existing businesses;
- to provide physical facilities for the ethnic minority business community;
- to support the development of appropriate facilities elsewhere in Scotland.

Executive Secondment Ltd (EXSEC), Treforest Industrial Estate, Pontypridd, Mid-Glamorgan, CF37 5UT (044-385 2666) *Contact: George Atkins.* Financially sound businesses with between 10 and 150 employees in Wales could have an Executive on secondment from EXSEC. Secondments last up to six months and it will only cost the firm about £15.00 per day.

Federation of Medium and Small Employers, Enterprise House, Pack and Prime Lane, Henley-on-Thames, Oxon RG9 1YU (04912 6161)

The Forum of Private Business Ltd, Ruskin Chambers, Drury Lane, Knutsford, Cheshire WA16 6HA (0565 4467). This is a non-profit-making organisation with the objectives of promoting and preserving a system of free competitive enterprise in the UK, and also of giving private people a greater voice in the legislations, that affects their business. The forum researches and distributes a Referendum nine times a year, keeping members informed and asking their views on a number of topical and important business issues. It makes government aware of these views both directly and by various public relations activities. The forum also plays a role by initiating training programmes in schools and colleges to show the importance of free enterprise in our society. Voting membership rises to a maximum if £250.00 per annum.

The Institute of Directors, 116 Pall Mall, London SW1Y 5ED (01-839 1233). The institute represents the interests both of the directors of large companies and owner directors of smaller ones. In particular, it has a service for putting those looking for funds or other resources in touch with those with funds to invest.

Institute of Management Services, 1 Cecil Court, London Road, Enfield, Middlesex EN2 6DD (01-363 7452)

The Institute of Small Business, 57/61 Mortimer Street, London W1N 7TD (01-637 4383) Offers an advisory service, fact sheets and two monthly publications to its members.

Intermediate Technology Development Group, 9 King Street, London WC2E 8HN (01-836 9434)

Job Creation Ltd, 17/18 Old Bond Street, London W1X 3DA (01-409 2229) *Contact: Patrick Naylor, Chairman.* Sets out to create new job opportunities in these areas:

- by establishing and managing the physical and psychological environment in which new businesses can start up and prosper, often by the conversion of old buildings into new business centres;
- by helping existing local businesses to take opportunities for expansion or diversification;
- by attracting mobile projects to areas of concern.
- through consultancy by conducting feasibility studies for job creation programmes, and also by undertaking major strategic studies;
- by developing, setting up and managing advanced business centres and science parks, an area in which Job Creation Ltd and its associates are exceptionally qualified;
- in the field of property by disposing of or converting redundant industrial sites often combining job creation with turning a property liability into a valuable asset;
- by European Community Representation, working on behalf of UK companies, assisting them to obtain maximum grants and loans from EEC funds.

They already have an impressive client list of major companies and councils, and a very high powered team of executives and associates.
Regional offices are:

Job Creation Ltd, Belfast Enterprise Zone Office, Clarendon House, 9–21 Adelaide Street, Belfast BT2 8DJ (02322 48449) *Contact: Denis Myles*

Gosport Job Creation Project, 15 Lees Lane, Gosport, Hampshire PO12 3UL (07017 80711/24331) *Contact: Jeff Rattle*

Wirral Business Centre, Gorsey Lane/Dock Road, Birkenhead, Merseyside L41 1JW (051-639 6393) *Contact: Vic Jones*

Job Creation bv, Korte Poten 7, 2511 EB the Hague, Netherlands (010 31 70 65 3338) *Contact: Dick Ponsen*

Job Creation Inc., c/o Mott Foundation, Mott Foundation Building, FLINT, Michigan 48502, USA (010 1 313 238 5651) *Contact: Peter Hardwick*

Job Creation Ltd, Lilienthalstrasse 7–25, 3500 Kassel-Bettenhause, West Germany (010 49 5061 50951) *Contact: Keith Freestone*

Job Creation Ltd, Melitta Road, Kildare, Eire (Eire 345 21522) *Contact: Gerry Wycherley*

Job Creation Ltd, c/o Zimbabwe Project, Old Shell House, Baker Avenue, Harare, Zimbabwe (010 2630 703239) *Contact: D. H. O'Brien*

Local Enterprise Trusts Co-ordinator, 10 Grenfell Road, Beaconsfield, Bucks (04946 3080)

Local Initiatives Support Ltd, The Adderbury Rookery, Banbury, Oxon OX17 3NA (0295 810993)

The National Federation of Self-employed and Small Businesses Ltd, 32 St Annes Road, West Lytham, St Annes, Lancashire FY8 1NY (0253 720911) Press and Parliamentary office: 140 Lower Marsh, Westminster Bridge, London SE1 7AE (01-928 9272). The federation is a campaigning pressure group in business to promote and protect the interests of all who are either self-employed or who own or are directors of small businesses. Formed in 1974, it now has some 50,000 members in 300 branches throughout the UK. The federation has the funds to take major test cases of importance to small business through the expensive legal process leading to the House of Lords (or European Court of Human Rights). They have been particularly effective in taxation and VAT matters.

Amongst other benefits, members are covered by a legal expenses compensation cover scheme. The cover includes:

- VAT tribunal representation and costs up to £10,000 per case to appeal in VAT disputes;
- defence of health and safety prosecutions, covering costs of prosecution under the Health and Safety at Work Act, 1974;
- in-depth investigation cover to meet accountants' fees in helping to deal with Inland Revenue investigation;
- Industrial Tribunal Compensation Awards to meet unfair dismissal awards. (This is supported by a telephone legal advice service.)

Full membership costs £18.00 per annum; £10 joining fee.

New World Business Consultancy, 2a Camberwell Green, London SE5 7AA (01-708 0130) *Contact: Jonathan Emanuwa* This is an advisory service focusing on the business development potential of economically disadvantaged groups, such as members of ethnic minorities wanting to start up a business. The consultancy operates as an autonomous unit within South Bank Polytechnic Centre for Employment Initiative.

PACE (PA Creating Employment), c/o PA Management Consultants Ltd, Hyde Park House, 60a Knightsbridge, London SW1X 7LE (01-235 6060) This organisation aims at two particular areas: the managed 'industrial village'; and the attraction of jobs into the UK through the initiative of PA's international network of offices.

Scottish Enterprise Foundation, University of Stirling, Stirling FK9 4LA (0786 3171) *Contacts: Tom Cannon, Jack Denny and Bob Hale* Founded in 1982 to encourage enterprise programmes and research, its main initiatives are the Graduate Enterprise Programme, Enterprise Agency Directors Programmes and Action Learning in Small Businesses. It houses a new Small Business Resource Centre charged with bringing together teaching materials, publications and research resources.

The Small Business Bureau, 32 Smith Square, London SW1P 3HH (01-222 9000). Formed in 1976, the bureau aims to serve the needs of the small business community. Membership costs £15 per annum and gives you access to its advisory service and a copy of its monthly newspaper *Small Business*. It also represents the small business point of view to Government, organises trade delegations and provides European opportunities through its involvement with EMSU (the European Medium and Small Business Union).

Small Business Research Trust, 3 Dean Trench Street, Westminster, London SW1P 3HB (01-222 6484/5). The trust intends to become an independent research organisation for small businesses in the UK. Formed in 1983 with a wide base of industrial, institutional and professional support.

Small Firms Information Service of the British Institute of Management, Parker Street, London WC2B 5PT (01-405 3456) The BIM runs a small firms information service to help with the management problems the smaller firm might encounter, and a signposting service to other sources of assistance in the area of general business information. Their publication *Setting* *up in Business* is a package of articles, pamphlets, check lists, reading lists and other material put together for loan to the member who is considering setting up in business for the first time. The material highlights both the problems and the advantages of being self-employed, the various considerations involved in registering a company, tax planning, employing staff, credit control, obtaining finance and gaining help from bank managers and accountants. The service is for members, although non-members may have photocopies of information sent to them for a modest cost.

Trade Associations, to be found through Directory of British Assoc., CBD Research Ltd, Beckenham, Kent. Most business fields have a trade association, such as the Brewers Society, the Federation of Fish Friers, or the Booksellers Association. They are a useful source of help and advice to potential new entrants to their trade. This directory lists all such associations.

The Union of Independent Companies, Alan Randall, 71 Fleet Street, London EC4 (01-583 9305) telex: 298681 ComSerG – This is a non-political organisation formed in 1977 by a number of small independent industrialists in the south west of England. Its aim is to create an environment which will stimulate the independent sector of the economy and generally to further the interests of the small independent company, in both the manufacturing and servicing sectors.

The UIC works through small groups who run independent companies in many parliamentary constituencies to research the problems affecting small independent companies and their potential growth and to develop methods of mutual assistance and combination. The UIC has a small effective headquarters in Fleet Street, London, where it maintains active contact with Whitehall, Westminster and the press. It disseminates literature, information and a monthly newsletter to members.

BUSINESS OPPORTUNITIES

If you know what kind of business you want and you plan either to start from scratch, or, if you are already in business, to grow from your existing base, then these ideas and opportunities may not be for you. There are, however, a very large number of people who simply know that they would like to work for themselves – quite what at they are not sure.

There is nothing unusual about this phenomenon, sometimes an event such as redundancy, early retirement or a financial windfall may prompt you into searching for a business opportunity, or perhaps into extending the scope of an existing business idea. Business ideas themselves very often come from the knowledge and experience gained in previous jobs, but they take time to germinate. More usually people only really start to think seriously (and usefully) about an idea when it becomes an opportunity.

NEW PRODUCTS OR BUSINESSES

Although you may not know exactly what you want to do, you will have certain resources and skills. Contacting people with complementary 'features' is one way of getting into business, or expanding an existing business.

There are a number of organisations and publications that put people in touch with business opportunities and new products.

Organisations
BAR (Agents Register) Ltd, 23 Victoria Avenue, Harrogate (0423 60608) Caters for commercial, distributive and buying agents. Membership costs £20.00. Their publication, *The Guide to Agency Agreements and Contracts* (£4.00) is a must. See also the Manufacturers Agents Association later in this section.

The Business Co-operation Centre, rue Archimède 17, B-1040 Brussels. This centre was set up in 1972 to assist small and medium-sized firms to contact and co-operate with companies with similar interests in the EEC. The centre was established on an experimental basis for a period of three years, but proved sufficiently popular to become a permanent service providing information to companies on economic, legal, tax and financial aspects of cross-frontier co-operation and integration. In addition, the centre acts as a marriage bureau for small and medium-sized firms, putting potential partners in touch with one another and assisting in preliminary discussions.

Any firm seeking the centre's help is asked to provide certain information about itself, and to define exactly what type of partner or what type of co-operation it wants. All the information supplied, and any queries received, are treated as strictly confidential, and no names are revealed without the agreement of all parties. The centre will search its files for a suitable partner and, if the application cannot be matched, will, if the firm agrees, circulate a summary of its requirements, with no names mentioned, to its 'correspondents' in all EEC countries.

Business Link-up, 33 St George Street, London W1R 9FA (01-499 4714) A contact agency for those wishing to find a new partner for a business enterprise.

Ideas and Resource Exchange Ltd (IREX), Snow House, 103 Southwark Street, London SE1 0JF (01-633 0424); telex 25187 SM1 W1LG IREX, founded in 1981, and extensively enhanced in January 1982 'deals' in saleable resources. These are the elements of a business broadly classified as ideas, skills, finance, capacity and markets. These resources (or any combination of them) are offered or sought by members, using a computer-based exchange. A member's entry in the exchange data box is called a proposition. This entry is based on a short statement written by the proposer giving the basic details of what he wants, either to receive or to offer. This information is coded, entered into the computer, which then carries out a matching run. When the computer finds that a member is offering what another is looking for, it records a match, after which the respective members' propositions are printed out. Contact can then be made in a way that ensures whatever level of security and confidentiality the respective members want. Membership costs £100 for one year's subscription, this includes 20 introductions.

This seems a sound, economical and quick way of putting your under-used resources to work in exploiting a business opportunity. The Directors of IREX have an impressive past track record. They include Sir Alexander Smith (Chairman), who until 1981 was the Director of Manchester Polytechnic, and Colin Lyle, a Director of Tate & Lyle.

Since the index began in February 1981, members have recorded nearly 10,000 matches, and there is now over £8.5

million on IREX's data-base available to help finance new or existing business. The Skills Register is a register of people with professional, executive or technical skills who are seeking employment or work assignments on contract.

At present the system deals only with people whose skills are broadly in the areas of Accountancy, Computing, Data-processing, Engineering (all specialisations) and Management Consultancy. The range will be extended.

The Manufacturers' Agents Association (MAA), 13a West Street, Reigate, Surrey (07372 43492), can advise you on becoming an Agent in almost any trade. Membership costs £32.20. If you are choosing this route to self-employment take on more than one agency. And make sure you have a written agreement, preferably using the standard MAA Agreement Form which costs 60p.

Marriage Bureau, The London Enterprise Agency (LENTA), 69 Cannon Street, London EC4N 5AB (01-236 2676/7 or 01-248 4444). Each month a bulletin is produced in which subscribers can advertise anonymously, either offering a resource, product, service or idea, or appealing for one themselves. Companies or individuals interested in a box number – in this way things are kept confidential – write to the bureau, who then set about arranging contact between the parties.

LENTA has no involvement in any negotiations resulting from the 'Marriage Bureau' introduction. Nor do they accept responsibilities for what happens later. Their service costs £30.00 per annum for registered investors and £20.00 for businesses seeking finance, and with over 100 advertisements in one issue you should find an interesting range of new opportunities.

There are also organisations that provide new products or business opportunities in the area of high technology. More details of these are given in Section 4.

Tourism – The National Tourist Board provide a service advising potential investors and operators of new business opportunities. The last English Tourist board annual report listed 200 possible projects.

English Tourist Board, 4 Grosvenor Gardens, London SW1 WODU (01-730 3400)

Welsh Tourist Board, Brunel House, 2 Fitzalen Road, Cardiff CF2 1UY (0222 499909)

Scottish Tourist Board, 23 Ravelston Terrace, Edinburgh EH4 3EH (031-332 2433)

Northern Ireland Tourist Board, River House, 48 High Street, Belfast BT1 2DS (0232 231221)

Publications

Business Ideas Letter This is published by Stonehart Publications, Hainault Road, Little Heath, Romford, Essex (01-597 7335) Each month this publication reviews, step by step, the process of starting up a selection of businesses. For example, in one month their articles included 'How to Start a Small Hotel' and 'Starting a Picture-framing Business'. All the critical steps were examined and useful advice was given. Contact addresses for finding more detailed information is provided at the conclusion of each article. From September 1984 this has been re-titled *New Business Ideas*.

Business Opportunities Digest, 11–12 Bloomfield Street, London EC2M 7AY. A monthly subscription magazine, price £19.50 for 12 issues. Introduces and explains business ideas and how to make them work for you.

How To Buy a Business This is a guide for the small businessman by Peter Farrell, published in 1983 by Kogan Page Ltd, 120 Pentonville Road, London N1. This book examines the advantages and risks of buying a business. It looks at why and when you should buy, how to judge a business's track record, why it is for sale, how to evaluate its assets and what it is worth. Finally there is a chapter on how to finance a purchase. *Contents*: 1 Why buy? 2 Why is it for sale? 3 What are you buying? 4 Judging the track record. 5 Evaluating the assets. 6 What is the right price? Can you afford it? 7 Paying for it. Price £4.95.

Chartsearch Ltd, 11–12 Bloomfield Street, London EC2M 7AY (01-623 5242). These are publishers of a series of books on starting or improving a small business. Prices range from £4.00 to £15.00.

The Entrepreneur, Alston, Cumbria CA9 3RP. Published monthly at £32.50 p.a.

Entrepreneur, published by Chase Revel Inc., 2311 Pontins Avenue, Los Angeles, California 90064, USA. UK price is £1.50 per issue (monthly). The publication gives a very invigorating view of American business opportunities, by the hundred.

The Insolvency Supplement, published fortnightly by Venture Capital Report, 2 The Mall, Bristol BS8 4DR (0272 737222), is a detailed directory of receiverships, liquidations and auctions, providing many opportunities to acquire going concerns and business assets. Price £45.00 p.a.

Just For Starters. A handbook of small-scale business opportunities, by Alan Bollard, published in 1984 by Intermediate Technology Publications, 9 King Street, London WC2E 8HN, price £12.50. A detailed survey of opportunities in the UK market followed by statistical surveys of nearly 50 industries and profiles of 33 of them.

New Product/New Business Digest, published by General Electric USA, Business Growth Services, 120 Erie Boulevard, Room 144, Schenectady, New York 12305, USA. The digest began 14 years ago as an outlet for GE's developments only, but now it is an extensively researched book. It describes, and in many cases illustrates, over 500 products and processes that are available for acquisition or licensing. The products/businesses, large and very small, range from new inventions and R & D spin-offs, to fully developed and tooled-up products. The opportunities come from Universities, R & D firms, USA Government agencies (such as the Small Business Bureau) entrepreneurs and major companies (including GE). A very useful source either to get you started or to extend your existing product range.

The digest consists of 67 pages and costs around $60.00 including postage to the UK.

Opportunities, A Handbook of Business Opportunity Search, by Edward de Bono, published in 1980 by Penguin Books, 536 King's Road, London SW1, price £2.25. This will certainly get you started. The whole book is thought-provoking, and the final part, 'Thinking for Opportunities', has a hundred pages that set out to answer two vital questions: 'How do you set about looking for business opportunities?' and 'Where do you start to look for those opportunities?'. It is mind-bending but it will open your eyes. An opportunity only exists when you can see it.

Venture Capital Report, 2 The Mall, Bristol BS8 4DR (0272 737222). This is a publication that gives details of entrepreneurs and their business ventures, inviting people with money to invest, often on a partnership basis, £150.00 per annum.

Working for Yourself, by Godfrey Golzen, published by Kogan Page, 120 Pentonville Road, London N1. This is the very successful *Daily Telegraph* book, in its sixth edition (August 1983). Apart from useful sections on the general mechanics of starting a business, tax, raising money, etc., there is a Directory of Opportunities. In this section you are given an insight into the pros and cons of some 60 different types of business, together with addresses and contact points to follow up those of interest to you. Price £5.95 (This is a good starting point in the opportunity search.)

Newspapers One of the best ways to keep abreast of current business opportunities is to read a selection of national and local papers. Start off with as wide a range as you can afford (or visit your library) to get the flavour of each. Then once you have made a selection, keep searching. Many articles give details of useful follow-up addresses.

Paper	Day and Writer	Section
Birmingham Mail and Post (021-236 3366)	Monday–Friday Stephen Keeling	Business page Business & Industrial Mail and Post
Bradford Telegraph and Argus (0274 729511)	Monday–Friday Chris Holland	Industry Page
Coventry Evening Telegraph (0203 25588)	Monday–Friday Ken Read	Business News, plus 16-page supplement every month called Business Life
Daily Express (01-353 8000)	Monday Tim Blackstone	Finance Page
Daily Mail (01-606 1234)	Wednesday David Lewis	Moneymail Moneywise; 2 & 3; Questions Answers; Current Accounts
Dalton's Weekly (01-949 6199)	Thursday	Extensive coverage of businesses for sale and business opportunities, partnerships, etc.
Exchange & Mart (01-680 6800)	Thursday	Business opportunities section
Financial Times (01-248 8000)	Tuesday Christopher Lorenz Tim Dickson	The Management Pages – two pages of business opportunities and companies for sale and wanted
The Guardian (01-278 2332)	Friday Clive Woodcock	Small Business Section Frequent stories of small business success and the new sources of help and advice
Hull Daily Mail (0482 27111)	Wednesday John Simpson	Industrial Note-book

Lancashire Evening Post (0524 66226)	Monday Bill Carmichael	Business Post
Liverpool Post (051-227 2000)	Monday–Friday Keith Ely	Business News Business supplement 1st Wednesday of every month
Manchester Evening News (061-832 7200)	Monday–Friday Mr Lomax	Business World
Newcastle Journal (0632 327500)	Monday–Saturday Ronnie Harrison	Business News Money on Monday, Business Journal on Tuesday, Thursday, Friday and Saturday; Northern Business on Wednesday
Nottingham Evening Post (0602 45521)	Monday–Saturday Richard Cox Clive Brett	Business Post Monthly Business Magazine (Martin Stevenson)
The Observer (01-236 0202)	Sunday Melvyn Marckus	Observer Business
Sheffield Telegraph (0742 78585)	Monday–Saturday Fraser Wright	Business Business extra on Wednesday
Sunday Telegraph (01-353 4242)	Sunday Ivan Fallon	City Page
Sunday Times (01-837 1234)	Sunday (and Saturday) Roger Elgin	Business News Business to Business section, extremely comprehensive range of business opportunities
The Times (01-837 1234)	Friday (and Saturday–see above)	Your Own Business, new issues in small business field
Western Mail (Cardiff & S Wales) (0222 33022)	Monday–Friday Ken Rice/John Foscolo	Business News
Wolverhampton Express (0902 22351)	Monday–Friday Gordon Key/Brian Blakley	Business Page

Yorkshire Post   Monday–Saturday   Business Post
(0532 432701)   Bernard Dineer/
                 Charles Pritchard/
                 Robin Morgan

CO-OPERATIVES

Although the most commonly known co-operatives are the high street shops and supermarkets, there is another, lesser-known variety, the workers' co-operatives – where workers share control and decision-making equally, and not in relation to their financial stake. They split off from the more successful retail movement, reached a peak of 100 or so outlets at the turn of the century, then declined (almost to the point of extinction).

The Industrial Common Ownership Act, 1976, and the formation of the Co-operative Development Agency (and subsequently the local CDAs) in 1978 gave workers' co-operatives a much needed shot in the arm. Various estimates put the number of workers co-operatives operating in the UK at the end of 1984 at around 1000. Rather more than double the number in 1982. They also seem to be a safer bet than conventional small businesses. Out of 593 co-operatives listed before August 1982, only 95 had ceased trading or become traditional companies. About a fifth of all co-operatives are in the Greater London area, and at the last count these employed some 1600 people. Certainly if the growth of supporting organisations and agencies is anything to go by, this seems a conservative estimate. In order to meet the legal requirements a co-operative must conform to the following rules.

Conduct of business The members must benefit primarily from their participation in the business, i.e. as workers, not merely as investors.

Control Each member has equal control through the principle of 'one person one vote'. Control is not related to the size of financial stake in the business.

Interest repayments A co-operative cannot pay an unlimited return on loan or share capital. Even in good years, interest payments will be limited in some specified way.

Surplus This may be wholly retained in the business or distributed in part to the members in proportion to their involvement, e.g. according to hours worked.

Membership This must be open to anybody satisfying the qualifications for membership.

The main attraction to co-operatives lies in the belief that shared control and decision-making leads to a greater level of work satisfaction. It is an unlikely path to wealth. There may be many partnerships and limited companies that operate close to the lines of a co-operative. They usually recognise that, in order to grow and survive, the door to larger funds than co-operatives can attract must be kept open.

The Co-operative Development Agency and local CDAs are a good starting point in the search for more information on workers' co-operatives.

Co-operative Development Agency (01-839 2988) The agency was established by Parliament in 1978 with all-party support to promote the concept of co-operatives. It gives advice on the mechanics and philosophy of co-operatives to people starting a new business or wanting to convert an existing business that might otherwise be sold or closed down.

Either from the central office or through its growing network of local Co-operative Development Agencies, the CDA can advise on local opportunities for co-operatives, and will evaluate specific projects from a commercial as well as a co-operative point of view. It can also give advice on sources of finance, legal and taxation problems, education, training and publicity. The CDA has no money of its own to finance co-operatives, and those who are able to pay are charged the cost of the advice and assistance given.

Details can be sent on request of a series of publications which cover various aspects of the co-operative movement.

Local Co-operative Development Agencies. A variety of bodies have been set up in local areas to promote co-operatives. Some have full-time staff funded by a local authority: some are based on existing co-operatives; others are run solely by volunteers. None of them is an agent of the national Co-operative Development Agency, but many have close working relationships with it.

Co-operative Development Agencies

Co-operative Development Agency (CDA), Broadmead House, 21 Panton Street, London SW1Y 4DR (01-839 2987) *Contact: Ian Brierley, Tony Marris, Ken Lucas*

CDA Belfast Office, c/o Ulster People's College, 30 Adelaide Park, Belfast 9 (0232 665368/665161) *Contact: Gerry Finnegan, Paul Kelly*

CDA Manchester Office, c/o Co-op Union, Holyoake House, Hanover Street, Manchester M60 0AS (061-832 4300 ext 288) *Contact: Ian Brierley, Tony Marris, Philip Riley*

Local Co-operative Development Agencies

Afan Co-operative Development Agency, 2nd Floor Royal Buildings, Talbot Road, Port Talbot, West Glamorgan (0639 895173)

Antur Broydd Cymru/Welsh Community Enterprise, c/o 3 Christina Street, Swansea SA1 4EW (0792 53498)

Antur Teifi, Graig Chambers, Newcastle Emlyn, Dyfed (0239 710238)

A.T.E.C., 4 Grove Terrace, Bradford, Yorkshire (0274 394083)

Avon Co-operative Development Agency, c/o Planning Department, Avon County Council, PO Box 46, Avon House North, St James Barton, Bristol BS99 7EU (0272 290777)

Barnet and Enfield Co-operative Development Steering Committee, c/o Mr John Gibson, 33 Ashbourne Court, Woodside Park Road, London N12 (01-446 3172)

Basildon District Co-operative Development Agency, Nevendon School, Burnt Mills Road, Basildon, Essex (0268 286436)

Berkshire Co-operative Development Steering Committee, Constables, Windsor Road, Ascot, Berkshire SL5 7LF (0990 21167)

Berkshire Co-operative Development Steering Committee, Reading Centre for the Unemployed, 4–6 East Street, Reading, Berkshire (0734 596639)

Birmingham Co-operative Development Agency, 3rd Floor, Bridge House, Bull Ring Centre, Smallbrook, Queensway, Birmingham B5 4JP (021-643 3531)

Black Country Co-operative Development Agency, Lich Buildings, 44 Queens Square, Wolverhampton, W Midlands (0902 773506/7)

Brent Co-operative Development Agency, 192 High Road, Willesdon, London NW10 2PB (01-451 3777)

Brighton Area Co-operative Development Agency, c/o John Woolham, Brighton CVS, 17 Ditchling Rise, Brighton BN1 4QL (0273 692664)

Cambridge Co-operative Development Agency, Office 5, 25 Gwydir Street, Cambridge CB1 2LL (0223 60977)

Cardiff and Vale Co-operative Development Association, 5 Mountstuart Square, Cardiff CF1 6EE (0222 494411)

City of Manchester Co-operative Development Agency (MANCODA), 61 Bloom Street, Manchester M1 3LY (061-236 1274)

Cleveland Co-operative Agency, 10A Albert Road, Middlesborough, Cleveland (0642 210224)

Community Initiatives Centre: Wansbeck, Station Villa, Kenilworth Road, Ashington, Northumberland (0670 853619)

Coventry Co-operative Development Agency, Unit 15, The Arches Industrial Estate, Spon End, Coventry CV1 3JQ (0203 714078)

Croydon Co-ops Group, c/o Unemployed Resource Centre, St Mary's Crypt, 70A Wellesley Road, Croydon CRO 2AR (01-686 1222)

Delyn Co-operative Development Agency, c/o Mr S. Hatch, Bryn Mywion Bach, Llanarmon-yn-Ial, Nr Mold, Clwyd (0352 2121 ext 542) (work) (08243 728) (home)

Derbyshire Co-operative Development Agency, 3 The Strand Arcade, Derby DE1 1BQ (0332 380515) Also at: Glossop (04574 3547) Chesterfield (0246 208953)

Devon and Cornwall Co-operative Development Agency, c/o Ms J. Thomson, Co-operative Retail Services Ltd, 2 Fore Street, Bodmin, Cornwall (0208 5457/77512)

Devon and Cornwall Co-operative Development Agency, c/o Mr D. Rees, CoSIRA, Matford Lane, Exeter EX2 4PS (0392 52616)

Devon and Cornwall Co-operative Development Agency, c/o Ms J. Reynolds, Co-operative Retail Services Limited, 30–37 East Street, Taunton, Somerset (0823 73477)

Doncaster Co-operative Development Agency Steering Group, c/o Marisa Graziano, 9 Ulverston Avenue, Askern, S Yorkshire DN6 0RB (0302 700564)

Durham (County) Co-operative Development Agency Steering Committee, c/o Kingsley Matthews, 124 Pentland Close, Peterlee, Co Durham (0783 862014)

Ealing Co-operative Development Agency, Charles House, Bridge Road, Southall, Middlesex UB2 4BD (01-574 4724)

Essex Co-operative Support Group, c/o 33 Clockhouse Way, Braintree, Essex

Essex Co-operative Development Agency, 64 Rothmans Avenue, Great Baddow, Chelmsford, Essex (0245 74039)

Glastonbury Co-operative Development Group, c/o Assembly Rooms, Glastonbury, Somerset

Gloucester Co-ops Group, 24 St Mark Street, Kingsholm, Gloucester GL1 2QQ (0452 502718)

Greenwich Employment Resource Unit, 311 Plumstead High Street, London SE18 1JX (01-310 6695)

Guildford Co-operative Development Agency, c/o GAUPC, 3A Leapale Road, Guildford, Surrey GU1 4JX (0483 33942)

Gwent Common Ownership Association, 78 Bridge Street, Newport, Gwent NPT 4AQ (0633 51868)

Hackney Co-op Developments, 16 Dalston Lane, London E8 3AZ (01-254 4829)

Hammersmith and Fulham Community Enterprise Development Agency, c/o CVS, Bishops Creighton House, 378 Lillie Road, London SW6 7PH (01-381 4446)

Hampshire Co-operative Development Agency, Co-op Party Education Centre, Nancy Road, Portsmouth, Hants (0705 822211 ext 321)

Haringey Co-operative Development Agency, 23 Hornsey Park Road, London N8 (01-889 3998)

Harrow Co-ops Group, c/o Mr T. Louki, 11 Tenby Avenue, Kenton, Harrow HA3 8RU, Middlesex (01-748 1319)

Hull Co-operative Development Steering Committee, c/o Mr T. Topham, Industrial Studies Unit, Department of Adult Education, University of Hull, 195 Cottingham Street, Hull, W Yorkshire (0482 497468)

ICOM London, 245 Coldharbour Lane, London SW9 (01-274 7700 ext 22)

ICOM North, 2 Jesmond Road, Newcastle-upon-Tyne NE2 4PQ (0632 816632)

Islington Co-operative Development Agency, 326–328 St Pauls Road, London N1 2LF (01-226 2783)

Kingston Co-operative Development Agency, Clarence Chambers, Fairfield West, Kingston-on-Thames, Surrey KT2 6QH (01-549 9159)

Lambeth Co-operative Development Agency, 460 Wandsworth Road, London SW8 (01-720 1466)

Lancashire Co-operative Development Agency, c/o Lancashire Enterprises Ltd, Lancashire House, Watery Lane, Preston, Lancashire (0772 735821)

Leeds Co-op Federation, c/o Major Minor Repairs Ltd, 78 Railway Street, Leeds 9, W Yorkshire (0532 444969)

Leicester and County Co-operative Development Agency, 30 New Walk, Leicester LE1 6TF (0533 554464)

Lewisham Co-operative Development Agency Steering Committee, c/o 38 Forestholme Close, Taymount Rise, London SE23 (01-699 7508)

Lewisham Co-operative Development Agency Steering Committee, c/o Rye Express, 8 Hatcham Park Road, London SE14 (01-732 5356)

Lewisham Co-operative Development Agency Steering Committee, c/o Sheila Ryan, Women and Employment Project, 179 Deptford High St, London SE8 (01-691 3550)

Llanelli Co-operative Development Agency, c/o Llanelli Community Services Agency, Castle Buildings, Murray Street, Llanelli, Dyfed (05542 55949)

Manchester (Greater) Co-operative Development Agency, c/o Co-op Union, Holyoake House, Hanover Street, Manchester M60 0AS (061-833 9496)

Medway Towns Co-operative Development Steering Committee, c/o John Black, Medway Towns Young Unemployment Project, 16a New Road Avenue, Chatham, Kent (0634 45555)

Merseyside Co-operative Development Agency, c/o Unemployed Resource Centre, Hardman Street, Liverpool 1 (051-709 4363/4/051-709 3995 ext 142)

Merseyside Federation of Workers Collectives, 9 Kelvin Grove, Liverpool 8 (051-727 4608)

Milton Keynes Co-operative Development Steering Committee, Co-op Research Unit, Open University, Walton Hall, Milton Keynes, Buckinghamshire (0908 652102/3)

Newham Co-operative Development Agency, 55 West Ham Lane, London E15 (01-519 2377)

North Cheshire Co-operative Development Agency, c/o Nigel Cooper, 3 Springfield Street, Warrington WA1 1BB, Cheshire (0925 35961 ext 115)

Northamptonshire Co-operative Development Association, 21–29 Hazelwood Road, Northampton NN1 1LG (0604 24040)

North Hertfordshire and Stevenage Co-operative Development Agency, c/o Martin Stears, 40 Kings Hedges, Hitchin, Hertfordshire (0462 55680 home) (0438 356111 ext 151 work)

Northern Region Co-operative Development Association, Bolbec Hall, Westgate Road, Newcastle-upon-Tyne NE1 1SE (0632 610140)

North Staffordshire Co-operative Development Agency, c/o Mr D. T. Ward, Town Hall, Stoke-on-Trent ST4 1HH, Staffordshire (0782 48241 ext 201)

North West Co-operative Development Council, c/o Greater Manchester CDA, Co-operative Union Ltd, Holyoake House, Hanover Street, Manchester M60 0AS (061-830 4300)

Norwich Co-operative Development Steering Committee, c/o Mike Foster, 1 Onley Street, Norwich

Notting Dale Co-operative Development Agency, c/o Ms J. O'Grady, 32 Addison Avenue, London W11 (01-727 4298)

Nottinghamshire Co-operative Development Agency, Dunkirk Road, Dunkirk, Nottingham NG7 2PH (0602 705700)

Ouse Co-operative Development Agency, c/o Rev. T. Desert, 87 Beverley Cresent, Bedford

Oxford Co-operative Development Association, Ms S. Stramer, c/o 146 Park End Street, Oxford

Salford Community Enterprise Development Agency, c/o Salford Central Mission, Broadway, Salford, Greater Manchester (061-872 0387)

Scottish Co-operatives Development Committee, Templeton Business Centre, Templeton Street, Bridgeton, Glasgow G40 1DA (041-554 3797)

Scottish Co-operatives Development Committee, Aberdeen Business Centre, Willowbank House, Willowbank Road, Aberdeen AB1 2YG

Sheffield Co-operative Development Group, Palatine Chambers, 22 Pinstone Street, Sheffield S1 2HN (0742 734563)

Southampton Co-operative Development Agency Steering Group, c/o Southampton Community Co-op Ltd, 92 St Mary's Road, Southampton SO2 0AH (0703 32583/332421)

Southampton Co-operative Development Steering Group, c/o Mr J. Ellis, 195A Derby Road, Southampton, Hants (0703 332421)

Southwark Co-operative Development Agency, 135 Rye Lane, London SE15 4ST (01-639 0134)

South West Co-ops Group, c/o Mr G. Micklewright, 5 Southville Road, Southville, Bristol (0272 633170)

Sunderland Common Ownership Enterprise Resource Centre (SCOERC), c/o John Blackburn, 44 Mowbray Road, Hendon, Sunderland (0783 650476)

Telford Co-operative Development Agency, c/o Cllr G. Bould, 9 Telford Road, Telford, Shropshire

Tower Hamlets Co-operative Development Agency Steering Committee, c/o Steven & Matilda Tennants Co., 50 Matilda House, St Katherine Way, London E1 (01-481 2557)

The Vaynor Alternative, Trefechan Community Centre, Beechwood Avenue, Trefechan, Merthyr Tydfil, Mid Glamorgan (0685 70357)

Wales Co-operative Development and Training Centre, 55 Charles Street, Cardiff CF1 4ED, South Glamorgan (0222 372237/25141)

Wales Co-operative Development and Training Centre, Morfa Hall, Church Street, Rhyl, Clwyd LL18 3AA (0745 55336)

Waltham Forest Co-operative Development Agency, 160 High Street, Walthamstow, London E17 (01-520 4621)

Wandsworth Enterprise Development Agency, Unity House, 56–60 Wandsworth High Street, London SW18 4LN (01-870 2165)

Warwickshire Co-operative Development Group, c/o Tony Fry, 23 Gordon Street, Leamington Spa, Warwicks CV31 1HR

West Cumbria Co-operative Development Group, c/o Roger Hopcraft, 13 Derwent Row, Broughton Cross, Nr Cockermouth, Cumbria (0900 823741)

West Glamorgan Common Ownership Development Association, 3 Christina Street, Swansea SA1 3EW, West Glamorgan (0792 53498)

Westminster, Kensington and Chelsea Co-operative Development Agency, 58A Oxford Gardens, North Kensington London W10 5UJ (01-968 7744)

York Co-ops Group, c/o York Community Bookshop, Shelf 9, 73 Walmgate, York (0904 37355)

Local Authority Officers With Specific Remit to Promote Co-operatives

Barnsley Metropolitan Council Peter Milford, Co-operatives Co-ordinator, Barnsley Metropolitan Council, Barnsley Enterprise Centre, Pontefract Road, Barnsley, S Yorkshire (0226 298091)

Calderdale Metropolitan Council Chris Green, Strategy Section, Chief Executives Department, Calderdale Metropolitan Council, Town Hall, Halifax (0422–57257) *also* 49 Halifax Road, Todmorden

London Borough of Camden Steve Angove, Economic Development Unit, London Borough of Camden Town Hall, Euston Road, London NW1 2RU (01-278 4444 ext 2825)

Cardiff City Council Peter Fortune, Industrial Development Officer, Cardiff City Council, 5 Mounstuart Square, Cardiff CF1 6EE (0222 494411)

London Borough of Hammersmith and Fulham Andy Flockhart, Economic Development Unit, London Borough of Hammersmith & Fulham, Town Hall, King Street, London W6 9JU (01-748 3020 ext 5319)

London Borough of Haringey Desmond Shield, Economic Development Unit, London Borough of Haringey, 98–100 High Road, Wood Green, London N22 (01-881 3000 ext 3386/3343)

London Borough of Hounslow Neil Miller, London Borough of Hounslow, The Civic Centre, Lampton Road, Hounslow, London TW3 4DM (01-570 7728 ext 3020)

Hull City Council David Gay, Department of Industrial Development, City of Hull, 76/78 Lowgate, Hull, W Yorkshire (0482 222627)

Kirklees Metropolitan Council Michael McGowan, Co-operative Development Officer, Employment Development Unit, Kirklees Metropolitan Council, Estate Buildings, Railway Street, Huddersfield, W Yorkshire HD1 1JU (0484 22133 ext 633)

Leeds City Council Chas Ball, Co-operative Development Officer, Department of Industry & Estates, Leeds City Council, 44 The Headrow, Leeds LS1 8EA (0532 463208/463170)

London Borough of Lewisham Sarah Glenn, Employment Promotion Unit, London Borough of Lewisham, Town Hall Chambers, Lewisham, London SE6 (01-690 4343 ext 630)

Greater London Council Jay Thakker, Ethnic Minorities Unit, Greater London Council, Room 686A County Hall, London SE1 7BP (01-633 1274)

Merthyr Tydfil Borough Council Geoff Pride, Self-Employment Initiative Officer, Merthyr Tydfil Borough Council, Town Hall, Merthyr Tydfil, Mid Glamorgan (0685 3201)

West Midlands County Council Rob Jackson, Co-op Team, Economic Development Unit, West Midlands County Council, County Hall, 1 Lancaster Circus, Queensway, Birmingham B4 7DJ (021-300 6667)

Rhymney Valley District Council Alan Bruce, Industrial Development Officer, Rhymney Valley District Council, Park Road, Hengoed, Mid Glamorgan CF8 7YB (0443 812241)

South Yorkshire County Council Phil Nicholls, Employment Promotion & Development Unit, South Yorkshire County Council, County Hall, Barnsley, S Yorkshire (0226 86141 ext 554)

Local Enterprise Agencies With Co-op Responsibilities

Powys Self Help Trust, The Old Town Hall, Temple Street, Llandrindod Wells, Powys (0597 4576) *Contact: Sheila Bailey*

Northern Ireland Local Enterprise, Development Unit, 17/19 Linenhall Street, Belfast BT2 8AB (0232 242582) *Contact: David Eynon*

Mendip & Wandsdyke Local Enterprise Group, Ammerdown, Nr Radstock, Bath BA3 5SN (0761 35321) *Contact: Mr P. A. Whiting*

Greater London Enterprise Board, 63/67 Newington Causeway, London SE1 6BD (01-403 0300) *Contact: Laura McGillivray and John Berry*

Camden Enterprise, 57 Pratt Street, London NW1 0DP (01-482 2128) *Contact: Bill Ball*

Other Organisations

Beechwood College, Elmete Lane, Roundhay, Leeds LS8 2LQ (0532 720205) The College, itself an independent co-operative, was founded in 1979 to meet the growing demand for education and training. Their courses are modestly priced at around £18.00 per day (residents) and £12.00 per day (non-residents) and cover most topics from how to start a co-operative to how to cope with expansion. They also have a consultancy service

(£120 per day + VAT and expenses) available to co-operatives, networks, voluntary groups and unemployment centres.

A leaflet is available which sets out the course programmes for each quarter, and also a booklist.

The Commonwork Centre, Bore Place, Tiddingstone, Edenbridge, Kent TN8 7AR (073 277 255) Commonwork is based on a farm in the Kent countryside, and was formed in 1976. It has gathered together learning material, and is using this in courses and workshops for co-operators. The centre can be used for groups of up to 17 to stay for 'tailor-made' courses at very modest prices.

The Co-operative Bank PLC, Head Office, 1 Balloon Street, Manchester M60 4EP (061-832 3456 ext 2803/2) In 1978 this bank launched a special start-up scheme aimed at encouraging viable new co-operatives. This consisted of an offer by the bank to match, pound for pound, the capital raised by members. Interest and other charges are at the prevailing commercial rate. Although this offer in itself is not particularly generous (given a sound business proposition any bank would lend in this ratio), their appreciation of the mechanics of a co-operative may make them a more understanding audience.

The Co-op Bank has been looking after the banking requirements of the co-operative movement for over 100 years. The full range of 'clearing bank' services are also available, including the Government Loan Guarantee Scheme. There are also more bank outlets than you may have thought: 75 regional branches (rising to over 100 over the decade) and 1000 Handybanks.

The Co-operative Union Ltd, Publication Sales Section, Holysake House, Hanover Street, Manchester M60 0AS. Their booklist is probably the most comprehensive on the subject in the UK, covering both the theory and the practice.

The Co-operative Union Ltd, Education Department, Stanford Hall, East Leake, Loughborough, Leicestershire LE12 5QR (050982 2333). This is the supreme body in the traditional co-operative movement. The Co-operative College is based here, and it offers a variety of courses for managers. In 1982 it launched a new one-year course for mature students from inside or outside the co-operative movement (grants available).

This is also a contact point for the union's 50 full-time and 70 part-time education secretaries. They cover the country and are a useful starting point for anyone wanting to find out more about co-operatives, courses, books or organisations.

Industrial Common Ownership Finance Ltd, 4 St Giles Street, Northampton NN1 1AA (0604 37563) Formed by ICOM (Industrial Common Ownership Movement) in 1973, ICOF Ltd now operates independently. It provides short- to medium-term loans from six months to six years and repayments can be made at regular periods – for example, monthly or in a lump sum at the end. The minimum sum it will consider is £1000 and the maximum is £50,000, though usually loans range between £2500 and £10,000.

The loan application form itself is a refreshingly simple but effective document. ICOF Ltd is quite a modest operation, having made a total of around 40 loans, with a little over half of these still outstanding, totalling some £130,000. Deposits in ICOF come in the main from larger co-operatives, such as Scott-Bader, and the Department of Industry.

Sources of Finance for Small Co-operatives by John Pearce, is ICOM pamphlet No. 7, price 25p.

Job Ownership Ltd, 9 Poland Street, London W1V 3DL (01-437 5511). Chairman: The Rt Hon. Jo Grimmond, MP; Director of Operations: Robert Oaksholt. Job Ownership was formed in 1978 to encourage the formation of all types of worker-owned business.

Apart from promoting the ideas of worker ownership, JOL is a consultancy. It advises people who are considering what sort of 'co-operative' to set up (for there are several quite different forms of worker ownership, of which the JOL model is only one). JOL's advice may include the preparation of a feasibility study/business plan, to help with a presentation to a source of loan funds, or help in forming a network of contacts. Normally they do not charge for initial consultation, and if they do their charges are modest compared with those of more conventional management consultancies.

New University of Ulster, The Co-operative Education, Research and Training Unit, Magee University College, Londonderry, BT48 7JL (0504 265621). Director: Ray Donnelly; Declan Jones.

Registry of Friendly Societies, 17 North Audley Street, London W1Y 2AP (01-629 7001). The register can give information about the legal requirements of forming a co-operative.

Assistant Registrar of Friendly Societies, 58 Frederick Street, Edinburgh EH 2NB (031-226 3224).

Wales Co-operative Development and Training Centre, Wales TUC, 1 Cathedral Road, Cardiff, CF1 9SD. Set up in 1983 to provide technical assistance and managerial expertise to develop and support new worker-owned enterprises.

Publications

A Handbook for Workers' Co-operatives This is a simple and understandable guide to starting up and running a co-operative venture. It is published by Aberdeen People's Press (1980) and written by Peter Cockerton, John Pearce, Ian Gilmour White and Anna Whyatt.

Management Accounting for Co-operatives by P. C. Norkett in Management Accounting (UK), February 1983.

Running Your Own Co-operative by John Pearce, published in 1984 by Kogan Page Ltd, 120 Pentonville Road, London N1 9JN (01-278 3393). Price £4.95.

Starting a Workers' Co-operative by Mark Roberts, published by Lambeth CDA (1983, 2nd ed.), 460 Wandsworth Road, London SW8 (01-720 1466). Price £1.00.

Work Aid-Business Management for Co-operatives and Community Enterprises by Tony Naughton, published by Beechwood College, Elmete Lane, Roundhay, Leeds LS8 2LQ (0532 72025). Price £2.95. This book covers the legal, accounting, taxation, financial and marketing aspects of running a co-operative.

FRANCHISING

Franchising accounts for about a third of retail sales in the USA including household names such as Coca-Cola, Avis Rent-a-Car and the ubiquitous McDonalds (over 5000 franchisees in the US alone). It is also viewed as one of the safest types of business (in the USA) with only 60 firms failing in 1982. You have, of course, to remember that these statistics only represent franchisors that have been established long enough to get into the statistics in the first place. Many don't even see out their first year.

Between 1978 and 1984 retail franchise outlets in the UK grew from approximately 2000 to about 5000. By 1985 the 200 or so franchise organisations are expected to have sales approaching £1 billion. These include such names as Prontaprint, Home Tune and Kentucky Fried Chicken. The franchise method involves three elements: a business (franchisor), which grants to others (franchisees) a right or licence (franchise).

Franchising is a marketing technique used to improve and expand the distribution of a product or service. The franchisor supplies the product or teaches the service to the franchisee, who in his turn sells it to the public. In return for this, the franchisee pays a fee and a continuing royalty, based usually on turn-over. The advantage to the franchisee is a relatively safe and quick way of getting into business for himself, but with the support and advice of an experienced organisation close at hand. The franchisor can expand his distribution with the minimum strain on his own capital and have the services of a highly motivated team of owner-managers. Franchising is not a path to great riches, nor is it for the truly independent spirit, as policy and profits will still come from 'on high'.

Before taking out a franchise it is essential that you consult your legal and financial advisers. You must also ask the franchisor some very searching questions to prove his competence. You will need to know if he has operated a pilot unit in the UK – an essential first step before selling franchises to third parties. Otherwise, how can he really know all the problems, and so put you on the right track? You will need to know what training and support is included in the franchise package, the name given to the start-up kit provided by franchisors to see you successfully launched. This package should extend to support staff over the launch period and give you access to backup advice. You will need to know how substantial the franchise company is. Ask to see their balance sheet (take it to your accountant if you cannot understand it). Ask for the track record of the directors (including their other directorships).

In the USA there are specific disclosure rules that oblige a franchise organisation to give very extensive details of its operations to prospective franchisees; details are available from the Federal Trade Commission, 6th and Pennsylvannia Avenue, NW, Washington DC 20580.

In the UK there are no such rules; however, the British Franchise Association (more details below) does lay down some guidelines. They can let you know something of the reputation of the organisation you are negotiating with. It might also be useful to ask one of the banking organisations (also listed below) if the franchisor has been vetted by them and given a clean bill of health.

Associations

The British Franchising Association, 75A Bell Street, Henley-on-Thames, Oxon RG9 2BD (0491 578049). The Association was formed in 1977 to establish a clear definition of ethical franchising standards and to help members of the public, press, potential investors and government bodies to differentiate between sound business opportunities and suspect business offers. It currently has some 60 members. Although being a member of the BFA does not guarantee the likely success of a franchise, it does show acceptance of a code of practice. The association will provide a check-list of questions to ask a franchisor and will answer questions on non-BFA companies if they have the information.

The International Franchise Association, 1025 Connecticut Avenue NW, Suite 1005, Washington DC 20036, USA. Founded in 1960, this is a non-profit organisation representing 350 franchising companies in the USA and around the world. It is recognised as the spokesman for responsible franchising. It could be particularly useful in providing information on the growing number of 'new' franchises arriving in the UK with claims of USA parentage.

National Franchise Association Coalition, PO Box 366, Fox Lake Illinois 60020, USA. This was formed in 1975 by franchisees in order to provide a centre for the expression of the franchisees' viewpoint, as distinct from that of the franchisors. No such organisation exists in the UK, but the American experiences provide some interesting lessons. There are areas of problems and dispute even between ethical and established franchise organisations and their franchisees. If you do run into such problems, this association may be able to give you some ideas and advice.

Banks and Financial Institutions

Barclays Bank plc, Marketing Dept, Juxon House, 6th floor, 94 St Paul's Churchyard, London EC4M 8EH (01-248 9155). *Contact: F. P. Salaun, Franchise Marketing Manager.* Either through a term loan, or a business expansion loan, Barclays can provide anything from £5000 to £500,000 to new or established franchisees. Of course, the business proposal must meet certain standards of performance and finance.

Barclays and the other institutions listed below have built up a considerable amount of experience in assisting franchisees, and they know the opportunities and advantages that exist in the 'right' franchise operations.

Lloyds Bank plc, 71 Lombard Street, London EC3P 3BS (01-626 1500). *Contact: Alan Pope*

Midland Bank plc, Independent Business Banking Unit, Business Development Division, Head Office, Poultry, London EC2P 2BX (01-606 9911)

National Westminster Bank plc, Domestic Banking Division, 6th floor, 4 Eastcheap, London EC3 1JH (01-726 1000)

Also:

First National Securities Ltd, First National House, College Road, Harrow, Middlesex HA1 1FB (01-861 1313) *Contact: D. E. B. Owen.* First National have agreed a finance package with a considerable number of franchise companies. This package can form part of the franchisor's offer to prospective franchisees.

Education

The following organisations regularly run courses on franchising, intended to explain the process to potential franchisees.

The British Franchising Association, 75A Bell Street, Henley-on-Thames, Oxon RG9 2BD (0491 578049)

Crown Eagle Communications Ltd, 2 Bloomsbury Place, London WC1A 2QA (01-636 0617) *Contact: J. K. Van Wycks (Seminar Division)*

Franchise World, James House, 37 Nottingham Road, London SW17 7EA (01-767 1371)

The Institute of Marketing, Moor Hall, Cookham, Maidenhead, Berks SL6 9HQ (06285 24922)

Thames Polytechnic, School of Business Administration, Riverside House, Beresford Street, London SE18 6BH (01-854 2030) *Contact: Jackie Severn*

See also the education section on page 298.

Publications

This field is still dominated by American publications. The American books listed here have direct relevance to the UK.

United Kingdom

Franchise Opportunities Directory, available from Unit 10, Wreford Yard, Ransome Road, Northampton (0604 68691). Updated and published each quarter, price £20.00 p.a. Gives the names and addresses of around 100 UK franchisors, a couple of lines description of the business and the minimum investment required.

Franchise Reporter, published by Franchise Publications, James House, 37 Nottingham Road, London SW17 7EA has eight issues a year, price £25.00 p.a. It is intended to keep you up to date with UK franchise news between the quarterly issues of *Franchise World*.

Franchise World, published by Franchise Publications, James House, 37 Nottingham Road, London SW17 7EA has all the latest news on new franchise opportunities, new consultancies and sources of finance. Each issue has a franchise directory, which describes the franchise organisations. The cost of entry is £25.00.

The Guide to Franchising, by Martin Mendelsohn (1982, 3rd ed.), published by Pergamon Press, Heddington Hill Hall, Oxford (0865 64881).

Taking Up A Franchise: The Daily Telegraph Guide (1985, 2nd ed.), published by Kogan Page Ltd, 120 Pentonville Road, London N1 (01-278 3393). This is the definitive guide to the subject in the UK. It provides potential investors with a comprehensive checklist of questions to ask franchisors and analyses each franchise in depth. It also covers financial analysis and includes specimen contracts. Price £5.95.

The Law and Practice of Franchising, by Martin Mendelsohn and Antony Nicholson (1982), published by Franchise Publications. The book has three parts: an overview of franchising, precedents of franchising agreements and clauses with commentary, and the law applicable to franchising. The areas dealt with range from trade marks, trade names and goodwill to the UK and EEC competition laws.

Sunday Times – the Business to Business section has a small but growing franchises sub-section which started in June/July 1982.

United States
The Complete Handbook of Franchising, by David D. Selz, published by Addison-Wesley. Price $35.00. This book is not for franchisees, but if you want to turn your existing business into an equally successful franchise organisation, the handbook may help.

The Dow Jones-Irwin Guide to Franchises, by Peter G. Norback and Crain Norback (1982). This is a thorough investigation of franchising, organised by franchise categories. Once again it covers only the American scene, but it does provide some useful pointers.

Franchising in the Economy 1981–1983, published in 1984 by the US Department of Commerce, Bureau of Industrial Econ-omies, Washington, DC, USA. Although completely based on the USA, it provides an extremely authoritative view of the role of franchising in an advanced industrial economy. It describes the business environment and the successes and fail-ures in each sector of franchising.

Franchising and the Ominous Buy Back Clause, by Burr, Burr and Bartlett, in the *Journal of Small Business Management*, vol. 13 (4), October 1975. The article helps with the crucial question: what happens if I want to sell out?

The Franchise Opportunity Handbook, published by US Government Printing Office, Administrative Division (SAA), Washington DC 20402, USA. Price $9.50. The handbook provides an interesting insight into the official American views on franchising and also gives an idea of the scope of the franchising phenomenon.

Franchise Rights, A Self Defense Manual for the Franchisee, published in 1980 by Alex Hammond, Hammond and Marton, 1185 Avenue of the Americas, New York, New York 10036, USA. Price $29.95. The manual contains perceptive insight into franchisee/franchisor relationships – forewarned is forearmed.

The INFO Franchise Newsletter, from INFO Press, 736 Center Street, Lewiston, New York 14092, USA. Does for the world (mainly North America) what Franchise Reporter sets out to do for the UK. INFO gives advance information on what new franchises are intending to start up in the UK, so it is a way of keeping ahead of the game, but makes sure they have piloted their franchise in the UK before they launch.

Consultancies

Some management consultancies have specialised in the franchising field. They are usually experienced both in launching new franchise businesses and in finding suitable opportunities for those wanting to take out a franchise. They are not necessarily legal and financial experts, so it is still important to get independent professional advice before acting.

The AFL Deeson Partnership Ltd, 151 Dulwich Road, London SE24 (01-733 6201/4); telex 916317. *Contact: Dr A. F. L. Deeson*
Andrew James Franchise Consultant, Hilltop House, 24 Cairnmuir Road, Edinburgh EH12 6LP (031-334 8040). *Contact: Andrew James*
Caltain Associates Ltd, Rothamstead, Broken Gate Lane, Denham, Uxbridge, Middlesex UB9 4LB (0895 834 200). *Contact: Dick Crook*
The Centre for Franchise Marketing, 34 Jarvis Street, London W1M 5HS (01-486 9957). *Contact: John Gooderham*
Franchise Concepts Ltd, 118 High Street, Sevenoaks, Kent, TN3 1GL (01-228 4743). *Contact: Bryan Wilkes*

Three important questions you should ask anyone offering their services in this field are:
- Has the consultant been involved in successful franchising at a high level?

- Has he demonstrated his ability to advise? Ask to speak to some of his past clients.
- If the consultant is taking commission on the sale of the franchises his client is launching, there could well be an undesirable conflict of interest.

Franchise Directory

Franchising is an extremely dynamic market, so things change very rapidly. Using this directory, at the side of each entry you will see how long the franchise has been established, whether or not it is a BFA member, or Associate, how many UK outlets it has, and whether or not it has a pilot operation, how much you will need in order to purchase and start up each franchise.

Use the information as a rough guide only. For example, the investment required in a franchise outlet in Oxford Street, London W1, will be very different from that of a similar operation in a small town. If you think the business area is interesting, get more information on all the franchises in that field and compare them. Do use professional advice before entering into any agreements. Some franchisors are subsidiaries of larger organisations, where this information is known it is listed after the description of the franchise.

	Minimum Start Up Capital £'000	1st UK Franchise	UK Franchise Outlets in 1984	UK Company Operated/Pilot	BFA member
AIDS, Elscot House, Arcadia Avenue, Finchley Central, London N3 2JE (01-349 3191) *Contact: Mike Salinger and Ivor Davis*	8	1983	16	0	Asso
Anicare Group Services (Veterinary) Ltd, 27 Buckingham Road, Shoreham-by-Sea, W Sussex BN4 5UA (079 17 63022) *Contact: J. Sheridan*	15½	1972	7	1	Yes
Apollo Window Blinds Ltd, Johnstone Avenue, North Cardonald Industrial Estate, Glasgow G52 4YH (041-810 3021) *Contact: James Watson, Franchise Manager*	13	1975	65	1	Yes

AIDS, Elscot House, Arcadia Avenue,
Finchley Central, London N3 2JE (01-349 3191)
Contact: Mike Salinger and Ivor Davis
AIDS has been providing a monthly management accounting service to small businesses for 12 years. AIDS takes the client's normal book-keeping figures, feeds them to its mainframe computer and supplies the client with a complete set of management accounts promptly every month. It is managed by accountants who have designed, tested and proven their service, which is complementary to the services normally provided by conventional accounting firms.
Parent Co: AIDS Computer Services Ltd

Anicare Group Services (Veterinary) Ltd, 27 Buckingham Road, Shoreham-by-Sea, W Sussex BN4 5UA (079 17 63022)
Contact: J. Sheridan
Promotes the establishment of small animal veterinary services using franchise agreements to establish groups of self-employed veterinary surgeons utilising the managerial, administrative, financial, promotional and organisational services provided.

Apollo Window Blinds Ltd, Johnstone Avenue, North Cardonald Industrial Estate, Glasgow G52 4YH (041-810 3021)
Contact: James Watson, Franchise Manager
Sell fashion window blinds through their high street retail outlets to homes and businesses. Shops provide total custom made blind service from measuring windows to installation. Company has

three factories manufacturing blinds
and 60 outlets in the North. Site selection, shopfitting, training and support
provided.

	Minimum Start Up Capital (£'000)	1st UK Franchise	UK Franchise Outlets in 1984	UK Company Operated/Pilot	BFA member
Auto-Smart Ltd, Basin Lane, Glascote, Tamworth, Staffs (0827 54291) *Contact: Mr M. E. Fidler, Managing Director* Auto-Smart distributors are self-employed, their business from either their own homes or a warehouse. They sell specialised products to the Automotive and Transport Industry from a 'Mobile Showroom'—a custom-built vehicle specially designed to carry the products—cases and bulk.	9	1981	90	0	No
Badge Man Limited, 544 Chiswick High Road, Chiswick, London W4 5RG (01-994 0826) *Contact: David Mackie, Sales & Marketing Manager* A fast service for high quality, personalised name badges on laminated plastic in any quantity. Can be operated from home. Customers range from large companies to local companies and retailers.	8½	1980	10	1	Yes
Balloon, 26 High Street, Merstham, Surrey RH1 3EA (07374 4211/3) *Contact: John Gooderham, Hervie Courvoisier (France)* Paris-based franchise, retails up-market maternity wear and accessories, exclusively designed and manufactured in France. Garments include shirts, blouses, cocktail dresses, day dresses, trousers, jeans, swimsuits, underwear and lounge wear. Also sells baby wear and children's clothes up to two years.	25	1984	2	1	No UK Yes Fr

Has 42 shops (22 in France) most of which are franchised.
Parent Co: La Redoute, France

	Minimum Start Up Capital £'000	1st UK Franchise	UK Franchise Outlets in 1984	UK Company Operated/Pilot	BFA member
Baskin-Robbins Ice Cream Europe Ltd, Glacier House, Brook Green, London W6 7BT (01-603 2040) *Contact: Susan Brocklehurst, Operations Manager* Choice of type of outlet from complete shops, shops within shops or kiosks. Varying range of 31 flavours. Full training and support given. Parent Co: Allied Lyons plc	12	1976	30	None	No
The Big Apple, 10–11 Great Newport Street, London WC2H 7NS (01-240 1701) *Contact: Mr Jim Lewis* Health studios/gymnasium.	45	1984	1	1	No
The Big Orange, 51 Chorley New Road, Bolton BL1 4QR *Contact: Miss Yuette All* Kiosk juice dispenser business	12	1982	3	1	Asso
British School of Motoring, 40 North St, Romford, Essex *Contact: Mr D. Haddon* Gives driving instruction. The franchises are existing businesses with accessible trading information but new areas may be developed. Training for all kinds of staff is given. The cars are modified and checked for serviceability before issue. Guidance is available on various aspects of the business. Part of the management services levy goes on publicity. Parent Co: Taurus Vehicle Leasing	N/A	N/A	160+	N/A	Yes

	Minimum Start Up Capital £'000	1st UK Franchise	UK Franchise Outlets in 1984	UK Company Operated/Pilot	BFA member
Bruce & Co., 43 Bridge Street, Leatherhead, Surrey KT28 3BM (0372 375161) *Contact: C. B. Jermyn and Mr I. W. Lynch, Partners* Business transfer agents for the sale of businesses, shops, hotels etc.	16	1981	13	None	No
Budget Rent-A-Car International Inc., International House, 85 Great North Road, Hatfield, Herts AL9 53F (07072 68266) *Contact: B. Glover and G. Barkatollah, Directors* World's largest franchised vehicle rental system which operates in 90 countries. Package includes support from national sales and marketing activities, modern business systems and training. Parent Co: Transamerica Corp.	50	1966	120	1	Yes
Burger King Ltd, 20 Kew Road, Richmond, Surrey TW9 2NA (01-940 6046) *Contact: R. C. M. Booth* Fast-food restaurants which the corporation services. There are own-brand sandwiches and plans to move into breakfast and other meals. Three types of cooking facility available according to market potential. The site can be corporation- or franchisee-owned. Full training is given and follow-up advice is available. Parent Co: Pillsbury Co.	250	N/A	N/A	N/A	Yes
The City Bag Store, 10 Northfield Industrial Estate, Beresford Avenue, Wembley, Middx (01-903 9448) *Contact: Brian Davies, Franchise Director* Seeking more franchises throughout UK to run own successful up-market handbag and leathergoods shop. Can be run by one person with a little part-time assist-	15	1983	9	5	No

ance. Full training given as is help and
assistance in finding suitable shop unit.
Parent Co: The City Bag Store Ltd

	Minimum Start Up Capital £'000	1st UK Franchise	UK Franchise Outlets in 1984	UK Company Operated/Pilot	BFA member
City Link, 13/14 Ascot Road, Clockhouse Lane, Feltham, Middx TW14 8QF (07842 43721) *Contact: M. D. Farback, Director* National same day/next morning parcels collection and delivery service, operated in conjunction with the British Rail 'Red Star' and 'Night Star' parcel services. Parent Co: City Link Transport Holdings	20	1972	26	6	Yes
Clentech, Abbots Barton House, Worthy Road, Winchester, Hants SO23 7SJ (0962 63577) *Contact: Derek Ayling and Ray Childs* Ceiling cleaning specialists. Parent Co: Conder International plc	12½	1983	24	1	Asso
Command Performance, High End, Troutstream Way, Loudwater, Herts WD3 4LQ (0923 777636) *Contact: Iain MaCaulay* A full service hair salon franchise new to the UK, but the largest chain in the USA with 400 outlets.	22	1983	2	4	Yes
The Complete Cookshop, The Warehouse, Rabans Lane, Industrial Estate, Aylesbury HP19 3RT (0296 31296) *Contact: Ron Faulkner* Retails pottery, glass and gifts over a wide range. Three types of franchise are available. Much of the stock is bought from clearance lines and need not be from the company. Training is given in preparation for trading.	30	1981	6	–	No
Cookie Coach, Greyhound House, 23–24 George Street, Richmond, Surrey TW9 1HY (01-940 3323)	13½	1983	22	None	Asso

	Minimum Start Up Capital £'000	1st UK Franchise	UK Franchise Outlets in 1984	UK Company Operated/Pilot	BFA member
Contact: Frank Grindell or Jack Liquorish Vends a range of 'giant cookies' made under licence. Franchisees have a specified area and carry the product in a replica 1901 New York bakery van. The concept is to sell direct on sites of the franchisee's choosing and to top up product supplies at retailers initially serviced by the company. Equipment includes lease of van, starter stock and staff uniform. Training given.					
Computerland, 19 Rue Theodore Eberhard, 1451 Luxemburg (010-352 437 751) *Contact: Frank Lech* An international network of retail outlets specialising in the sale and servicing of small computers.	165	1982	14	No	No
Cover Right Ltd, Unit 10, Bancombe Industrial Estate, Martock, Somerset (0935 824866) *Contact: Mr P. O'Leary* The company markets and lays a floor- (and wall-) covering material, which is seamless, non-skid, minimises maintenance and is available in a range of colours and designs. Franchisees have a defined area and are given full training and equipment.	7½	1981	3	–	No
Descamps, 197 Sloane Street, London SW1X 9QX (01-235 7165) *Contact: G. Gagny* Sells fine household linen. Colours co-ordinated between bed linen, towelling,	40	1980	N/A	N/A	No

table linen and nursery linen. All designs by Primrose Boidier of France.
Parent Co: Descamps Deuneestive (France).

	Minimum Start Up Capital £'000	1st UK Franchise	UK Franchise Outlets in 1984	UK Company Operated/Pilot	BFA member
Despatch Post, TNT Despatch Post, 3rd Floor, Blackburn House, Bondgate, Nuneaton, War CV11 4DU (0203 347932) *Contact: Mr R. Crofts and Mr R. McClellan* The reception point for parcels which are delivered on any of TNT's express parcel services within the UK, Europe and worldwide. Parent Co: TNT Roadfreight (UK) Ltd.	3–4	1981	305	None	Yes
Drips Plumbing, 143 Maple Road, Surbiton, Surrey (01-549 9711) *Contact: Mr P. M. Slinn* All year round plumbing service intended to give corporate image to existing plumbing organisations. Parent Co: Dyno-Rod Ltd	3	1981	26	None	Yes
Dyno-Rod plc, 143 Maple Road, Surbiton, Surrey KT6 4BJ (01-549 9711) *Contact: Mr R. G. Taylor and Mr R. Stoner* Offers service on pipe work of various kinds. The services include cleaning, clearance, testing, tracing and emergency work. There is also an Industrial Jetting Division and an Off Shore Division. Media coverage varies by area.	7½	1965	80	3	Yes
Entré Computer Centres, 17 Bath Road, Slough, Berkshire (0753 3122) *Contact: Fiona Samson* Their concept is a 'consultative sale' approach, selling computer hardware and software to solve business problems.	200	1984	9	No	No

	Minimum Start Up Capital £'000	1st UK Franchise	UK Franchise Outlets in 1984	UK Company Operated/Pilot	BFA member
'Enviraflo', Weststone House, 9/11 Horton Street, St Phillips, Bristol BS2 0LD (0272 28966) *Contact: Roger Davidge, Franchise Manager* Structural cleaning service which utilises a revolutionary wet abrasive surface cleaning system. Used to prepare steel surfaces on offshore oil platforms and to clean exterior of buildings.	9½	1982	3	4	No
Foto Inn Ltd, 12 Oxford Street, London W1N 9FL (01-580 0434) *Contact: A. Khorshid* 60-minute high quality colour print service using the latest technology. Shops are equipped with easy to operate mini labs which can handle all popular sizes of colour film and some black and white film.	40	–	N/A	4	Asso
Global Cleaning Contracts, Global House, Lind Road, Sutton, Surrey (01-642 0054) *Contact: K. L. P. Wearn and A. N. Hinwood* The Global franchisee sells cleaning contracts to contractors. The contractor then has to supply the labour, equipment and materials. Parent Co: Global Cleaning Contracts (Holdings) Ltd	30	1980	18	2	Yes
Holland & Barrett (Franchising) Ltd, Healthways House, Station Approach, West Byfleet, Surrey KT14 6NE (0932 41133) *Contact: Ken Mullarkey, Chief Executive* Europe's largest health food retailer which manufactures, markets and distributes a wide range of health foods. Owns a number of brands such as Allinson and Prewetts. Holds headlease while granting an underlease to the franchisee. Parent Co: Booker McConnell	45	1982	10	150	Yes

114

	Minimum Start Up Capital £'000	1st UK Franchise	UK Franchise Outlets in 1984	UK Company Operated/Pilot	BFA member
Home Tune, Home Tune House, Guildford Road, Effingham, Surrey KT24 5QS (0372 56656) *Contact: Mr Duncan Whitefield, Managing Director* It is an on-site motor vehicle tuning service. Mobile vans, with testing equipment and spares, carry the service to the customer. Full training is given and all vans and equipment are supplied through the company on hire. Central buying is used to obtain tools and vehicle parts. There is vehicle livery and a logo. During the first year of trading the franchise is advertised locally.	10	1968	236	–	Yes
House of Fraser International, 1 Howick Place, London SW1P 1BH (01-828 9044) *Contact: B. A. Evans* Provides a total franchising service to create and operate major department stores overseas. Franchises name, retailing expertise and provides senior management, merchandising and promotion, purchasing and delivery and advice on location and design of stores.	4.5m	N/A	None	None	No
Identicar, Identicar House, Wolverhampton Road, Warley, West Midlands B69 4RL (021-541 1141) *Contact: J. H. Harris and D. A. Morcom* Vehicle security systems, principly the irremovable marking of registration number on to the vehicle windows. Free car rental and reduced insurance premiums are part of the retail package. Parent Co: Identicar (Holdings) Ltd.	15	1979	100	10	Yes
Intacab, Clock House, Service House, High Road, Laindon, Basildon, Essex SS15 6NV (0268 415891) *Contact: Peter Dance, Franchise Director*	50	1982	8	2	No

A taxi service under a company logo. A comprehensive package including advice and instruction is provided. There is also a company marketing campaign using press advertising, mailing shots and leaflets.

	Minimum Start Up Capital £'000	1st UK Franchise	UK Franchise Outlets in 1984	UK Company Operated/Pilot	BFA member
Interlink Express Courier Parcels, Portland House, 22/24 Portland Square, Bristol, Avon BS2 8RZ (0272 40257) *Contact: Mrs R. A. Bugden and Mr R. G. Gabriel* Guaranteed, nationwide overnight parcel delivery service. Provides a door-to-door service for industry and commerce.	21½	1981	93	3	Yes
Isodan, 12 Mount Ephraim Road, Royal Tunbridge Wells, Kent TN1 1EE (0892 44822) *Contact: S. John Holt, Managing Director* A system of cavity-wall insulation using dry granules. It involves no on-site hazards or expensive equipment.	7½	1975	55	Nil	No
In-Toto, Wakefield Road, Gildersome, Leeds LS27 0QW (0532 524131) *Contact: Ian Wilkie and Sue Cass* Quality fitted kitchen showrooms, furniture by Wellman and electrical fittings by Phillips.	30	1980	30	Nil	Yes
Jet Cleen, Prospect House, Bloxwich Road, Walsall, West Midlands WS3 2UZ (0922 491920) Wash and prepare vehicles on site; de-wax and clean engines; also clean factories and machinery.	5	1981	12	No	No

	Minimum Start Up Capital £'000	1st UK Franchise	UK Franchise Outlets in 1984	UK Company Operated/Pilot	BFA member
Kall-Kwik Printing, Victoria Road, South Ruislip, Middx HA4 0JF (01-841 5151) *Contact: John B. Atkinson, Franchising Manager* Sole licensee for US Kwik-Kopy system. Have 100 high street shops in UK. Provide financial start-up package, site selection layout planning, training, pre- and post-opening support and marketing assistance.	20	1979	115	1	Yes
Kenprest, RE Tyre & Rubber Co. Ltd, Mill Lane, Alton, Hants GU34 2QG (0420 82122) *Contact: Mr R. J. Rata* Franchise is based on a patented system for retreading truck tyres and also the Kentred system for both car and truck tyres.	20	1962	38	None	No
Kentucky Fried Chicken (GB) Ltd, Wicat House, Camberley, Surrey GU15 3HL (0276 686151) *Contact: Mrs Jenny Bassett* Retails fast food to eat or take away. The company helps in finding and assessing the site and provides drawings for planning permission. Company policy is on shop fittings and equipment, these being proved before use by franchisees. Full training is given and media coverage is provided. Franchisees can be elected to the board responsible for advertising expenditure. Parent Co: Heublein Inc. (in USA)	70	1962	307	61	Yes
Kwik Strip, Units 1/2, The 306 Estate, 242 Broomhill Road, Brislington, Bristol BS4 5RA (0272 772470) *Contact: Ivor Chivers* Specialises in serving the growing stripping/restoration market with a process which will strip paint, varnish	8	1983	None	1	No

and polyurathenes from all types of
wood and metal. The company offers a
comprehensive package which includes
a starter-pack and continuous back-up
from the Head Office in Bristol.

	Minimum Start Up Capital £'000	1st UK Franchise	UK Franchise Outlets in 1984	UK Company Operated/Pilot	BFA member
Lasalign, D.S.B. House, 135 High Street, Bromley, Kent BR1 1JF (01-466 6021/2/3) *Contact: Graham Ross* Offers load haulage industry and large fleet operators of articulated vehicles a mobile low assisted trailer axle alignment service. Uses latest laser based equipment.	6	1983	7	2	No
Leaders Health Food Stores, 105 London Road, Brighton, East Sussex (0273 695001) *Contact: Roy Harris* Health food stores located in the high streets of the South of England. Full training given at existing stores and own training school. £1000 deposit (returnable) secures town of choice. Parent Co: Holgran Ltd and Southern Health Foods Ltd.	20	1983	3	35	No
The Maids, 4–6 Lind Road, Sutton, Surrey (01-642 0054) *Contact: K. C. P. Wearn and H. Brogden* Home cleaning service. Supervised team with special cleaning equipment and materials. Thoroughly clean the home. Additional services include spring cleaning, emergency cleaning and carpet and upholstery cleaning. Parent Co: Global Cleaning Contracts (Holdings) Ltd	10	1983	1	0	No
Med-Ped, Plaza Med-Ped, Palma Nova, Mallorca, Spain (010-34-71-68-16-32) *Contact: Daniel C. Denby*	35	1980	15	1	No

Two-wheeled vehicle hire in Spanish
tourist resorts. Expanding soon to
France, Italy, Greece, Portugal etc.
Parent Co: Mediterranean Mopeds S.A.

	Minimum Start Up Capital £'000	1st UK Franchise	UK Franchise Outlets in 1984	UK Company Operated/Pilot	BFA member
Mixamate Ltd, Station Yard, Bourne Way, Hayes, Kent BR2 7EY (01-462 8011)	50	1979	6	3	Asso
Mobile Tuning Ltd, 7A Nelson Road, London SE10 9JB (01-853 1520)	11	1977	42	2	Yes
Mopps & Co., Coniscliffe House, Coniscliffe Road, Darlington DL3 7EX (0325–84727): also known as Poppies	4½	1983	4	1	No

Mixamate Ltd, Station Yard, Bourne
Way, Hayes, Kent BR2 7EY (01-462 8011)
Contact: Peter Bates, Managing Director
Mixamate supplies concrete for builders
and the DIY market. Franchisees
should have HGV operating experience
as a specialised vehicle, supplied by the
company, carries cement, aggregate and
water to mix, in amounts as required,
on site. A territory is allotted and full
training given. There is company policy
on appearance of staff and vehicles.

Mobile Tuning Ltd, 7A Nelson Road,
London SE10 9JB (01-853 1520)
Contact: Anton Rowntree
Car tuning company which specialises in
using Crypton electronic engine tuning
equipment at customer's homes or places
of work. Provides comprehensive training, a fully equipped van, spare parts,
diagnostic equipment and tuning data
for the different makes of cars. Also
receive continuous promotional and
technical support.

Mopps & Co., Coniscliffe House,
Coniscliffe Road, Darlington DL3 7EX
(0325–84727): also known as Poppies
Contact: S. Rorstad and C. Sorensen
Based on a range of high quality domestic
and commercial cleaning services. Franchisee has sole rights to territory, use of
Mopps & Co. name and logo and associated goodwill. Training is provided and
constant help and support is available
from Head Office.
Parent Co: Prontaprint Ltd.

	Minimum Start Up Capital £'000	1st UK Franchise	UK Franchise Outlets in 1984	UK Company Operated/Pilot	BFA member
Mr Fish on Wheels Ltd, 26 High Street, Merstham, Surrey RH1 3EA (07374 4211) *Contact: Michael Way* Selling fresh sea-food to the housewife and food trade using well equipped, eye-catching sales and delivery vehicles. Fleets range from 10 to 14 vehicles.	30	1983	5	–	No
Mr Slade Franchises Ltd, Maritime Chambers, Howard Street, North Shields NE30 1AR (0632 596421) *Contact: Eunice Hesslegrave* Dry cleaning units, sited in existing retail outlets. Additionally, agents pass work to the unit. In future the franchisees, who should have business experience, will have independently sited premises. Preparation training is given and the opening phase supported with a launch programme. Parent Co: Mr Slade Ltd	12	1983	11	17	Asso
Nature's Way Ltd, 1 Clifford Road, Bex-hill, East Sussex TN40 1QA (0424 222125) *Contact: Barry Howell, Managing Director* They retail and serve health food. Franchisees should have an interest in the products. A defined area is allotted and company assistance is available on choice of sites. Company policy covers layout and fittings and stock must be bought from an approved list. Promotion is funded from a turnover levy.	20	1978	8	21	No
Olivers Hot Bread & Coffee Shops, Leeds House, 64 George Street, Luton, Beds LU1 2BD (0582 417408) *Contact: Gordon Paterson* Combination of units comprising a bakery, take-away and coffee shops with seating of 70–150. Shops have a range of in-store	50	1982	14	5	Yes

equipment and are supplied with special bakery mixes and other ingredients.

	Minimum Start Up Capital £'000	1st UK Franchise	UK Franchise Outlets in 1984	UK Company Operated/Pilot	BFA member
The Pancake Place, 30 New Road, Milnathort, Kinross KY13 7XT (0577 63969) *Contact: Mr A. Miller and Mr R. Kay* 'Olde-worlde' style restaurants aimed at popular end of market. Menu consists of pancake-based snacks and three course meals. Parent Co: The Pancake Place Ltd	35	1981	15	4	Yes
Pass & Co., Passco House, 635 High Road, Leytonstone, London E11 4RD (01-539 1105) *Contact: J. Frankling, Franchise Director* Specialises in the remedial treatment of woodworm, dryrot and rising damp giving a guarantee each time.	12½	1983	18	2	No
PDC Copyprint, Head Office, 103 Oxford Street, London W1H 9DL (01-439 8937) *Contact: Mr D. Campbell Nisbet, Mr H. Stokes and Mr W. Slade* Experienced quickprint company with unique features. Reducing royalty – buying out licence, full training, holiday relief, private insurance, site finding, shop fitting, machinery installation and supply. Parent Co: PDC Holdings	15	1979	15	1	No
Phildar UK Ltd, 4 Gambrel Road, Westgate Ind. Estate, Northampton NN5 5NF (0604 583111) *Contact: G. C. Houston or T. Moreav* Makes and retails own brand knitting wools, rug making and tapestry work supplies together with related hobbies accessories. Interest in handicrafts would be an advantage. Premises have a company logo and colours, with layout	10	1979	10	82	Yes

and interior design plans drawn up by
the company. Training is given and
support is provided on promotion, legal
and financial guidance.
Parent Co: Phildar Ltd

	Minimum Start Up Capital £'000	1st UK Franchise	UK Franchise Outlets in 1984	UK Company Operated/Pilot	BFA member
Pip Instant Printing, Security House, Sumatra Road, London NW6 1NG (01-794 7850) *Contact: Ivor Freedman* Shops provide a full instant-print service from copiers and offset presses; with over 700 locations worldwide it is the largest instant printers.	20	1982	32	6	Yes
Pizza Express Ltd, 29 Wardour Street, London W1 (01-437 7215) *Contact: Ian S. Neill* These restaurants offer a choice of 14 pizzas, a selection of desserts and Italian wines and beer. Comprehensive training and advice on running a Pizza Express.	105	1972	26	9	Yes
Prodata, Churchfield Road, Frodsham, Cheshire (0928 35110) *Contact: C. I. Piff* Specialised, professional book-keeping service for small to medium sized firms. They visit their clients regularly taking a compact microcomputer with them which is used to record current financial information.	2½	1981	12	–	No
Prontaprint, Coniscliffe House, Coniscliffe Road, Darlington DL3 7EX (0325 55391) *Contact: Peter Brennan and John Atkinson* High-speed printing and instant copying shops. Printing experience is not required, as full training is offered and all equipment is tested for suitability. Parent Co: Prontaprint Holdings Ltd.	48	1971	251	1	Yes

	Minimum Start Up Capital £'000	1st UK Franchise	UK Franchise Outlets in 1984	UK Company Operated/Pilot	BFA member
Pronuptia de Paris Bridalwear, 70/78 York Way, London N1 9AG (01-278 7722) *Contact: Edward Young, Chairman* It has international outlets retailing bridal wear exclusive to the company. There is a commercial association with Young's menswear. Training is given in various aspects of the business. Company advice is available on suitable locations and shopfitting. National advertising in women's magazines, with fashion shows, point of sale aids and local publicity. Parent Co: Young's Dress Hire Ltd	20 to 40	1978	64	15	Yes
Safeclean, Pound House, Stream Road, Upton, Didcot, Oxon (0235 850387) *Contact: Desmond Cook, Managing Director* Offers an on-site service to clean upholstery and carpets. Materials can be treated for anti-static and flame retarding. Hand cleaning methods are used and the equipment is patented. Franchisees must be fit and could start business on a part-time basis. Training is given both before and after start-up. Parent Co: D. G. Cook Ltd	5	1972	50	–	Yes
Servicemaster Ltd, 50 Commercial Square, Freemans Common, Leicester LE2 7SR (0533 548620) *Contact: Mr J. R. Major* A carpet and upholstery cleaning organisation specialising in on-site cleaning of carpets and upholstery in domestic, commercial and disaster situations. Parent Co: Service Master Industries Inc.	8½	1959	159	None	Yes

	Minimum Start Up Capital £'000	1st UK Franchise	UK Franchise Outlets in 1984	UK Company Operated/Pilot	BFA member
Silver Shield Windscreen, 38–42 Holbrook Lane, Coventry CV6 4AB West Midlands (0203 661311) *Contact: John Oliver* Offers on-site motor vehicle windscreen replacement. The service is day and night throughout the year and contact can be made by freefone. A complete training, promotional and advice package is given. Company equipment and materials are provided.	15 to 25	1978	54	1	Yes
Singer, 255 High Street, Guildford, Surrey GU1 3DH (0483 5771144) *Contact: Angela Auger* It is a retail outlet for the sale, and after-sale servicing, of the Singer company sewing machines and related products. The franchise can be added to an existing business or started independently. Full training is given and a pre- and post-trading advice package is available. Parent Co: The Singer Company (USA)	8	1965	N/A	N/A	No
Snap-on-Tools Ltd, Dunham House, 85/99 Cross Street, Sale, Cheshire M33 1FU (061-969 0126) *Contact: Jonathan Ward* Retail tools for the motor vehicle garage trade, the role of the franchisee being to sell a range of company-supplied products to appropriate outlets. Full training is given but someone with previous sales experience is envisaged as a franchisee.	5	1965	306	–	Yes

	Minimum Start Up Capital £'000	1st UK Franchise	UK Franchise Outlets in 1984	UK Company Operated/Pilot	BFA member
Sovereign Services (SE), 39 Osborne Road, Eastbourne, East Sussex BN20 8JJ (0323 20814) *Contact: B. R. Southon* Offers a private ambulance service with fully qualified medical attendance. Vehicles and staff move patients, including out-patients, to and from hospitals and nursing homes over any distance. Repatriation abroad can be provided. Parent Co: Sovereign Medical Services Ltd	12½	1982	13	2	No
Sperrings Convenience Store, Sperring House, 1 Spring Crescent, Portswood, Southampton SO2 1FZ (0703 552550) *Contact: Mike Trusler and Debi Bunker* Large chain of convenience stores, more than 45 outlets. It is a full business format franchise.	80	1983	3	45	Yes
Spud-u-Like, 34–38 Standard Road, London NW10 6EU (01-965 0181) *Contact: G. Heath and R. Patmore* Restaurants specialising in a large variety of filled baked potatoes. Parent Co: British School of Motoring.	40	1980	40	4	Yes
Stop A Thief, Knightsford House, Church Road, Wombourne, Wolverhampton, West Midlands WV5 9EX (0902 893870) *Contact: Phil Aston* Security marking of vehicles and property. System is easily operated by one person who operates from a fully equipped, signwritten vehicle. Full training and on-going assistance are provided.	6	1982	21	1	Asso
Strikes Restaurant, 289 Oxford Street, London W1R 2AD (01-629 4680) *Contact: Mr John Connell and Miss R. Eliades*	35	1982	7	31	Yes

Licensed table service restaurants, with take-away facilities. Possible outlets are considered for viability and suitable premises are prepared with company advice. Although training is given franchisees are expected to select their own staff. At time of opening publicity is given but later franchisees must pay for advertising.

	Minimum Start Up Capital £'000	1st UK Franchise	UK Franchise Outlets in 1984	UK Company Operated/Pilot	BFA member
Tandy Corps (Branch UK), Tameway Tower, Bridge Street, Walsall, West Midlands (0922 648181) *Contact: Bob Cleaver, National Manager* A retailer of consumer electronics, whose range includes hi-fi, radios, microcomputers, electronic components and general electronic durables. Parent Co: Radio Shack in the USA.	4	1973	118	228	No
J. W. Thornton, Derwent Street, Belper, Derbyshire DE5 1WP (077382 4181) *Contact: Mr R. E. Smith, Commercial Sales Manager* Retails own-brand sugar and chocolate confectionery. The franchise can be run independently or in an existing business retailing compatible products. Shops are stocked and fitted exactly as company-owned outlets. Training is given. This is a Fractional Franchise and only of interest to people looking for add-on products.	7	1975	70	150	Yes
Tie Rack Ltd, 2 Montpelier Street, London SW7 1EZ (01-584 8129) *Contact: Mr T. D. Jennings and Mr J. S. W. Tonks* Retailing of quality ties through rented premises with stock supplied from Franchisor. Parent Co: Associated Investments Ltd	15	1983	3	11	No

	Minimum Start Up Capital £'000	1st UK Franchise	UK Franchise Outlets in 1984	UK Company Operated/Pilot	BFA member
Torlink, C & J Clark Ltd, Street, Somerset BA16 0YA (0458 43131) *Contact: J. E. Dixon, Torlink Manager* Effects the assisted Venture Scheme of the Clarks footwear organisation to install franchisees as retailers of company footwear products. Training is given. Company policy covers selection and fitting of retail outlets, which are sub-let to franchisee. There is a comprehensive franchise package. Products are nationally advertised. Parent Co: C. J. Clark Ltd	25	1966	130	–	No
Trace Heat Pumps Ltd, Trade House, Eastways Ind. Park, Witham, Essex CM8 3YU (0376 515511) *Contact: G. A. Sills, N. R. Smart and T. J. Cook* Sells, installs and services own heat pumps. Have largest range of pumps in UK, over 350. Will provide training and ongoing support. Parent Co: Trace Cleveland Ltd	17	1983	17	1	Asso
Uticolor, Sheraton House, 35–37 North Street, York TO1 1JD (0904 37798) *Contact: Eric S. Bottomley, Director* An invisible repairing service for vinyl- and leather-covered furniture. The bonding technique is taught. Customers include schools, pubs, hotels and offices.	5	1978	33	2	Yes
Vinyl Master (UK) Ltd, Avonbridge, King Johns Island, Tewkesbury, Glos GL20 6EB (0684 295511) *Contact: Mr N. Scanlan* Offers an on-site repair and re-covering service for vinyl-covered upholstery. Market includes homes and businesses of various kinds.	5	1981	28	1	No

	Minimum Start Up Capital £'000	1st UK Franchise	UK Franchise Outlets in 1984	UK Company Operated/Pilot	BFA member
Watertite Ltd, Unit 4, Wall End Close, Leamore, Walsall, West Midlands WS2 7PH (0922 409178) *Contact: J. Oliver and C. Evans* Installation of new and replacement guttering with aluminium guttering formed on site in 'bespoke' lengths.	14	1983	7	–	Yes
Wetherby Training Services, 2 Hastings Court, Collingham, Wetherby, West Yorkshire LS22 5AW (0937 73079) *Contact: D. G. Button* Secretarial training centre	4	1984	1	No	No
Wimpy, 214 Chiswick High Road, London W4 1PD (01-994 6454) *Contact: Ian Petrie, Managing Director* A world-wide network of hamburger restaurants. Wimpy offers franchise in its new counter-service style outlets.	300	1958			Yes
Counter Service			36	19	
Table Service			367	2	
Parent Co: United Biscuits.					
Youngs Formal Wear for Men, 70/78 York Way, London N1 9AG (01-278 7722) *Contact: Edward Young, Chairman* Retail and hire out men's formal morning and evening wear. Menswear can also be ordered in Pronuptia bridal wear shops. Training is provided as is promotion and various forms of guidance and advice.	25–54	1978	54	17	Yes

	£'000 Minimum Start Up Capital	1st UK Franchise	UK Franchise Outlets in 1984	UK Company Operated/Pilot	BFA member
Yves Rocher Beauty Centres, Chapel Court, 169B Borough High Street, London SE1 (01-403 4944) *Contact: Mr S. Partridge, Managing Director* Attractively designed and equipped small shops offering a complete range of cosmetic products and treatments. Over 600 outlets world-wide. Parent Co: Yves Rocher	15	1980	33	1	Yes
Ziebart Appearance & Protection Services, Zeegard Car Care Ltd, Crescent House, Crescent Road, Worthing, Sussex (0903 203170) *Contact: L. F. Smith, Managing Director* Specialists in the treatment of rust protection of new and used vehicles. Backed by Ziebart International Corporation, Ziebart UK is able to offer total protection for vehicles, inside and out. Parent Co: Ziebart International Corporation.	3½	1971	30	–	Yes

EXPLOITING HIGH, AND NOT SO HIGH, TECHNOLOGY

Technology presents considerable opportunities to inventors and users alike. It also presents a number of problems. Inventors have difficulty in communicating their ideas to commercial organisations. These ideas are often a long way from being a recognisable product at the time when most help (financial or otherwise) is needed. A growing number of institutions, organisations and services now aim to provide just this understanding and assistance.

On the other hand, there are many small businesses which could make considerable use of new technology, if only they knew how. Microcomputers are the most obvious development, where dull, repetitive tasks can be done quickly, leaving the entrepreneur free to perform more important tasks.

The following material should give you an appreciation of what is happening to solve these technological communication problems.

SCIENCE PARKS, INNOVATION AND TECHNOLOGY CENTRES

In 1973 an experiment began to encourage the growth of technical innovation in the USA. The basic idea was to bring inventors, entrepreneurs and academics together physically on or near the college campus. By adding some government funds to provide buildings, materials and equipment, it was hoped that the right environment to identify and stimulate new products and services would then be created. Although at the start these 'Innovation Centres' would be heavily subsidised, they were expected to become substantially self-supporting. This, no doubt, was the motivation in ensuring that a good business school was on the campus too (a lesson that UK emulators have not universally followed). The American experiment seems to show that the college-industry centres can and do flourish. By 1978 these centres had played a major part in forming some

30 new and largely technology-based businesses. They employed on average 40 people each, and some had sales returns of well over $1 million per annum. By the end of 1983, some 40 centres were operating around the USA based on such colleges as Carnegie-Mellon and the Massachusetts Institute of Technology.

In the UK (and elsewhere) similar deliberations were taking place. For example, in 1969 a decision was taken to encourage the expansion of science-based industry close to Cambridge. This would take advantage of the considerable concentration there of scientific expertise, equipment and libraries. The resultant Science Park was officially opened in 1975.

A growing number of organisations are now concerned with improving the lot of the inventor-entrepreneur. Some of these seem to offer little more than premises and a sympathetic ear. Others are rather less than high-technology based. However, most of them are extremely young, at least half have expressed a desire to provide practical as well as technological help to small, new innovation-based businesses. This situation represents a considerable improvement when compared to the UK inventors' lot in the 1970s.

SCIENCE PARKS

	Opening Date	Area	Range of Unit Sizes	Number of Companies	Campus Based	Business School
Aston Science Park, Birmingham Technology Ltd, Love Lane, Birmingham B7 4BJ	1982	22 acres	300– 10,000 sq ft	9	Yes	Yes

Aston Science Park,
Birmingham Technology Ltd,
Love Lane, Birmingham B7 4BJ
(021-359 0981)
Contact: Peter H. Cross
This was established by Aston
University and Birmingham
City Council. It makes use of
refurbished and adapted factory
premises and provides nursery
accommodation for small firms.
Special technologies: micro-
processing, computing, biotechnology, biodeterioration, pharm-
aceuticals, tribology and
robotics.
Other help to the users of the
Science Park includes access to
venture and loan capital, administrative services, business
advice, technical support on
product development, and advice
on licensing and patenting.

Birchwood Science Park	1973	75 acres	500– 50,000 sq ft	50	No	No

Birchwood Science Park, Birchwood, Warrington, Cheshire
(0925 51144)
Contact: C. W. Cawley
This science park is not on university campus, although Liverpool and Manchester Universities Joint Research Unit is
nearby. The universities themselves, together with UMIST
and Salford, are within a radius
of 20 miles. The Northern Area
Headquarters of the UK Atomic
Energy Authority is based at
Birchwood, as are the British
Nuclear Fuels, the Nuclear

Power Company, the National Centre for Tribology, the European Space Tribology and the Risley Materials Laboratory. The units can be tailor-made to meet the needs of a wide variety of science- and technology-based companies, and can be used as a laboratory, a workshop, sales office or demonstration area.

	Opening Date	Area	Range of Unit Sizes	Number of Companies	Campus Based	Business School Link
Brunel Science Park, Brunel University, Uxbridge (0895 39234) *Contact: Mr Burkitt* The park was opened in collaboration with the GLC.	1983	N/A	1000–5000 sq ft	20	Yes	No
Cambridge Science Park, Trinity College, Cambridge (0223 358201)	1975	52 acres	1300–122,600 sq ft	24	Yes	No

The use of buildings on the park is limited to applied research and light industry production that needs regular scientific consultation with the college or other local institutions and appropriate ancillary services.

The businesses are in the following fields, among others: genetic engineering, contract research and development, computer systems and software, specialist biochemicals, lasers and a firm that consults on the causes of fire, accidents and explosions.

The companies on the park employ from 4 to 200 people. The average is something like 40 per company, with around 10% being directors of the businesses.

Hull Innovation Centre, Guildhall Road, Queens Gardens, Hull HU1 1HJ (0482 226348)
Contact: Dr W. K. Donaldson
The centre was set up by the Kingston-upon-Hull City Council to operate as an advice office. Its objectives are to encourage and assist small firms, especially new ventures. Occupancy is assumed for one year.
Although the Innovation Centre works closely with local firms, the University of Hull, the city's other colleges and the Department of Industry, it has some very useful 'self-contained' resources. The centre makes available floor space, engineering staff and well equipped machine shop, electronics equipment, plastics machinery, operational support, technological consultancy and contact with other sources of advice, education and help. When they are established, clients move out to commercial premises, some of which are also being provided by the City Council. The licence includes an undertaking to pay, over the first seven years of successful operation, a levy calculated to make Hull Innovation Centre independent of public-sector help.

Opening Date	Area	Range of Unit Sizes	Number of Companies	Campus Based	Business School
1981		150–450 sq ft	24	No	Yes

	Opening Date	Area	Range of Unit Sizes	Number of Companies	Campus Based	Business School Link
Listerhills High Technology Development at Bradford University, 1 Campus Road, Bradford BD7 1HR (0274 306017) Contact: C. Monck and Lawrence West, Director of Industrial Liaison Services on 0274 733466 ext 8284	1983	42,000 sq ft	1000–8000 sq ft	13	No	Yes
Lynch Wood, Peterborough Development Corporation, Touthill Close, Peterborough PE1 1UJ (Peterborough 68931) Contact: D. E. Bath	1983	116 acres	—	0	No	Yes
Merseyside Innovation Centre, 131 Mount Pleasant, Liverpool L3 5TF (051-708 0123) Contact: F. B. Hollows Sponsored by the University of Liverpool, Liverpool Polytechnic and Merseyside County Council, its purpose is to foster closer liaison between academic research activities and the economic development objectives of the council. It provides facilities ranging from advice on protecting a new product through to its commercial exploitation. They can organise consultancy research, design and testing facilities, and project management. Its fields of interest include small scale micro-electronics, new materials development and computer technology.	1982	16,000 sq ft	200–1000 sq ft	10	Yes	No

	Opening Date	Area	Range of Unit Sizes	Number of Companies	Campus Based	Business School I
Peel Park Campus, Atholl House, East Kilbride G74 1LU (03552 41111) *Contact: Alistair Dalziel*	1983	120 acres	1–15 acres	—	No	Yes
Salford Science Park, Wynne Street, Salford 6 (061-794 4711) *Contact: Mr Henry* The science park was launched jointly by Salford University and Salford City Council.	1980	6.25 acres	1250 sq ft	N/A	N/A	N/A
Somerset Innovation Centre, 1 The Crescent, Taunton TA1 4EA (0823 76905)	1982	N/A	N/A	N/A	No	No

The centre is jointly sponsored by CoSIRA and Somerset County Council. It is intended to act as a focal point for those who have an invention but lack the expertise to make or market the product.

Confidential, impartial advice is available on technical evaluation, patent licensing design, design and drawing facilities, models and prototype production, production planning, marketing finance, supply sourcing, and setting up a new business.

In particular, the following facilities are available to those inventors who can show that they have a potentially commercial product:

■ Engineering facilities: as well as having close links with local engineering colleges, CoSIRA has its own experimental work-

Opening Date | Area | Range of Unit Sizes | Number of Companies | Campus Based | Business School Link

shops in Salisbury where staff specialise in engineering problem-solving. By making use of the skilled and professional staff at these centres, CoSIRA can help inventors realise their original ideas.

■ Marketing: advice can be given on test marketing, advertising, packaging and joint ventures with existing manufacturers.

■ Finance: apart from CoSIRA's own loan facilities, their accountants are familiar with all the many schemes available from the high street banks, the City and various government aids for investment. Budgeting and cash-flow forecasts can be prepared for presentation to other lenders. In addition, they are aware of individuals and firms looking for new products.

■ Patents and other protection: Advice on patents, copyrights and trade marks is available through links with several local firms of patent agents. The initial discussion is free or at a low charge.

What will it cost? An initial discussion costs nothing, and much of the necessary explanatory talks will be at a low charge. Should engineering or prototype production be involved, then costs will be incurred but at a subsidised level. Patent fees and the full costs of employing a patent agent are your responsibility. *The award scheme*: In addition to the package of advice, a limited number of cash awards are made to help with the costs of patenting, market research or prototype production. Awards are made to a maximum of £500 per applicant. The awards are open to individuals, small firms and new businesses and companies of all sizes. The new product or process must incorporate an innovation but need not be patented or patentable. It must either not yet have come into production or have been produced within the last year. The awards given will be on the merits of commercial viability, market potential, originality and technical merit. Financial need may also be taken into account.

	Opening Date	Area	Range of Unit Sizes	Number of Companies	Campus Based	Business School I:
South Bank Technopark, Polytechnic of the South Bank, London Road, London SE1 (01-223 8977)	1985	110,000 sq ft	200+ sq ft	Nil	Yes	Yes

Contact: Mr Jeff Jeffers
The services are aimed at new start high technology businesses that would benefit from interfacing with the Polytechnic's facilities, e.g. use of computer, laboratories, recreational facilities, etc.

South Bank Technopark company manage the development and provide professional back-up services such as book-keeping. The funding of £5.8 million was provided by the Prudential.

	Opening Date	Area	Range of Unit Sizes	Number of Companies	Campus Based	Business School Link
Stowell Technical Park, FEARNEY Industrial Development Ltd, 445 Bolton Road, Pendlebury, Manchester M27 2TD (061-736 4576)	1983	6.5 acres	1400–11,700 sq ft	15	No	No
Surrey Research Park, University of Surrey, Guildford, Surrey (0483 579626) Contact: Dr Malcolm Parry	1983	68 acres	600–12,000 sq ft	N/A	Yes	Yes
Tyne and Wear Innovation and Development Company Ltd, Unit 3, Green Lane Buildings, Heworthway, Pelaw, Gateshead NE10 0UW (0632 380500 or 0632 382468) Contact: Dr J. A. Hedley	1982	5000 sq ft		30–40	No	Yes

The park was developed by Fearney Industrial Development Ltd, in co-operation with the City of Salford. It is close to Salford University but is not on the campus. However, there are links with the University's Research and Development Faculty. The site has the benefits of an enterprise zone, and provides offices, laboratory, workshop, research and development and servicing accommodation.

139

This is the umbrella for the Innovation Centre, sponsored by Tyne and Wear County Council, the North Regional TUC, Tyne and Wear Chamber of Commerce and Industry, and Newcastle and Sunderland Polytechnics.

The centre includes among its objectives the introduction of new products and processes by inventors and small businesses, particularly those that will improve employment prospects in the county. It has space, advice, facilities and, most importantly, encouragement to offer, together with practical help in moving inventions or innovations to the prototype stage. Help is on hand with patent application procedures and the centre has strong links with local companies on the look-out for new products to license.

Alternatively, the centre will introduce the innovator to other organisations who will help them to set up their business. The first practical piece of advice comes with their introductory leaflet. Bold red type advises you to patent your idea as soon as possible and warns you not to talk to anyone until they have signed a 'non-disclosure agreement'.

	Opening Date	Area	Range of Unit Sizes	Number of Companies	Campus Based	Business School Link
Unilink, Heriot Watt University, Riccarton, Edinburgh EH14 4AS	N/A	22 acres	N/A	N/A	Yes	No

(031-449 5111 ext 2299/2330)
Contact: Mr I. G. Dalton (031-226 6436)
Unilink is the division of the university that works to establish links with both the private and state business communities. The Board of Management, headed by the university's Principal, has 10 directors drawn in equal proportions from the university and the business community. Apart from an extensive range of consultancy activities, the Director of Unilink is responsible for the following:
The Research Park. Here companies are encouraged to build their own research departments on the campus. The university's particular areas of expertise are electronics and micro-electronics, computer-aided engineering, offshore and petroleum engineering, and bio-technology.
Unlike some science parks, this facility is not intended for production or mass manufacturing units. The site is available only to companies who want to establish their own research and development groups.

	Opening Date	Area	Range of Unit Sizes	Number of Companies	Campus Based	Business School Link
Upton Science Park, Metropolitan Borough of Wirral, Municipal Offices, Brighton Street, Wallasey, Wirral L44 8ED (051-638 7070 ext 376)	N/A	50 acres	5–50 acres	N/A	No	No

Contact: John Thompson
Their literature forecasts 'prestige

	Opening Date	Area	Range of Unit Sizes	Number of Companies	Campus Based	Business School I.

developments' and clean, low-
level modern buildings. The map
of the site shows the GPO site
and Champion Spark Plugs, but
there is no sign of the
university.

	Opening Date	Area	Range of Unit Sizes	Number of Companies	Campus Based	Business School I.
University of Warwick Science Park, Barclays Venture Centre, University of Warwick Science Park, Coventry CV4 7EH (0203 24011)	1983	24 acres	400–30,000 sq ft	15	Yes	Yes

Contact: Mr D. N. E. Rowe
The science park is wholly owned
by the university, Coventry
City Council, West Midlands
County Council and Warwickshire County Council. The site
will be used to attract high technology firms wanting to take
advantage of a close relationship with the university and
other institutions, such as
Manchester Polytechnic, the
Motor Industry Research
Association; the National Agriculture Centre, the National
Vegetable Research Station,
Lucas Group Services, British
Leyland, Rolls-Royce, Talbot
and Courtaulds.
Specific expertise includes bio-
technology, CAD/CAM,
robotics, industrial controls and
systems, industrial software,
metrology etc.
Companies can either build
their own premises, rent a unit
or take a space in the 'incubator'
building. This is a 25,000 square

foot building designed to house a number of small companies, sharing common central services such as administrative and computing services. Barclays Bank has invested £1 million in this project.

Residents of the science park may be able to get loan and equity capital from either the West Midlands County Council or Coventry City Council. The latter can provide loans of up to £100,000 at low level interest rates, for the first two years. Otherwise, close relationships are maintained with ICFC and the British Technology Group (see next section for more details of these organisations).

	Opening Date	Area	Range of Unit Sizes	Number of Companies	Campus Based	Business School Link
West of Scotland Science Park, Kelvin Campus, West of Scotland Science Park, Glasgow G20 0SP (041-946 7161) *Contact: Dr Colin Bond*	1983	70 acres	830– 12,500 sq ft	2	Yes	Yes
Whitechapel Technology Centre, 75 Whitechapel Road, London E1 *Contact: Rodney Willis (01-633 5350) Alistair Hanman (01-633 5133)* at The County Hall, London SE1 7PB (01-633 2344) This is the first of a series of new technology centres that the GLC plan to open in London. It is intended for small companies supplying technologically inno-vated products or services. There	1982		8 units 1950– 4000 14 units 240– 1130 monthly tenancy	14	No	No

143

are nine units available on 10-
year leases.

A rent-free period of three
months will be considered as a
contribution towards the cost of
fitting the units. The unit is not
on a university or college
campus (though Queen Mary
College Industrial Research
Unit is close), but their innovation centre will help.

An innovation centre will
occupy one of the units at the
technology centre. This will
provide information and advice
on new technology, link firms to
existing networks of advice,
information and support, and
generally help new ventures to
get off the ground.

The Genesis units provided are
intended to appeal particularly
to firms at an early stage of their
development. This product or
service should be based on a
patented invention or a technological innovation.

Opening Date

Area

Range of Unit Sizes

Number of Companies

Campus Based

Business School Lin'

FINANCIAL AND ADVISORY SERVICES FOR TECHNOLOGY

Apart from science parks, there are a number of other organisations and services useful to the innovator. In this section you can find out how to meet other inventors; how to get someone else to do all the work of developing, patenting and marketing your product, and then pay you a fee; how to find financial institutions that understand technology and can give more than just financial help. (See also pages 269–274.)

Hi-tech Sources of Finance

A growing number of financial institutions are prepared to take the plunge and invest in High-technology businesses. Some are prepared to go further and put management and production expertise at the entrepreneurs disposal. Naturally these efforts are not philanthropic. They are intended to improve the chances of success and so 'insure' the investors stake. (See also page 243.)

Anglo-American Venture Fund, 8th Floor, Bank House, Charlotte Street, Manchester M1 4ET (061-236 7302). *Contact: Mr E. R. D. Duckworth*

Advent Eurofund Ltd, Trinity House, Bath Street, St Helier, Jersey (0534 75151). *Contact: Gillian Holl*

Advent Technology plc (Advent Management Ltd), 48 Manor Place, Edinburgh EH3 7EH (031-225 5784). *Contact: Mr Michael Moran*

Alta Berkeley Associates, 25 Berkeley Square, London W1X 5HB (01-629 1550).

Baronsmead Associates Ltd, 59 London Wall, London EC2M 5TP (01-638 6826).

Biotechnology Investments Ltd, N. M. Rothschild & Sons Ltd, PO Box 185, New Court, St Swithins Lane, London EC4P 4DU (01-280 5000). *Contact: Mr Jeremy Hayward*

Birmingham Technology Ltd, Aston Science Park, Love Lane, Birmingham B7 4BJ (021-359 0981). *Contact: Mr Peter Cross*

British Technology Group, 101 Newington Causeway, London SE1 6BU (01-730 8600). (Funded by national government) In 1981 the British Technology Group was formed out of the late National Enterprise Board and the National Research Development Corporation. The two organisations have a combined portfolio of 400 investments in industrial companies.

In addition, about 200 research and development projects are being funded at British universities.

BTG can provide finance for technical innovation in any field of technology. This finance is available to any company or individual entrepreneur, either as equity or loan capital. BTG is the main channel for exploiting technology from universities, polytechnics, research councils and government research establishments. It has a portfolio of 1800 UK patents, 600 licences and over 400 revenue earning innovations.

For small companies they have two schemes:

- The Small Company Innovation Fund (SCIF). This was established in September 1980 to provide finance where the business as a whole is innovative. Despite having advanced only £1 million spread over two dozen projects since its inception, BTG are keen to hear from innovative entrepreneurs needing the services of SCIF.

- Oakland Finance Ltd, established in March 1981, provides loans of up to £50,000 for technological or more traditionally based companies.

Clydebank Enterprise Fund, Clyde House, 170 Kilbowie Road, Clydebank (041-952 0084/5/6). This is a joint venture between the Bank of Scotland and the SDA to promote through low interest loans enterprising business projects within Clydebank and the Enterprise Zone. The fund offers unsecured loans up to £25,000 at a 5% rate of interest.

Granville Venture Capital, 27/28 Lovat Lane, London EC3 8EV (01-621 1212)

IFH Technology Fund, 1 Princes Gate, Knightsbridge, London SW7 (01-584 5628)

Innotech Investments Ltd, 39 Buckingham Gate, London SW1E 6BS (01-834 2492).

Innovation-Linked Investment Scheme (ILIS). Offers assistance to independent small and medium-sized firms (up to 500 employees) that are developing innovative products or processing in the high-tech field. Further details from your nearest Department of Trade & Industry Regional Office (see pages 64–65).

INTEX Executives (UK) Ltd & EP Woods Investments Ltd, Chancery House, 53/64 Chancery Lane, London WC2A 1QU (01-831 6925/01-242 2263). *Contact: Mr D. Bruce Lloyd*

Oakland Management Holdings Ltd, Ramsbury House, High Street, Hungerford, Berkshire RG17 0LY (0488 83555). *Contact: Mr J. F. Hall-Craggs*

P.A. Development Ltd, Bowater House East, 68 Knightsbridge, London SW1K 7LJ (01-589 7050). *Contact: Mr Peter Grundy*

Prutec, 17 Buckingham Gate, London SW1E 6LN (01-828 2082).

3i Ventures, is the high-technology arm of Investors in Industry plc, 91 Waterloo Road, London SE1 8XP (01-928 6394). Generally its approach is effective for situations calling for investments of £200,000 or more. In whatever form its funds are provided it expects them to be at substantial risk. Other than in exceptional circumstances they ask for a significant, but minority shareholding in the business.

Advisory Services for Technology

American Inventors Corporation, 82 Broad Street, Dept SL Westfield, Massachusetts 10186, USA. They offer a link between UK inventors and American Industry via a free confidential disclosure registration and an initial consultation in London to discuss your business idea.

University of Bath, School of Management, Claverton Down, Bath BA2 7AY (0225 61244). *Contact: Graham Ray (accountant) or Nicholas Crawford (marketing and new products)*. This is the home of a Levhume trust funded research project into how small firms can make use of technology and product licensing to help them expand.

The Calderdale Innovation Centre, Calder College, Todmorden, West Yorkshire (070681 4399). They select promising inventions from ideas submitted and then provide extensive advice on technical and marketing matters. They can also help with prototypes and design work.

The Centre for Innovation in Industry, 18 Adam Street, London WC2H 6AH (01-930 3258/01-839 4901). *Contact: Bingham Dore*. CII has a new products data-bank that links inventors with manufacturers and investors.

The Chartered Institute of Patent Agents, Staple Inn Buildings, High Holborn, London WC1V 7PZ (01-405 9450). The institute itself does not run an advisory service, although it will give advice on patents, trade marks and designs where possible. It publishes The Register of Patent Agents (price £2.00), which lists the names and business addresses of all the patent agents qualified to practise before the Patent Office.

The patent agent will be able to give advice on all aspects relating to making application for patents, trade marks and designs, as well as on infringement of these or of protection and on passing off matters. He may also be able to give advice on the exploitation of any invention protected by patent, although this is not specifically within his field of operation. The patent agents will work to a fixed scale of charges relating to the work done, in the same way as a solicitor charges, rather than taking a share in the commercial success of an invention.

Co-operative Research Grants Scheme, Science Research Council, Polaris House, North Star Avenue, Swindon (0793 26222). This scheme promotes co-operation between firms who wish to develop new products that require research beyond their capabilities, and academics in universities and polytechnics. The SRC will support the academic contribution but the firm must pay its share.

Coventry Innovation Centre, c/o Coventry Chamber of Commerce and Industry, St Nicholas Street, Coventry, Warwickshire (0203 51777). Gives advice and help to inventors. Prototypes can be produced by local firms and may even be paid for by the City Council. It also has a workshop which was recently set up so that the inventors can work, under supervision, on their own prototypes.

The Design Council, 28 Haymarket, London SW1Y 4SU (01-839 8000). A number of Design Advisory Officers are available to advise on design of products and to investigate the technical problems of an existing product. These Records of Engineering Expertise hold information about sources of specialist technical advice of use to engineering designers.

The Design Council has four regional offices at the following addresses:

The Design Council: Scottish Design Centre, 72 St Vincent Street, Glasgow G2 5TN (041-221 6121).
The Design Council: Design Centre Wales, Pearl Assurance House, Greyfriars Road, Cardiff CF1 3JN (0222 395811/2).
The Design Council: Midlands, Norwich Union House, 31 Waterloo Road, Wolverhampton WV1 4BP (0902 773631).
The Design Council: Northern Ireland, Windsor House, 30 Victoria Street, Belfast BT1 3GS (0232 338452).

If you employ between 60 and 1000 people you could have up to 15 days' free design consultancy and a further 15 days at half price.

For details of this contact John Benson, Department of Industry, PO Box 702, London sw20 8s2 (01-930 8655).

Institute of International Licensing Practitioners Ltd, 105 Onslow Square, London sw7 (01-584 5749). Licensing practitioners can help you find customers to licence your invention to, if you cannot exploit it yourself. They keep a register of members and their specialist areas of expertise. Copies are available from the secretary.

The Institute of Inventors, 19 Fosse Way, Ealing, London w13 0BZ (01-998 3540/4372/6372). This is a self-supporting institute run by inventors for inventors. It can help with patent application, prototypes and commercialisation of suitable inventions.

The Institute of Patentees and Inventors, Staple Inn Buildings South, 335 High Holborn, London wc1v 7px (01-242 7812). The institute was founded in 1919 to further the interests of patentees and inventors. It gives advice and guidance to members on all aspects of inventing, from idea conception to innovation and development. Its journal, *The Inventor*, comes out quarterly and helps to keep members up to date. Its *New Patents Bulletin* acts as a liaison with industry, bringing members' inventions to the notice of specialised manufacturing firms. Exhibitions of new inventions are organised frequently by UPI. Membership costs £20.00 per annum.

Inventors Development Ltd, Tress House, Stamford Street, London se1 9NT (01-393 9305). Formed by a group of inventors to make socially worthwhile but economically viable inventions.

IRS – Dialtech, Department of Trade and Industry, Room 204, Ebury Bridge House, 2–18 Ebury Bridge Road, London, sw1w 8qd (01-730 9678 ext 297). This is a computer-based information service covering science and technology. Users dial into the service, using their own terminals. A typical 10-minute search would cost £6.00. For users without terminals, a TECH-SEARCH service is offered at a cost of about £25.00.

Malcolm Hedley – Saw Design Group, Cust Hall, Toppesfield, Nr Halstead, Essex co9 4eb (0787 237704). These are designers and engineers who can take an invention and turn it into a manufacturable product. The group frequently deal with individual inventors and small firms.

The National Westminster Bank operate a Technical Advisory Service which can prepare a report on the technical viability of a product or a project, using outside academics and research institutes. The customer and the bank share the costs of this work equally. To find out about the service contact your local branch initially.

New Technology Appraisal Project, Interwork, Cranfield Institute of Technology, Cranfield, Bedfordshire, MK4 3OAL (0234 752767). *Contact: Brian Wilson.* Using this scheme, managers of Lloyds Bank can refer new technology projects to interwork for appraisal. Any business, whether an existing or new customer of Lloyds Bank, which requires finance, could qualify for this free feasability study. Users get a copy of the report sent to the bank.

Overseas Technical Information Unit, Department of Trade and Industry, Room 230, Ebury Bridge House, Ebury Bridge Road, London SW1W 8QD (01-730 9678 ext 403). The unit keeps industry and government departments up to date with significant technological development overseas. Free reports and newsletters are circulated.

PA Patcentre International, Cambridge Division, Melbourn, Royston, Herts SG8 6DP (0763 61222). Their major role is the development of commercially successful products for companies.
The service begins with a clear definition of the commercial and market constraints and extends through initial concept development, technical and commercial feasability studies, ergonomic design and styling, prototype design and construction, production and manufacturing engineering, market research and market launch, packaging and supporting graphics. Each project is managed by an experienced team of senior consultants who are recognised authorities in their field and have in-depth experience in international project and business development.

Prutec, 17 Buckingham Gate, London SW1E 6LN (01-828 2082). Prutec is a wholly owned subsidiary of Prudential Assurance. Since opening its doors for business in 1981 with some £20 million venture capital, it has sought out investment opportunities in technological innovation in the UK. The company has close links with PA International, and has several PA executives on its board. The rest of the management consists of a small, highly qualified team with wide experience in science and technology, and in business methods. Prutec's investments strategies include basic research developing technological applications and commercialising such developments.
This is an unusual source of finance, with Prutec Executive setting out to speak the same language as technologists. They expect not just to invest money but to give technological and

commercial expertise as well. They have a number of technology areas of particular strategic interest, and they will actively promote the development of products to meet market needs they have identified.

QMC Industrial Research Ltd, 229 Mile End Road, London E1 4AA (01-709 0066). QMC Ltd is a wholly owned company of Queen Mary College, University of London, which makes available the invention expertise and equipment of the college to industry. They have available some 250 highly qualified staff and their supporting technicians.

QMC have very active links with the local small business community and have carried out work in the following fields:

- Testing Services. Chemical, physical and biological tests ranging from strength and fatigue of metals and plastics to safe development of crops in polluted waste ground;
- Materials Expertise. Safety of materials and products, particularly organic materials like upholstery foams exposed to fire; and substitution of cheaper new materials with adequate performance in traditional products;
- Engineering Expertise. Wide range of services, including strength of structures, more efficient energy utilisation, geotechnical surveys and soil mechanics, process improvements;
- Product Liability investigation. Advice and laboratory service from a reputable, independent, expert organisation (the university) which carries weight in court proceedings;
- Specialised ('one-off') services. Prototype development, project management, economic appraisals of technical markets, adaptation of computer software to specific needs, etc.

Research Engineers Ltd, Orsman Road, Shoreditch, London N1 5RD (01-739 7811). This organisation specialises in making prototypes for inventors.

Technology Advisory Point, Ebury Bridge House, 2–18 Ebury Bridge Road, London SW1W 2QD (01-730 9678 ext 588). *Contact: Ian Melville.* TAP's primary purpose is to help UK industry to increase its productivity and profitability by taking advantage of the UK's its vast R&D expertise. This service is not confined to the department's own research establishments, as TAP has detailed knowledge of the expertise, experience and facilities in associations and academic institutions.

The aim is simply to provide one point of contact for businesses looking for help when faced with a technological problem. In this way, they hope to remove the frustration felt when enquiries are passed from one person to another.

Information which TAP can provide includes the best contact

to deal with a particular problem, establishments which can carry out work in a particular area; establishments which have certain testing or calibration facilities; and laboratories which have available certain specialised equipment or facilities.

Three telephone lines are open for enquirers to contact TAP staff to discuss the details of their problems and the sort of expertise they are looking for. There is no charge for using TAP, and the same will normally apply to preliminary enquiries to the chosen organisation. Their charges will vary with the nature of the services provided and the charging policy of the establishment concerned. Information on this will normally be provided at an early stage.

TECH ALERT, Department of Trade and Industry, Ebury Bridge House, Ebury Bridge Road, London SW1W 8QD (01-730 9678 ext 513). Selected research information published monthly, abstracted from 10 technical journals. Can report the supplier as potential licenser of the technology in question.

Technology Policy Unit, Department of Industry, 29 Bressenden Place, London SW1E 5DT (01-213 5433). *Contact: Dr Bob Wiggins.* This is the base for the governments Support for Innovation activity. Schemes include:

CADCAM	Computer-aided Design and Conputer-aided Manufacture in the mechanical and electrical engineering industries.
CADMAT	Computer-aided Design, Manufacture and Testing in the electronics sector.
FMS	Flexible Manufacturing Systems for computer-controlled batch production.
FOS	The Fibre Optics and Opto-Electronics Industries Scheme.
MAP	the Microelectronics Application Project to encourage the use of microelectronics in products and processes in any sector of manufacturing industry.
MISP	the Microelectronics Industry Support Programme.
INDUSTRIAL ROBOTS	to encourage the application of robots and the manufacture of British machines.
SPS	the Software Products Scheme to promote computer software products and packages.

For literature only, write freepost to their address.

Techtrade Europe, 53–55 Frith Street, London W1A 2HG (01-323 3211). *Contact: Angie Laycock.* A technology transfer service for establishing worldwide contacts between buyers and sellers of technology.

Transmission Systems Ltd, Airport Road, St Brelade, Jersey, British Isles (0534 45626). *Contact: Derek Bernard, Managing Director.* TSL's business was originally based on its involvement with the WORKMATE workcentre project which is licensed to Black & Decker and manufactured and marketed by them throughout the world with enormous success.

From the various ideas submitted to TSL by outside inventors, they select those which would appear to pass the following criteria:

1   Appear to be technically and economically feasible;

2   Appear to hold out the prospect of effective potential protection by Patents and/or Design Registrations;

3   Seem to hold out the prospect of sufficient commercial potential to justify the high risks involved;

4   Are of a nature and size which is likely to be within TSL's capacity within a reasonable time frame.

If an Invention Submission appears to satisfy these criteria then TSL will make the inventor a specific offer setting out the basis on which it would be prepared to become involved in the project. Each project tends to be different but it is not unusual for the Agreement to give the inventor 50% of any net royalties arising from the product sales – that is after development, patent and administrative expenses have been deducted.

This may be one of the few ways in which an inventor with little money or commercial expertise can hope to achieve commercial success with his invention without taking on extra risks, such as borrowing substantial sums of money, in order to do the job on his own.

In the first instance anyone wishing to consider this approach should write to Transmission Systems Limited and ask for their Invention Submission Form.

RESEARCH ASSOCIATIONS

There are some 50 research organisations in the UK, which are the centres of knowledge in their respective fields. If the product or idea that you are developing (or want to use) comes within their sphere of interest, they may well be of use. They have extensive information systems, and can usually guide enquirers to appropriate sources of data or other help.

ASLIB (Association of Social Libraries Information Bureau), 3 Belgrave Square, London SW1X 8PL (01-235 5050) *Contact: Dr Dennis A. Lewis, Director*

BHRA Fluid Engineering, Cranfield, Bedfordshire MK43 0AJ (0234 750422) *Contact: Mr G. F. W. Alder, Director*

Brick Development Association, Woodside, Winkfield, Windsor, Berkshire SL4 2DX (0344 885651) *Contact: Rear Admiral A. J. Monk, CBE, Director-General*

British Brush Manufacturer's Research Association, c/o Department of Textile Industries, The University, Leeds LS2 9JT (0532 31751) *Contact: Mr D. I. Fothergill, Director*

British Carbonization Research Association, Wingerworth, Chesterfield, Derbyshire S42 6JS (0246 76821) *Contact: Mr J. P. Graham, OBE, Director*

British Ceramic Research Association, Queens Road, Penkhull, Stoke-on-Trent ST4 7LQ (0782 45431) *Contact: Dr D. F. W. James, Director*

British Glass Industry Research Association, Northumberland Road, Sheffield S10 2UA (0742 686201) *Contact: Dr E. A. Kellett, Director*

The British Internal Combustion Engine Research Institute Ltd, 111–112 Buckingham Avenue, Slough SL1 4PH (0753 27371) *Contact: Mr I. A. G. Brown, Director and Secretary*

British Leather Manufacturers' Research Association, King's Park Road, Moulton Park, Northamptonshire NN3 1JD (0604 494131 or 0604 494990 after 17.15) *Contact: Dr R. L. Sykes, Director*

Building Services Research & Information Association, Old Bracknell Lane West, Bracknell, Berkshire RG12 4AH (0344 426511) *Contact: Dr D. P. Gregory, Director*

Construction Industry Research and Information Association, 6 Storey's Gate, London SW1P 3AU (01-222 8891) *Contact: Dr L. S. Blake, Director*

Cranfield Unit for Precision Engineering, Cranfield Institute of Technology, Cranfield, Bedfordshire MK43 0AL (0234 750111) *Contact: Professor P. A. McKeown, Director*

Cutlery & Allied Trades' Research Association, Henry Street, Sheffield S3 7EQ (0742 79736) *Contact: Mr E. A. Oldfield, Director*

Drop Forging Research Association, Shepherd Street, Sheffield S3 7BA (0742 27463) *Contact: Dr S. E. Rogers, Director*

Fabric Care Research Association, Forest House Laboratories, Knaresborough Road, Harrogate HG2 7LZ (0423 8803210) *Contact: Mr E. J. Davies, Director*

Fire Insurers' Research & Testing Organisation, Melrose Avenue, Boreham Wood, Hertfordshire WD6 2BJ (01-207 2345) *Contact: Mr R. W. Pickard, Director*

Furniture Industry Research Association, Maxwell Road, Stevenage, Hertfordshire SG1 2EW (0438 313433) *Contact: Mr D. M. Heughan, Director*

HATRA (Hosiery and Allied Trades Research Association), Thorneywood, 7 Gregory Boulevard, Nottingham NG7 6LD (0602 623311/2) *Contact: W. N. Bignall, Director*

Lambeg Industrial Research Association, The Research Institute, Lambeg, Lisburn, Co. Antrim, Northern Ireland BT27 4RJ (084 622255/6) *Contact: Dr W. W. Foster, PA to Director of Research*

Machine Tool Industry Research Association, Hulley Road, Macclesfield, Cheshire SK10 2NE (0625 25421/3 and 26189) *Contact: Mr M. E. Hadlow, Director*

National Computing Centre, Oxford Road, Manchester M1 7ED (061-228 6333) *Contact: Mr David R. Fairbairn, Director*
London Office: 11 New Fetter Lane, EC4A 1PU (01-353 4875) *Contact: Mrs Fleming, Regional Officer*

The Paint Research Association, Waldegrave Road, Teddington, Middlesex TW11 8LD (01-977 4427/9) *Contact: Dr G. de W. Anderson, Director*

Paper & Board, Printing & Packaging Industries Research Association, Roundalls Road, Leatherhead, Surrey KT22 7RU (0372 376161) *Contact: Dr N. K. Bridge, Director*

Processors' & Growers' Research Organisation, The Research Station, Great North Road, Thornhaugh, Peterborough PE8 6HJ (0708 782595) *Contact: Mr A. J. Gane, Director and Secretary*

Production Engineering Research Association of Great Britain, Melton Mowbray, Leicestershire LE13 0PB (0664 64133) *Contact: Professor W. B. Heginbotham, OBE, Director-General*

Rubber & Plastic Research Association of Great Britain, Shawbury, Shrewsbury, Shropshire SY4 4NR (0939 250 383) *Contact: Dr J. P. Berry, Director*

Shirley Institute, Wilmslow Road, Didsbury, Manchester M20 8RX (061-445 8141) *Contact: Dr Alasdair Maclean, Managing Director, Dr J. Honeyman, Director of Research*

Shoe & Allied Trades' Research Association, Satra House, Rockingham Road, Kettering, Northamptonshire NN16 9JH (0536 516318) *Contact: Mr J. Graham Butlin, Director*

Spring Research and Manufacturers' Association, Henry Street, Sheffield S3 7EQ (0742 760771) *Contact: Mr J. A. Bennett, Director*

Steel Castings Research and Trade Association, 5 East Bank Road, Sheffield S2 3PT (0742 28647) *Contact: Dr J. A. Reynolds, Director*

Timber Research and Development Association, Stocking Lane, Hughenden Valley, High Wycombe, Bucks HP14 4ND (0240 243091) *Contact: Mr J. G. Sunley, Director*

Water Research Centre, PO Box 16, Henley Road, Medmenham, Marlow, Bucks SL7 2HD (062 84 16653) *Contact: Mr J. L. van der Post, Chief Executive*

WIRA (Woollen Industry Research Association), Wira House, West Park Ring Road, Leeds LS16 6QL (0532 781381) *Contact: Dr B. E. King, Director*

Other Research Institutes include:

Association of Independent Contract Research Organisations (AICRO) represents a large and comprehensive concentration of

155

UK based research and development skills. Their spread of activities ranges from aerodynamics to alternative energy; and from geotechnics to toxicology. They aim to give customers access to the best expertise and facilities available.

Their members can undertake complete programmes or supplement in-house R&D. They have considerable experience in working with small businesses. Contact AICRO at 7 Catherine Place, London SW1E 6EB (01-834 0292)

British Association for the Advancement of Science, Fortress House, 25 Savile Row, London W1X 1AB (01-734 6010)

The Research and Development Society, 47 Belgrave Square, London SW1X 8QX (01-235 6111)

COMPUTERS

If you have not already bought a computer then there are a number of organisations, periodicals and books that may help you to make the best decisions. You will need to know something of what a computer can and cannot do, and exactly what work you want done. If your business is or is likely to involve repetitions, routinised, time-consuming and usually boring tasks, the chances are that a computer could do them better. Typically, small businesses put their book-keeping, management accounts, payroll, mailing and price lists and, more recently, wordprocessing functions on to a computer. Systems are available to analyse customers: how long they take to pay up; how much on average they order; and when their next order is due.

Finding your solution. Once you have decided what you want done, then you have to find the software and hardware to meet your needs. The software is the programme or instructions that have to be given to the computer in order to process your data and produce the information that you want.

Finding out about software means reading the computer magazines, talking to manufacturers and users, going to exhibitions and getting demonstrations from software houses.

An increasing number of 'standard' software packages are available for specific trades and professions. Packages include those for small shops, such as pharmacies, and for medical practices and estate agents. Your trade association will be watching these developments, and they should be able to help you find out more. Keeping a watch in your trade magazine will also show you what enterprising people are getting up to in this area. It is highly likely that your needs and the available software will not quite match. In this case you will need to customise the software to your own requirements by writing, or having written, additional programmes.

Finally, you will have to decide on the hardware – the computer itself. Your choice of software will pre-select the computer best-suited to your needs, but you can still choose whether to buy (or lease) your own, or to use a computer bureau on a time-sharing basis.

It is very likely that the complexities and unfamiliarity of the field, combined with overwhelming apparent choice of systems, will leave you confused. Help is at hand, either from the following organisations, or by referring to the publications listed afterwards.

Organisations

Association of Independent Computer Specialists, c/o BEAMA, Leicester House, 8 Leicester Street, London WC2H 7BN (01-437 0678 telex 263536) *Contact: AICS Public Relations Officer: Dr S. G. Beech (0732 460420); AICS Microsystems Group: Alan Mayne (01-883 7703)*

The association was formed in 1972 with the twin objectives of improving the professional standards of computer consultants, and of making sure that clients receive independent advice. There are now some eighty members. Contact can be made either by sending for the AICS Handbook or by asking for a specific service. The handbook, as well as telling you about AICS, has the names, addresses and details of the fields of experience and specialisation of members. It also tells you when the members' consultancy was established, who the principals are, and the geographical area of operations.

AICS maintains links with similar organisations – for example, the Association of Independant Computer Professionals. AICP was formed in Birmingham in 1981 and now has about 20 members.

Barclays Microprocessor Applications Unit, Department of Computer Science, University of Manchester, Oxford Road, Manchester M13 9PL (061-273 7121)

British Computer Society, 13 Mansfield Street, London W1H 0BP (01-637 0471) Can advise across the whole field and produces a number of authoritative journals.

Brixton Information Technology Centre, c/o ICFC Ltd, 91 Waterloo Road, London SE1 8XP (01-928 7822, ext 387) In the period 1984/85 there will be approximately 140 of these Information & Technology Centres. (Contact the Manpower Services Commission for local details.)

City Technology Centre, 165 Shoreditch High Street, London E1 6HU (01-739 8856) *Contact: Mr R. Dowry.* The centre was set up in 1982 to encourage and help firms in Hackney to make use of microcomputers in their business. The centre runs training courses and other education and awareness programmes.

Computing Services Association, 73–74 High Holborn, London WC1V 6LE (01-405 2171/3161)

Computer Town UK, 14 Rathbone Place, London W1P 1DE

Institute of Data Processing Management, 50 Goschen Buildings, 18 Henrietta Street, London WC2E 8NU (01-240 3304)

The National Computing Centre, backed by government and industry provides; public and in-house training courses; teaching materials; supplies software packages; publishes a comprehensive range of books; offers information; and operate an Enquiry/Advisory service:

Their addresses are:

Head Office, Oxford Road, Manchester M1 7ED (061-228 6333 telex 668962)

London and South East, 11 New Fetter Lane, London EC4A 1PU (01-353 4875)

Midlands, 7th Floor, Devonshire House, Great Charles Street, Birmingham B3 2PL (021-236 6283)

North and North Wales, (same address as Head Office)

Northern Ireland, 117 Lisburn Road, Belfast BT9 7BP (0232 665997)

Scotland, 2nd Floor, Anderston House, 389 Argyle Street, Glasgow G2 8LR (041-204 1101)

South West and South Wales, 6th Floor, Bristol and West Building, 41 Corn Street, Bristol BS1 1HG (0272 277077)

The Software Products Scheme, administered by The National Computing Centre Ltd, Oxford Road, Manchester M1 7ED (061-228 6333). A free comprehensive booklet describes this scheme.

Microsystems Centres (MSC) A Federation of Microsystem Centres is being established, supported by the Government and the National Computing Centre. These centres are an independent, authoritative, practical and individual source of assistance, advice and information for anyone who is considering using a microcomputer in business. Small and new businesses will find the range of services particularly helpful.

The services of each centre will include:

Training The centres' flexible training programmes are aimed at specific needs, from clerical staff through to financial advisers. They run self-instruction and taught courses at most times including weekends, evenings and lunch-times.

Consultancy and advice This is available to help you choose the right computer; to analyse and select from available software;

or to commission specific or modified software. This consultancy extends from the feasability study designed to find out if a computer will help to solve your business problem, through to acceptance tests on installing any system you may decide to buy. The centres do not sell hardware or software, so the advice given is independent. The cost per hour for this consultancy advice is around £50.

Demonstrations by their trained staff can be given on a range of microcomputer systems on permanent display at centres.

Information is available from the centres' comprehensively stocked book shop, which carries a range of books, magazines and articles on most aspects of the subject.

The London Centre is: Microsystems Centre, 11 New Fetter Lane, London EC4A 1PU (01-353 0013/4/5) *Contact: Colin Harris*

Centres are open or will open shortly as below and a Centre also be opening in Birmingham.

Avon Microsystems Centre Ltd, Bank of England Chambers, Wine Street, Bristol BS1 2DN (0272 277774)

Coventry Microsystems Centre, Henley College of Further Education, Henley Road, Bell Green, Coventry CV2 1ED (0203 611021)

East Midlands Microsystems Centre, Trent Polytechnic, Burton Street, Nottingham NC1 4BU (0602 48248)

Edinburgh: Waverley Microsystems Centre, INMAP, 21 Lansdowne Crescent, Edinburgh EH12 5EH (031-225 3141)

Greater Manchester Microsystems Centre, Salford University Industrial Centre Ltd, Salbec House, 100 Broughton Road, Salford M6 6GS (061-736 5843)

Hertfordshire Microsystems Centre, De Havilland Cottage, Elstree Way, Borehamwood, Hertfordshire WD6 1JE (01-953 6024)

Merseyside Microsystems Centre, Merseyside Innovation Centre, 131 Mount Pleasant, Liverpool L3 5TF (051-708 0123)

Milton Keynes Microsystems Centre, Information Technology Exchange, Midsummer House, 429 Midsummer Boulevard, Saxon Gate West, Central Milton Keynes MK9 2HE (0908 668866)

South Wales Microsystems Centre, Computer Centre, Polytechnic of Wales, Pontypridd, Mid Glamorgan CF37 1DL (0443 405133)

South Yorkshire Microsystems Centre, Sheffield City Polytechnic, Dyson House, Suffolk Road, Sheffield S1 1WR (0741 73862)

Strathclyde Microsystems Centre, Paisley College of Technology, 72 George Street, Paisley, Renfrewshire PA1 2LF (041-887 1241 ext 379)

Tyne and Wear Microsystems Centre, Coach Lane Campus, Newcastle-upon-Tyne Polytechnic, Newcastle-upon-Tyne NE7 7XA (0632 700504)

Ulster Microsystems Centre, Ulster Polytechnic, Shore Road, Newtonabbey, Co. Antrim BT37 0QB (0231 65131)

West Yorkshire Microsystems Centre, Queenswood House, Beckett Park, Leeds LS6 3QS (0532 759741)

The Federation will have the addresses as they come on stream. Their address is:
Federation of Micro Centres, The National Computing Centre Ltd, Oxford Road, Manchester M1 7ED (061-228 6333, telex 668962) *Contact: John Turnbull, Federation Manager*

As well as these centres, a network of associated centres will be set up, offering either a more limited or more specialised service. These centres will complement the activities of the major centres and they will work closely with them. In this way both wider and deeper coverage will be attained quickly.

Neath Information Technology Centre, ITEC Centre, Neath (0639 4141 ext 176) *Contact: Mr Emlyn Williams.* Jointly sponsored by Metal Box PLC and Neath Borough Council, with educational, administrative and technical support from the West Glamorgan Institute of Higher Technology. (See Brixton for details of ITEC's.)

Publications

Computing Marketplace, Gower Press, 1983 501pp; Gower House, Croft Road, Aldershot, Hants GU11 3HR. This is a directory of computing services, software suppliers, micros, minis, mainframes, computer training establishments, DP staff recruitment, computer equipment financing and leasing, system maintenance. Price: £29.50

Infotech Survey, carried out in January 1984 for Your Business, 60 Kingley Street, London W1R 5LH (01-437 5678). It examined microcomputers for small business applications. Hardware examined, costs listed and brief appreciation of each system given.

The Micro-Computer Users' Handbook 1983, published by Macmillan, 4 Little Essex Street, London WC2R 3LF (01-836 6633), 400pp. Covers the essential decisions to be made in understanding the computer, buying it and making effective use of it. Many of the more popular systems and programmes are described in some detail. Such as: Visicalc, dBase II and UNIM. Price: £16.95

Small Business Computers for First-Time Users, by I. R. Beaman, published by National Computing Centre (1983), marketed by John Wiley & Sons Ltd, Baffins Lane, Chichester, Sussex PO19 1UD. It highlights the key aspects of computer selection and offers guidance on evaluating proposals and implementing the selected system. Price: £7.95

Small Computers in Small Companies, published by Easton and Lawrence (1981), Department of Marketing, University of

Lancaster, Gillow House, Lancaster LA1 4YX (0524 65201). It surveys the experiences of 100 small organisations that have installed small computer systems. It tells you how they chose, what they chose and how happy (or unhappy) they are with their decisions. Price: £25.00

Specialised Software, published by VNU Business Publications (1983), 62 Oxford Street, London W1A 2HG (01-636 6890) A survey carried out by *Micro-Decision*, the monthly UK computer journal. The survey lists details of software written for over 325 different types of business application. The following should give a flavour of the industries covered:

Advertising Database; Animal Performance Monitoring; Bakers; Bar Stock; Bill of Materials; Boat Sales; Book Shops; Car Sales; Coach Tour Operations; Debt Collection; Dry Cleaners; Employment Agencies; Export Documentation; Garment Industry; Kitchen Retailers; Mail Order; Recipe Costing; Newsagents; Petrol Stations; Pharmacists; Property Management; Retailing Management; Time Records and Travel Agents.

Software File, Durrant House, 8 Herbal Hill, London EC1R 5JB. A monthly directory of existing specialist software – prices and suppliers. Subscription rate £50 per annum.

See also page 298 for courses on computers and the Open University, page 331.

INDUSTRIAL ORGANISATIONS

Further sources of information on the application of technology are listed below:

British Safety Council, 62–64 Chancellors' Road, London W6 9RS (01-741 1231)

British Standards Institution, 2 Park Street, London W1A 2BS (01-629 9000)

Cambridge Information and Research Services Ltd, Grosvenor House, High Street, Newmarket CB8 9AL (0638 663030)

Ergonomics Information Analysis Centre, Department of Engineering Production, University of Birmingham, PO Box 363, Birmingham B15 2TT (021-472 1301 ext 2731)

Institute of Industrial Managers, 45 Cardiff Road, Luton, Beds LU1 1RQ (0582 37071)

Institute of Management Services, 1 Cecil Court, London Road, Enfield, Middx. EN2 6DD (01-363 7452) *Contact: Barbara Goreham.* Leaders in the work-study field; their technical information service can give advice to small businesses.

Institute for Operational Research, Tavistock Centre, 120 Belsize Lane, Hampstead, London NW3 5BA (01-435 7111)

Institute of Production Control, National Westminster House, Wood Street, Stratford-upon-Avon, Warwicks, CV37 6JS (0789 205266)

Institute of Production Engineers, 66 Little Ealing Lane, London W5 4XX (01-579 9411)

Institute of Quality Assurance, 54 Princess Gate, Exhibition Road, London SW7 2PG (01-584 9026)

Institute of Science Information, 132 High Street, Uxbridge, Middx UB8 1DP (0895 30085)

Institute of Value Management, c/o Delta Executive Development Centre, 22 Cavendish Avenue, Buxton, Derbyshire SK17 9AE (0298 2284)

Intermediate Technology Development Group, 9 King Street, London WC2E 8HN (01-836 9434)

Local Government Operational Research Unit, 229 Kings Road, Reading, Berks RG1 4LS (0734 661234)

Low Cost Automation Centres Established by the Department of Industry to encourage the use of low cost aids to automation, the centres now run independently, and have developed considerable micro-electronics expertise. Department of Industry, Electric Application Division, Room 406, 29 Bessenden Place, London SW1E 5DT *Contact: Dr Flaherty on* (01-213 5290)

There are centres for Scotland – Paisley College of Technology, Automation and Control Centre (041-887 1241 ext 354) *Contact: John Wyle*; North West – Stockport College of Technology (061-480 3897); Yorkshire and Humberside – Sheffield Polytechnic (0742 20911 ext 335); West Midlands – University of Birmingham, Department of Engineering Production (021-472 1301 ext 3404); London and the South East – Kingston Polytechnic (01-549 1366 ext 241); South West – Bristol Polytechnic (0272 41241 ext 73) and Gloucester College of Art Technology (0452 3588); Northern Ireland – Queen's University of Belfast, Ashby Institute (0232 661111 ext 4281); Northern Ireland Automation Centre.

Manufacturing Advisory Service (MAS), PERA (Production Engineering Research Association) Melton Mowbray, Leicestershire LE13 0PB (0664 64133). Open to small firms (80–100 employees) in certain sectors of manufacturing industry, the service includes free advice on methods of improving manufacturing efficiency; answers to three enquiries on technical problems in the manufacturing field; limited assistance with training.

The Manufacturing Advisory Service (North Western Region only), Salford University, Industrial Centre Ltd, Salford M45 4WT (061-736 8921)

Micro-electronics Industry Support Programme (MISP), Department of Industry (same address as MAP, below) (01-213 5818) The scheme, announced in July 1978, is mainly intended to help UK firms create the capability to meet the demands for micro-electronic components and ancilliary equipment, materials and services. MISP provides grants towards the cost of product/process development and manufacturing. It will run until March 1984 at least.

MicroProcessor Application Project (MAP), Electronics Application Division, Room 514, 29 Bressenden Place, London SW1E 5DT

(01-213 3982) MAP's aim is to encourage UK industry to apply microprocessor techniques to a wide range of products and production processes. Grants are available for training, feasability studies and product development.

National Industrial Fuel Efficiency Service Ltd (NIFES), Head Office, Nifes House, Sunderland Road, Broad Heath, Altringham, Cheshire (061-928 5791) and at Birmingham WA14 5HQ (021-454 4471); Buntingford, Herts (0763 71154); Leeds (0532 505943); Newcastle-upon-Tyne (0632 813776); Nottingham (0602 625841); and Aberdeen (0224 642343)

National Federation of Industrial Association Ltd, Bridge House, Bewdley, Worcestershire DY12 1AB (0299 403741)

National Terotechnology Centre, c/o BIS Man House, Cottingham, Corby (05363 4222) *Contact: Mr Todd or Mr Horsley*

Operational Research Society, Neville House, Waterloo Street, Birmingham B2 5TX (021-642 0236)

Plastics Advisory Service, 5 Belgrave Square, London SW1X 6PH (01-233 9888) Free advice to users of plastic materials; on suitable materials; sources of supply; appropriate manufacturers; commercial advice on UK and Export Markets.

Quality Assurance Consultants in the UK, a directory, published free and available from DTI, Research and Technology Policy Division, Room 816, 29 Bressenden Place, London SW1E 5DT (01-213 4500)

The Small Firms Technical Enquiry Service, was launched in June 1982 and is operated for the Department of Industry by the Production Engineering Research Association. A funding of £2.2 million has been made available for three years. Aid is obtainable to any small manufacturing firm employing no more than 200 people. The service could be used, for example, in helping to find the source of a particular component, in improving the quality of a product, or in helping to increase the efficiency of a process, and for many other problems. Firms can make use of the service by ringing PERA at Melton Mowbray (066 64133 ext 444)

Technical Indexes Ltd, Willoughby Road, Bracknell, Berkshire RG12 4DW (03444 26311) Specialists in producing or disseminating technical information. Founded in 1965, they provide essential technical data to design engineers, draughtsmen and buyers in the following fields: electronic engineering, chemical engineering, laboratory equipment, materials handling, engineering components and materials, British Standards, defence standards, American Industry Standards, Mil Specs, American Catalogues and Japanese Catalogues.

FINDING OUT ABOUT YOUR MARKET

Forty organisations or important new publications have been added to this section since the first edition of this guide, which reflects the growing interest in small business marketing problems.

In contrast to the raising of money, where problems and their solutions can be treated in a relatively general way, everyone's products and markets are specialised, if only geographically so. Unless you are prepared to spend a lot of cash early on, perhaps even before you are sure whether you have a product or service to sell, you will have to find out about your market yourself. Your market-place is made up of customers, actual and potential; competitors; suppliers; distribution channels; and communication media. In order to succeed, you will have to find out all you can about these elements of your market-place and use that knowledge to your advantage. There is a vast amount of information freely available, or at a comparatively low cost – much cheaper than the cost of a relatively small mistake, which could be fatal early in the life of a business.

There are also many organisations, which, though not expressly set up to help you, have services, facilities or resources that you can tap, and so improve your knowledge and skills.

To make this complex subject digestible it is divided into six topics. 'The Information Available' will give you a flavour of the great mass of data on companies, at home and overseas, and on products and markets. There are almost 4000 current British directories and this section pulls together the ones of most use to you.

'Finding the Information' tells you how to make use of the country's substantial information and library services. The main business libraries in London, for example, are the most extensive in their fields in Europe.

'Marketing Organisations and their Services' provides details of the prominent professional bodies in the field together with some other organisations of special interest, and, where appropriate, how they might help you. One organisation, for example, can put you in front of a marketing expert in your field of interest for half a day at a cost of only £15.00.

There are also sections on exporting and importing, giving details of important organisations and services.

The final topic covers general marketing books and periodicals that can give you a broad background knowledge on the subject. These books have been chosen as much for their readability as for their direct usefulness. (See also page 279 for legal issues in marketing.)

THE INFORMATION AVAILABLE

You will need a regular flow of information on your market to help you make decisions about such matters as what to sell, at what price, your likely competitors, or to find what is going on in markets overseas. You will also need to know something on the size, shape, rate of growth and profitability of your chosen market.

In this section the hundred or so key directories, indexes, reference works and services that hold much of this valuable raw marketing data are identified and described. The ready availability of these publications has been as much a consideration in including them as their usefulness.

Interpreting that information is a harder problem, but some of these reference works contain analyses of the data provided. Otherwise, organisations in the other sections in this book may be able to help, particularly those offering a counselling or advice service, such as Enterprise Agencies, the Marketing Advisory Service, or the Warwick Statistical Service.

This section is divided into four areas: Company and Product Data, UK; Company and Product Data, Overseas; Market and Industry Data, UK; and Market and Industry Data, Overseas.

Company and Product Data provides information on home and overseas companies, their products or services, profiles and profitability. Market and Industry Data provides information on the markets serviced by those companies, their size, growth and other characteristics. There are a number of reference sources that do not rest easily in one section, and they will have been placed in the most suitable location and cross-referenced in order to help you find your way around.

Company and Product Data The range of readily held data on UK companies is bewildering, and on overseas companies only a little less so. At first glance many of the directories and information sources seem to duplicate one another's efforts, or at any rate to overlap. However, once you are faced with a particular problem their differences become apparent. *Kelly's Manufacturers & Merchants Directory* is a most useful tool for finding suppliers or competitors on a national basis. Their

Regional Directories, however, go into much finer detail for each region, but they omit the global picture.

The Retail Directory will tell you, street by street, the names and business of every shop, and another section will tell you each buyer's name. None of these will tell you much about who owns the business or about their financial performance. This information is given in *Who Owns Whom* and the Extel Card services, respectively. If you want to compare one company with another in the same line of business, *Jordans* or *ICC Business Ratios* are two useful sources. To find out what has been said in the press about a company, you could use *McCarthy's Information Services* or *Research Index*. If you want to confine your search to comment in the *Financial Times*, then their monthly index provides a cross-reference by company, general business area and by personality. If you want to know who has gone bankrupt lately, then *The London Gazette* gives out an official notice.

For overseas companies, much the same information is available, but some of the sources' names are different. There is very little you cannot find out about a company or business if you set your mind to it. The publications listed below are not exhaustive, but they are among the most important and authoritative.

Company & Product Data, UK

The Centre for Interfirm Comparison Ltd, 8 West Stockwell Street, Colchester, Essex CO1 1HN (0206 562274) and 25 Bloomsbury Square, London WC1A 2PJ (01-637 8406) This is a non-profit-making organisation, established in 1959 by the British Institute of Management and the British Productivity Council to meet the need for a neutral, expert body to conduct interfirm comparisons on a confidential basis, and to help managers to improve business performance. Participating firms feed a range of information into the centre, who in turn feed out yardsticks for them to compare systematically the performance of every important aspect of their business with other, similar firms. Together with the yardstick ratios come written reports on the findings and ideas for action – but only, of course, to the participating firms, and even then only on a 'comparative' basis so that no one company's data can ever be identified. The uniqueness of this method rests in part on the data itself. It goes far beyond anything supplied in companies' annual returns to Companies House or production monitor figures.

Thousands of companies, large and small, have participated, and comparisons are made in over 100 industries, trade, services and professions both in the UK and abroad.

The centre publishes a number of free booklets that explain their activities, the ratios they use, why they use those particular ratios and, more importantly, how you can use them to improve performance.

Commercial Names and Number (UK) Ltd, 11th Floor, Riverside House, Woolwich High Street, London SE18 6DN (01-855 7821) Suppliers of business list classifications – A selective commercial mail order mailing list source, by trade and area.

Credit Ratings Ltd, 51 City Road, London EC1Y 1AY (01-251 6675/6) This company provides an ad hoc, subscription service Credit Report. The cost varies from £18.50 to £12.50 for each report, which can normally be provided within 48 hours.

Each Credit Report provides a company profile, financial performance figures for the past two years, and eight credit ratios (including an estimate of how long they normally take to pay their bills). These ratios are then compared with the average for that industry, and are followed by a short commentary bringing important factors to the reader's attention.

Companies Registration Office keeps records of all limited companies. For England and Wales these records are kept at Companies House, 55–71 City Road, London EC1 (01-253 9393) and for Scotland at the Registrar of Companies for Scotland, 102 George Street, Edinburgh EH2 3JD. For Northern Ireland the same service is available from The Department of Commerce, Chichester House, 43/47 Chichester Court, Belfast BT1 4PJ (0232 234121)

The records kept include financial statements, accounts, directors' names and addresses, shareholders, and changes of name and structure. The information is available on microfiche at £1.00 per company, and can be photocopied at 10p per sheet. This service is available to visitors only. There are a number of commercial organisations who will obtain this information for you. Two such organisations are:

The Company Search Centre, 1/3 Leonard Street, London EC2A 4AQ (01-251 2566)
Extel, 37/45 Paul Street, London EC2A 4PB (01-253 3400)

The charges for this service are about £3.00 to £3.50 for a microfiche of each company, or for a photocopy of the report and accounts, around £8.00.

Extel Quoted Service, cards published each year by the Exchange Telegraph Co. Ltd. Cards for each of the 3000 UK companies quoted on the Stock Exchange contain the following information: name and business of the company together with details of subsidiaries and associates; the date on which the company was registered (formed), along with any change of name or status (eg, private to public); directors – their positions (chairman, managing director, etc) and their shareholdings, as well as the names of the company secretary, bankers, auditors and solicitors. Ten years' profit and loss accounts and at least three years' balance sheets are given, together with a sources and applications of funds statements. The highest and lowest share price over the ten-year period is also given, as well as the chairman's latest statement on the company position. A news card is published three or four times a year, giving details of dividends declared, board changes, acquisitions, liquidations, loans raised and other elements of operating information. A selection of these cards is held in many reference libraries. Individual cards can be bought for £2.40 from Extel Statistical Services Ltd, 37/45 Paul Street, London EC2A 4PB (01-253 3400, telex 262687) or Manchester Office (061-236 5802)

Extel's Handbook of Market Leaders, brings together details on 750 major quoted companies. Though not a substitute for the cards it does provide a quick reference guide to the financial performance of major companies. Published twice a year, in January and July, at £35.00 an issue.

Extel Unquoted Service provides a similar service for some 2000 ordinary companies. These cards cost £5.85 each, as considerably more work has to be done to get at this information, and the call for it is less.

Financial Times Index, introduced in 1981, provides a monthly and yearly index to the references to some 35,000 companies. Instead of thumbing through back issues, you can locate the abstract of each story by using the corporate index, the general index covering products and industries, or the personality section covering key people. This series costs £250.00 per annum, and is available from Financial Times Information Ltd, Minster House, Arthur Street, London EC4R 9AX. The index is also available on microfiche, floppy discs and magnetic tape.

First Clue, The A–Z of Finding Out, published by Pan Books Ltd, Cavage Place, London SW10 9PG. Written by Robert Walker, a Fleet Street journalist, it gives hundreds of first ports of call, in your search for organisations. Price £2.50.

ICC Business Ratios produce 150 business sector reports analysing the performance of some 12,000 leading UK companies over a three-year period. For each sector (for example, window manufacturers, retail chemists, the toy industry or computer equipment) key performance ratios are shown for each company in the sector and an average for the sector as a whole. You can therefore use this information to compare your performance, actual or projected, against an industry standard. There are nineteen key ratios, and they cover profitability, liquidity, asset utilisation, gearing, productivity and exports. Growth rates are monitored, including sales, total assets, capital employed, average wages and exports. It is thus possible to see quickly which company is growing the fastest in your sector and to compare your growth against the best, the worst or the average. Reports are priced at about £105.00 each, and further details are available from The Business Ratio Manager, ICC Business Ratios, 28–42 Banner Street, London EC1Y 8QE (01-253 3906)

Jordan's Business Information Service, Jordan House, 47 Brunswick Place, London N1 6EE (01-253 3030) They also have offices in Bristol, Cardiff, Edinburgh and the Isle of Man. Their Company Search Department can get you information on any UK company in 'Companies House', and their Rapid Reply Service can guarantee despatch within a few hours. Alternatively, if you really are in a hurry, they have a telex and telephone service. They also produce a range of annual business surveys covering some fifty industries. These are priced between £25.00 and £95.00.

Jordan's new Companies Service could be particularly useful for a small company looking for sales leads. Over 25,000 new companies are incorporated each year, and Jordan's reports on about half. They eliminate the companies with convenience directors and registered offices (each of which offers no contact point), which leaves several thousand 'genuine' new potential customers each month. Naturally, these companies could be anywhere in the UK, so in order to make the service more useful to small business, they have produced a county by county service, with London split into eight. These selected services cost from £150.00 to £700.00 per annum. The whole UK service could cost around £6000, and London alone around £2500. At 24p a 'lead', this could prove a cost-effective way to expand sales.

Kelly's Manufacturers and Merchants Directory, published by IPC Business Press, 40 Bowling Green Lane, London EC1R ONE has an alphabetical list of manufacturers, merchants, wholesalers and firms, together with their trade descriptions, addresses, telephone and telex numbers. In addition, entries are listed by trade classification. A section lists British Importers under the goods they import. Exporters are listed by the products they export and the continent and countries in which they sell.

The directory covers 90,000 UK firms classified under 10,000 trade, product or service headings.

Kelly's Regional Directory of British Industry is published in eight volumes each October. It provides an exhaustive, town-by-town guide to industry and the products and services offered. This really is most useful if you want to confine your interests to one particular area, perhaps as an aid to a concentrated sales blitz.

Kelly's Post Office London Directory provides business listings by street, so a company's immediate neighbours can be identified. It is useful for finding concentrations of a particular type of business, or for finding gaps in provisions of a particular type of business.

Key British Enterprises, published by Dunn and Bradstreet Ltd, 26/32 Clifton Street, London EC2P 2LY (01-377 4377) Information on 20,000 UK companies that between them are responsible for 90 per cent of industrial expenditure. KBE is very useful for identifying sales prospects or confirming addresses, monitoring competitors and customers or finding new suppliers. As well as giving the names, addresses, telephone and telex numbers of the main office of each company, it gives branch addresses, products indexed by SIC code, sales turnovers (UK & overseas), directors' names and responsibilities, shareholders, capital structure, trade names, and number of employees.

KBE is in two volumes, alphabetical and geographical. By using the directory you can quickly establish the size of business you are dealing with and what other products or services they offer. It is very often important to know the size of a firm, if, for example, your products are confined to certain types of business. A book-keeping service is unlikely to interest a large company with several hundred employees; they would have their own accounts department. Conversely, a very small company may not need a public relations consultant.

Kompass is published in association with the CBI in two volumes: Volume I is indexed by product or service to help find suppliers, indicating whether they are manufacturers, wholesalers or distributors. It can be very useful indeed on certain occasions to be able to bypass a wholesaler and get to the manufacturer direct.

Volume II gives basic company information on the 30,000 suppliers identified from Volume I. These include the addresses, telephone and telex numbers, bankers, directors, office hours and the number of employees.

The London Gazette, published by HMSO four times a week,

provides the official notices on companies, including bankruptcies and receiverships. It may be too late for you to do much by the time it reaches the Gazette.

McCarthy Information Services provide a comprehensive press comment service monitoring the daily and financial press. From some fifty papers and journals they extract information on quoted companies each day and unquoted companies each week.

The service is provided on subscription, and a modestly priced Back Copy Service seems the most likely one to appeal to small business. The subscription is £37.50 per annum, and 55p per page copied. McCarthy Information Ltd, Manor House, Ash Walk, Warminster, Wilts BA12 8PY (0985 215151)

Research Index is an index to news, views and comments from the UK national daily papers plus around 150 periodicals in every field. The material is chosen carefully to include most items that would interest the business user, both on individual companies and on industries. Over a period of a year it includes around 130,000 items, and since the first edition over a million references have been made.

Research Index has always given good value at a modest price, currently £83.00 per annum, including binder and postage. By using it, even the smallest business can have at its fingertips the knowledge for information retrieval equivalent to the most sophisticated libraries. Published by Business Surveys Ltd, PO Box 21, Dorking, Surrey RH5 4EE (0306 87857)

The Retail Directory, published by Newman, 48 Poland Street, London W1V 4PP (01-439 0335) gives details of all UK department stores and private shops. It gives the names of executives, and merchandise buyers as well as addresses and telephone numbers, early closing days, etc. It also covers multiple shops, co-operative societies, supermarkets and many other retail outlets. If you plan to sell to shops, this is a useful starting point, with around 1305 department stores and large shops and 4821 multiple shop firms and variety stores listed in 1346 pages. If you are already selling retail, this directory could help you expand your prospects list quickly. The directory also identifies high turn-over outlets for main product ranges. There is a useful survey, showing retail activities on each major shopping street in the country. It gives the name and nature of the retail businesses in each street.

A separate volume contains shop surveys for the Greater London area, with 27,830 shops listed by name, street number and trade. The head offices of 1130 multiples are given, as are 233 surveys showing what sort of shops are in any area. This can be used for giving sales people useful contacts within their territory.

Sell's Directory, Sells Publications Ltd, Sell's House, 39 East Street, Epsom, Surrey KT17 1BQ and the Institute of Purchasing Management. It lists 65,000 firms alphabetically, with name, trade, address, telephone number and telex numbers. Using a classified cross-reference system, it covers 25,000 products and services. There is a guide to several thousand trade names cross-referenced back to each company. The two remaining sections include a contractors' section, advertising firms seeking contract work, and a business information section.

If you only know the trade name and want to find out who makes the product, then this directory will help you. You can then use it to find competitive sources of supply of similar products or services.

SOURCEFINDER, Morgan-Grampian Videotex Services, 30 Calderwood Street, Woolwich, London SE18 6QH (01-855 7777) An electronic directory using the British Telecom Prestel network, lists products and services, and where to find them under several hundred category headings. Prices to advertisers start at £180.00.

Stubbs Directory, published by Dunn and Bradstreet Ltd, lists 130,000 UK firms, their addresses, phone numbers and the product or service provided. Some 4000 categories of suppliers of goods and services are given, making this the most useful tool for identifying competitors and suppliers throughout the whole country – a sort of one-edition Yellow Pages. Although it does not have the depth of information of some other directories, it certainly has one of the widest spreads. You can use this as a starting point to find what companies you would like to look at in much more detail, or it may well be enough in itself.

Stubbs Name Matching Service, 6–8 Bonhill Street, London EC2A 4BU (01-377 4377) A new (1983) early warning system to alert companies to customers who might be getting into financial difficulties. A check is made on official, public and commercial records each day on: county court judgements; meetings of creditors; companies that have secured a mortgage or charge on assets; appointment of liquidators; winding up orders and appointment of receivers. You supply Stubbs with the names of the companies you want monitored, customers, competitors or even suppliers. It costs £2.00 per name and the information is sent to you within 48 hours.

Who Owns Whom, (UK) pub. David Bradstreet. Vol. I lists

parent companies, showing the structure of a group as a whole and the relationship with member companies. Vol. II lists subsidiaries and associates showing their parent companies.

Company and Product Data, Overseas

DTI Export Data Branch holds 50,000 status reports on overseas businesses. As well as telling you what the company does, each report gives a guide to the company's local standing and suitability for acting on behalf of a UK business. It is very useful if you want an overseas agent or wish to establish their reliability generally, e.g. as a customer. (See also page 186.)

European Companies is a comprehensive guide to sources of information on business enterprises throughout Europe. Published by CBD Research Ltd, 154 High Street, Beckenham, Kent BR3 1EA (01-650 7745)

European Report (A4/6) (published in Europe and available in main UK business libraries) comes out twice a week and provides a brief review of business and economic events.

Extel European Companies Service See listing in UK section for more details (pages 167–8).

Funk and Scott International and European Indexes provide a worldwide index to company news appearing in several hundred English language papers and journals. They have an index for the USA too. You can use this service to find out what has been happening to a company that has not shown up in its figures, for example, new products cancelled, strikes, acquisitions, divestments and board changes.

ICC American Company Information Service, 81 City Road, London EC1Y 1BD (01-251 4941) They can provide reports on 12,000 US public companies. The report includes the Annual Report and Accounts and the IOK Corporate Structure report on subsidiaries, directors, prominent shareholders and company properties. These cost £36.00 and £27.50 respectively for each company.

ICC European Company Information Services, 81 City Road, London EC1 1BD (01-251 4942) Through company registries and information services throughout Europe, ICC can provide various reports, including financial accounts, status reports and annual returns on companies registered in Belgium, Denmark, France, Germany, Holland, Norway, Sweden, Channel Islands, Italy, Portugal and Spain. A thousand European company accounts are kept on file in the UK ready for immediate despatch. The cost of the information ranges from £12.50 to £37.50 per company.

Jordan's Overseas Company Information (see page 169, for address) covers the whole world with an international network of agents and information sources. Information on companies varies from country to country, as does the speed with which that information can be retrieved. Still, this is certainly one of the best ways of finding out about a company that is not included in a general directory either because it is too small or too new. Of course, you may need much more detailed information on a particular company than is normally provided in a directory, and this information service may be able to provide it.

KOMPASS Directories, similar to the UK directories, are available for Belgium and Luxemburg, Denmark, West Germany, France, Holland, Italy, Australia, Brazil, Indonesia, Morocco, Norway, Singapore, Spain, Sweden and Switzerland (see page 170).

McCarthy's Australian Service
McCarthy's European Information Service
McCarthy's North American Service
See listing in UK section for more detail of above three services (see page 171).

Principal International Business, published by Dunn and Bradstreet, gives the basic facts about 50,000 businesses in 135 countries. As well as the business name, address and telex and its main activities, it tells you if the company is a subsidiary of a larger corporation; whether they import or export; how many employees they have; their latest sales volume; and the name of the chief executive. Its cover of companies in each country is not great: nearly 8000 in the USA; 6000 in Germany; 5500 in France; 4000 in Japan; and 2000 businesses in the UK. This represents only a small percentage of the businesses in any one country, but they are the principal ones.

Standard and Poor's Register of Corporations, Directors & Executives. The Corporation Record, Volume I, has a wealth of information on the financial structure and performance of 38,000 of the most significant American corporations. There is also a list of the subsidiary companies cross-referenced to parents. Volume II contains the individual listings of 70,000 people serving as officers of these corporations, together with some personal details on their education and fraternal membership. Volume III contains a series of indexes that complement the first two volumes.

Stores of The World Directory, 1984/85 edition, covers 7550 department stores, chains, co-ops and variety stores in 121 countries. (See Retail Directory UK for sources and more details, page 171.)

Thomas's Register of American Manufacturers, consists of 16 volumes, making it probably the most comprehensive directory on the market. Volumes 1–8 list products alphabetically, giving the manufacturer's name. Volume 9 and 10 give company names, addresses with zip codes and telephone numbers listed alphabetically, together with branch offices, capital ratings and company officials. An American trade-mark index is given in Volume 10.

Volumes 11–16, called *Thomcat*, contain catalogues of companies, bound alphabetically and cross-referenced in the first ten volumes. In all a formidable work, this is useful either to find an American source of supply or a potential customer for your product. The catalogues provide an insight into the way in which American companies market their wares.

WALL STREET's Corporate and INDUSTRY RESEARCH REPORTS, prepared by leading analysts and UK brokerage and institutional investment firms. In-depth analysis and data on 5000 companies and 150 industries, prepared by 40 research departments. Published by Research Publications Ltd, PO Box 45, Reading RG1 8HF (0734 583247)

Wall Street Journal Index provides a monthly and annual review of published material on the USA. It is in two sections. The first gives company news, and second gives general business news. Both are alphabetical and provide brief abstracts of the activities in question. It is somewhat similar to what the FT has to say about a company, product or personality.

Who Owns Whom (Australasia and Far East). Details are as below.

Who Owns Whom (Continental Europe) is published in two volumes. The first is similar to the UK volume, and the second volume has a section on foreign investment. (See listing in UK section for more details, page 172.)

Who Owns Whom (North American edition) is perhaps the definitive directory of US Multinational subsidiaries. Canadian companies are also covered.

Market and Industry Data

Businesses have to take part in censuses in much the same way as do individuals. This information, showing purchasers, stocks, capital expenditure and so on, is available for all the main UK industries, in the Annual Report on the Census of Production. The *Business Monitor Series* covers this and other areas in considerable detail each month and quarter. *Mintel Retail Business* is a monthly publication that examines consumer goods markets. By taking an area at a time it can produce quite comprehensive studies on spending patterns and the underlying reasons for them. The market share held by various businesses is given in *The A–Z of UK Marketing Data* and *UK Market Size* lists the output of the UK manufacturing industry under thousands of headings.

If you want a piggy back on someone else's research, then *Reports Index* is a quick reference guide to several thousand market studies, carried out on UK products and markets, available for purchase at quite modest prices. If you do not find a reference book in this section covering the field you are interested in, then the Guide to *Official Statistics* from HMSO, or *Sources of UK Marketing Information* by Tupper and Wills, will probably show you where to find it.

Overseas markets are particularly well covered with the *Euromonitor* publications, which provide comprehensive comparative information on European and international markets. *Market Data Reports on European Industries* shows growth and size trends of twenty-four industries in eight countries over the past seven years. The *International Directory of Published Market Research* provides a useful insight into who has done what in the market research field, and a number of useful indexes on other international data sources are also identified.

Market and Industry Data, UK

The A–Z of UK Marketing Data, published by Euromonitor Publications Ltd, 18 Doughty Street, London WC1N 2PN.

It provides basic market data for several hundred UK markets, from adhesives to zip fasteners, by product area, market size, production, imports, exports, the main brands, their market share and a market forecast. A good glimpse at a wide range of markets.

Annual Abstract of Statistics, published by the Central Statistical Office, is the basic source of all UK statistics. Figures are given for each of the preceding ten years, so trends can be recognised.

ASLIB Directory, Volume I. Information sources in science, technology and commerce, edited by Ellen M. Coldlin, 5th edition, 1982. A valuable reference tool if you need to track down information over a wide range of subjects. This edition has over three thousand entries from a large number of sources, professional, amateur, big and small. A major factor in including sources was their willingness to make the information available.

BBC Data Enquiry Service, Room 3, The Langham, The British Broadcasting Corporation, Portland Place, London W1A 1AA. This is a personal information service drawing on the world-wide resources of the BBC. It is an inexpensive and speedy way of checking facts and drawing on a statistical data bank which covers people, products, countries and events. The service could tell you the price of a pint of milk in 1951 or the current state of the Dutch economy. *Ad hoc* enquiries can cost as little as £5.00, or an annual subscription, £100.00.

Benn's Press Directory, published by Benn Publications Ltd, Sovereign Way, Tonbridge, Kent TN9 1RW (0732 364422) Published in two volumes. Volume I is the standard reference work on the UK media, giving detailed descriptions. Volume II covers the media in other countries.

British Business, published weekly by the Department of Industry and Trade (£1.10) provides basic statistics on UK markets. These include retail sales, cinemas, hire purchase, engineering sales and orders, industries production, catering, motor trade, textiles and man-made fibre turn-overs.

British Planning Data Book, by Taylor and Redwood, published January 1983 by Pergamon Press Ltd, Headington Hill Hall, Oxford OX3 0BW. Price £20.00. Wide ranging source of information on Market and Industry topics.

British Rate & Data Advertisers & Agency List is produced four times a year, and lists all advertising agencies, their executives and their customers' brand names. It also covers market research and direct mail companies.

British Rate & Data, updated monthly. Whatever market you are interested in, it is almost certain to have a specialised paper or journal. These will be an important source of market data. *BRAD* lists all newspapers and periodicals in the UK and Eire, and gives their frequency and circulation volume, price, their executives, advertising rates and readership classification.

Business Monitors are the medium through which the Government publishes the business statistics it collects from over 20,000 UK firms. They are the primary, and very often the only source of detailed information on the sectors they cover. The *Monitors* can help businessmen to monitor trends and trace the progress of 4000 individual products, manufactured by firms in 160 industries. *Monitors* can also be used to rate your business performance against that of your industry and measure the efficiency of different parts of your business.

The *Monitors* are published in three main series. The *Production Monitors* are published monthly, quarterly and annually. The quarterly is probably the most useful, with comprehensive yet timely information. *The Service and Distributor Monitors* cover the retail market, the instalment credit business, the motor trade, catering and allied trades and the computer service industry, amongst others. Finally, there are *Miscellaneous Monitors* covering such topics as shipping, insurance, import/export ratios for industry, acquisitions and mergers of industrial and commercial companies, cinemas and tourism.

The *Annual Census of Production Monitors* covers virtually every sector of industry, and include data on total purchases, total sales, stocks, work in progress, capital expenditure, employment, wages and salaries. They include analyses of costs and output, of establishments by size, of full- and part-time employees by sex, and of employment, net capital expenditure and net output by region.

You can use the information – particularly that from the size analysis table – to establish such ratios as gross output per head, net output per head, net to gross output, and wages and salaries to net output. With these as a base, you can compare the performance of your own business with the average for firms of similar size and for that with your particular industry as a whole. For example, you can discover your share of the market, and compare employment figures, increases in sales and so on.

Most of the libraries listed later in this section will have a selection of the *Business Monitor Series*. Individual monitors can be bought from HMSO Books, PO Box 569, London SE1 9NH. They are all individually priced.

Financial Times Business Information Service, published by the FT at Bracken House, 10 Cannon Street, London EC4P 4BY (01-236 4000) (Most details are given under *Information Services* in the next section, page 189.)

Guide to Official Statistics is the main guide to all government-produced statistics, including *ad hoc* reports. It is published by HMSO. However, a brief, free guide is available from the Press and Information Service, Central Statistical Office, Great George Street, London SW1 3AQ. Price £18.50.

Index to Business Reports, edited by R. N. Hunter, Librarian, Bradford University Management Centre, published by Headland Press. Provides the key to thousands of market and industrial reports. Latest volumes published Jan 1983–Dec 1984. Price £29.95.

Key Note Publications Publishers of the same name at 28–42

Banner Street, London EC1Y 8QE (01-253 3006) produce concise briefs on various sectors of the UK economy.

Each *Key Note* contains a detailed examination of the structure of an industry, its distribution network and its major companies; an in-depth analysis of the market, covering products by volume and value, market shares, foreign trade and an appraisal of trends within the market; a review of recent developments in the industry, highlighting new product development, corporate development and legislation; a financial analysis of named major companies, providing data and ratios over a three-year period together with a corporate appraisal and economic overview; forecasts on the future prospects for the industry, including estimates from *Key Note*'s own database and authoritative trade sources. There is a very useful appendix detailing further sources of information – recent press articles, other reports and journals.

Over 100 market sectors are covered, including such areas as adhesives, after-dinner drinks, bicycles, butchers, commercial leasing, health foods, road haulage, public houses, travel agents and woman's magazines.

Each *Key Note* costs £60.00, falling to £30.00 for users of their voucher system.

Marketing & Distribution Abstracts, published eight times a year by Anbar Publications Ltd, PO Box 23, Wembley HA9 8DJ (01-902 4489) This surveys 200 journals world-wide and provides an index to abstracts of appropriate articles and reports in the field.

McCarthy's Industrial Services provides a similar service on products and markets as their service on quoted and unquoted companies. The industry service is classified into thirteen industry groups: agricultural and animal and vegetable raw materials; building and civil engineering; finance; general engineering; electrical and electronic engineering; chemicals and chemical engineering; miscellaneous industrial manufacturers; consumer goods manufacture; transport and transport equipment; marketing; distribution and consumer services; communications and communications equipment; mining and minerals and energy. Within the main industry group lie about 350 subsections. Marketing for example, ranges from auto vending, franchising to street markets, as well as the more predictable department stores and supermarket groups.

Press cuttings are provided at 55p per copy. A phone call to McCarthy will tell you how many pages are involved, as naturally the size varies with the volume of news in a given area. The Back Numbers Service seems good value for small businesses. (See also page 171.)

MGN Marketing Manual, published by the Mirror Group of Newspapers (01-353 0246) provides a survey of UK social and economic conditions, including market data on 90 products.

Mintel is a monthly publication providing reports on the performance of new products and a wide range of specific areas of consumer expenditure. It covers five specific consumer goods markets each month, combining published data and original research to make the studies as exhaustive as possible. Comprehensive data on Leisure and Retail markets is also given. £295 per annum for marketing data and £395 per annum for Leisure and Retail.

Further details from *Mintel*, 20 Buckingham Street, The Strand, London WC2N 6EE (01-379 6118)

Office of Population, Census and Surveys produce demographic statistics for each county in England and Wales from the 1981 census. These provide data not only on total populations in each area, but also on occupations, economic groups, etc. Similar reports for Scottish and Northern Ireland regions are also available. There is a reference library at OPCS, St Catherine House, 10 Kingsway, London WC2B 6JP (01-242 0262)

More information and answers to general enquiries on these reports are also available from this number on ext 2009/2013.

Overseas Trade Statistics published by the Department of Industry and Trade, provide a monthly statement of UK imports and exports by volume and value for each product group and individual country.

The Bill Entry Services, operated by HM Customs and Excise, Portcullis House, 27 Victoria Avenue, Southend-on-Sea SS2 6AL (49421 ext 310) will provide more detailed information at a fee.

Principal Sources of Marketing Information, by Christine Hull. The Times Information and Market Intelligence Unit, New Printing House Square, Gray's Inn Road, London WC1 (01-837 1234) Price £2.50

Reports Index More recently Business Surveys Ltd introduced its bi-monthly Reports Index. This is an index to reports in every field published and available for sale. Its sources include Government publications, HMSO as well as non-HMSO, market research organisations, trade and professional associations, public bodies, stockbrokers, educational establishments, EEC, industrial and financial companies. Again, at £94.00 per annum, the cost is modest. (Address: see Research Index, page 171.)

Retail Business, published monthly by the Economist Intelligence Unit, covers the economic aspects of the UK retail trade, with emphasis on consumer-goods market research, distribution patterns and sales trends. £165.00 per annum plus p&p. (See also page 182.)

Retail Intelligence is a quarterly publication also from Mintel, covering the consumer goods marketed in considerable depth.

Sources of UK Marketing Information, by Tupper & Wills, published by E. Benn, 24 New Street Square, London EC4 (01-353 3212) A comprehensive guide to the main source of data on over 1000 products. Price £20.00

Stockbrokers' Research and Information Services, compiled by Hilton and Watson, third edition (1982) from The Library, Oxford Centre for Management Studies, Kennington, Oxford OX1 5NY Price £4.00. Has the details of research specialisations of 54 leading UK stockbroking firms, who all produce regular analysis of UK market sectors.

UK Market Size, published by IMAC Research, Lancaster House, More Lane, Esher, Surrey (63121) This report lists the output of UK manufacturing industry under 5000 separate headings. It costs £75.00 and is produced each year.

Market and Industry Data, Overseas

British Business magazine's European Community Information Unit offers a free service to businesses in Britain by answering general enquiries about EEC matters and referring business enquiries to experts in official circles. (See also page 177.)

Concise Guide to International Markets is now published in four volumes, covering Europe, the Americas, the Far East and Australia, and the Middle East and Africa. It is updated every two years, and contains 4000 facts about 109 world markets. There are 550 pages of up-to-date information on population, literacy, languages, religion, climate, working hours, currency, main towns, income, retail and wholesale structures, advertising agencies, commissions, associations, advertising controls, advertising expenditure, media of all types, market research facilities, together with over 100 maps. £15 per volume, £50.00 for all four including free binder.

This guide provides a useful overview to markets, and could be helpful in choosing markets to look at more closely later.

It is published by Leslie Stinton & Partners, 39a London Road, Kingston-upon-Thames, Surrey KT2 6ND in conjunction with the International Advertising Association (01-549 3476)

Economist Intelligence Unit, 22 St James Place, London sw1A 1NT (01-493 6711) produces each quarter some 83 separate reviews covering 160 countries, evaluating growth prospects, assessing opportunities and examining local and international problems. It provides a business-orientated analysis of the economic state of the countries examined.

European Marketing Data & Statistics, published by Euromonitor Publications Ltd, is an annual handbook containing comparative information about European Markets. International Marketing Data & Statistics is a companion volume that covers North and South America, Asia, Africa and Australasia.

Findex, published by ICC Information Group Ltd, 28/42 Banner Street, London EC1Y 8QE (01-253 6131)

This is a reference guide to 7000 world-wide market research reports, polls, studies and surveys from 300 leading research publishers. It gives rather more details on each research study than some other publications. It is extremely well cross-indexed, by subject, geography and publisher.

It is produced in the spring of each year, and an update is produced between publications. Price: £127.00.

International Directory of Published Market Research, 8th edition, 1984, by British Overseas Trade Board in association with Arlington Management Publications Ltd, 87 Jermyn Street, London sw1 6JD (01-930 3638) Price: £22.25.

The directory is in three parts. Part I is the Master Index, assigning a code number to each product. Part II contains 6000 study listings in numerical order according to the British Standards Industrial Classification Scheme. This has the advantage of keeping related subjects close together. The studies themselves cover industrial and consumer markets and are briefly described together with the date when they were completed, how much each study costs and who is selling it. Part III gives the names, addresses and phone numbers of the 375 research firms who carried out the studies. None of the studies is earlier than 1978, and some were produced in 1984.

Market Data Reports on European Industries are published by Market Studies International, 28–42 Banner Street, London EC1Y 8QE (01-253 6131 telex 23678)

Twenty-four European industries are included in this series. Each study gives the growth, size and competitive potential over seven years, in eight European countries. The studies are priced between £75.00 and £175.00.

Published Data on European Industrial Markets, published by
Industrial Aids Ltd, 14 Buckingham Palace Road, London
SW1W OQP (01-828 5036) Part I lists over 1900 market research
reports available for purchase at prices from as low as £10.00
up to several thousand pounds. Although the directory is entitled 'industrial', the interpretation is fairly wide. It covers
consumer goods as markets for industrial products, and
financial and economic planning studies, where they are considered of possible interest to industry. This could be a relatively
inexpensive way of finding out about a distant market-place.
The market studies are indexed, and the most frequent entries
are food and drink, machinery and equipment, chemicals, plastics and polymers, transport, pharmaceutical, medical, veterinary and dental, metals, metal powders, paper board, paper
chemicals, computers and data processing, fuels, oil, energy,
feedstocks, furniture and fittings, electronic, electrical, building and construction packaging, printing and graphics
(including inks and publishing), fibres and textiles, clothing
and agriculture (excluding fertilisers).

Part II is a guide to other sources of information on European
industrial markets. It covers East Europe and the USSR as
well as the more obvious European countries. It gives sources
of international statistics and a few pages on each country's
key sources of information. These are grouped under six main
headings: national statistics, and government and non-
governmental organisations, the press, banks, company information libraries and similar organisations. Price: £35.00.

Published Data on Middle and Far East Industrial Markets,
also published by Industrial Aids Ltd. The first edition came
out in 1983, in roughly the same style as its European sister.
It lists over 700 multiclient market research reports available
for purchase. Price: £30.00.

Statistics – Europe (£42.50), *Africa* (£25.00), *America* (£43.50),
Asia and Australasia (£44.00) are four guides to sources of
statistics for social, economic and market research. They are
published by CBD Research Ltd, 154 High Street, Beckenham,
Kent BR3 1EA (01-650 7745)

*Subjects Index to Sources of Comparative International Statistics
(SISCIS)*. For any activity or commodity it shows in what form
the statistics are presented, in what unit and for what countries.
From this it is possible to identify which of 350 major stat-
istical serials contain the required figures. Also published by
CBD Research Ltd (see above for address).

FINDING THE INFORMATION

Now that you have an idea of the considerable mass of data that is available about companies, their products and markets, the next problem that remains is to track it down. Fortunately, many of the directories and publications are kept in reference sections of major libraries up and down the country.

If you know exactly what information you want, then your problem is confined to finding a library or information service that has that information.

Specialist Libraries

Apart from your local library there are hundreds of specialist libraries concentrated in government departments, major industrial companies, trade organisations, research centres and academic institutes.

Two useful publications that will help you find out about these are listed below.

ASLIB Economic and Business Information Group Membershire Directory, published by the group and available from the London Business School Library, Sussex Place, Regent's Park, London NW1 4SA (01-262 5050) It provides a list of over 300 specialist business libraries throughout the country, and gives a very useful guide to their area of specialist interest.

Guide to Government Departments and Other Libraries The 26th edition, published in 1984, is the latest, and it is available from the Science Reference Library, 25 Southampton Buildings, Chancery Lane, London WC2A 1AY (01-405 8721) Price: £10.00. As the title indicates, this book concentrates on libraries in government departments and agencies, and particularly avoids duplicating the ground covered by the ASLIB Directory. The entries are arranged by subject covered, supplemented by an alphabetical index of the libraries, their locations, phone numbers and opening hours.

Not all the libraries covered in these directories are open to the public for casual visits. However, many will let you use their reference facilities, by appointment.

British Institute of Management Library and Management Information Centre, Management House, Parker Street, London WC2B 5PT (01-405 3456 ext 126/7/8/9) open Monday to Friday, 09.30 to 17.30. The Library houses one of the largest specialised collections of management literature in Europe. This includes much valuable information not generally available. The services are for BIM members who can use the library in person or make enquiries by letter or telephone.

The Library also produces extremely valuable reading lists covering a wide range of topics. These provide a selective guide to books, directories and periodicals in any of 170 specific areas. They also publish *A Basic Library of Management*, which lists 300 or so of the more useful books in the management field.

Business Statistics Office Library, Cardiff Road, Newport, Gwent NPT 1XG (0633 56111 ext 2973, telex 497121/2) open Monday to Friday, 09.00 to 17.00. This Library keeps all the data produced in published form by the Business Statistics office, together with a substantial quantity of non-official material. The coverage extends beyond UK statistics to include foreign information and an extensive range of company data and trade directories. The library is freely open to the public, who can enquire personally or by telephone, telex or letter.

Science Reference Library, Department of the British Library, 25 Southampton Buildings, Chancery Lane, London WC2A 1AY (01-405 8721 ext 3344 or 3345; patent enquiries ext 3350, telex 266959) This is the national library for modern science and technology, for patents, trade marks and designs. It has the most comprehensive reference section of this type of literature in Western Europe. If you do not have an adequate library close at hand a visit here could save you visits to several libraries. It should also be able to provide you answers if most other places cannot do so.

The Library's resources are formidable. It has 25,000 different journals, with issues back to 1960 on open shelves and the rest quickly available. It has 85,000 books and pamphlets and 20¼ million patents. It has a world-wide collection of journals on trade marks, together with books on law and design. Most of the major UK and European reports are held, as is trade literature and around 1000 abstracting periodicals.

The services are equally extensive. It is open from Monday to Friday, 09.30 to 21.00, and on Saturday from 10.00 to 13.00. You can visit without prior arrangement or a reader's ticket. Telephone requests for information, including the checking of references, are accepted. Once at the library, staff are available to help you find items and to answer general queries. Scientific staff are also on hand for specialised enquiries. There is even a linguist service to help you inspect material written in a foreign language, though for this service you must make an appointment.

The Business Information Service of the Science Reference Library (01-404 0406) This was set up in January 1981, primarily to support the activities of other business and industrial libraries. However, it will help individual users as much as possible. Staff here can extract reference information quickly, advise on the use of business literature and suggest other organisations to contact. For extensive research you will have to call in person, but they can let you know if a visit would be worth while.

There are three locations, one at Southampton Buildings (address above), which holds company information, industry, country and market surveys. The other two are listed below.

Official Publication Library, The British Library, Great Russell Street, London WC1B 3DG (01-636 1544 ext 234/5) open Monday, Friday and Saturday from 09.30 to 16.45, and Tuesday to Thursday 09.30 to 20.45 (please phone first). Virtually all official British publications are held here, together with an extensive intake from all other countries of the world from international organisations. All the UK and major overseas series complementing the Statistics and Market Intelligence Library are here too. An extensive world-wide collection of legislative publications and a complete set of all current UK electoral registers are kept here.

The Newspaper Library, The British Library, Colindale Avenue, London NW9 5HE (01-200 5515) A comprehensive set of British (national and local) newspapers and most major foreign and commonwealth newspapers are kept here. It is best to telephone and check they have what you want, or you can send for a catalogue and price list.

Statistics and Marketing Intelligence Library, of the Overseas Trade Board, 1 Victoria Street SW1 (01-214 5444/5, telex 8811074DTHQG) Reading room open 09.30 to 17.30, Monday to Friday.

This library is primarily concerned with statistics and directories from overseas countries and import/export data on the UK. As such, it is the most important source of international statistics and business information. It also has a very comprehensive collection of other UK statistics and directories.

In addition to these special libraries, major chambers of commerce, such as those in London, Birmingham, Manchester and Glasgow, have their own substantial business collections.

Local Reference Libraries For most purposes you will find that one of the major local libraries with a good business information section will do. Among the libraries with a strong commitment to business information and experienced staff are the following (Manchester Central appointed a Small Firms Officer in the spring of 1984):

ABERDEEN: Central Library, Rosemount Viaduct, Aberdeen AB9 1GU (0224 634622) Open: 09.00–21.00 Monday–Friday, 09.00–17.00 Saturday

BIRMINGHAM: Central Libraries, Chamberlain Square, Birmingham B3 3HQ (021-235 4511) Open: 09.00–18.00 Monday and Friday, 09.00–20.00 Tuesday, Wednesday and Thursday, 09.00–17.00 Saturday

BRADFORD: Central Library, Prince's Way, Bradford, W Yorks BD1 1NN (0274 753600) Open: 09.00–20.00 Monday–Friday, 09.00–17.00 Saturday

BRISTOL: Central Library, College Green, Bristol BS1 5TL (0272 276121) Open: 09.30–20.00 Monday–Friday, 09.30–17.00 Saturday

CAMBRIDGE: Central Library, 7 Lion Yard, Cambridge CB2 3QD (0223 65252) Open: 09.00–19.00 Monday–Saturday

CHATHAM: Chatham Library, Riverside, Chatham MA4 5SN (0634 43589) Open: 09.00–19.00 Monday, Tuesday and Friday, 09.00–17.00 Wednesday, Thursday and Saturday

CORNWALL: County Information Library, Union Place, Truro, Cornwall (0872 72702) Open: 09.30–17.00 Monday–Wednesday, 09.30–19.00 Friday, 09.30–12.30 Saturday

COVENTRY: Reference Library, Bayley Lane, Coventry CV1 5RG (0203 25555) Open: 09.00–21.00 Monday–Friday, 09.00–16.30 Saturday

DURHAM: Branch Library, Reference Department, South Street, Durham City DH1 4QS (0385 64003) Open: 10.00–19.00 Monday–Friday, 09.30–17.00 Saturday

EDINBURGH: Central Library, Reference Section, George IV Bridge, Edinburgh (031-225 5584) Open: 09.00–21.00 Monday–Friday, 09.00–13.00 Saturday

EXETER: Central Library, Castle Street, Exeter EX4 3PQ (0392 77977) Open: 09.30–20.00 Monday–Friday, 09.30–18.00 Wednesday, 09.30–16.00 Saturday

GLASGOW: Commercial Library, Royal Exchange Square, Glasgow (041-221 1872) Open: 09.30–17.00 Monday–Saturday

INVERNESS: Inverness Branch Library, Reference Section, Farraline Park, Inverness (0463 236463) Open: 09.00–19.30 Monday, 09.00–18.30 Tuesday, 09.00–17.00 Wednesday, 09.00–18.30 Thursday, 09.00–19.30 Friday, 09.00–17.00 Saturday

IPSWICH: Central Library, Northgate Street, Ipswich IP1 3DE (0473 214370) Open: 10.00–17.00 Monday–Thursday, 10.00–19.30 Friday, 09.30–17.00 Saturday

LEEDS: Central Library, Calverley Street, Leeds LS1 3AB (0532 462067) Open: 09.00–17.00 Thursday–Friday, 09.00–21.00 Monday, Tuesday and Wednesday, 09.00–16.00 Saturday

LIVERPOOL: Commercial Library, William Brown Street, Liverpool, Merseyside L3 8EW (051-207 2147 and 207 0036) Open: 09.00–21.00 Monday–Friday, 09.00–17.00 Thursday and Saturday

LONDON: City Business Library, Gillett House, 55 Basinghall Street, London EC2B 5BX (01-638 8215) Open: 09.30–17.00 Monday–Friday

Deptford Reference Library, 140 Lewisham Way, Deptford, London SE14 6PF (01-692 1162) Open: 09.30–20.00 Tuesday–Friday

Holborn Library, 32/38 Theobalds Road, London WC1X 8PA (01-405 2706) Open: 09.30–20.00 Monday–Thursday, 09.30–18.00 Friday, 09.30–17.00 Saturday

Westminster Reference Library, St Martin's Street, London WC2H 7HP (01-930 3274) Open: 10.00–19.00 Monday–Friday, 10.00–17.00 Saturday

LUTON: Reference Library, Bridge Street, Luton (0582 30161) Open: 09.00–20.00 Monday–Friday, 09.00–17.00 Saturday

MANCHESTER: Central Library, St Peter's Square, Manchester M2 5PD (061-236 9422) Open: 09.00–21.00 Monday–Friday

NEWCASTLE-UPON-TYNE: Central Library, Princess Square, Newcastle-upon-Tyne, Northumberland NE99 1HC (0632 610691) Open: 09.00–21.00 Monday–Friday, 09.00–17.00 Thursday and Saturday

NOTTINGHAM: Central Library, Angel Row, Nottingham NG1 6HP (0602 43591) Open: 09.30–20.00 Monday–Friday, 09.00–13.00 Saturday

OXFORD: Central Library, Westgate, Oxford OX1 1DJ (0865 815509) Open: 09.15–19.00 Monday–Friday, 09.15–17.00 Thursday and Saturday

PORTSMOUTH: Central Library, Guildhall Square, Portsmouth PO1 2DX (0705 819311–7) Open: 10.00–19.00 Monday–Friday, 10.00–16.00 Saturday

SHEFFIELD: Sheffield Business Library, The Central Library, Surrey Street, Sheffield S1 1XZ (0742 734711) Open:

SOUTHAMPTON: Central Library, Civic Centre, Southampton SO9 4XP (0703 23855) Open: 09.00–19.00 Monday–Friday, 10.00–16.00 Saturday

SWANSEA: Central Reference Library, Alexandra Road, Swansea SA1 5DX (0792 55521) Open: 09.00–19.00 Monday, Tuesday, Wednesday, Friday and 09.00–17.00 Thursday and Saturday

Before making a special journey it would be as well to telephone and make sure the library has the reference work you want.

Do not neglect your local library. A recent visit to Kensington and Woolwich libraries was a very pleasant surprise. Gloucestershire is also among a growing band of progressive County Libraries aiming to serve local business needs in the information field. Their librarian has produced a very useful guide to their free commercial service for the county's business communities.

Information Services

In addition to the many excellent business libraries up and down the country, there are an increasing number of organisations that will do the searching for you. The benefits to you are twofold: professionals search out the data, and can alert you to sources that you may not have thought of; they save you time, not just the time you would spend searching. If you are not near a good business reference library you may have a consider-

able and expensive journey to make. Mostly, these organisations have substantial libraries of their own, but, for example
Warwick, will search elsewhere if they cannot find it in their
stocks. They claim the largest statistics collection in the UK,
after the Statistics and Market Intelligence Library in London,
and they have access to several on-line data bases.

The Financial Times Business Information Service,
Bracken House, 10 Cannon Street, London EC4 (01-248 8000)
The service offers impartial, authoritative facts – facts about
companies, industries, statistics and people. They keep press
cuttings on some 25,000 prominent people in industry, politics
and business. They also have a Business Information Consultancy, which can offer an on-demand information service to meet
individual information requirements.

The service costs £36.00 per hour, with a minimum charge
of £3.00. Subscriptions can be taken out on a six-month or annual
basis. The annual rate is £250.00 plus VAT. This is, in effect a
deposit, with charges for using the services debited against it.

Industrial Aids Ltd, Enquiry service at 14 Buckingham
Palace Road, London SW1W 0QP (01-828 5036 telex 918666
CRECON G) This service is geared to supply commercial and
technical information, such as Who makes what/where/how
much? Who is company A's agent in country X? Where are
custom manufacturing sources? Details are given of company
financial data, affiliations, product literature, consumption
patterns, end users, prices, discounts and trading terms, as well
as new legislation and standards, trade and industrial economic
statistics, conference papers, proceedings and lists of delegates.

The cost is £33.00 per hour, excluding VAT. You can use the
service by telephone, telex or by letter, and the response is
fast.

Market Location Ltd, 17 Waterloo Place, Warwick Street,
Royal Leamington Spa, Warwicks CV32 5LA (0926 34235)
Contact: M. J. Griffiths. Market Location is a research organisation studying manufacturing industry in the UK. It gathers
its information through field research. Its team of researchers
travel the country, marking each manufacturing unit on maps
and conducting a face-to-face interview with a representative
of the company in order to obtain accurate, first-hand
information.

The data gathered is published on a series of large-scale maps
with accompanying indexes, giving the company name,
address and telephone number; the name of the location
manager and his position; the activity of the company and its
SIC main-order heading; the size of the workforce and its group
structure.

Clients of Market Location are usually companies with a sales force selling to manufacturing industry. They use the service to improve their sales performance by finding new prospects, by increasing salesmen's call rates, reducing travelling expenses, and eliminating potentially abortive cold-calling.

Market Location produces statistics tables for each county, showing the number of factories, broken down by SIC code and number of employees (including percentages).

Copies of the statistics tables for all the counties researched cost £50.00.

The Marketing Shop, 18 Kingly Court, Kingly Street, London W1R 5LE (01-434 2671, telex 2625437) This organisation provides a wide range of marketing services, but its Information Service is perhaps the most useful facility for small businesses. It can provide data on practically any topic, either using its own library or outside sources, and will also monitor the media for information on companies, products or markets. Charges are £35.00 an hour for *ad hoc* work. The more usual arrangement is for customers to take a block of hours to be used over the year. Block fees start at around £500.00, which works out at £35 per hour. In general they give quotes for any research they do.

The Trade Opening Bureau (TOB), Confederation of British Industry, Centre Point, 103 New Oxford Street, London WC1A 1DU (01-379 7400) The aim of this free service is to help British Companies, particularly, but not exclusively CBI members by identifying purchasing and tendering opportunities for their goods and services in the UK and abroad.

The service covers a comprehensive range of trading and commercial matters including: raw materials; trade names; new and existing products; industrial and commercial services and consultancies; research and commercial organisation; trade associations; journals and directories; exhibitions and trade fairs.

To make contact with the TOB either phone or write to the address above. The bureau's staff are there to help you find the answer to your particular enquiry and the service is completely free of charge.

Warwick Statistics Service, University of Warwick Library, Coventry CV4 7AL (0203 418938, telex 31406) *Contact: Jennifer Carr or David Mart.* The service offers a range of commercial and economic information based on published sources including international statistics, both official and non-official, market research, periodicals, reports, directories, company reports and on-line services. The service can be particularly helpful to a small business with information on market size and share, locating particular types of company and finding out about them, tracing recent articles on a particular product or process, on consumer expenditure data, imports and exports, economic conditions, price trends, advertising expenditure and production and sales figures.

The service will also undertake analysis of the data in question, and provide a written report on their desk research. In general, enquiries are dealt with on the telephone, telex or by post; however, personal visits are welcomed. If you telephone beforehand, documents can be assembled for you to look at.

Annual subscribers to the service pay £350.00 for 25 hours' search time and publication. Occasional users of the service can get information or research assistance on an *ad hoc* basis at a cost of £25.00 per hour pro rata, with a minimum charge of £6.00. All in all, it is very good value.

Their monthly journal, *Market & Statistics News*, provides a regular source of information on statistical and marketing topics, and costs £25.00 per annum.

The service holds regular one-day seminars on Information Sources for Business Planning and Market Research, costing £35.00–40.00.

Dialog, Data star and Textline are three on-line, computer-based business information retrieval systems. They require the user to have a terminal (keyboard) and a Modem or Acoustic coupler. That is the device that lets you use your telephone to connect up to the data base.

Dialog and Data star have extensive American information data bases, and are building up their UK information file. They could be worth a look for a small business if you already have the hardware, and are very interested in the USA business scene.

Data star, Willoughbey Road, Bracknell, Berks RG12 4DW (0344 489151)

Dialog, Information Retrieval Service, PO Box 8, Abingdon, Oxford OX13 6EG (0865 730969, telex 837704 Inform G)

Textline is a computerised business information service provided by Finsbury Data Services, 68–74 Carter Lane, London EC4V 5EA (01-236 9771) Users can retrieve summaries of daily press stories on financial, business and industrial matters. The service covers the business news published in the leading UK daily and weekly newspapers, and from other sources. (See also 'Which Databank?' on page 193.)

Abstracting Services If you do not know exactly what you are looking for but know the subject area, then you need to find out what is in print on that subject. Simply to scan the shelves, apart from being time-consuming, will not produce direct results. Only a fraction of the books, periodicals, directories and other reference works are likely to be in any one library. For these reasons you need to use one of the main abstracting systems. An abstract is a brief summary of the publication itself, usually just enough to let you know if it is worth reading. Only a few are mentioned here, but one or more such services are available at many major county libraries. Alternatively, you could search the one that best suits your needs by reading:

Inventory of Abstracting and Indexing Services Produced in the UK, by G. Burgen, A. Vickery and S. Keenan, published by the British Library Research and Development Department. This is the definitive guide to abstracting and indexing services. Otherwise, useful abstracting services are listed below.

Anbar Bibliography gives details of the main business management books published each year. Anbar Publications, 65 Wembley Hill Road, Wembley, Middx (01-902 4489)

Anbar Abstracting Journals cover accounting and data processing; marketing and distribution; personnel and training; top management; work study and O & M.

These abstracts are a selective guide through the literature, provided by subject experts, and include brief summaries of the articles listed from the 200 or so journals searched.

British National Bibliography, published weekly by the British Library Bibliographic Services Division, provides a subject list of all books published in Britain.

Business Periodicals Index, published by G. H. W. Wilson (New York), provides a guide to articles published in some 300 international business journals, and are indexed by the service.

London Business School Small Business Bibliography, arranged under appropriate subject headings, lists and indexes about 2600 books and articles on small business management. First published in 1980, it is up-dated at nine-monthly intervals.

SCIMP (Selective Co-operative Index of Management Periodicals) is produced by the Manchester Business School Library, but covers mainly European periodicals.

It may be useful to know something of other types of written information that is not generally published. Two such abstracts are:

Research in British Universities, Polytechnics and Colleges, from the British Library Lending Division. There is a section on business and management with a comprehensive guide to current research indexed by topic and college.

Selected List of UK Theses and Dissertations in Management Studies, compiled by N. R. Hunter, University at Bradford Library.

Four useful books on researching for business information are:

Business Information Services, published in 1981 by Clive Bingley Ltd. The author is Malcolm J. Campbell of the City Business Library. It is an extremely useful book and illustrates clearly the range of business information that is available.

The Manager's Guide to Getting Answers (1983), The Library Association, 7 Ridgmount Place, London WC1E 7AE (01-636 7543) Price: £4.75.

Use of Management and Business Literature, edited by K. D. C. Vermont, published by Butterworths, 88 Kingsway, London WC2B 6AB (01-405 6900)

Which Databank? by Allan Foster of Preston Polytechnic, provides an evaluative guide to online numeric databases in business, finance and economics. The latest edition was published in Autumn 1983 by Headland Press. Price: £7.95.

MARKETING ORGANISATIONS AND THEIR SERVICES

The organisations that look after the interests of professional marketeers can also give considerable help to newcomers and small businesses. At least two of these organisations, the Institute of Marketing and the British Overseas Trade Board, have unrivalled libraries and information banks in their respective fields. The Institute of Marketing, with its unique low-cost advisory service, is one particularly useful organisation. Many others, including the Market Research Society, the Institute of Management Consultants and the Society of Business Economists, provide specialist members' directories. These can put you in touch with someone with recent experience in the areas of your concern. Although you will have to pay for their services, you will improve the chances of solving your problem first time round.

Education is also a strong point of many organisations. The Institute of Sales and Marketing and the British Direct Marketing Association hold frequent short courses on most aspects of sales and marketing, as does the Institute of Marketing itself.

Some new and localised organisations are also listed here, if their services seem unique and important. The Small Firms

Service, the SDA, WEDA and LEDU can all also help with marketing expertise (see pages 14–16).

The Advertising Association, Abford House, 15 Wilton Road, London SW1V 1NJ (01-828 2772) The association was formed in 1926, and is primarily a federation of organisations with a major interest in advertising. As such it sets out to promote greater awareness of the effectiveness and purpose of all types of 'paid-for-space' in the media. Two services of possible interest are its publications of advertising expenditure statistics and forecasts in all media; and its education programme, run through CAM, listed later.

British Consultants Bureau, Westminster Palace Gardens, 1–7 Artillery Row, London SW1P 1RJ (01-222 3651) This is an independent, non-profit-making association of British consulting firms of all disciplines. BCB's main purpose is to promote the interest of British consultants overseas. However, the bureau publishes a comprehensive directory, giving detailed information about all their members, their experience and their expertise. This is available to commercial firms.

The British Direct Marketing Association, 1 New Oxford Street, London WC1A 1NQ (01-242 2254) The association brings together the three main groups of people who influence the way in which products and services are marketed direct to customers. These groups are: direct mail houses, who prepare and market lists of prospective customers; financial, insurance, commercial and manufacturing firms; publishers and professional organisations that market direct (ie not via retailers), and advertising agencies and consultancies that specialise in direct marketing methods.

The BDMA is growing rapidly both in size and stature. It has played an important role in helping the customer to choose whether or not he wants to receive more advertising mail through the post. Its education programmes of short courses and work-shops, covering the use of direct mail, is extensive. In October 1982 the first Diploma in Direct Marketing programme was launched at Kingston Polytechnic.

The BDMA also produces a number of useful books that introduce the subject to the novice, or sharpen up older hands.

British Institute of Management, Management House, Parker Street, London WC2B 5PT (01-405 3456) Their services to members include information and advisory functions, and a research and education programme. They also have a Centre for Physical Distribution Management, which covers transport, warehousing, inventory control, materials handling and packaging matters.

This is more an institute for professional managers than just for marketeers, but its wider vision is particularly useful for small businesses.

Communication Advertising and Marketing Education (CAM) Foundation, Abford House, 3rd Floor, 15 Wilton Road, London SW1V 1NJ (01-828 7506) This is the authoritative body on what and where to study in the marketing field.

Direct Selling Association, 44 Russell Square, London WC1P 4JP

IMAGE Marketing Services, 359 The Strand, London WC2 (01-836 7086) *Contact: Andrew Ferguson.* They run a scheme called Sharex, to help small firms take part in exhibitions.

The Instant PR Service for Small Businesses (INSTA-PRESS), Suite 36, 26 Charing Cross Road, London WC2 (01-836 7653) Offers small businesses the chance to have their own professionally written press releases circulated to the right publications for as little as £100.00.

Institute of Management Consultants, 23–24 Cromwell Place, London SW7 2LG (01-584 72856) The institute has 3000 individual members, and publishes the journal Innovation and Management. As a free service to industry it operates a professional register, putting enquirers in contact with members with appropriate skills.

Institute of Marketing, Moor Hall, Cookham, Maidenhead, Berks SL6 9HQ (06285 24922) The institute has nearly 23,000 members, and is the largest and most comprehensive body in the field. It has a substantial library and a wide range of publications, including its series Checklists for Sales and Marketing (details from Leviathan House Ltd, 80 East Street, Epsom, Surrey KT17 1HF (Epsom 28300)

Its annual Marketing Year Book also provides a useful range of information sources.

There are few subjects in the field to which the institute cannot provide a useful pointer.

The Marketing Advisory Service, reachable at the Institute of Marketing, was established to enable British companies of any size to get marketing advice from highly experienced professional marketeers. The service itself is free, although an administration charge of £15.00 is made, and you will have to meet any travelling expenses incurred by the advisers.

It works like this; you get a list of 50 advisers, a brief description of their qualifications, experience and areas of particular knowledge and skill, and from that list you choose who you would like to speak to. Seeing that list, it is hard to think of an area of marketing or type of product that is not covered.

Your meeting with the adviser will not resolve all your marketing problems, but it will help you decide what to do next. If you think that some professional consultancy is needed, then your advisers should be able to put you in touch with the right people. It is important to note that these advisers are not consultants themselves. If you want to discuss the scheme before committing yourself, first send for their booklet, then talk to Peter Blood, The Director General of the Institute.

Industrial Market Research Association, 11 Bird Street, Lichfield, Staffs, WS13 6PW (05432 23448) The association represents some 800 members of the profession of Industrial Market Research in the UK. Although it does produce a directory of members, this is not generally available.

The Institute of Public Relations, Gate House, St John Square, London EC1M 4DH (01-253 5151) The institute is mainly concerned with keeping professional standards high and promoting general awareness of the role of public relations.

The Institute of Sales Promotion, Panstar House, 13–15 Swakeleys Road, Ickenham, Middx UB10 8DF (08956 74281/2) This is the recognised professional body of their branch of marketing. Their *Consultants' Register* is available to non-member prospective clients, as is their information service, which holds a comprehensive reading list on the subject.

The Mail Order Traders Association of Great Britain, 25 Castle Street, Liverpool L2 4TD (051-227 4181)

The Marketing Society, Derwent House, 35 South Park Road, London SW19 8RR (01-543 5191) The society was formed twenty years ago. One of its main objectives is to raise the reputation and understanding of marketing among general management, government, the Civil Service, trade unions and educationalists.

The Market Research Society, 15 Belgrave Square, London SW1X 8PF (01-235 4709) This is the professional body for those concerned with market, social and economic research. It has 3500 members, and is the largest body of its kind in the world.

Apart from a programme of education, research and publications of primary interest to members, the society produces a directory of organisations providing market research services. The directory provides background information on the 210 research agencies, their executives, experience and the size in sales turn-over. Some of the organisations are quite small, with turn-overs below £50,000 per annum, whereas others have a turn-over of several million pounds.

They also publish the *International Research Directory*.

The Post Office, provides an introductory offer for first-time users of their Direct Mail, Business Reply, Freepost and Overseas direct mail shot services. As a small business you would be prudent to think of using Direct Mail and with the Post Office paying for the first 1200 of your letters, you can save money too. *Contact: Kay Manley*, Post Office Direct Mail Section, Room 604, 22–25 Finsbury Square, London EC2B 2QQ.

Public Relations Consultants Association, 37 Cadogan Street, Sloane Square, London SW3 2PR (01-581 3951) The association produces a wide range of guidance papers and other publications, which extend from the useful – *Selecting a PR Consultancy and Consultancy/Client Agreement*, to the esoteric – *How to Set up for a Royal Visit*.

It publishes together with the *Financial Times*, the most authoritative book in the field, *Public Relations Yearbook*. This gives profiles of 150 PR consultancies and their clients. There are also several useful articles on other aspects of public relations.

From Financial Times Publishing, 102 Clerkenwell Road, London EC1 (01-405 6969) Price: £15.00.

Regional Newspaper Advertising Bureau Ltd, Grosvenor House, 141 Drury Lane, London WC2B 5TD (01-836 8251) *Contact: Peter Edwards*. Single point of entry to book advertising in any of 1000 local newspapers. They offer a computerised data-base service that can provide all relevant facts and figures about these local papers and the areas in which they operate.

Small Firms Marketing Centre, London Road, Warmley, Bristol BS15 5JH (0272 677807) The centre has a small full-time staff and a team of part-time specialist consultants on tap. It was established in 1983 to provide practical help to small and young enterprises at a modest cost.

Their range of service includes: Market Research and Assessment; Preparing a Market Plan; Product Design; Advertising and Promotion; Market Contacts – and general Marketing Advice. *Contact: Rona Wagstaffe and Angela Davis*

The Society of Business Economists, 11 Bay Tree Walk, Watford, Herts WD1 3RX (0923 37287) The society was formed in 1953 to allow businessmen and other economists to discuss ideas, problems and other matters of common interest.

It produced a *Register of Freelance Economists* who are members of the society. This register has now been taken over by P. E. Consultancy Group Appointment Division, Foxglove House, 166 Piccadilly, London W1V 9ED (01-409 2669) *Contact: Maurice Honey*. The register costs £5.00, and contains details of some 30 economists, their experience, specialist skills and fees.

The fees range from around £100.00 to £250.00 per day, and several express a specific interest in the small business field.

SPECIALIST SERVICES FOR EXPORTING

The British Overseas Board, with its wide range of expertise and services, is of considerable use to first-time exporters. Apart from a wealth of information and statistics, its Market Entry Guarantee Scheme can provide an important part of the funding which a small firm needs to enter a new market.

The Institute of Export is the professional body in the field, and two other services are particularly interesting. Scanmark, run from Buckinghamshire College of Higher Education, undertakes research into overseas markets at a fraction of the cost of the commercial research organisations. The Export and Overseas Trade Advisory Panel Ltd performs a rather different role. Using their panel of expert advisers, they not only help you to evaluate an overseas market opportunity but will guide you through the red tape, too.

SITPRO (the Simplification of International Trade Procedures Board) will also be able to help with export documentation systems that will save exporters time and money, and the BBC Service to Exporters is always keen to hear interesting exporting stories.

Organisations

Berlitz, 321 Oxford Street, London W1A 3BZ (01-629 7360) Perhaps the best known name in the language business.

The Brain Exchange, Aisec Great Britain Ltd, Seymour Mews House, Seymour Mews, London W1H 9PE (01-486 4853) Can provide an overseas business studies student to work on your project for between 8 weeks and 18 months. Administrative fee of £100 and student must be paid £80.00 per week.

BBC Data Enquiry Service, Room 3, The Langham, British Broadcasting Corporation, Portland Place, London W1A 1AA. This service draws on the world-wide resources of the BBC to provide up-to-the-minute, accurate information, fast. It can provide information on the social, economic and political aspects of every country in the world. It can also supply career details of leading foreign politicians and other public figures overseas. It is quite inexpensive too; a relatively simple enquiry could cost as little as £5.00.

BBC Service to Exporters, Export Liaison Unit, BBC External Services, Bush House, London WC2B 4PH (01-240 3456 ext 2039/2295) Which of your products could make a good story? Which programme would be the right one for you? Any overseas enquirers will be put in touch with you.

British Overseas Trade Board, 1–19 Victoria Street, London SW1H OET (01-215 7877) The board provides a considerable amount of information, advice and help to the exporter. In particular it gathers, stores and disseminates information on overseas markets; gives advice and help to individual firms; organises collective trade promotions; and stimulates export publicity.

The board really does know all there is to know about the process of exporting, and it can help with some of the costs. For example, its Export Market Research Scheme can provide up to a third of the costs of carrying out market-research studies overseas. The market Guarantee Scheme can fund a large part of the cost of your export drive. Half of such costs as overseas office accommodation, staff costs, training, travel expenses, sales promotions, overseas warehousing and commercial and legal costs can be met by the board, which could pay up to £150,000 towards such costs.

The board's Export Intelligence Service, Lime Grove, Eastcote, Middlesex (01-866 8771) costs £52.50 for a subscription. This will keep you up to date on events in any market area you choose. The service publishes a very comprehensive booklet outlining its services, and can provide more information on any area of particular interest.

Regional Offices

North-eastern Regional Office, Stanegate House, 2 Groat Market, Newcastle-upon-Tyne NE1 1YN (0632 324722, telex 53178)

Yorkshire and Humberside Regional Office, Priestley House, 1 Park Row, Leeds LS1 5LF (0532 443171, telex 557925)

West Midlands Regional Office, Ladywood House, Stephenson Street, Birmingham B2 4DT (021-632 4111, telex 337021)

North-west Regional Office, Sunley Buildings, Piccadilly Plaza, Manchester M1 4BA (061-236 2171, telex 667104)

East Midlands Regional Office, Severns House, 20 Middle Pavement, Nottingham NG1 7DW (0602 56181, telex 37143)

South-west Regional Office, The Pithay, Bristol BS1 2PB (0272 291071, telex 44214)

Scottish Regional Office, Alhambra House, 45 Waterloo Street, Glasgow G2 6AT (041-248 2855, telex 777883)

Welsh Regional Office, New Crown Buildings, Cathays Park, Cardiff CF1 3NQ (0222 825111)

Clothing Export Council, Academy House, 26–28 Sackville Street, London W1X 2QT (01-434 1881) Advises members on export sales and marketing matters in the knitting and clothing fields.

Durham University Business School, Export Studies Centre, Mill Hill Lane, Durham DH1 3LB (0385 41919) *Contact: Mike Willis*. The Centre was set up in 1980, particularly to help small firms to enter export markets. They are developing a national network of export centres, so there may be one nearer to you than Durham. Also see the Education Section for other institutions running courses in exporting (page 298).

'The European Project', Department of Languages, Napier College, Sighthill Court, Edinburgh EH11 4BN (031-443 6061 ext 376) *Contact: J. R. Megson* Language/Marketing students are available to carry out 2 week marketing tasks in one european market. No fees are charged, but firms using students are expected to make a £200.00 contribution to expenses.

Export Houses See under their heading in the finance section (page 228 in the Finance Section). These provide the most comprehensive range to exporters and potential exporters.

The Export Overseas Trade Advisory Panel Ltd, World Trade Centre, London E1 9AA (01-481 1962) *Contact: David Royce*. This company has a panel of advisers with substantial knowledge of overseas markets. They have experience of finding and developing profitable opportunities for exporting and trading overseas. They also have experience in handling all aspects of finance, insurance and shipping. The panel themselves have among their number recently retired members of the Diplomatic Service, the Department of Trade and the Export Credit Guarantee Department. Their service could be particularly attractive to a company exporting for the first time, or considering a move into a new market.

It will cost £75.00 per day for each panel member forming the advisory team, plus any out-of-pocket expenses. This could be a lot cheaper than going to the country in question.

Exporters Workshops, are held by the Small Firms Group of the London Chamber of Commerce, 69 Cannon Street, London EC4N 5AB (01-248 4444) Provides information, education and contacts to help small firms to start exporting. Your local chamber may do the same.

The Institute of Export, World Trade Centre, London E1 9AA (01-488 4766) The institute aims to contribute to profitable exporting by providing a forum for the exchange of experience and information between exporters. It also promotes education and training throughout the whole field of exporting. Its regular journal, *Export*, is a good way of getting into the export picture. Price: £10 for 10 issues.

Institute of Freight Forwarders Ltd, Suffield House, 9 Paradise Road, Richmond, Surrey TW9 1SA (01-948 3141)

Institute of Linguists, 24a Highbury Grove, London N5 2EA (01-359 7445) Will advise on industrial and technical translations – ask for the Translator's Guild.

International Business Unit, University of Manchester Institute of Science and Technology (UMIST), PO Box 88, Sackville Street, Manchester M60 1QD (061-236 3311)

International Chamber of Commerce, Centre Point, 103 New Oxford Street, London WC1 (01-240 5558)

Joint Ventures Overseas. More than 100 companies are listed in the register of North-west companies who wish to participate in joint ventures with overseas companies compiled by the North-west Industrial Development Association.

Details can be obtained from Chris Proudfoot, North-west Industrial Development Association, Brazennose House, Brazennose Street, Manchester M2 5AZ (061-834 6778)

The London Chamber of Commerce, runs residential beginners' courses in French, Arabic, German, Spanish and Portuguese, Italian, Japanese and Mandarin Chinese, which guarantee to teach you to speak and write 450 words of the new language in six days. It does not sound a lot, perhaps, but when used in multiple combinations 450 words provide an extremely useful basic preliminary vocabulary of expressions and phrases. Also available are intermediate and advance courses in French and intermediate courses in German and Spanish starting in 1985.

The courses have been designed by Professor Robert Boland specifically for the mature student, and make a complete departure from the school language-lab routine.

For more information contact Mrs K. Allerman, LCCI, 69 Cannon Street, London EC4A 5AB (01-248 4444 ext 337)

The Post Office, provides an introductory offer for first time users of their Overseas Direct Mail Service. *Contact: Kay Manley*, Post Office Direct Mail Section, Room 604, 22–25 Finsbury Square, London EC2B 2QQ.

Scanmark, Buckinghamshire College of Higher Education, High Wycombe, Bucks HP11 2JZ (0494 444640) *Contact: L. S. Collins*. Established in 1974, Scanmark is a team of postgraduate students in the final year of an export marketing course.

Their first disciplines include accountancy, agriculture, business studies, chemistry, economics and psychology. They also have a combined fluency in French, Spanish, German, Russian, Italian and Portuguese.

Recognised by the British Overseas Trade Board and the London Chamber of Commerce, Scanmark has carried out over 100 research projects in 20 countries.

Its clients have included small businesses launching their first product, and larger companies moving into new markets. This really is a low-cost way of getting the fundamental facts on overseas markets.

Service 800, Buckingham Court, 78 Buckingham Gate, London SW1E 6PE (01-222 3011), is a worldwide toll-free telephone system available in 50 cities. It lets your overseas customers (or potential ones) engage in international business with you for the cost of a local phone call. You appear to people, say in New York, as having a New York number. They dial that, pick up the local call bill, and are routed automatically through the international network to you. Service 800 costs £300 to install, £200 a month rental and the normal telephone charges. A lot cheaper than keeping a sales office in New York, but you have to remember the Time Zones!

Simplification of International Trade Procedures Board, SITPRO, Almark House, 26–28 King Street, London SW1Y 6QW (01-930 0532, telex 919130 Sitrog) This is an independent body set up by the Department of Trade. Its objective is to simplify trade documents and procedures and so make international trade easier for British companies.

The board would like to know of any persistent problems in international trade documents and procedures, to help it decide on future priorities for action. *SITPRO News* is available on request. SITPRO also produces a range of publications, one of which, *Systematic Export Documentation*, is a useful guide through a complex process.

The board has an advisory consultancy service which will visit sites and help with specific problems.

Technical Help to Exporters, from the British Standards Institution, Linford Wood, Milton Keynes MK14 6LE (0908 320033) Marketing any product overseas means that you will have to comply with all the technical requirements of the country to which you want to sell. You will have to comply with the laws of the land (safety and environmental); national standards; certification practices; and customer needs. This service can supply detailed information on foreign regulations; identify, supply and assist in the interpretation of foreign standards and other technical requirements; provide translations; and help with obtaining foreign approval.

A technical enquiry service is operated specifically to deal with the day-to-day problems of exporters, many of which are answerable over the telephone. The charge depends on the amount of research and the time involved. Many queries are answered free of charge to members.

Membership costs £120 plus VAT per annum, with an initial registration fee of £20.00 plus VAT. A publications list is issued twice a year, free of charge. A free introductory offer was available throughout 1983. It may be repeated.

Technical Translations International Ltd, Imperial House, 15–19 Kingsway, London WC2B 6UU (01-240 5361)

Publications

Barclays Bank International, Barclays House, 1 Wimborne Road, Poole, Dorset BH15 2BB (0202 671212) Barclays Bank International has produced a new 1983 series of booklets entitled 'Support for World Trade': *Introduction to Exporting, Export Finance – Barclays and ECGD, Documentary Letters of Credit, Currency Deposits SDRs and ECUs*, and *Introduction to Importing*. The publications deal in detail with such subjects as how to find markets abroad; where to obtain reliable, up-to-date information about those markets; the British Overseas Trade Board and export factoring; the Export Credits Guarantee Department; buyer/supplier credits; documentary letters of credit; and bills of exchange. Specimen documents and diagrammatic guides complement the text.

These booklets were produced not only for companies thinking of exporting for the first time but also for those already established in the overseas markets. They explain, in a clear, concise manner, the steps along the export road. Copies of the booklets are available to companies through any branch of Barclays or by writing to the Marketing Department (address above).

The Business Traveller's Handbook: How to get along with people in 100 countries, compiled by Foseco Minsep Ltd. Gives complete advice on etiquette and codes of behaviour in over 100 countries. An ideal handbook for the business traveller who wants to create the best possible impression. Available from Graham & Trotman Ltd, Sterling House, 66 Wilton Road, London SW1V 1DE (01-821 1126) Paperback price: £3.95.

Croner's Reference Book for Exporters, from Croner House, 173 Kingston Road, New Malden, Surrey KT3 3SJ (01-942 8966) This is a loose-leaf and regularly up-dated service that keeps exporters up to date on all exporting procedures. It is available on a ten-day free approval offer; price: £35.90.

Directory of Export Buyers, 1981, published by Trade Research Publications, 6 Beech Hill Court, Berkhamstead, Herts HP4 2PR (044 273951) A new 3rd edition coming out late 1984. The conventional wisdom of successful exporting recommends that you should travel abroad to contact buyers. However, firms abroad are increasingly establishing buying offices in this country in order, amongst other reasons, to look for new sources of supply. It is estimated that orders for about 20% of British exports are negotiated and signed in the UK, and mainly by people listed in this directory. The entries are indexed by countries bought from, products bought and foreign firms bought for; price: £29.00.

Doing Business in the European Community, 2nd edition 1983 by John Drew, published by Butterworth & Co, Borough Green, Sevenoaks, Kent TN15 8BR (0732 884567); price: £17.50.

The Europa Year Book 1984, A world survey (25th edition). Europa Publications Ltd, 18 Bedford Square, London WC1B 3JN. In two large volumes this annual provides factual information about every country in the world, and 1650 of the principal international organisations. Price: £90.00 (UK) the set.

European Business Directory, British Telecom Enterprises (BTE), 23 Howland Street, London W1P 6HQ (01-631 2345) Has launched in 1983 a European business directory listing 130,000 exporting companies in six countries. The directory will be issued free (£20.00 to the rest of us I'm afraid) to 38,000 companies in the UK listing businesses in Belgium, West Germany, France, Italy and the Netherlands.

The annual directory is being simultaneously published in the other five countries and contains the names of 13,000 British exporters.

Export for the Small Business, by Henry Deschampsneufs 1984, published by Kogan Page Ltd, 120 Pentonville Road, London N1 (01-837 7851) Price: £5.95.

Export Handbook, 1983/84. Invaluable guide from the British Overseas Trade Board for all seeking to explore and boost their export potential. It provides an introduction to governmental and non-governmental services, which give advice and assistance and gives much useful information on UK import and export regulations, overseas tariffs, credit insurance and finance, freight forwarding and international transport. Available from HMSO Bookshops and Agents (see Yellow Pages). Price: £4.95.

Handbook of International Business, edited by Ingo Walter, published in 1982 by John Wiley, Baffins Lane, Chichester, Sussex PO19 1UD (0243 784531) It contains 44 sections covering virtually every area of international business. Price: £39.50.

Handbook of International Trade, from Kluiver Publishing Ltd, 1 Harlequin Avenue, Great West Road, Brentford, Middx TW8 9EW (01-568 6441) The handbook concentrates on facts about key markets and sources of further information in those markets. It can be sent on approval. Price: £85.00.

Selecting Agents and Distributors, by J. Thorn in Industrial Marketing Digest (UK) Volume 8 No. 1 (1983) warns of the pitfalls and problems and suggests how to overcome them.

The Small Firms Service of the Department of Industry produces a free booklet, *How to Start Exporting*. It is a very useful twenty-six pages, and includes a market check-list to help choose which market to tackle first. There is also a reading list and a section giving other useful organisations.

The service's counselling and information service can also provide practical advice on exporting for beginners.

Both the booklet and the counselling service can be reached on Freephone 2444. (See also pages 173, 181, 190 (TOB) and 194 (British Consultants Bureau).)

SPECIALIST SERVICES FOR IMPORTING

British Importers Confederation, 69 Cannon Street, London EC4N 5AB (01-248 4444) The confederation was founded in 1972, and represents some 3500 importers. It is the only organisation protecting the interests of importers whatever the goods concerned.

Membership fees start at £90.00, plus VAT, and members include a significant number of one-man importers or smaller firms, as well as such companies as Shell and Unilever.

Because of its close relationship with the UK Government and the EEC Commissions, the confederation is usually aware of likely changes in import procedures long before they occur. This knowledge and other information form an important part of the service that the confederation can provide for small businesses.

Croner's Reference Book for Importers accurately spells out the regulations and procedures to import goods of any nature into the UK. It covers import controls, exchange controls, VAT, marking of goods, customs and excise, and transit and tran-shipment insurance. The book is in loose-leaf form and the service includes a regular supply of amendments. From Croner Publications Ltd, Croner House, 173 Kingston Road, New Malden, Surrey KT3 3SS (01-942 8966) price £25.00.

Directory of British Importers, 1983, published by the British Importers Confederation and Trade Research Publications of 6 Beech Hill Court, Berkhampstead, Herts HP4 2PR (04427 3951) 4th edition out in late 1984. The directory gives a considerable amount of information about importing firms, and whether you simply want to find out more about your competitors or to find an alternative source of supply, this directory will give you the answers. Price: £39.00.

Importing for the Small Business, by Mag Morris (1984). Published by Kogan Page Ltd, 120 Pentonville Road, London N1. Price: £5.95.

Importing Handbook, published by the British Importers Confederation and Trade Research Publications (address above), 2nd edition 1984. Price: £15.00.

See also *The Exporting Handbook* in previous section.

BOOKS AND PERIODICALS ON MARKETING

Advertising, What It Is and How to Do It, by Roderick White, published by McGraw-Hill Book Co (UK) Ltd, Shoppenhangers Road, Maidenhead, Berks SL6 2QL (0628 23431) in association with the Advertising Association. Starting from 'Should you advertise and if so how much?' the book covers media, agencies, ad designs and choice, economics and the law. It tells you what questions to ask, and whether and where the answers can be provided. Price: £7.50.

Advertising Yourself, by Alison Corke (ex Saatchi & Saatchi) (1984) published by Words, 148 Stockton Lane, York YO3 OBX A basic manual for the smaller advertiser. Price: £7.50.

Basic Marketing, 2nd Edition 1982 by Tom Cannon, published by Holt, Rinehart and Winston Ltd, 1 St Annes Road, East Sussex BN21 3UN A first class backdrop to modern marketing matters.

Be Your Own PR Man, a public relations guide for the small businessman, by Michael Bland, published by Kogan Page Ltd, 120 Pentonville Road, London N1 (01-837 7851) Price: £4.95.

Campaign, Haymarket Publications Ltd, 22 Lancaster Gate,

London W2 (01-402 4200) A weekly mainly concentrating on advertising and agency matters. Price: 60p.

The Creative Handbook, published by Creative Handbook Ltd, 100 St Martin's Lane, London WC2N 4AZ (01-379 7399) Listing of all creative services, eg illustrators, model makers, photographers, cartoonists etc. Annual, latest edition April 1984. Price: £28.00.

Effective Marketing for the Smaller Business, by Geoffrey Lace (1982), Scope Books, 3 Sandford House, Kingsclerc, Newbury, Berkshire RG15 8PA A useful working book for the new firm and perhaps even the not so new. The writer is Managing Editor of *Marketing Magazine*. Price: £12.00.

Focus, The European Journal of Advertising and Marketing launched January 1982. More details from Advertising Age's Focus, Crain Communications Inc., 20–22 Bedford Row, London WC1 4EB (01-831 9621) Price: £17.50 per annum.

Getting Sales, by Smith & Dick, published in 1984 by Kogan Page, 120 Pentonville Road, London N1 9JN A useful introduction to the selling process and for those managing a small sales team for the first time. Price: £4.95.

The Headline Business, a businessman's guide to working with the media, published in 1981 by Abbey Life Assurance and the CBI, Centre Point, 103 New Oxford Street, London WC1A 1DU Not so much 'how to do PR', more an appreciation of who the media organisations are and what they do. Price: £2.50.

How to make an Exhibition of Yourself, by Lathan & Morcels. Published in April 1982 and available from Wards Colour Printers, Halifax Road, Dunston Industrial Estate, Gateshead (0632 605915) A useful 45 page booklet for people who have never exhibited before, or who got it wrong last time. Price: £2.00.

How to Win More Business by Phone, by Bernard Katz, published in 1983 by Business Books (address below). Everything about telephone selling, a vital technique no small businessman can be without. Price: £14.40.

How to Win Profitable Business, A Sunday Telegraph Guide, by Tom Cannon, 1984. The entrepreneurs guide to practical marketing for profit. Covers 24 key marketing topics with action guidelines after each. Business Books, 17–21 Conway Street, London W1P 6JD. Price: £5.95.

Introducing Marketing by Christopher, McDonald and Wills, Pan, 18 Cavaye Place, London SW10 (01-373 6070) 1980. Refreshing, practical and set firmly in the UK environment. Price: £1.75. (A new edition is due to be published late 1984.)

Managing for Results, Peter F. Drucker, Pan (address as above), 1964. Not strictly marketing, but a classic with many important pointers for the person running his own business.

Managing Sales Team, January 1982, by Neil Sweeney, published by Kogan Page, 120 Pentonville Road, London N1. It presents 12 management tasks and 100 management skills of use to small organisations with a sales force. Price: £11.95.

Map Marketing Ltd, 92–194 Carnwath Road, London SW6 3HW (01-736 0297) Offer a range of Bartholomews Maps, showing area, district and sector post codes. The range of 63 maps covers the whole of the UK priced at £12.95 each. The maps are laminated so you can write on and rub off information. Useful for sales and territory planning.

Marketing A weekly subscription-only publication from Haymarket Publications (address above). Price: 60p weekly and £40 per annum.

Marketing for Accountants and Managers by R. J. Williamson, published by Heinemann, 10 Upper Grosvenor Street, London W1X 9PA (01-493 4141) A very good book, despite the slightly off-putting title. It covers the ground efficiently and readably, giving very useful pointers towards additional reading at the end of each section. Price: £8.95.

Marketing for Business Growth, by Theodore Levitt, published by McGraw-Hill (address above). An extremely readable book on the strategic level. Price: £28.25.

Marketing, Management, Analysis, Planning and Control, by Philip Kotler, published by Prentice-Hall, 66 Wood Lane End, Hemel Hempstead, Herts HP2 4RG (0442 58531) 5th edition 1984. The most lucid and comprehensive book on the subject. Generally accepted as the standard text, and though illustrated liberally with American examples, the theory is both readable and understandable. Price: £28.45.

The Marketing Research Process, by Margaret Crimp, published by Prentice-Hall, (address as above) 1981. Useful coverage of the whole area of market research in such a way that the layman will have no trouble in understanding it. Price: £8.50.

Marketing Today, by Gordon Oliver, published by Prentice-Hall (address as above) 1980. An extremely good and comprehensive marketing book set in the UK environment. Price: £9.95.

Marketing Week, 60 Kingly Street, London W1R 5LH In most newsagents. It provides a general review of main-current marketing topics. Price: 50p.

Selling to the Ministry of Defence, a booklet published in 1983 to help small firms to compete for MOD business. Free from: Industrial Policy Division 1, Room 2328 Main Building, Ministry of Defence, Whitehall, London SW1A 2HB (01-218 2695)

Small Business, Marketing To be published in 1984 by Macmillan Press Ltd, Brunel Road, Houndhill Industrial Estate, Basingstoke RG21 2XS (0256 29242) In the Warwick Small Business Series, so it should be good, if a little pricey.

Successful Retailing through Advertising, by Eric Lowe, published by McGraw-Hill (address above) in 1983. It is a step-by-step approach to improving retailers' sales and profits, and advertising. Price: £7.95. (See also page 281 for books on the legal aspects of marketing.)

RAISING THE MONEY

PREPARING YOUR CASE

There does not seem to be a shortage of money to finance the launching of new business and the growth of existing ones. What are scarce are good, small company propositions. At least, that is the argument put forward by the financial institutions themselves. There is certainly an element of truth in this view, but the quality of the propositions owes much to the poor groundwork and planning of some budding entrepreneurs.

The starting point for any search for funds is to determine how much is needed, and then to demonstrate the security that the likely investor will then enjoy.

The accepted way in which proposals for funds are put forward is through a Business Plan. The Business Plan brings together the marketing and operational aspects of the business or proposed business, and expresses these actions in terms that a financial institution will understand. Not surprisingly, these institutions will expect the plan to contain financial statements both actual and projected.

Banks as Advisers

As well as being a possible source of money, the banks, through their national network of branch managers, can help with the preparation and evaluation of business plans.

They see hundreds of new business proposals each year and are a mine of local knowledge.

If you want advice on your business plan, and they are usually only too pleased to help, you need some facts to hand first.

The National Westminster Bank has prepared a useful business plan presentation check list, which is reproduced below.

CHECK LIST

About you

☐ Very brief synopsis for your own banker, detailed for approach to others: age, education, experience.

☐ Personal means eg property, liabilities guarantees. Other business connections.

☐ For a type of business new to you, or start-up situation, outline experience, ability and factors leading up to your decision.

Your business

☐ Brief details of: when established, purpose then and now, how the business has evolved, main factors contributing to progress.

☐ Reputation, current structure and organisation. Internal accounting system.

☐ Past 3 years audited accounts if available, and latest position.

☐ Up to date Profit and Loss figures, including details of withdrawals.

☐ Up to date liquid figures, ie debtors, creditors, stock, bank balance etc.

☐ Borrowing history and existing commitments, eg HP, leasing loans. Bankers.

☐ Description of major assets, and any changes.

Your key personnel

☐ Age, qualifications, experience, competence, of directorate/ senior management. Directors' Bankers.

☐ Emergency situation, someone to run the business in your absence.

☐ List of principal shareholders/relationships.

Your purpose

☐ Explain fully your business plan, the use to which the money will be put, eg expansion, diversification, start-up.

- [ ] Describe the practical aspects involved and the how and when of implementation.

- [ ] Diagrams, sketches, photographs etc. are usually helpful, eg property purchase and conversion to your use.

- [ ] Consider: planning permission, legal restrictions, government policy.

- [ ] Contingency plans for setbacks: reliability of supplies/raw materials/alternative sources, other factors outside your control, eg weather.

- [ ] Relevance to existing operations, (if any) opportunity for shared overheads, disruption of current business.

- [ ] Personnel, are more staff required, availability of specialist skills/training. Management ability for expanded/different operation?

Your Market

- [ ] Estimated demand, short and long term. External verification of market forecasts, eg from trade associations, market research publications.

- [ ] Competition, who from, likely developments.

- [ ] Describe your competitive advantages, eg quality, uniqueness, pricing (justify) location-local/national.

- [ ] Marketing included in costings?

- [ ] If new, or technology based or highly specialised business – detail and perspective necessary.
  NB A banker does not need to know how it works (though he may be interested), just that what it does, is reliable, and has good sales prospects.

Your profit

- [ ] Demonstrate how profits will be made, include detailed breakdown of costings, timing, projected sales, orders already held.

- [ ] Profit projections should attempt to cover the period of a loan, however sketchy.

- [ ] For capital investment – profit appraisal. Capital allowances eg new small workshop scheme.

☐ Everything included in costings? eg tax, stamp duty, legal fees, bank interest.

The amount

☐ State precisely the amounts and type of finance required and when it will be needed. Is type of finance correct? eg overdraft to finance working capital, term loan for capital expenditure.

☐ Is the amount requested sufficient? eg increased working capital requirements/margin for unforeseen circumstances.

☐ Detail the amount and form of your contribution to the total cost.

☐ Justify all figures – Cash flow forecast for next 12 months: show maximum range. All outgoings considered eg net VAT, holiday pay, bank interest and repayments, personal drawings.

Repayment

☐ Relate projected profitability and cash flow to expected repayments, Justify fully the term requested. Is it long enough?

☐ How quickly will the business generate cash? Is a repayment 'holiday' necessary and what turnover needs to be achieved to break-even?

☐ Consider the worst situation, feasibility of contingency plans, irretrievable losses.

☐ Interest rate – What is the effect of variation in base rate on plans?

Security

☐ What assets are/will be available as security?

☐ Are any assets already used for security elsewhere?

☐ Independent/realistic valuation of assets offered. Leasehold considerations, any unusual features/saleability. Support for guarantees.

☐ Agreement of other interested parties/realistic awareness of loss of asset.

☐ Insurance eg life, property, business.

If you can provide a satisfactory and comprehensive answer to most of these points, you will certainly find yourself at the head of most queues for funds.

Your first point of contact should be the local branch of any bank you choose. If you have any difficulties then speak to the bank's small firms adviser. These are listed on page 226.

Accountants and Your Business Plan

You might think of accountants as people who can only help once your business has got off the ground, or if you run into tax problems.

Northing could be further from the truth. Most accountancy firms can help you with your initial business plan. Some have departments that only look after new and small businesses. Usually the first consultation is free and at least one major accountancy firm offers new businesses a discounted rate of fees, up to the time they can appoint their own accountant. The type of services an accountant can offer in the businesses planning field include:

- Help in preparing cash flows, forecasts and budgets.
- A critical appraisal of your business plan.
- Advice on the most suitable legal forms for your business.
- Raising capital.
- Obtaining Government grants and assistance.
- Feasibility studies.
- Staff recruitment and employment advice.
- Training in book-keeping and the use of computers.

The following firms are amongst those that have departments, groups or partners responsible for providing services to new and small businesses. Whilst only the head offices of these are given below, they all have branches throughout the UK that can give a similar service locally.

Arthur Anderson & Co., 1 Surrey Street, London WC2R 2TS (01-836 1200) *Contact: J. O. Ormerod*

Arthur Young McClelland Moores & Co., Rolls House, 7 Rolls Buildings, Fetter Lane, London EC4A 1NH (01-831 7130) *Contact: John E. Smith*

Binder Hamlyn, Chartered Accountants, 7–15 Lansdowne Road, Croydon CR9 2PL (01-688 4422) *Contact: M. H. T. Gairdner*

Coopers and Lybrand, Chartered Accountants, Business Services Group, Chesterfield House, Bloomsbury Way, London WC1A 2TP (01-243 3366) *Contact: J. P. E. Taylor*

Dearden Farrow, Chartered Accountants, 1 Serjeant's Inn, London EC47 1JD (01-353 2000) *Contact: Hamish S. Renton*

Deloitte Haskins & Sells, Chartered Accountants, PO Box 207, 128 Queen Victoria Street, London EC3P 4JX (01-248 3913) *Contact: G. Whitehead*

Neville Russell, Chartered Accountants, Regent House, Heaton Lane, Stockport, Cheshire SK4 1BS (061-477 4750) *Contact: J. C. G. Pickering*

Peat, Marwick, Mitchell & Co., 1 Puddle Dock, Blackfriars, London EC4V 3PD (01-236 8000) *Contact: J. R. Hustler*

Price Waterhouse, Independent Business Group, Southwark Towers, 32 London Bridge Street, London SE1 9SY (01-407 8989) *Contact: Simon Bruce-Smythe*

Spicer and Pegler, Chartered Accountants, Financial Services Department, PO Box 498, 12 Booth Street, Manchester M60 2ED *Contact: Christopher Wheatcroft*

Thomson McLintock and Co., Chartered Accountants, UK Proprietary Business Group, 70 Finsbury Pavement, London EC2A 1SX (01-638 2777) *Contact: P. D. Bailey*

Thornton Baker, Chartered Accountants, Business Services Group, Fairfax House, Fulwood Place, London WC1V 6DW (01-405 8422) *Contact: Paul D. Reed*

Touche Ross & Co., Chartered Accountants, Hill House, 1 Little New Street, London EC4A 3TR (01-353 8011) *Contact: P. Carpenter*

Other help to prepare your financial plans

The Small Firms Service, CoSIRA and the Enterprise Agencies listed in Section 2, can also help you put together a proposal to raise money, as can some of the bodies listed on page 243–51.

Many of the courses run at the colleges listed in Section 8, will take you step-by-step through the process of preparing your case for finance. In all about 1000 organisations that could help you in your plans to raise money, are listed in the guide.

Books that can help you with business plans are included at the end of this section.

WHAT ARE THE DIFFERENT TYPES OF MONEY?

Small businesses need to borrow money for a variety of reasons: in order to start up, expand, re-locate, to start exporting or importing, to innovate or carry out research and development, or to meet the unexpected, such as the collapse of a major customer or supplier. The level of borrowing that you can secure will be related in some way to your abilities, the nature of your business and how much you have put into the business. Few lenders like to see themselves much more exposed to financial risk than the owner(s), who after all expect to make the most gain.

In the eye of most lenders, finance for the small business fits into two distinct areas: short-term, which does not necessarily mean that you only want the money for a short term, but rather the life of the asset you are buying is itself relatively short; and long-term, which is the converse of that. The table below may help you get a clearer picture.

Now, of course, starting up or expanding a small business will call for a mix of short-term and long-term finance. You may be able to get all this from one source; more likely, though, once you start to trade you will find that different sources are better organised to provide different types of money.

All methods of financing have important implications for your tax and financial position, and appropriate professional advice should always be taken before embarking on any financing exercise.

Term	Business need (eg)	Financing method
Short (up to 3 years)	For raw materials or finished goods; to finance debtors; equipment with a short life or other working capital needs; for dealing with seasonal peaks and troughs; to start exporting; or to expand overseas sales	Overdrafts Short-term loans Factoring Invoice discounting Bill finance Trade credit Export & import finance
Medium to Long (3 years plus)	Acquiring or improving premises; buying plant and machinery with a long life; buying an existing business, including a franchise; for technological innovations or developing a 'new' product or idea.	Mortgage Sale and leaseback Loan finance Long-term leasing Hire purchase Equity & venture finance Public-sector finance

Overdrafts Bank overdrafts are the most common type of short-term finance. They are simple to arrange; you just talk to your local bank manager. They are flexible with no minimum level. Sums of money can be drawn or repaid within the total amount agreed. They are relatively cheap, with interest paid only on the outstanding daily balance.

Of course, interest rates can fluctuate. So what seemed a small sum of money one year can prove crippling if interest rates jump suddenly. Normally you do not repay the 'capital'. You simply renew or alter the overdraft facility from time to time. However, overdrafts are theoretically repayable on demand, so you should not use short-term overdraft money to finance long-term needs, such as buying a lease or some plant and equipment. Overdrafts are more usually used to finance working capital needs, stocks, customers who have not paid up, bulk purchases of materials and the like.

Term Loans (Short, Medium and Long) These are rather more formal than a simple overdraft. They cover periods of 0–3, 3–10 and 10–20 years respectively. They are usually secured against an existing fixed asset or one to be acquired, or are guaranteed personally by the directors (proprietors). As such, this may involve you in a certain amount of expense with legal fees and arrangement or consultants' fees. So it may be a little more expensive than an overdraft, but unless you default on the interest charges you can be reasonably confident of having the use of the money throughout the whole term of the borrowing.

The interest rates on the loan can either be fixed for the term or variable with the prevailing interest rate. A fixed rate is to some extent a gamble, which may work in your favour, depending on how interest rates move over the term of the loan. So, if general interest rates rise you win, and if they fall you lose. However, a variable rate means that you do not take that risk. There is another benefit to a fixed rate of interest. It should make planning ahead a little easier with a fixed financial commitment, unlike a variable overdraft rate, in which a sudden rise can have disastrous consequences.

Government Loan Guarantees for Small Businesses were first introduced in March 1981 and are still available. To be eligible for this loan, your proposition must have been looked at by an approved bank and considered viable, but should not be a proposition that the bank itself would normally approve. You can be a sole trader, partnership, co-operative or limited company wanting funds to start up or to expand. The bank simply passes your application on to the Department of Industry, using an approved format.

This is an elementary business plan, which asks for some details of the directors, the business, their cash needs and profit performance or projection of the business. There are no formal rules on size, number of employees or assets, but large businesses and their subsidiaries are definitely excluded from the scheme. The other main exclusions are businesses in the following fields: agriculture, horticulture, banking, commission agents, education, forestry (except tree-harvesting and saw-milling), house and estate agents, insurance, medical and veterinary, night-clubs and licensed clubs, pubs and property, and travel agencies.

The loans can be for up to £75,000 and repayable over 2 to 7 years. It may be possible to delay paying the capital element for up to two years from the start of the loan. However, monthly or quarterly repayments of interest will have to be made from the outset. The loan itself, however, is likely to be expensive. Once approved by the Department of Trade, the bank lends you the money at bank rate plus 4 or 5% and the Government guarantees the bank 70% of its money if you cannot pay up.

In return for this the government charge you a 5% 'insurance' premium on the 70% of the loan it has taken on risk. Borrowers would be expected to pledge all available business assets as a security for the loan, but they would not necessarily be excluded from the scheme if there are no available assets.

Also on the plus side, directors will not normally be asked to give personal guarantees on security, an undertaking they may have to make for other forms of borrowing.

There are now some 30 banks operating the scheme, and by mid 1984 some 14,648 loans worth £481 million had been granted. The average loan has remained at about £33,000 for the past two years. To date 2000 of the businesses have already gone into liquidation, and various estimates of the ultimate casualty rate range from an optimistic one in five, to a pessimistic one in three.

The rule certainly seems to be to ask for as much as you need, plus a good margin of safety. Going back for a second bite too soon is definitely frowned upon. You do not have to take all the money at once. At the discretion of your bank manager, you can take the money in up to four lots. However each lot must be 25% or more.

Encouraging, too, is the evidence that these loans were fairly evenly split between 'start-ups' and growing young businesses.

One final point on term loans. Banks tend to lump overdraft facilities and loans together into a 'total' facility, so one is often only given at the expense of the other.

Mortgage Loans   These operate in much the same way as an ordinary mortgage. The money borrowed is used to buy the freehold on the business premises. That then acts as the main security for the loan, with regular repayments made up of interest charges and principal paid to the lender.

The main suppliers are the insurance companies and pension funds, who generally prefer to deal in sums above £50,000. Some of the smaller companies will lend as little as £5000, particularly if the borrower is a policyholder. As well as the regular payments, a charge of about 2% will be made to cover the survey, valuation and legal work in drawing up agreements. (See National Association of Pension Funds, page 258.)

Sale and Leaseback   This involves selling the freehold of a property owned by a business to a financial institution, which agrees to grant you a lease on the premises.

The lender will want to be sure that you can afford the lease, so a profit track record will probably be needed, and all expenses involved in the negotiations are met by the borrower. The borrower then has the use of the value of the asset in immediate cash to plough into the business.

The tax aspects of sale and leaseback are complex and work more in the favour of some types of business than others, so professional advice is essential before entering into any arrangement.

As with other forms of finance, it is a competitive market and a few 'quotes' are worth getting.

Trade Credit   Once you have established creditworthiness, it may be possible to take advantage of the trade credit extended by suppliers. This usually takes the form of allowing you anything from seven days to three months from receiving the goods, before having to pay for them.

You will have to weigh carefully the benefit of taking this credit against the cost of losing any cash discounts offered. For example, if you are offered a 2½% discount for a cash settlement, then this is a saving of £25 for every £1000 of purchases. If the alternative is to take six weeks' credit, then the saving is the cost of borrowing that sum from, say, your bank on overdraft. So if your bank interest is 16% per annum, that is equivalent to 0.31% per week. Six weeks would save you 1.85%. On £1000 of purchase you would only save £18.50 of bank interest. This means that the cash discount is more attractive. However, you may not have the cash or overdraft facility, so your choice is restricted.

Bill Financing   This is rather like a post-dated cheque which can be sold to a third party for cash, but at a discount. Once you have dispatched the goods concerned to your customer you can draw a trade bill to be accepted by him on a certain date. This, in effect, is a commitment by him to settle his account on that date, and he is not expected to pay until then. You can sell this bill to a bank or a discount house and receive immediate cash. Of course, you have to pay for this service. Payment takes the form of a discount on the face value of the bill, usually directly related to the creditworthiness of your customer. It has several advantages as a source of short-term finance.

Firstly, it is usually competitive with bank overdrafts. Secondly, you can accurately calculate the cost of financing a transaction, because the discount rate is fixed and not subject to interest rate fluctuations. This is particularly important if the time between dispatch of the goods and payment by the customer is likely to be several months. Thirdly, by using bill finance, you can free up overdraft facilities for other purposes. For example, you can get on with making up more products for other customers – something you may not have been able to do if you were waiting for the last customer to pay.

Factoring   This is an arrangement which allows you to receive up to 80% of the cash due from your customers more quickly than they would normally pay. The factoring company buys your trade debts and provides a debtor accounting and administration service. In other words, it takes over the day-to-day work of invoicing and sending out reminders and statements. This can be a particularly helpful service to a small, expanding business. It can allow the management to concentrate on growing the business, with the factoring company providing expert guidance on credit control, 100% protection against bad debts, and improved cash flow.

You will, of course, have to pay for factoring services. Having the cash before your customers pay will cost you a little more than normal overdraft rates. The factoring service will cost between ½ and 3½% of turn-over, depending on volume of work, the number of debtors, average invoice amount and other related factors. You can get up to 80% of the value of your invoice in advance with the remainder paid when your customer settles up, less the various charges just mentioned.

If you sell direct to the public, sell complex and expensive capital equipment or expect progress payments on a long-term project, then factoring is not for you.

If you are expanding more rapidly than other sources of finance will allow, then this may be a useful service. All other things being equal, it should be possible to find a factor if your turn-over exceeds £25,000 per annum, though the larger firm will look for around £100,000 as the economic cut-off point.

Invoice Discounting   This is a variation of factoring open to businesses with a net worth of £30,000. Unlike factoring, where all your debtors are sold to the factor, in this service only selected invoices are offered. This can be particularly useful if you have a few relatively large orders to reputable, 'blue-chip'-type customers in your general order book.

Up to 75% of the value of the invoices can be advanced, but you remain responsible for collecting the money from your customers. This you forward to the discounting company, who in turn sends you the balance less a charge on the assigned invoices. This charge will be made up of two elements. You will pay interest on the cash advanced for the period between the date of the advance and your refunding the discount company.

You will also have to pay a factoring charge of between ¼ and ¾%.

The twist is that, if your customer does not pay up, you have to repay the discount house their advance. Unlike normal factoring, however, your customer will never know that you discounted his invoice.

Export Finance   This is a specialist subject in itself. The range of possibilities open to the exporter is described in considerable detail in the Bank of England booklet referred to at the end of this section. The central feature of most forms of export financing is ECGD (Export Credits Guarantee Department) credit insurance. This is a government-backed credit insurance policy that gives cover against the failure of your foreign customers either to take up the goods you have dispatched or to pay them. The cover includes loss caused by war and trade sanctions. Although the government themselves do not provide export finance, ECGD credit insurance will put you in a highly favourable position with, for example, your bank. They in turn would be able to provide finance with a greater degree of security than they could normally expect. (ECGD addresses are at the end of the section.)

Some banks, notably the Midland, operate a Smaller Exporters' Scheme providing ECGD-backed post-shipment finance for small exporters who may find it uneconomic to take out an ECGD policy on their own. In certain cases, an Export house may be willing to manage your overseas business for you, acting as your agent in finding customers, or even as a merchant actually buying the goods from you for re-sale in certain overseas markets.

Import Finance   This includes such elements as a produce or merchandise advance. In this case the imported goods themselves are offered as security for a loan. There are some obvious limitations on the type of goods that could be accepted. Fruit and vegetables, and other perishable goods or commodities in volatile markets are excluded. However, under the right circumstances up to 80% of the value of sold goods and 50% of unsold goods can be realised in cash quite quickly.

Leasing   This is a way of getting the use of vehicles, plant and equipment without paying the full cost at once. Operating leases are taken out where you will use the equipment for less than its full economic life – for example, a car, photocopier or vending machine. The lessor takes the risk of the equipment becoming obsolete, and assumes responsibility for repairs, maintenance and insurance. As you, the lessee, are paying for this service, it is more expensive than a Finance lease, where you lease the equipment for most of its economic life and maintain and insure it yourself.

Leases can normally be extended, often for fairly nominal sums, in the later years.

The obvious attractions of leasing are that no deposit is needed leaving your working capital for more profitable use elsewhere. Also, the cost of leasing is known from the start, making forward planning more simple.

Hire Purchase   This differs from leasing in that you have the option at the start to become the owner of the equipment after a series of payments have been made. The interest is usually fixed and often more expensive than a bank loan. However, manufacturers (notably car makers) often subsidise this interest, so it pays to shop around both for sources of HP finance and manufacturers of equipment.

Private Equity Finance   This is only relevant if your business is or is shortly to become a limited company, and it refers to the sale of ordinary shares to investors. Unlike other forms of 'borrowing', where interest has to be paid whether or not the business makes a profit, shares usually only attract a dividend when the business is profitable.

This makes it extremely important to get as large an equity base as possible at the outset. Although it does mean giving up some control, you may gain some valuable business expertise, and your reputation can be enhanced if the investors are respected themselves.

Apart from equity finance you provide yourself, you can attract outside investment from outside sources.

Individuals: unlike publicly quoted companies, which have a stock-exchange facility, you will have to find investors yourself. Recent tax changes – in particular, those incorporated in the Government's 'Business Expansion Scheme' (described below) – have made it attractive for high taxpayers to invest in new business. Several organisations have been established to acquire such funds and find suitable investments.

Institutions: such as ICFC, subsidiaries of the clearing banks and venture capital organisations, provide equity capital, usually for companies with exceptionally high growth potential. In general equity financing from people other than those known well by you is the most difficult money to raise.

The Business Expansion Scheme,   introduced in April 1983, replaces the Business Start Up Scheme. It is designed to make it attractive for UK income taxpayers to invest in new or growing businesses. It is intended to run until April 1987.

The investors at whom the scheme is aimed are UK taxpayers who are not connected with the business they are going to invest in. They cannot be paid directors or employees of the business, nor can they own more than 30% of the business. They could, however, be unpaid directors or take fees for professional services. The investor gets tax relief on up to £40,000 invested in any one year. The minimum investment is £500.00 and the funds must be left in for at least five years. The effect of this scheme is that a top-rate taxpayer could be putting as little as £2500 of his own money into a business in return for a £10,000 share, the balance being effectively paid by the Inland Revenue.

Your solicitor, accountant or bank manager may be able to put you in touch with interested individuals.

Alternatively, a number of financial institutions are offering 'portfolio' facilities to investors. This means that investors put their funds into an approved organisation which seeks out potential investment opportunities on their behalf. This spreads their risk, and gives them the benefit of 'professional' management.

Many of the institutions keep a 'register' of business proposals that they have not invested in. People with funds can use the register to seek out private investment opportunities. So it is well worth sending your business plan.

Public Equity Finance 1983 saw the establishment of the Unlisted Securities Market (USM) as a major source of finance for small and growing companies. The USM works in a similar way to the Stock Exchange, in offering shares to a wide public market. There is no minimum size for a company looking for a USM Quote, although a three year track record is expected. Under certain conditions the Stock Exchange will let a completely new venture come in. A company entering the USM can expect to pay expenses of between 5% and 10% of the amount raised.

To find out more contact either the Stock Exchange, or a stockbroker (see page 258).

Venture Capital This is start-up capital usually associated with businesses involved in technological and technical innovation. The sums involved are usually up to £100,000 over periods of five years or more. With this capital usually comes management expertise, often in the form of a board member from the financial institution. So you are going to have to be able to work with him, and probably give a personal guarantee for the sums involved.

Perhaps the greatest benefit coming from the provider of

venture capital is their expertise at keeping your financial structure in line with your changing needs.

Development Capital   These are funds to help established firms grow and diversify. Like venture capital, the period involved is five years or so, and the investing institution expects to be able to sell its stake either to the directors or possibly through an eventual Stock Exchange quotation. Generally you will need to have a pre-tax profit of £30,000 per annum and be looking for more than £50,000 additional finance. The investor will want to put a director on your board – as much to help you and the company as to keep an eye on its investment.

Management Buy-outs   This is not a type of money. It is, however an increasingly popular activity that involves the existing managers of a business buying out the business from its owners. As both the business and the managers will have a 'track record', it may be easier to find equity finance for such ventures; an increasing number of lending organisations have moved into this field (see pages 227, 242 and 258).

Public-sector sources   These include central and local government, certain agencies and EEC funds. There are over 111 different types of funds available, with differing types of eligibility. In the main, they are concentrated on providing regional and local assistance, encouragement for specific industries, ranging from agriculture to encouraging tourism in Wales; and assistance for specific purposes such as research and development, employment or exporting. The booklet Financial Incentives and Assistance for Industry, referred to at the end of this section, covers this subject comprehensively.

Individual schemes of particular relevance and importance to small businesses, are explained under the appropriate sponsoring bodies heading, in the section headed 'Where you can get the money'.

WHERE YOU CAN GET THE MONEY

There are now several hundred institutions that provide start up and development capital for new and small businesses. They are clustered into a score or so groups, usually called 'Houses'. Some of them, as their names imply, provide only one type of finance. However in the main, they cover a spread of the different types. The functions of each 'house' are briefly described, before their main members are listed.

For most of us, borrowing money usually means either a visit or a letter to our local bank manager. Although he is by no means the only source of finance for a new or small business, the local bank manager is a good starting point.

Clearing Banks This is the general name given to the high street bankers. We immediately think of the big four banks – Barclays, Lloyds, Midland and the National Westminster – when we think of 'clearers'. However, there are another dozen or so that fit within the general meaning of 'clearing and domestic deposit bank'.

The banks offer a wide range of services in their own right. Through wholly or partially owned subsidiaries they cover virtually every aspect of the financial market. These services include overdrafts, term loans, trade bill finance, factoring, leasing, export and import finance, the Government Loan Guarantee Scheme, and equity financing.

In addition to providing a source of funds, the clearing banks have considerable expertise in the areas of tax, insurance and financial advice generally. Very little of this expertise will rest in your local branch office. The bank's regional and main head offices are where these centralised services are provided.

As you probably already have a bank account, this may be your starting point in looking for money for business. Do not forget, however, that the banks are in competition with one another and with other lenders. So shop around if you do not get what you want first time. Incidentally their charges to commercial customers vary too, so ask for figures before signing up.

The banks are becoming quite adventurous in their competition for new and small business accounts. Barclays Bank Business Start Loan is one such adventurous scheme. It is aimed exclusively at providing some, though not all, of set-up costs of a new business. The amount needed should be between £5000 and £100,000. The period of the loan is three to five years, and the capital is to be repaid in full at the end of the fifth year. Not only do borrowers get the advantage of deferring capital repayments for up to five years, but interest charges are taken in the form of royalty on sales. In this way you pay only when you can best afford to, and so ease early cash-flow problems.

Some of the banks have a small firms specialist, one of whose tasks is to help new, small-business clients get the best out of their banking services. To get an opinion from one of these specialists would be a good way of finding the possibilities of getting finance and how best to go about it.

Clearing and Other Domestic Deposit Banks	Small Firms Adviser (if any)
Allied Irish Banks Ltd, 64/66 Coleman Street, London EC2R 5AL (01-588 0691)	*Area Advance Controller, Frank Sullivan*
Bank of Ireland, Advances Dept, 36 Moorgate, London EC2R 6DP (01-628 8811/9)	*Assistant General Manager, Andrew Roger*
Bank of Scotland, PO Box No 5, The Mound, Edinburgh EH1 1YZ (031-229 2555)	*Business Development Co-ordinator, James Winterbottom .*
Barclays Bank plc, Small Business Unit, Marketing Department, 6th Floor, Juxon House, 94 St Paul's Churchyard, London EC4H 8EH (01-248 9155)	*Manager, Small Business Unit, P. E. J. Jackson*
Clydesdale Bank plc (a member of the Midland Banking Group), 30 St Vincent Place, Glasgow G1 2HL (041-248 7070)	*Business Development, A. K. Denholm*
Co-operative Bank plc, 1 Ballon Street, Manchester M60 4EP (061-832 3456)	*Corporate Business Manager, Peter Walker, ext 282*
Coutts & Co. (a member of the National Westminster Bank Group), 440 Strand, London WC2R 1QS (01-379 6262)	
Lloyds Bank plc, Head Office, PO Box 215, 71 Lombard Street, London EC3P 3BS (01-626 1500)	*Manager, Small Business Unit, D. B. Good*
Midland Bank plc, Small Business Unit, Head Office, Poultry, London EC2P 2BX (01-606 9911)	*Head of Unit, Stuart White*
National Girobank, Director of Customer Services, 10 Milk Street, London EC2V 8JH (01-600 6020)	*Director of Customer Services, P. Gottlieb*
National Westminster Bank plc, Small Business Section, 3rd Floor, 116 Fenchurch Street, London EC3M 5AN (01-726 1000)	*Noel Dearing and Malcom Keeting*
Northern Bank Ltd (a member of the Midland Bank Group), Corporate Finance Department, PO Box 183, Donegall Square West, Belfast BT1 6JS (0232 245277)	*John Sherrard*
The Royal Bank of Scotland Ltd, PO Box 183, 42 St Andrew Square, Edinburgh EH2 2YE (031-556 8555)	*Business Development Managers, J. Byers and J. Payne*
Ulster Bank Ltd (a member of National Westminster Bank Group), Planning and Marketing Division, 47 Donegall Place, Belfast BT1 5AU (0232 220222)	

Williams & Glyn's Bank plc (a member of the Royal Bank of Scotland Group), Marketing Department, 20 Birchin Lane, London EC3 (01-623 4356)

Yorkshire Bank plc, 20 Merrion Way, Leeds LS2 8NZ (0532 441244)

Controller (Marketing), J. Howley

Central Trustee Savings Bank Ltd, PO Box 99, St Mary's Court, 100 Lower Thames Street, London EC3R 6AQ (01-623 5266)

Head of Corporate Lending, D. Morton

Accepting Houses provide some, or all of these services; domestic and international banking; credit finance, export credits, leasing, debt factoring, medium term finance, buyouts and some development capital for the small firm. They are unlikely to be interested in propositions for amounts less than £50,000, but they are worth a try. The Accepting Houses Committee is at 101 Cannon Street, London EC4N 5BA (01-283 7332)

Baring Brothers & Co. Ltd, 8 Bishopsgate, London, EC2N 4AE (01-283 8833) Branches: Birmingham and Liverpool

Brown, Shipley & Co. Ltd, Founders Court, Lothbury, London EC2R 7HE (01-606 9833)

Charterhouse Japhet plc, 1 Paternoster Row, St Paul's, London, EC4M 7DH (01-248 3999) Representative Office: Manchester

Robert Fleming & Co. Ltd, 8 Crosby Square, London EC3A 6AN (01-638 5858)

Guiness Mahon & Co. Ltd, PO Box 442, 32 St Mary-at-Hill, London EC3P 3AJ (01-623 9333)

Hambros Bank Ltd, UK Department, 41 Bishopsgate, London EC2P 2AA (01-588 2851)

Hill Samuel & Co. Ltd, 100 Wood Street, London EC2P 2AJ (01-628 8011) Branches: Birmingham, Bristol, Glasgow, Leeds and Manchester

Kleinwort Benson Ltd, PO Box 560, 20 Fenchurch Street, London EC3P 3DP (01-623 8000) Branches: Birmingham, Edinburgh and Manchester

Lazard Brothers & Co. Ltd, 21 Moorfields, London EC2P 2HT (01-588 2721)

Samuel Montagu & Co. Ltd, 114 Old Broad Street, London EC2P 2HY (01-588 6464)

Morgan Grenfell & Co. Ltd, 23 Great Winchester Street, London EC2P 2AX (01-588 4033)

N. M. Rothschild & Sons Ltd, PO Box 185, New Court, St Swithin's Lane, London EC4P 4DU (01-280 5000) Branches: Leeds and Manchester

J. Henry Schroder Wagg & Co. Ltd, 120 Cheapside, London EC2V 6DS (01-588 4000)

Singer & Friedlander Ltd, 21 New Street, Bishopsgate, London EC2M 4HR (01-623 3000) Branches: Birmingham, Bristol, Glasgow, Leeds and Nottingham

S. G. Warburg & Co. Ltd, 30 Gresham Street, London EC2P 2EB (01-600 4555)

Discount Houses These are the specialist institutions that provide bill financing. There are eleven members of the London Discount Market Association, whose Honorary Secretary is Mr S. J. Dare, 39 Cornhill, London EC3V 3NU (01-623 1020) Bill financing is a bit of a long shot as a source of finance for a small business. Although bills may be as little as a few thousand pounds, the average is nearer £25,000. Nevertheless, given a good proposition, discount houses will be happy to listen. Gerald Quin, Cope & Co. Ltd and Page & Gwyther Ltd may be the most responsive at the small end of the bill market.

London Discount Market Association Members

Alexanders Discount plc, 1 St. Swithin's Lane, London EC4N 8DN (01-626 5467)

Cater Allen Ltd, 1 King William Street, London EC4N 7AU (01-623 2070)

Clive Discount Co. Ltd, 1 Royal Exchange Avenue, London EC3V 3LU (01-283 1101)

Gerrard & National plc, 32 Lombard Street, London EC3V 9BE (01-623 9981)

Jessel, Tonybee and Gillett plc, 30 Cornhill, London EC3V 3LH (01-623 2111)

King & Shaxson plc, 52 Cornhill, London EC3V 3PD (01-623 5433)

Page & Gwyther Ltd, 1 Founders Court, Lothbury, London EC2R 7DB (01-606 5681)

Gerald Quin, Cope & Co. Ltd, 19/21 Moorgate, London EC2R 6BX (01-628 2296)

Seccombe Marshall & Campion plc, 7 Birchin Lane, London EC3V 9DE (01-283 5031)

Smith St. Aubyn & Co. Ltd, White Lion Court, Cornhill, London EC3V 3PN (01-283 7261)

The Union Discount Co. of London plc, 39 Cornhill, London EC3V 3NU (01-623 1020) and 24a Melville Street, Edinburgh EH3 7MS (031-226 3535)

Export Houses There are some 800 export houses operating in the UK, offering almost every service possible to exporters and foreign importers. Some 230 of them belong to the British Export Houses Association, and they are actively interested in working with small firms.

Three types of company will find an export house particularly useful: firstly, those that are considering exporting for the first time; secondly, those that want to expand outside their existing overseas markets; and thirdly, those that have to extend credit to their customers to a greater extent than they are willing or able to do (this may be to meet competition or currency problems).

Export houses are specialists in financing and servicing exports and are divided into four main types.

Export agents and managers sell a manufacturer's goods in selected countries where they have expert knowledge. They work very closely with their clients, and can in effect become the manufacturer's own export department. This can save a small company money and provide a greater level of expertise than could realistically be afforded. Payment for these services is usually by commission, but sometimes a retainer or even a profit-sharing scheme can be used.

Confirming houses, buying or independent houses and stores buyers work as follows. Confirming houses represent foreign buyers in the UK and can confirm, as a principal, an order placed by that buyer with a British supplier. Buying or independent houses buy, pay for and ship goods for their overseas principals. A stores buyer is a particular type of buying house dealing only with departmental stores. Being linked to such houses costs you nothing but can open up many new overseas markets for your products.

Merchants, as the word implies, both buy and sell as a principal. They specialise in certain products and markets. One of the largest sells in 120 different countries. Others operate in a much narrower sphere. Dealing with a merchant is little different from selling in the UK, and, even better, there is no credit risk.

Finance houses can provide you with non-resource finance and allow your foreign buyer time to pay. This gives the exporter absolute security and makes the deal attractive to an overseas buyer. Normally only the foreign buyer pays a commission for the service.

The British Export Houses Association, 69 Cannon Street, London EC4N 5AB (01-248 4444) is the best starting point for contacting an export house. The association secretary is Mr H. W. Bailey. They produce a Directory of British Export Houses, which tells you all about each house and its particular expertise. Last edition was brought out in 1978/79 and a new edition will be released in late 1984/early 1985. Alternatively you can include full details of your requirements in the association's monthly Export Enquiry circular. This will cost £25.00 plus VAT for the first insertion, and £10.00 plus VAT for each repeat. The circular goes to all members and is considered to be a very effective way of communicating quickly in a rapidly changing environment.

Some Leading Export Houses

Adam & Harvey Ltd, 15/16 Bonhill Street, London EC2P 2EA (01-628 7711)

Balfour Williamson & Co. Ltd, Roman House, Wood Street, London EC2Y 5BP (01-638 6191)

Booker Merchants International Ltd, 63–69 New Oxford Street, London WC2 6DN (01-836 4994)

British Markitex Ltd, PO Box 52, Deneway House, Potters Bar, Herts EN5 1AH (0707 57281)

Coutinho Caro & Co. Ltd, Walker House, 87 Queen Victoria Street, London EC4V 4AL (01-236 1505)

Dalgety Ltd, Dalgety Export Service Division, Corn Exchange Building, 52/57 Mark Lane, London EC3R 7SR (01-488 3100)

Dominion Shippers Ltd, 17 Stamford Street, London SE1 9NG (01-633 0066)

Gellatly Hankey & Co. Ltd, International House, Mitre Spire, London EC3A 5ED (01-621 0388)

Gillespie Brothers & Co. Ltd, Ling House, Dominion Street, London EC2M 2RT (01-606 6431)

Inchcape Exports Ltd, Dugard House, Peartree Road, Stanway, Colchester, Essex CO3 5UL (0206 44166)

W. H. Jones & Co. (London) Ltd, Tower House, 17 Oakleigh Park North, London N20 9AP (01-445 5006)

Keep Brothers Ltd, The Rotunda, New Street, Birmingham B2 4NQ (021-643 6851)

Lewis & Peat (Merchanting) Ltd, 32 St Mary at Hill, Eastcheap EC3P 3HA (01-623 9333)

Matheson & Co. Ltd, 142 Minories, London EC3N 1QL (01-480 6633)

Rabone Petersen & Co. Ltd, PO Box 326, 42 Hagley Road, Birmingham B16 8PU (021-454 5843)

Saltraco Ltd, Maridian House, 42 Upper Berkeley Street, London W1H 7PL (01-723 1222)

Scholefield Goodman & Sons Ltd, 135 Edmund Street, Birmingham B3 2HS (021-236 7471)

UAC International Ltd, UAC House, Blackfriars Road, London SE1 9UG (01-928 2070)

United City Merchants Ltd, UCM House, 3/5 Swallow Place, London W1A 1BB (01-629 8424)

Some Finance Houses

British Overseas Engineering & Credit Co. Ltd, Walker House, 87 Queen Victoria Street, London EC4V 1AP (01-236 6544)

Charterhouse Japhet Export Finance PLC, 1 Paternoster Row, St. Paul's, London EC4M 7DH (01-248 3999)

Grindlay Brandts Export Finance PLC, 23 Fenchurch Street, London EC3P 3ED (01-626 0545)

Manufacturers Hanover Export Finance Ltd, 7 Princes Street, London EC2P 2EN (01-606 8461)

Tennant Guaranty Ltd, 1 Seething Lane, London EC3N 4BP (01-488 1309)

Tozer Kemsley & Millbourn (Holdings) Ltd, 28 Great Tower Street, London EC3R 5DE (01-283 3122)

UDT International Finance Ltd, 51 Eastcheap, London EC3P 3BU (01-623 3020)

Factoring Companies   These financial institutions provide a full sales accounting service, often including credit management and insurance against bad debts. 1983 saw Factoring Companies reporting an 18% increase in business. However, Barclays Bank withdrew from direct involvement and uses Anglo Factoring, a relative newcomer. The Association of British Factors is at Moor House, London Wall, London EC2 5HE Secretary Mr Michael Burke (01-638 4090)

ABF members charge between ¾ and 2½% of gross turnover for the sales ledger package and around bank overdraft rate for finance charges. They will advance about 80% of invoice price almost immediately the invoice is raised. They generally only consider customers with £100,000 per annum turnover, but may consider good cases from £50,000.

Members of the Association of British Factors

Alex. Lawrie Factors Ltd, Beaumont House, Beaumont Road, Banbury, Oxon OX16 7RN (0295 4491) (*Lloyds & Scottish Group*) Branches: Bristol, Coventry, Edinburgh, London, Manchester, Newcastle and Stockport

Anglo Factoring Services Ltd, 44 Old Steine, Brighton, Sussex BN1 1NH (0273 722532) (*J. Rothschild & Co.*)

Arbuthnot Factors Ltd, Arbuthnot House, Breeds Place, Hastings, Sussex TN34 3DG (0424 430824) (*Arbuthnot Latham Bank & Yorkshire Bank*)

Credit Factoring International Ltd, Smith House, PO Box 50, Elmwood Avenue, Feltham, Middx TW13 7QD (01-890 1390) (*National Westminster Bank Group*)

Griffin Factors, Forward Trust Group Ltd, Griffin House, 21 Farncombe Road, Worthing, Sussex BN11 2BW (0903 205181) (*Midland Bank Group*)

H and H Factors Ltd, Randolph House, 46–48 Wellesley Road, Croydon, Surrey CR9 3PS (01-681 2641) (*Walter E. Heller Overseas Corporation & Hambro Bank*)

Independent Factors Ltd, International Factors Ltd, Sovereign House, 98–99 Queen's Road, Brighton BN1 3WZ (0273 21211) (*Lloyds & Scottish Group*)

Invoice Factors

The Association of Invoice Factors, 109/113 Royal Avenue, Belfast BT1 1FF (0232 224522) *Mr A. M. Selig*

This may be a better bet for a small business. Their members' average client has a turn-over of £100,000 per annum, and they would be prepared to look at propositions from £1000 per month gross sales value. They advance 70 to 80% of the value of the invoice, and charge between ½ and 3½% for maintaining the sales ledger. Between advancing you the money and getting it in from your client, their financing rate charges are similar to overdraft rates.

Members of the Association of Invoice Factors

Anpal Finance Ltd, PO Box 37 Kimberly House, Vaughan Way, Leicester LE1 9AX (0533 56066)

Century Factors Ltd, Vincent Chambers, 60 Princes Street, Yeovil, Somerset BA20 1HL (0935 76501)

Gaelic Invoice Factors Ltd, Finlay House, 10–14 West Nile Street, Glasgow G1 2PP (041-248 4901)

Larostra Ltd, 296 Kingston Road, London SW20 8LX (01-543 3322)

London Wall Factors Ltd,15 South Moulton Street, London W1Y 1DE (01-629 9891 and 01-573 3783)

Ulster Factors Ltd, Northern Bank House, 109–113 Royal Avenue, Belfast BT1 1FF (0232 224522)

Alternatively, arrangements can be made through a factoring broker, who will charge the factor rather than the client.

Expansion Finance & Investments Co., Tudor House, Heath Road, Weybridge, Surrey KT13 8TZ (0932 47682) *J. L. A. Ormisten*

Leasing Companies   These may be a little more adventurous in dealing with new and small businesses than other sources of finance. The Equipment Leasing Association is the main organisation in this field. It is located at 18 Upper Grosvenor Street, London W1X 6PB (01-491 2783)

Most leasing companies are subsidiaries of much larger financial institutions, including the clearing banks. Some of them operate in specialist markets such as aircraft or agriculture, as their names imply. Many would not look at anything under £1 million. A phone call to the association will put you in touch with a selection of appropriate companies. Four companies that have a spread of business between a few hundred pounds and £50,000 are Anglo Leasing, FC Finance, Hamilton Leasing, and Schroder Leasing.

Airlease International Management Ltd, 24–28 St Mary Axe, London EC3A 8DE (01-626 9393)

Allied Irish Finance Co. Ltd, 10–12 Neeld Parade, Wembley Hill Road, Wembley HA9 6QU (01-903 1383)

American Express Equipent Finance (UK) Ltd, PO Box 171, 12–15 Fetter Lane, London EC4A 1PT (01-583 6666)

Anglo Leasing Ltd, 2 Clerkenwell Green, London EC1R 0DH (01-253 4300)

Arbuthnot Leasing International Ltd, 20 Moorgate, London EC2R 6HH (01-628 9876)

Barclays Mercantile Industrial Finance Ltd, Elizabethan House, Great Queen Street, London WC2B 5DX (01-242 1234) (*A member of the Barclays Bank Group*)

Baring Brothers Co. Ltd, 8 Bishopsgate, London EC2N 4AE (01-283 8833)

Robert Benson Lonsdale & Co. Ltd, 20 Fenchurch Street, London EC3P 3DB (01-623 8000)

BNP (Finance) Ltd, 8–13 King William Street, London EC4P 4HS (01-626 5678)

British Credit Trust Ltd, 34 High Street, Slough SL1 1ED (0753 73211)

British Industrial Corporation (Leasing) Ltd, PO Box 243, 30 Gresham Street, London EC2P 2EB (01-600 4555)

Capital Leasing Ltd, 4 Melville Street, Edinburgh EH3 7NZ (031-226 4071) (*A member of the Bank of Scotland Group*)

Carolina Leasing Ltd, 14 Austin Friars, London EC2N 2EH (01-588 9133)

Chartered Trust plc, 24–26 Newport Road, Cardiff CF2 1SR (0222 484484)

Chase Manhattan Ltd, PO Box 16, Woolgate House, Coleman Street, London EC2P 2HD (01-638 6999)

CIN Leasing Ltd, 19–23 Moorgate, London EC2R 6AR (01-920 0446)

Citicorp International Bank Ltd, 335 Strand, London WC2R 1LS (01-836 1230)

City Leasing Ltd, 23 Great Winchester Street, London EC2P 2AX (01-588 4545)

Commercial Credit LeasingLtd, Railway Approach, Wallington, Surrey, SM6 0DY (01-773 3111)

CTSB Leasing Ltd, PO Box 99, St Mary's Court, 100 Lower Thames Street, London EC3R 6AQ (01-623 5266) (*A member of the Trustee Savings Bank Group*)

Eastlease Ltd, 8 Surrey Street, Norwich, Norfolk NR1 3ST (0603 22200 ext 2555)

ELCO Leasing Ltd, 41 Bishopsgate, London EC2P 2AA (01-588 2851)

European Banking Co. Ltd, 150 Leadenhall Street, London EC3V 4PP (01-638 3654)

First Co-operative Finance Ltd, 1 Balloon Street, Manchester, M60 4EP (061-832 3300)

Forward Trust Group Ltd, Broad Street House, 55 Old Broad Street, London EC2M 1RX (01-920 0141) (*A member of the Midland Bank Group*)

GKN Sankey Finance Ltd, PO Box 31, Albert Street, Bilstom, West Midlands WV4 0DL (0902 44456)

Gray Dawes Leasing Ltd, 22 Bevis Marks, London EC3A 7DY (01-283 8765)

Grindlays Bank Group, Leasing Department, Minerva House, London SE1 9DH (01-626 0545)

Guinness Mahon Leasing plc, PO Box 442, 32 St Mary-at-Hill, London EC3P 3AJU (01-623 9333)

Hambros Bank plc, Equipment Leasing Department, 41 Bishopsgate, London EC2P 2AA (01-588 2851)

Hamilton Leasing Ltd, Hamilton House, 80 Stokes Croft, Bristol BS1 3QW (0272 48080)

Highland Leasing Ltd, Elstree House, Elstree Way, Boreham Wood, Hertfordshire WD6 1DW (01-207 4488)

Hill Samuel Leasing Co. Ltd, 100 Wood Street, London EC2P 2AJ (01-628 8011)

ICFC Leasing, 91 Waterloo Road, London SE1 8XP (01-928 7822)

Lease Plan UK Ltd, Pembroke House, Pembroke Road, Ruislip, Middlesex HA4 8NQ (08956 30891)

Lloyds Bowmaker Finance Group, 9–13 Grosvenor Street, London W1X 9FB (01-491 3236) *(A member of the Lloyds Bank Group)*

Lloyds Leasing Ltd, 57 Southwark Street, London SE1 1SH (01-403 1600) *(A member of the Lloyds Bank Group)*

Lombard and Ulster Leasing Ltd, Canada House, 22 North Street, Belfast BT1 1JX (0232 229261) *(A member of the National Westminster Bank Group)*

Lombard North Central plc, Lombard House, Curzon Street, Park Lane, London W1A 1EU (01-409 3434) *(A member of the National Westminster Bank Group)*

Lynn Regis Finance Ltd, 10 Tueay Market Place, King's Lynn, Norfolk PE30 1JL (0553 3465)

National Girobank, City Office, 10 Milk Street, London EC2V 8JH (01-600 6020)

Nordic Leasing Ltd, Nordic Bank House, 20 St Dunstan's Hill, London EC3R 8HY (01-621 1111)

North West Securities Ltd, North West House, City Road, Chester CH1 3AN (0244 315351) *(A member of the Bank of Scotland Group)*

Orient Leasing (UK) Ltd, 14 Curzon Street, London W1Y 7FH (01-499 7121/2)

Orion Leasing Ltd, 1 London Wall, London EC2Y 5JX (01-600 6222)

Premier Computers Ltd, Queen Anne's Court, Windsor, Berkshire SL4 1DG (07535 68133)

Rea Brothers (Leasing) Ltd, King's House, 36–37 King Street, London EC2V 8DR (01-606 4033)

Royal Bank Leasing Ltd, 26 St Andrew Square, Edinburgh EH2 1AF (031-556 8555) *(A member of the Royal Bank of Scotland Group)*

St Michael Finance Ltd, Michael House, Baker Street, London W1A 1DN (01-935 4422)

Scandinavian Leasing Ltd, Scandinavian House, 2–6 Cannon Street London EC4M 6XX (01-236 6090)

Schroder Leasing Ltd, Townsend House, 160 Northolt Road, Harrow Middlesex HA2 0PG (01-422 7101)

Shawlands Securities Ltd, 8 Christchurch Road, Bournemouth BH1 3NQ (0202 295544)

SocGen Lease Ltd, 105–108 Old Broad Street, London EC2P 2HR (01-628 6751)

Standard Chartered Merchant Bank Ltd, Company Secretary, 33–36 Gracechurch Street, London EC3V 0AX (01-623 711)

United Dominions Leasing Ltd, Endeavour House, 1 Lyonsdown Road, New Barnet, Hertfordshire EN5 1HU (01-440 8282) *(A member of the Trustee Savings Bank Group)*

S. G. Warburg & Co. (Leasing) Ltd, 30 Gresham Street, London EC2P
2EB (01-600 4555)
Williams & Glyn's Leasing Co. Ltd, 20 Birchin Lane London EC3P
3DP (01-623 4356) (*A member of the Royal Bank of Scotland Group*)
Yorkshire Bank Leasing Ltd, 2 Infirmary Street, Leeds LS1 1UL
(0532 442511)

Finance Houses   These provide instalment credit for short-
term credit facilities such as hire purchase. Their association
is at 18 Upper Grosvenor Street, London W1X 9PB (01-491 2783)

Finance Houses Association Members, Hire Purchase

Allied Irish Finance Co. Ltd, Wembley Hill House, 10/12 Neeld
Parade, Wembley Hill Road, Wembley HA9 6QU (01-903 1383)
Associates Capital Corporation Ltd, Associates House, PO Box 200,
Windsor, Berkshire SL4 1SW (07535 57100)
AVCO Trust Ltd, PO Box 154, 66–68 St Mary's Butts, Reading,
Berkshire RG1 2PE (0734 584241)
Beneficial Trust Ltd, Prudential House, Wellesley Road, Croydon CR0
9XY (01-680 5096)
Boston Trust & Savings Ltd Boston House, Lower Dagnall Street,
St Albans, Hertfordshire AL3 4PG (0727 32241)
British Credit Trust Ltd, 34 High Street, Slough SL1 1ED (0753 73211)
Cattle's Holdings Finance Ltd, 6 Wolfreton Drive, Springfield Way,
Anlaby, Hull HU10 7BZ (0482 659371)
Chartered Trust plc, 24–26 Newport Road, Cardiff CF2 1SR (0222
484484)
Charterhouse Japhet Credit Ltd, Alexandra Court, 27–29 Denmark
Street, Wokingham, Berkshire RG11 2AY (0734 775221)
Citibank Savings, St Martin's House, Hammersmith Grove, Hammer-
smith, London W6 9HW (01-741 8000)
Commercial Credit Services Ltd Commercial Credit House, Railway
Approach, Wallington, Surrey SM6 0DY (01-773 3111)
First Co-operative Finance Ltd, 1 Balloon Street, Manchester M60
4EP (061-832 3300)
First National Securities Ltd, First National House, College Road,
Harrow, Middlesex HA1 1FB (01-861 1313)
Forthright Finance Ltd, 114–116 St Mary Street, Cardiff CF1 1XJ
(0222 396131)
Forward Trust Group Ltd, Broad Street House, 55 Old Broad Street,
London EC2M 1RX (01-920 0141) (*A member of the Midland Bank
Group*)
HFC Trust Ltd, Cory House, The Ring, Bracknell, Berkshire RG12
1BL (0344 24727)
ICFC Leasing, 91 Waterloo Road, London SE1 8XP (01-928 7822)
Industrial Funding Trust Ltd, 1–3 Worship Street, London EC2A 2HQ
(01-377 1040)
KDB Finance Ltd, Oakvale House, Chatham Road, Sandling, Maid-
stone, Kent ME14 3BQ (0622 57294)
Lloyds Bowmaker Finance Group, 9–13 Grosvenor Street, London
W1X 9FB (01-491 3236) (*A member of the Lloyds Bank Group*)

Lombard and Ulster Ltd, Canada House, 22 North Street, Belfast BT1 1JX (0232 229261) (*A member of the National Westminster Bank Group*)

Lombard North Central plc, Lombard House, Curzon Street, Park Lane, London W1A 1EU (01-409 3434) (*A member of the National Westminster Bank Group*)

Lynn Regis Finance Ltd, 10 Tuesday Market Place, King's Lynn, Norfolk PE30 1JL (0553 3465)

Medens Ltd, 46–50 Southwick Square, Southwick, Brighton BN4 4UA (0273 593358)

Mercantile Credit Company Ltd, PO Box 75, Elizabethan House, Great Queen Street, London WC2B 5DP (01-242 1234) (*A member of the Barclays Bank Group*)

M. H. Credit Corporation Ltd, Director and General Manager, 50 East Street, Epsom, Surrey KT17 1HQ (03727 41011)

North British Finance Group Ltd, King William House, Market Place, Hull HU1 1RB (0482 224181) (*A subsidiary of Yorkshire Bank plc*)

North West Securities Ltd, North West House, City Road, Chester CH1 3AN (0244 315351) (*A member of the Bank of Scotland Group*)

St Margaret's Trust Ltd, The Quadrangle, Imperial Square, Cheltenham GL50 1PZ (0242 36141) (*A member of the Royal Bank of Scotland*)

Security Pacific Trust Ltd, 308–314 Kings Road, Reading, Berkshire RG1 4PA (0734 61022)

Service Finance Corporation Ltd, Winston Hall, 20 East Park Road, Blackburn, Lancashire BB1 8BD (0254 56521/2)

Shawlands Securities Ltd, 8 Christchurch Road, Bournemouth BH1 3NQ (0202 295544)

United Dominions Trust Ltd, Endeavour House, 1 Lyonsdown Road, New Barnet, Hertfordshire EN5 1HU (*A member of the Trustee Savings Bank*)

Vernons Finance Corporation, Vernons Building, Mile End, Liverpool L5 5AF (051-207 3181)

The Wagon Finance Ltd, 3 Endcliffe Crescent, Sheffield S10 3EE (0742 664466)

Yorkshire Bank Finance Ltd, 2 Infirmary Street, Leeds LS1 2UL (0532 442551)

Investment Trust Companies, invest mainly in public equity shares. Some will provide equity finance for private companies, perhaps for amounts down to £25,000.

The Association of Investment Trust Companies is at 6th Floor, Park House, 16 Finsbury Circus, London EC2M 7JJ (01-588 5347)

Their members, that may consider smaller companies are:

Aberdeen Trust plc, Investment Manager, 10 Queen's Terrace, Aberdeen AB9 1QJ (0224 29151)

The Ailsa Investment Trust plc, Chairman, 66 St James's Street, London, SW1A 1NE (01-493 8111)

Alliance Investment plc, The Cardinal Investment Trust plc, The Foreign & Colonial Investment Trust plc, General Investors and Trustees plc, Investment Manager, 1 Laurence Pountney Hill, London EC4R 0BA (01-623 4680)

The Alliance Trust plc, Secretary, Meadow House, 64 Reform Street, Dundee DD1 1TJ (0382 21234)

The Alva Investment Trust plc, Managers, 100 West Nile Street, Glasgow G1 2QU (041-332 8791)

Baillie, Gifford & Co., Secretary, 3 Glenfinlas Street, Edinburgh EH3 6YY (031-225 2581)

City Financial Administration Ltd, Director, Regis House, King William Street, London EC4R 9AR (01-623 4951)

Martin Currie Investment Management Ltd, 29 Charlotte Square, Edinburgh EH2 4HA (031-225 3811)

Edinburgh Fund Managers Ltd, Secretary, 4 Melville Crescent, Edinburgh EH3 7JB (031-226 4931)

The Edinburgh Investment Trust plc, Manager, 3 Charlotte Square, Edinburgh EH2 4DS (031-225 4525)

Electra Investment Trust plc, Chief Executive, Electra House, Temple Place, Victoria Embankment, London WC2R 3HP (01-836 7766)

The First Scottish American Trust plc, The Northern American Trust plc, Belsize House, West Ferry, Dundee DD5 1NF (0382 78244/5)

Fleming Enterprise Investment Trust plc, Fleming Technology Investment Trust plc, Investment Director, 8 Crosby Square, London EC3A 6AN (01-638 5858)

The Fleming Mercantile Investment Trust plc, Investment Director, 2nd Floor, P & O Building, 122 Leadenhall Street, London EC3V 4QR (01-283 2400)

Gartmore Investment Ltd, Secretary, 2 St Mary Axe, London EC3V 8BP (01-623 1212)

Glasgow Stockholders Trust plc, Investment Manager, Ashley House, 181–195 West George Street, Glasgow G2 2HB (041-248 3972)

John Govett & Co. Ltd, Secretary, Winchester House, 77 London Wall, London EC2N 1DH (01-588 5620)

G. T. Management Ltd, 1st Floor, Park House, 16 Finsbury Circus, London EC2M 7DJ (01-628 8131)

Hambros Bank Ltd, Investment Trust Department, 41 Bishopsgate, London EC2P 2AA (01-588 2851)

Hodgson Martin Ventures Ltd (see also under venture capital and other specialist investment institutions).

Ivory & Sime Ltd, Secretary, 1 Charlotte Square, Edinburgh EH2 4DZ (031-225 1357)

Kleinwort Benson Investment Management Ltd, Company Secretary, 20 Fenchurch Street, London EC3P 3DB (01-623 8000)

Lazard Securities Ltd, Secretary, 21 Moorfields, London EC2P 2HT (01-588 2721)

Montagu Investment Management Ltd, Secretaries, 117 Old Broad Street, London EC2N 1AL (01-588 1750)

Murray Johnstone Ltd, Executive Director, 163 Hope Street, Glasgow G2 2UH (041-221 5521)

Rights and Issues Investment Trust plc, Secretary, Dauntsey House, Frederick's Place, Old Jewry, London EC2R 8HN (01-606 2167)

RIT and Northern plc, Chief Executive, 66 St James's Street, London SW1A 1NE (01-493 8111)

Safeguard Industrial Investments plc 2a Pond Place, London SW3 6QJ (01-581 4455)

The Scottish Investment Trust plc, Secretary, 6 Albyn Place, Edinburgh EH2 4NL (031-225 7781)

Scottish National Trust plc, Investment Manager, Ashley House; 181–195 West George Street, Glasgow G2 2HB (041-248 3972)

Scottish Northern Investment Trust plc, Investment House, 6 Union Row, Aberdeen AB9 8DQ (0224 631414)

Second Alliance Trust plc, Secretary, Meadow House, 64 Reform Street, Dundee DD1 1TJ (0382 21234)

Stewart Fund Managers Ltd, 45 Charlotte Square, Edinburgh EH2 4HW (031-226 3271)

Touche, Remnant & Co., Mermaid House, 2 Puddle Dock, London EC4V 3AT (01-236 6565)

The Young Companies Investment Trust plc, Secretaries, 21 New Street, Bishopsgate, London EC2M 4HR (01-623 3000)

Business Expansion Funds There are now over thirty schemes launched. Some will invest in start-ups, even down to £30,000. Some keep registers putting individual investors in touch with specific companies.

So if you are looking for equity capital it will pay to put your proposal forward, even if the fund itself will not invest.

Alpha B E Fund: Laurence Prust & Co, 7–11 Moorgate, London EC2H 6HH (01-606 8811)

Baronsmead B E S Fund: Baronsmead Associates Ltd, c/o Cazenove & Co, 12 Tokenhouse Yard, London EC2 (01-588 2828)

Beechbank Farmers: Hill Samuel & Co. Ltd, 100 Wood Street, London EC2P 2AJ (01-628 8011)

Britannia: Britannia Group of Investment Companies, Salisbury House, 29 Finsbury Circus, London EC2M 5Q1 (01-588 2777)

Buckmaster Development Fund: Buckmaster & Moore, The Stock Exchange, London EC2P 2JT (01-588 2868)

Capital Ventures Ltd, The Priory, 37 London Road, Cheltenham, Glos. GL52 6HA (0242 584380)

Castleforth Fund Managers Limited: The Royal Bank of Scotland Group plc; Laing & Cruickshank, Northern Investment Trust plc, 26 St Andrew Square, Edinburgh EH2 1AF (031-556 8555)

Centreway B E Fund: Midland & Northern, 1 Waterloo Street, Birmingham B2 5PG (021-643 3941)

Charterhouse B E Fund: Charterhouse Japhet plc, 1 Paternoster Row, St Paul's, London EC4M 7DH (01-248 3999)

The Colegrave Fund; The Cave Fund; The Guinness Mahon Fund: Capital Ventures Ltd, 37 London Road, Cheltenham, Glos GL52 6HA

County Bank First B E Fund: County Bank Ltd, 11 Old Broad Street, London EC2N 1BB (01-638 6000)

Creative Capital Fund: c/o The British Linen Bank, 4 Milville Street, Edinburgh EH3 7NZ (031-226 4071)

Electra Risk Capital Funds 1 and 2: Electra Risk Capital plc, Electra House, Temple Place, Victoria Embankment, London WC2R 3HP (01-836 7766)

First and Second Basildon Funds: c/o Laurence Prust, Basildon House, 7–11 Moorgate, London EC2H 6HH (01-606 8811)

First, Second and Third Northern Venture Capital Syndicate: Hodgson Martin Ventures Ltd, 44A St Andrew Square, Edinburgh EH2 2BD (031-557 3560)

Granville Business Expansion Fund: Granville & Co. Ltd, 27–28 Lovat Lane, London EC3 8EE (01-621 1212)

Hill Woolgar B E Fund: Hill Woolgar Fund Managers, 5 Frederick's Place, London EC2 (01-606 2651)

Lazard Development Capital Fund: Lazard Development Capital Ltd, 88 Baker Street, London W1M 1BL (01-588 2721)

Melville Fund: British Linen Bank Fund Managers Ltd, PO Box 49, 4 Melville Street, Edinburgh EH3 7N2 (031-226 4071)

Mercia Venture Capital Scheme: Mercia Venture Capital Ltd, 126 Colmore Row, Birmingham B3 3AP (021-223 3404)

1983 Mercury B E Fund: S. G. Warburg & Co. Ltd, 30 Gresham Street, London EC2 (01-600 4555)

Minster Trust 1983/4 B E FUND: Minster Trust Ltd, Minster House, Arthur Street, London EC4R 9BH (01-623 1050)

Oak Venture Fund: Oak Venture Management Ltd, Virginia House, Cheapside, King Street, Manchester M2 2WG (061-834 8262)

Ravendale Bexfund: Ravendale BEM, 21 Upper Brook Street, London W1 (01-629 5983)

Risk Sheltered Venture Participants Fund: Bean Bower & Co. Ltd, 521/535 Royal Exchange, Manchester M2 7EW (061-832 4405)

Sabrelance B E Fund: Sabreland Ltd, 20/21 Princes Street, Hanover Square, London W1R 8PX (01-493 3599)

Singer & Friedlander B E Fund: Singer & Friedlander Ltd, National Westminster House, 8 Park Row, Leeds LS1 5BQ (0532 438073)

Stewart B E Fund: Rowan Investment Managers, City Gate House, 39–45 Finsbury Square, London EC2A 1JA (01-606 1066)

Valleys of Enterprise Trust Fund: Rossendale and Blackburn Enterprise Trusts, 29 Kay Street, Rawtenstall, Rossendale, Lancashire B4 7LS (0706 229 838)

Wessex Business Expansion Fund: Granville and Co. Ltd, 27–28 Lovat Lane, London EC3R ATB (01-621 1212)

Yordshire Venture Capital Fund: Capital for Companies Ltd, Bridge House, Westgate, Leeds 1 (0532 443794)

Public Sector Finance   There are over 100 different schemes operating, offering a wide range of assistance to new and small businesses. The important services and publications that will keep you up-to-date in this rapidly changing field are listed at the end of this section.

One scheme worthy of special mention is the Enterprise Allowance Scheme, under which 35,000 unemployed people will be encouraged to start their own business. They will be paid £40.00 per week for a maximum of 52 weeks.

The scheme is open to people who:
- are receiving unemployment or supplementary benefit
- have been unemployed for at least 13 weeks
- are over 18 and under retirement age
- have at least £1000 to invest in the business
- agree to work full-time in the business (at least 36 hours per week)

The business you plan to set up should be:
- new – if you have already started your business you are ineligible
- independent – you should not be a subsidiary of or supported by another business
- small – applications will not be accepted from people who intend to employ more than 20 workers during the first three months of the operation

If you think you may be eligible contact your nearest job centre.

Business Competitions   If you want some free money, you could enter a competition. Around a score of these are run each year, sponsored by Banks, Councils, and Big Companies. Prizes can range up to £15,000, and last year nearly £1 million was 'given away'. These organisations have run competitions in the recent past and may do so again.

Aycliffe and Peterlee Development Corporation, *The Make It In Business Award*, Peterlee, Co Durham SR8 1BR (0783 863366)

Bank of Ireland, *Start Your Own Business Competition*, Planning and Marketing Department, Bank of Ireland, Area Office, Donegall Place, Belfast BT1 5BX Prize Fund £30,000

Churchill College, *Churchill College Small Business Prize*, Cambridge CB3 0DS Dr R. C. Campbell. Prizes for 3000 word article of £400.00

Daily Telegraph and National Westminster Bank, *Through, Venture Capital Report*, 2 The Mall, Clifton, Bristol, BS8 4DR (0272 737222) Prizes of £20,000 cash

Design Council, *Design Award for Small Firms*, 28 Haymarket, London SW1Y 4SU (01-839 8000) Prize £10,000

Durham University and Shell UK, *'How's Business' Competition*, Mill Hill Lane, Durham DH1 3LB Three Prizes of £10,000

Greater Manchester Economic Development Corporation, *Greater Manchester Enterprise Competition*, Bernard House, Piccadilly Gardens, Manchester M1 4DD (061-247 3878)

Institution of Mechanical Engineers, *Manufacturing Effectiveness Competition*, 1 Birdcage Walk, London SW1 (01-222 7899) Prize £10,000

Lloyds Bowmaker and Accountancy Age, *National Award for Small Businesses*, Bowmaker House, Christchurch Road, Bournemouth BH1 3L6 Prizes of £25,000 cash

Design Council, *Opportunity Wales*, Pearl Assurance House, Greyfriars Road, Cardiff CF1 3JN Prizes to £4500

Development and Venture Loans and Capital Financial Institutions

There are now a considerable number of financial institutions under this heading. Many are subsidiaries of the clearing banks, insurance companies, pension funds, overseas banks; and even the Bank of England and the Government. Some of them can provide a range of services beyond equity and loan finance, although in general that is their speciality. A brief description of some of these institutions and their activities will give a flavour of the whole sector.

Industrial & Commercial Finance Corporation Ltd (ICFC) is part of Finance for Industry, was formed in 1945 and now claims to be the major source of long-term finance for new and small businesses.

ICFC's shareholders are the Bank of England (15%) and the English and Scottish clearing banks (85%). It operates as a private-sector organisation concerned exclusively with private-sector business. However, it also adminsters funds with low interest rates from the European Investment Bank (EIB), the European Coal and Steel Community (ECSC), and participates in the Government's loan guarantee scheme.

The corporation currently has over £400 million invested in some 3500 companies, £100 million of which was advanced to just over 1000 businesses in the year 1981/1982.

Funds for individual investments range from £5000 up to £2 million. About 70% of these were for £100,000. Indeed about half of all ICFC loans are far less than £50,000.

Finance is provided through long-term loans, or in the form of ordinary or preference shares, or in any combination of these. ICFC takes an equity stake in about a third of cases, the balance being term loans.

ICFC's close relationship with the clearing banks makes the negotiation of security cover easier. This is particularly true when, for example, the clearer already has a charge on the business's assets.

ICFC's main areas of activity are financing new business,

providing funds for expansion, and arranging management buy-outs. ICFC have completed over 200 buy-outs, and claim to be the pioneers of the technique. More recently they have moved into the leasing and hire-purchase fields, with over £24 million provided in 1981/1982. This spread of facilities allows ICFC to propose the best financial package for the company's current needs.

Midland Bank Venture Capital Ltd is, as the name implies, the venture capital area of the Midland Bank. Their operation is similar to the National Westminster Bank's Capital Loan Scheme. The starting threshold for the schemes are £5000 and £10,000 respectively, and both go up to £50,000.

Whilst the Midland Bank take equity and are rewarded with a dividend, the National Westminster Bank offers a loan on which interest is due. It is, however, a loan with a difference: when the loan is taken out, the National Westminster expect to take an option to buy the shares in the company at some future date. The loan itself then ranks next to the shareholders' equity and behind that of the other creditors.

Ranking closer to the shareholders' equity increases the riskiness, as they are paid last. If the money runs out, the shareholders get nothing, then the next in line lose out and so on. So, by placing their loan in this way, the bank has made it virtually capital – hence the term 'capital loan'.

The whole investment and lending field is extremely dynamic, so you would be well advised to look around carefully. Once you find the institution that has a package you like, find its competitor(s), and then you can negotiate the best deal for your needs.

The following list of institutions is not quite exhaustive, but should give you a good cross-section from which to find a source of long-term finance. The guide to their services is simply intended to give you a clue to their policies. The £25,000 threshold was selected because a vast majority of new businesses are not looking for a greater level of external long-term financing. A number of these bodies will help prepare business plans.

Some institutions service only existing businesses with a proven track record. Others insist on an equity stake or board participation either or both of which may be unacceptable. The mark against each institution in the list will give you answers to some of these questions. (See also page 145 for sources of finance for high-tech ventures.)

Institutions giving long-term finance

	Invest less than £25,000	Start-up loans provided	Equity stake not required	May not put a director on your board	No special restrictions	Help with Business Plan
Abingworth (various City Institutions, including Barclays Bank), 26 St James's Street, London SW1A 1HA (01-839 6745) *Contact: P. Dicks*	•					
Alan Patricof Associates Ltd, 24 Upper Brook Street, London W1Y 1PD (01-493 3633)	•					
Allied Combined Trust Ltd (Allied Irish Bank Group), Pinners Hall, 8/9 Austin Friars, London EC2N 2AE (01-920 9155) *Contact: Nicholas Condon*	•	•		•		
Anglo-American Venture Fund Ltd, (See under British Technology Group)						
A P Bank (Norwich Union), 21 Great Winchester Street, London EC2N 2HH (01-638 4711)						
Barclays Development Capital (Barclays Bank), 3rd Floor, Chatsworth House, 66/70 St Mary Axe, London EC3A 8BD (01-623 4321) *Contact: M. R. Cumming*			•		•	
British Railways Pension Funds, 50 Liverpool Street, London EC2P 2BQ (01-247 7600 ext 2784) *Contact: Peter Croft*				•	•	•
British Steel Corporation (Industry) Ltd, (BSC), NLA Tower, 12 Addiscombe Road, Croydon CR9 3JH (01-686 0366)	•	•	•	•		•
British Technology Group (Government financed organisation) 101 Newington Causeway, London SE1 6BU (01-403 6666) *Contact: D. M. James*	•	•	•	•		
Regional Offices:						
North East Regional Enterprise Office, Centro House, 3 Cloth Market, Newcastle-upon-Tyne NE1 1EH (0632 327068)	•	•	•	•		
North West Regional Enterprise Office, 8th Floor, Bank House, Charlotte Street, Manchester M1 4ET (061-236 9800)	•	•	•	•		
Merseyside Regional Enterprise Office, Richmond House, 1 Rumford Place, Liverpool L3 9QY (051-227 1366) *Contact: E. A. Payne*	•	•		•		•
BTG in Scotland, 87 St Vincent Street, Glasgow G2 5TF (041-221 1820)	•	•	•	•		
Anglo American Venture Management Ltd, 8th Floor, Bank House, Charlotte Street, Manchester M1 4ET (061-236 7302)	•	•	•	•		

Western Enterprise Fund Ltd, Shinners Bridge, Dartington, Totnes TQ9 6JE (0803 862271)

Brown Shipley Developments (BS 7 Co.), Founders Court, Lothbury, London EC2R YHE (01-606 9833) *Contact: Mrs C. Howlett*

Business Mortgages & Investment Trust plc, Manager, 1 Marlborough Road, Sherwell, Plymouth PL4 8LP (0752 669286) *Contact: R. V. A. Peachey*

Candover Investments, 4/7 Red Lion Court, London EC4A 3EB (01-583 5090) *Contact: P. Symonds*

Capital Partners International Ltd (private European investors), 40 Edgerton Crescent, London SW3 2EB (01-351 4899) *Contact: C. von Luttitz and P. Cammerman*

Castle Finance (Norwich Union), Norwich Union Insurance Group, Surrey Street, Norwich NR1 3TE (0603 22200)

Cayzer Ltd, Cayzer House, 2–4 St Mary Axe, London EC3A 8BP (01-623 1212) *Contact: Jonathan Hawksley*

Charterhouse Development Capital (Charterhouse Group), 65 Holborn Viaduct, London EC1A 2DR (01-248 4000) *Contact: Richard Duncan*

CIN Industrial Investments (National Coal Board Pensions Funds), 33 Cavendish Square, London W1M 0AL (01-629 6000)

Citicorp Development Capital Ltd, Melbourne House, 33 Melbourne Place, Aldwych, London WC2B 4ND (01-438 1277) *Contact: Jon Moulton*

Clydesdale Bank Industrial Finance Ltd (a member of the Midland Bank Group), 30 St Vincent Place, Glasgow G1 2HL (041-248 7070) *Contact: S. B. Keir*

Commercial Bank of the Near East (private shareholders mainly Greek), 107/112 Leadenhall Street, London EC3A 4AE (01-283 4041) *Contact: R. F. Coyle*

Company	Invest less than £25,000	Start-up loans provided	Equity stake not required	May not put a director on your board	No special restrictions	Help with Business Plan
Western Enterprise Fund Ltd						
Brown Shipley Developments		•	•	•		
Business Mortgages & Investment Trust plc	•	•	•	•		
Candover Investments			•	•		
Capital Partners International Ltd	•	•				
Castle Finance	•		•			
Cayzer Ltd	•	•	•	•	•	
Charterhouse Development Capital	•					
CIN Industrial Investments	•		•	•		
Citicorp Development Capital Ltd			•	•		
Clydesdale Bank Industrial Finance Ltd		•	•			
Commercial Bank of the Near East	•	•	•	•	•	

	Invest less than £25,000	Start-up loans provided	Equity stake not required	May not put a director on your board	No special restrictions	Help with Business Plan
CoSira Council for Small Industries in Rural Areas, 141 Castle Street, Salisbury, Wilts SP1 3TP (0722 336255) *Contact: Info. Officer*	•	•	•	•		•
County Bank, County Bank Ltd, 11 Old Broad Street, London EC2N 1BB (01-638 6000) *Contact: C. A. Bloomfield*	•	•	•	•		
Creative Capital Fund (British Linen Bank), c/o The British Linen Bank Ltd, 4 Melville Street, Edinburgh EH3 7NZ (031-226 4071)	•		•	•		
Dawnay, Day & Co. Ltd, Managing Director, Corporate Finance, Garrard House, 31 Gresham Street, London EC2V 7DT (01-726 4080) *Contact: B. Pincus*	•	•	•	•		
Development Capital Group Ltd, 88 Baker Street, London W1M 1DL (01-486 5021) *Contact: M. Burrell* Also Baker Street Investment Co. plc (BASIC) same address. Also Lazard Development Capital Ltd, 21 Moorfields, London EC2P 2HT (01-588 2721) *Contact: N. Falkner*	•					
East Anglian Securities Trust Ltd, 3 Colegate, Norwich (0603 660931) *Contact: John Cox, Group Secretary*	•	•		•	•	
East of Scotland Onshore plc (ESO plc), 42 Charlotte Square, Edinburgh EH2 4NQ (031-226 4471) *Contact: D. M. Munro*		•		•		
Electra Risk Capital (Electra Investments), Electra House, Temple Place, Victoria Embankment, London WC2R 3HP (01-836 7766) *Contact: O. J. H. Huntsman*	•			•		
English & Caledonian Investment plc, Cayzer House, 2–4 St Mary Axe, London EC3A 8BP (01-623 1212) *Contact: John Parkin*	•					
Equity Capital for Industry (City Institutes), Leith House, 47/57 Gresham Street, London EC2V 7EH (01-606 8513) *Contact: Tony Lorenz*	•			•	•	
European Investment Bank (EEC's long-term bank), 23 Queen Anne's Gate, London SW1H 9BU (01-222 2933) *Contact: Guy Baird*	•	•	•	•		
Exeter Trust Ltd (ET Ltd), Sanderson House, Blackboy Road, Exeter, Devon EX4 6SE (0392 50635)	•	•	•	•	•	

	Invest less than £25,000	Start-up loans provided	Equity stake not required	May not put a director on your board	No special restrictions	Help with Business Plan
F & C Management Ltd, Secretary, 1 Laurence Pountney Hill, London EC4R 0BA (01-623 4680) *Contact: J. Nelson*	•		•	•		
Fountain Development Capital Fund, Hill Samuel & Co. Ltd, 100 Wood Street, London EC2P 2AJ (01-628 8011) *Contact: D. Osborne*				•	•	
Greater London Enterprise Board, 63–67 Newington Causeway, London SE1 (01-403 0300) *Contact: Mrs J. Pegg*	•		•			
Gresham Trust (Gresham), Barrington House, Gresham Street, London EC2Z 7HE (01-606 6474) *Contact: T. A. Jones*			•		•	
Grainger & Co. Ltd, Managing Director, 18 Woodside Terrace, Glasgow G3 7NY (041-332 8751) *Contact: Adam I. Armstrong*	•	•	•	•	•	•
Growth Options Ltd, (Member of National Westminster Bank Group) Business Development Division, 6th Floor, 4 Eastcheap, London EC3M 1JH (01-726 1919) *Contact: Colin Peacock*	•	•		•	•	•
Guidehouse Ltd, 1 Love Lane, London EC2 7JJ (01-606 6321)				•	•	
Hafren Investment Finance Ltd, (Welsh Development Agency) Peal House, Greyfriars Road, Cardiff CF1 3XX (0222 32955)	•	•				
Hambros Advanced Technology Trust, 41 Bishopsgate, London EC2P 2AA (01-588 2851) *Contact: G. J. Chalk, A. Ryden*				•		
Highlands & Islands Development Board (HM Government & Scottish Office), Bridge House, 27 Bank Street, Inverness IV1 1QR (0463 234171)	•	•	•	•	•	•
Industrial and Commercial Finance Corporation (ICFC) (Bank of England & Clearing Banks), 91 Waterloo Road, London SE1 8XP (01-928 7822) *Contact: Miss S. L. Palmer*	•	•	•	•	•	•
Regional Offices:						
Aberdeen, 38 Carden Place, Aberdeen AB1 1UP (0224 638666) *Contact: Keith Mair*	•	•	•	•	•	•
Birmingham, 112 Colmore Row, Birmingham B3 3SA (021-236 9531) *Contact: Peter Williams, Malcolm Gloak*	•	•	•	•	•	•

	Invest less than £25,000	Start-up loans provided	Equity stake not required	May not put a director on your board	No special restrictions	Help with Business Plan
Brighton, 47 Middle Street, Brighton BN1 1AL (0273 23164) *Contact: Paul Waller*	●	●	●	●	●	●
Bristol, Pearl Assurance House, Queen Square, Bristol BS1 4LE (0272 277412) *Contact: John Kingston*	●	●	●	●	●	●
Cambridge, Jupiter House, Station Road, Cambridge CB1 2HX (0223 316568) *Contact: Richard Summers*	●	●	●	●	●	●
Cardiff, Alliance House, 18/19 High Street, Cardiff CF1 3TS (0222 34021) *Contact: Ray Braddick*	●	●	●	●	●	●
Edinburgh, 8 Charlotte Square, Edinburgh EH2 4DR (031-226 7092) *Contact: Jim Martin*	●	●	●	●	●	●
Glasgow, 9th Floor, Pegasus House, 375 West George Street, Glasgow G2 4AR (041-248 4456) *Contact: Sandy Walker*	●	●	●	●	●	●
Leeds, Headrow House, The Headrow, Leeds LS1 8ES (0533 25223) *Contact: David Thorp, Barry Anysz*	●	●	●	●	●	●
Leicester, Abacus House, 32 Friar Lane, Leicester LE1 5QU (0533 25223) *Contact: David Wilson*	●	●	●	●	●	●
Liverpool, Silkhouse Court, Tithebarn Street, Liverpool L2 2LZ (051-236 2944) *Contact: Jeremy Dawson*	●	●	●	●	●	●
London, 91 Waterloo Road, London SE1 8XP (01-928 7822) *Contact: Andrew Holmes, Brian Larcombe, Roger Lawson, Philip Marsden, Donald Workman*	●	●	●	●	●	●
Manchester, Virginia House, 5 Cheapside, Manchester M2 4WG (061-833 9511) *Contact: Peter Folkman*	●	●	●	●	●	●
Newcastle, Scottish Life House, Archbold Terrace, Jesmond, Newcastle-upon-Tyne NE2 1DB (0632 815221) *Contact: Colin Chadburn*	●	●	●	●	●	●
Nottingham, 38 The Ropewalk, Nottingham NG1 5DW (0602 412766) *Contact: Graham Spooner*	●	●	●	●	●	●
Reading, 43/47 Crown Street, Reading RG1 2SN (0734 861943) *Contact: Roger Cottrell*	●	●	●	●	●	●
Sheffield, 11 Westbourne Road, Sheffield S10 2QQ (0742 680571) *Contact: Paul Gilmartin*	●	●	●	●	●	●

	Invest less than £25,000	Start-up loans provided	Equity stake not required	May not put a director on your board	No special restrictions	Help with Business
Southampton, Capital House, 11 Houndwell Place, Southampton SO1 1HU (0703 32044) *Contact: Richard Scrase*	•	•	•	•	•	•
Industrial Common Ownership Finance Ltd, 4 St Giles Street, Northampton NN1 1AA (0604 37563)	•	•	•	•	•	
INTEX Executive (UK) Ltd & E.P. Woods Investments Ltd, Chancery House, 53/64 Chancery Lane, London WC2A 1QU (01-831 6925 or 01-242 2263) *Contact: D. Bruce Lloyd*	•	•	•	•	•	•
Investors in Industry Group plc See 3i Ventures						
James Finlay Corporation (James Finlay Group), 10/14 West Nile Street, Glasgow G1 2PP (041-204 1321)					•	
Larpent Newton & Co. Ltd, 7th Floor, 18 Breams Buildings, London EC4A 1HN (01-831 9991) *Contact: Simon Ashton*	•				•	•
Leisure Development Ltd, Mountbatten House, Victoria Street, Windsor, Berkshire SL4 1HE (07535 57181) *Contact: J. A. Knight*					•	
Leopold Joseph & Sons Ltd, 31–45 Gresham Street, London (01-588 2323) *Contact: Paul Thrussell*	•	•	•	•	•	•
Local Enterprise Development Unit, (Department of Commerce Northern Ireland), Lamont House, Purdys Lane, New Town Breda, Belfast BT8 4TB (0232 691031) *Contact: George Mackey*	•	•	•	•		•
London Wall Industrial Consultants Ltd (Smithdown Investments Ltd), Managing Director, 15 South Molton Street, London W1Y 1DE (01-408 1502) *Contact: G. L. Taylor*	•	•	•	•		•
Lovat Enterprise Fund (National Coal Board Pension Fund & Others), 27/28 Lovat Lane, London EC3R 8EB (01-621 1212) *Contact: Tom Sooke, Guy Eastman, A. Hawksley*						•
Mathercourt Securities Ltd, 1 Lincoln's Inn Fields, London WC2A 3AA (01-831 9001) *Contact: Ian Taylor*	•			•	•	•
Melville Street Investments (Edinburgh) Ltd, (British Linen Bank) 4 Melville Street, Edinburgh EH3 7NZ (031-226 4071)	•					

	Invest less than £25,000	Start-up loans provided	Equity stake not required	May not put a director on your board	No special restrictions	Help with Business Plan
Meritor Investments Ltd, (Midland Bank & Rolls Royce Pension Fund), 22 Watling Street, London EC4M 9BR (01-638 8861)				●		
Midland Bank Industrial Finance (Midland Bank), 22 Watling Street, London EC4M 9BR (01-638 8861) *Contact: J. R. Beevor*		●		●		
Midland Bank Venture Capital Ltd, 22 Watling Street, London EC4M 9BR (01-638 8861) *Contact: B. L. J. Warnes*	●	●		●	●	●
Minster Trust (Minster Assets), Minster House, Arthur Street, London EC4R 9BH (01-623 1050)		●				
Moracrest Investments Ltd (Midland Bank, Prudential and British Gas Pension Fund), 22 Watling Street, London EC4M 9BR (01-638 8861) *Contact: D. G. Hutchings*		●		●		
National Coal Board Pension Fund (NCB), Hobart House, Grosvenor Place, London SW1 (01-629 6000)			●	●	●	●
National & Commercial Development Capital (National & Commercial Banking Group), 88 Baker Street, London W1M 1DL (01-486 5021) *Contact: Mr Robinson*						
National Commercial & Glyns Limited, (Royal Bank of Scotland Group), 26 St Andrew Square, Edinburgh EH2 1AF (031-556 8555) *Contact: James S. Lindsay (ext 2621)*			●	●	●	●
National Westminster Bank, under the terms of Capital Loan Scheme. Approach through local branch but if guidance is needed to identify a suitable branch (01-726 1891)						
Newmarket Co. (1981) Ltd UK Subsidiary Newmarket (Venture Capital) Ltd, 57 London Wall, London EC2 (01-638 4551) *Contact: Tim Earl*						
Noble Grossart Investments (Scottish Investment Institute), 48 Queen Street, Edinburgh EH2 3NR (031-226 7011)	●					
Northern Venture Capital Syndicate, Hodgson Martin Ventures Ltd, 4A St Andrew Square, Edinburgh EH2 2BD (031-557 3560)	●			●	●	

	Invest less than £25,000	Start-up loans provided	Equity stake not required	May not put a director on your board	No special restrictions	Help with Business Plan
Norwich General Trust (Norwich Union Insurance), 12 Surrey Street, Norwich NR1 3NJ (0603 22200) Sister organisation: Castle Finance (01-493 8030)	•	•	•			
Oakwood Loan Finance Ltd (British Technology Group), 101 Newington Causeway, London SE1 6BU (01-403 6666)	•	•	•	•	•	•
P. A. Developments Ltd (P.A. Ltd), Managing Director, Bowater House East, 68 Knightsbridge, London SW1X 7LJ (01-589 7050) *Contact: P. T. Grundy, D. E. Hemming*				•	•	
Pegasus Holdings Ltd (a member of the Lloyds Bank Group), General Manager, 11–15 Monument Street, London EC3R 8JU (01-626 1500 ext 2231)				•		
Rainford Venture Capital, (Pilkington Brothers, Prudential Assurances, Community of St Helen's Trust and others) Prescott Road, St Helen's, Merseyside WA10 ETT (0744 682336)	•	•			•	
Royal Bank Development Ltd (Royal Bank of Scotland), Edinburgh House, 3–11 North St Andrew's Street, Edinburgh EH2 1AF (031-556 8555) *Contact: James S. Lindsay*			•	•	•	•
Safeguard Industrial Investments (Major Insurance & Pension Funds) 2a Pond Place, London SW3 6QJ (01-581 4455) *Contact: H. E. King*				•	•	•
Scottish Allied Investors, James Finlay plc, 10/14 West Nile Street, Glasgow G2 2PT (041-204 1321)						•
Scottish Development Agency (UK Government), 120 Bothwell Street, Glasgow G2 7JP (041-248 2700) *Contact: Mr J. Fisher*. Also: Small Business Division, Roseberry House, Haymarket Terrace, Edinburgh EH12 5EZ (031-337 9595) *Contact: Mr B. Rutherford*	•	•	•	•	•	•
Scottish Offshore Investors (James Finlay & others) 10/14 West Nile Street, Glasgow G2 1PP (041-204 1321)						•
Shandwick Consultants Ltd, Wamford Court, 29 Throgmorton Street, London EC2N 2AT (01-588 4278)						

	Invest less than £25,000	Start-up loans provided	Equity stake not required	May not put a director on your board	No special restrictions	Help with Business Plan

Sharp Unquoted Midland Investment (Legal & General Royal Insurance, Sun Life Assurance & others) Edmund House, 12 Newall Street, Birmingham B3 3ER (021-236 5801)

Small Company Innovation Fund (SCIF) (British Technology Group), 101 Newington Causeway, London SE1 6BU (01-403 6666)

Smithdown Investments (private individuals), 141 North Hyde Road, Hayes, Middlesex (01-573 3783). Also at: 15 South Moulton Street, London W1Y 1DE (01-408 1502) *Contact: G. L. Taylor*

Stewart Fund Managers Ltd, 45 Charlotte Square, Edinburgh EH2 4HW (031-226 3271) *Contact: J. H. Murray*

Thamesdale Investment & Finance Co. Ltd, Manager, Hamblin House, 1–2 Langham Place, London W1N 8HS (01-636 2557)

Thomson, Clive & Partners Ltd (TCP Ltd), 24 Old Bond Street, London W1X 3DA (01-491 4809) *Contact: Mr Fitzherbert*

3i Ventures, 91 Waterloo Road, London SE1 8XP (01-928 7822) *Contact: Vicki Bowman or Geoff Taylor*

Trust of Property Shares Ltd, Managing Director, 6 Welbeck Street, London W1M 8BS (01-486 4684)

UKP-EA Growth Fund Ltd, 7th Floor, 18 Breams Blds, London EC4A 1HN (01-831 9991) *Contact: Mr C. Breese*

Venture Founders Ltd (British Investment Trust), 39 The Green, South Bar Street, Banbury, Oxon OX16 9AE (0295 65881)

Welsh Development Agency (UK Government), Treforest Industrial Estate, Pontypridd, Wales (044 385 2666)

West Midlands Enterprise Board Ltd, Lloyds Bank Chambers, 75 Edmund Street, Birmingham B3 3HD (021-236 8855) *Contact: Mr N. R. Holmes*

Woodside Securities Ltd (See under Grainger & Co. Ltd)

CONTROLLING THE MONEY

Even with a good business plan and a reasonably willing provider of funds, your financial problems are not over. Indeed, in one sense they are just about to begin. Before you take on outside investors or lenders you only have your own money to lose. With other people's funds you will have to give an account of 'stewardship', as well as keep records to meet the needs of the Inland Revenue and the Customs and Excise.

In fact, you will probably have to show how you propose to control the finances of the business before anyone will part with any funds. They will want to know how you will keep track of the business.

There are four elements to successful financial control. Firstly, you should plan ahead. Have a budget that sets out clearly what you expect to happen over the next 12 months, month by month. This should be expressed in terms of money out and money in.

Secondly, you need management information that shows you what has actually happened at each stage in your plan.

Thirdly, you need to compare your budget or plan with the actual position.

Fourthly, you need to be able to use this comparison to take action – to control the business.

The single greatest reason that new and small businesses go out of business is lack of good financial control.

Choosing a Book-keeping and Accounting System

In order to get financial control you need to install a book-keeping system BEFORE you START TRADING. This should tell you how much you have in the bank; how much you owe; and how much you are owed (A bare minimum). All the systems reviewed can do this.

The following is a brief survey of some of the more 'popular' book-keeping systems. They are divided into five categories: 'shoe boxes'; do-it-yourself books; halfway houses; accountants only and computer based systems.

'Shoe box' systems This is for the simplest businesses, which need relatively little financial control beyond cash, bank accounts, accounts payable and accounts receivable.

At its simplest you need four shoe boxes, a bank paying-in book and a cheque book (the last two can tell you how much you have in the bank). You keep two boxes for unpaid invoices (one for sales, one for purchases, services and so on). You transfer the invoices into the other two boxes (one for sales, one for purchases, etc) when each invoice is paid. By adding all the invoices in one box (sales, unpaid invoices) you can find out how much you are owed, and by adding another (purchases, unpaid) you find out how much you owe.

You keep every record relating to the business, too.

This is a perfectly adequate system unless you need some form of cash control or some profit information and you need it fast. It is, however, not too good on credit control.

Essentially, this system is only for the smallest firms.

The DIY System These are normally hardback, bound books with several sections to them, each part ruled and already laid out for the entries. Each one has a set of instructions and examples for each section.

All the systems mentioned here have some advantages and disadvantages in common:

Advantages: Each one tries to assist the small business person by allowing some measures of financial control, especially over cash and bank balances. They almost always include VAT sections and Profit and Loss sections. They aim, in the large part, to make an accountant unnecessary, or at least to minimise your expense in that area.

Disadvantages: None of these systems will work unless it is kept up regularly – which means weekly at a minimum, and preferably daily. As a drawback this cannot be over-emphasised. Unless you currently regularly keep a diary, these books are probably not for you. If not kept properly, they can cost you more in accountancy fees rather than less. Other disadvantages are that they often assume some prior knowledge from the user, even though they give instructions. Their instructions sometimes leave much to be desired relying largely on worked examples that are difficult to follow. They compartmentalise people and business, and they tend to ignore such expenses as 'use of home as office' (for example, home telephone bills) many of which may be tax allowable. Finally, many people also find that they would rather not use these books as the basis for dealing with their Inspectors of Taxes, and would rather have their accountants do this. In these circumstances you are going to need an accountant anyway, and your inspector is much more likely to pay attention to him in any case.

The following tables show the basic information for some of the most common systems, and the conclusions as to their relative usefulness.

Finco Small Business Book-keeping System This system, at £35, may seem dear, but it has two years' supply of forms (compared to others which provide only one), and gives a large amount of financial control for a relatively small sum. This is first choice.

The Kalamazoo Set Up is the second choice. It would have been first choice had it not cost £92. You probably also need training to be able to use it, even with their book as support. It has been chosen because it can give the best financial control, if used properly. In addition, it can save time through being a single-write system (entering up to three records simultaneously).

DIY Accounting Books, Comparison Table

Name and availability	Approx. Cost	Financial Control Provided	Records Provided
Ataglance Ataglance Publications, 16 Sawley Avenue, Lytham St Annes, Lancs FY8 3QL (0253 727107)	£ 4	Bank	Payments, Receipts, VAT
Collins Self Employed Account Book W. H. Smith and other stationers	£ 9	Bank, debtors, creditors	Payments, receipts, VAT, subcontract
Collins Complete Traders Account Book W. H. Smith and other stationers	£ 9	Bank	Payments, receipts, VAT
Evrite Traders Account Book Commercial stationers or Evrite Publishing Co. Ltd, Hill Street Chambers, St Helier, Jersey, Channel Islands	£ 8	Bank debtors	Payments, receipts VAT
Finco Small Business Bookkeeping System Casdec Ltd, 11 Windermere Avenue, Garden Farm Estate, Chester-le-Street, Co. Durham DH2 3DU (0385 882906)	£35	Bank, cash, debtors, creditors, wages	Receipts, payments, sales, purchases, payroll, VAT
Kalamazoo Set Up Pack Kalamazoo Business Systems, Mill Lane, Northfield, Birmingham B31 2RW (021-475 2191)	£92	Bank, cash, debtors, creditors	Receipts
Simplex 'D' Cash Book Commercial stationers or George Viner (Dist. Ltd), Simplex House, Mytholmbridge Mills, Mytholmbridge, Holmfirth, Huddersfield HD7 2TA	£ 3	Bank, cash	Receipts, payments, profit and loss

General Comments

Ataglance: Few instructions, mostly related to VAT. But if you are thinking of opening a fish and chip shop they have prepared a special book-keeping ledger, costing £1.98.

Collins Self Employed Accounts Book: This seems to be aimed at sub-contractors and is reasonably comprehensive, but the instructions may call for prior knowledge.

Collins Complete Traders Account Book: For retail outlets only. The instructions are somewhat limited.

Evrite Traders Account Book: Brief instructions. Relies on worked examples. Assumes prior knowledge. Debtor control in total only (not by individual customers).

Finco Small Business Book-keeping System: Simple instructions, two years' supply of record sheets, loose-leaf. This is more easily adaptable to any business (there is less compartmentalisation), and gives detailed control over individual amounts outstanding, both receivable and payable. Because it is loose-leaf, your accountant can take the relevant records without depriving you of your control. It can also be used in conjunction with your accountant's minicomputer.

Kalamazoo Set Up: This is the most comprehensive system (as well as the most expensive). It provides everything that all other systems give you, two years' supply of records (loose-leaf) and a debtors/creditors ledger. Your £92 also buys you a basic book-keeping book which gives information on how to keep it up (and why you need to). The book is by John Kellock. A Practical Guide to Good Book-keeping and Business Systems, and is available separately.

Simplex 'D' Cash Book: This is the best known of this type of book. Its instructions are short, and it uses worked examples. There are separate books for VAT and wages, as well as a separate book, *Simplified Book-keeping for Small Business* at £3.00.

Halfway House Systems   The halfway-house systems lie between a simple DIY system and an 'accountant only' system. Pre-printed stationery tends to be used, but in loose-leaf form. They are more flexible than the DIY, and tend to be cheaper than using an accountant only. However, they do require some knowledge on the part of the person who keeps the books. Again, this need not be daunting, as your accountant can probably train you (or your office girl or boy) to keep them up. The major problem is that you need your accountant before you can use your records for more advanced financial control.

There are two common half-way house systems on the market: Twinlock and Kalamazoo.

Twinlock available at commercial stationers or the publishers at Twinlock Ltd, 36 Croydon Road, Beckenham, Kent BR3 4BH (01-650 4818)

Kalamazoo only from the publishers at Kalamazoo Ltd, Northfield, Birmingham B31 2WR (021-475 2191)

At the basic level the two systems seem remarkably similar, both in cost and financial control. The minimum systems will cost £200 to £400 and Kalamazoo offer training with their product. Both are single-write systems (where one writing can enter up to three records). You should talk to your accountant before installing one.

Accountant Only Systems The accountant only systems are those for the more complex (possibly larger) small businesses, and will be designed by your accountant. They often need trained book-keepers to run them. However, the training period can be relatively short (anything from one day upwards). The book-keeper handles the routine matters, and your accountant the non-routine.

Computer Systems There are many small computer systems that will carry out the book-keeping and accountancy functions needed by a small business. But, like all systems, they are only as good as the quality of information put in. The other major problems with computer systems are these: selecting the equipment in a market with many models with claimed advantages; making sure that you have the necessary extra equipment; making sure that you have the software (programmes) capable of handling your information and record needs; and, finally, ensuring that you can use the machine efficiently. This is fine for the enthusiast, but others tend to get lost in the jungle. It would certainly be safest to start off with an accounting book-keeping practice who have their own computer based system. This is also an area in which your nearest Micro-System's Centre could be of help (see page 158).

![black bar]

ORGANISATIONS AND PUBLICATIONS FOR FINANCE

Organisations

The Association of Authorised Public Accountants, 10 Cornfield Road, Eastbourne, East Sussex BN21 4QE (0323 641515/5)

The Association for Bankrupts, 4 Johnson Close, Lancaster. *Contact: John McQueen.* They try to give support to those who cannot cope with bankruptcy

The Association of Certified Accountants, 29 Lincoln's Inn Fields, London WC2A 3EE (01-242 6855)

Banking Information Service, 10 Lombard Street, London EC3V 9AR (01-626 8486)

British Insurance Association, Business Finance Information, Aldermary House, 10–15 Queen Street, London EC4 (01-248 4477) Some Insurance Companies will provide long term loans, mortgage loans, sale and leaseback arrangements and equity finance for new businesses. Contact the Secretary for more information

British Venture Capital Association, Leith House, 47–57 Gresham Street, London EC2V 7EH (01-606 8513) Acts as a clearing house for people wishing to make contact with a member venture capital company

Corporation of Mortgage, Finance & Life Assurance Brokers Ltd, PO Box 101, Guilford, Surrey GU1 2HZ (0483 35786/39126)

Credit and Guarantee Insurance Co. Ltd, Colonial House, Mincing Lane, London EC3R 7PN (01-626 5846) Provides domestic trade credit and can cover commercial risk for exporters

Export Credits Guarantee Department (ECGD), **Headquarters:**
Aldermanbury House, Aldermanbury, London EC2P 2EL (01-606 6699)

Regional Offices:

City of London, PO Box 46, Clements House, 14–18 Gresham Street, London EC2V 7JE (01-726 4050)

Belfast, River House, High Street, Belfast BT1 2BE (0232 231743)

Birmingham, Colmore Centre, 115 Colmore Row, Birmingham B3 3SB (021-233 1771)

Bristol, 1 Recliffe Street, Bristol BS1 6NP (0272 299971)

Cambridge, Three Crowns House, 72–80 Hills Road, Cambridge CB2 1NJ (0223 68801)

Cardiff, Crown Building, Cathays Park, Cardiff CF1 3NH (0222 824100)

Croydon, Sunley House, Bedford Park, Croydon, Surrey CR9 4HL (01-680 5030)

Glasgow, Fleming House, 134 Renfrew Street, Glasgow G3 6TL (041-332 8707)

Leeds, West Riding House, 67 Albion Street, Leeds LS1 5AA (0532 450631)

Manchester, Townbury House, Blackfriars Street, Salford N3 5AL (061-834 8181)

Government Assistance Information Service (GAINS), Bank of Scotland, Uberior House, 61 Grassmarket, Edinburgh EH1 2JF (031-229 2555) You put forward your project and the Bank runs it through their GAINS computer programme. This produces a printout listing the government assistance you may be eligible for. The service is free

Institute of Chartered Accountants in England & Wales, PO Box 433, Chartered Accountants Hall, Moorgate Place, London EC2P 2BJ (01-628 7060) The society provides a free booklet, *You Need a Chartered Accountant*

The Institute of Chartered Accountants of Scotland, 27 Queen Street, Edinburgh EH2 1LA (031-225 5673)

The Institute of Cost and Management Accountants, 63 Portland Place, London W1N 4AB (01-580 6542)

Institute of Credit Management, Easton House, Easton on the Hill, Stamford, Lincolnshire PE9 3NH (0780 56777) The professional body for people interested in credit management. Produce a quarterly journal, *Credit Management*

Intex Executives (UK) Ltd, Chancery House, 53–64 Chancery Lane, London WC2A 1QU (01-831 6925) Obtain funds for selected small scale new enterprises

Local Councils, can very often provide small sums of start up finance, or money for market research. Contact your local councils' Industrial Development Officer

London Enterprise Agency, 'The Marriage Bureau', 69 Cannon Street, London EC4 5AB (01-236 2676) Puts people with funds (amongst other resources) in contact with people with business ideas

The London Society of Chartered Accountants, 38 Finsbury Square, London EC2A 1PX (01-628 2567) The society will put you in touch with an accountant if you ring its client information service

Management Buy-out Association, The Chairman, 71 Padleys Lane, Burton Joyce, Notts NG14 5BW (060 231 2499) Founded in 1982 by George Bloomfield, to offer impartial advice to managers contemplating 'buy-outs'

National Association of Pension Funds, Sunley House, Bedford Park, Croydon CR0 0XF (01-681 2017) Some pension funds are prepared to invest in promising small businesses. The Secretary of this association could put you in touch with such a fund

PRESTEL CITISERVICE, Page 5991, provides a weekly update of important changes in the pattern of government finance for new projects. (Service provided by Peat, Marwick & Mitchell & Co.)

Regional Development Grants Office, Department of Industry, Room 431, Kingsgate House, 66–74 Victoria Street, London SW1E 6SJ (01-212 6712)

Small Business Management Resources Ltd, 13 Great Stuart Street, Edinburgh EH3 7TP (031-225 3567) Financial and Management Advisers

The Society of Company & Commercial Accountants, 11 Portland Road, Edgbaston, Birmingham B16 9HW (021-454 8791/2)

The Stock Exchange, The Quotations Department, Throgmorton Street, entrance, PO Box 119, London EC2P 2BT (01-588 2355) Can give advice on USM listing and other equity finance.

Regional Offices:

Belfast, 10 High Street, Belfast BT1 2BP (0232 21094)

Birmingham, Margaret Street, Birmingham B3 3JL (021-236 9181)

Dublin, 28 Anglesea Street, Dublin 2 (0001 778808)

Glasgow, 69 St George's Place, Glasgow G2 1BU (041-221 7060)

Liverpool, Silkhouse Court, Tithebarn Street, Liverpool L2 2LT (051-236 0869)

Manchester, 4 Norfolk Street, Manchester M2 1DS (061-833 0931)

Trade Indemnity plc, Trade Indemnity House, 12–34 Great Eastern Street, London EC2A 3AX (01-739 4311) Branches at: Birmingham,

Bradford, Bristol, Glasgow, Leicester, Manchester, Newcastle and Reading. Provides domestic trade credit and can cover commercial risk for exporters

Venture Capital (Business Start-up) Services, Suite 127, Pall Mall, Trafalgar Square, London WC2N 5EP (01-979 5593) Financial adviser specialising in start-ups

Publications

An Insight into Management Accounting, by John Sizer, published by Penguin, 1980. A good all round book for people with some financial knowledge. (01-351 2393) Price: £3.50

Blays Guide to Regional Finance for Industry & Commerce provides a guide to financial assistance available in Assisted Areas, Enterprise Zones, Inner Urban Areas, New Towns and EEC Assistance, throughout the UK. The guide was published in March 1982, costs £65, which includes a 12-month subscription to their up-dating service. Blays Guides Ltd, Churchfield Road, Chalfont St Peter, Bucks SL9 9EW (0753 889241)

Cash Flow – The Key to Business Survival published in November 1981 by Dun and Bradstreet Ltd, 26/32 Clifton Street, London EC2P 2LY (01-377 4377) It has a foreword by Sir Kenneth Cork, who should know the answers if anyone does.

Cost Accounting, by A. J. Tubb, first edition 1977, published by Teach Yourself Books, Hodder & Stoughton, Mill Road, Dunton Green, Sevenoaks, Kent TN13 2YA (0732 450111) A very useful book for anyone starting up a manufacturing business who wants to see how to set prices at a level that will not lose money. Price: £2.95

Directory of Grant Making Trusts, 1983 (new edition March 1985), published by Charities Aid Foundation, 48 Pembury Road, Tonbridge, Kent TN9 2JD (0732 356323) Lists 2300 grant making bodies, their objectives, policies and criteria. The purpose of the directory is mainly to help charities in their search for funds. In certain cases these trusts will make grants to individuals, very often in the educational fields.

Finance for New Projects in the UK, a guide to Government Grants, published by Peat, Marwich, Mitchell & Co., 1 Puddle Dock, Blackfriars, London EC4V 3PD (01-236 8000) September 1983 – 7th Edition. Price: £1.00

Financial Incentives and Assistance for Industry – A Comprehensive Guide, published by Arthur Young, McClelland Moore & Co, Rolls House, 7 Rolls Buildings, Fetter Lane, London EC4A 1NL (01-831 7131)

Financial Management for the Small Business, published in May 1984 by Kogan Page, 120 Pentonville Road, London N1 (01-837 7851) This is the Daily Telegraph Guide. It is a comprehensive guide to preparing profit and loss accounts, cash flow statements, financial control ratios, costing, pricing and break-even. Price: £5.95

Guide to Running a Small Business, (The Guardian), published by Kogan Page Ltd, 120 Pentonville Road, London N1 (01-837 7851) 4th edition May 1984. Price: £5.95

Guide to Venture Capital in the UK, by Lucius Carey, published December 1983 by Venture Capital Report, 2 The Mall, Clifton, Bristol BS8 4DR (0272 737222) A review of venture capital sources – in some detail. Price: £10.20

How to Collect Money That Is Owed to You, by Mel Lewis, published by McGraw-Hill Book Co. UK Ltd, Shoppenhangers Road, Maidenhead, Berks SL6 2QL (0628 23431) April 1982. This is a lively short book on the techniques which any business person can use to achieve prompt payment of money owed to him or her. It has a guide to credit insurance and factoring, examples of contracts, invoices and collection letters, lists of useful addresses and organisations and a guide to telephone collection techniques. It will be of great interest to the smaller trader. Price: £9.50

How to Survive the Recession, by Jeremy Prescott, published by the Institute of Chartered Accountants, 1982. Despite the slightly off-putting title, this book sets out in clear, simple and concise terms what basic business controls you need, how to get them and how to use them. It is written by someone at ICFC who has seen many companies experiencing financial problems that came directly from lack of financial control. Price: £4.95

Industrial Aids in the UK March 1984, a Businessman's Guide, by Gasa Walker and Kevin Allen, available from Centre for Study of Public Policy, McLance Building, University of Stra-thclyde, Glasgow G1 1XQ (041–552 4400) Describes 134 different industrial aids in a 'user orientated' manner. Price: £8.95

Leasing, by T. M. Clark published by McGraw Hill. This is a comprehensive guide to all aspects of leasing as a means of financing capital equipment. It traces the development of leasing to its present importance in finance for industry. It also deals with the principles of finance leasing, taxation, government policy, aspects of law and insurance, and with risks and problems involved, offering suggestions for evaluating and accounting for leasing transactions. Price: £15.00 Out of print at present – new edition approx. Autumn 1984.

Management Accounting, by Brian Murphy, second edition 1978, published by Teach Yourself Books, Hodder & Stoughton, Mill Road, Dunton Green, Sevenoaks, Kent TN13 2YA (0732 450111) A good book for beginners, it covers all the essential stages of the business plan, together with the elements of financial control systems. Price: £2.50

Management Buy-Outs and Incentive Financing, from Dept. MB, The Daily Telegraph, 135 Fleet Street, London EC4P 4BL (01-353 4242) Price: £5.50 post free in UK

Management Buy Outs, special report No. 115. Published by Economist Intelligence Unit, Spencer House, 27 St Jame's Place, London SW1A 1NT (01-493 6711) April 1984. It covers the commercial, financial, legal and tax aspects of completing a management buy-out

Money for Business, July 1983 edition, published by the Bank of England, Economic Intelligence Department, London EC2R 8AW (01-606 4444) A first class and comprehensive guide. Price: £2.50

A Practical Guide to Good Book-keeping and Business Systems, by John Kellock, published in 1982 by Business Books Ltd, 17–21 Conway Street, London W1P 6JD Written to accompany the Kalamazoo Book-keeping system for small businesses, but a valuable read on its own

Official Sources of Finance and Aid for Industry in the UK, by the National Westminster Bank Ltd, June 1984, available from Market Intelligence Unit, 41 Lothbury, London EC2P 2BP (01-725 1000) Price: £5.50

Raising Finance, The Guardian Guide by Clive Woodcock, published by Kogan Page, 120 Pentonville Road, London N1 (01-837 7851) First edition 1982. A very good and comprehensive book, but I should wait for the second edition. Price: £4.95

Small Business Software Series, McGraw–Hill, Shoppenhanger Road, Maidenhead, Berks SL6 2QL Six programs and accompanying books to explain different aspects of financial management. Prices from around £30.00.

UK Venture Capital Journal, Venture Economics, 37 Thames Road, London W4 3PF (01-995 7619) Price: £195 for annual subscription which includes 4 issues quarterly

Understanding Company Financial Statements, January 1982, by R. H. Parker, published by Penguin, 530 Kings Road, London SW10 (01-351 2393) It is an excellent, simple guide to the balance sheet and other important financial statements. Price: £2.95

Venture Capital Report, 2 The Mall, Clifton, Bristol BS8 4DR
(0272 737222) The report puts people with funds in touch with
people with business proposals

Working for Yourself (Daily Telegraph), by Godfrey Golzen,
Chapter 3, published by Kogan Page Ltd, 120 Pentonville
Road, London N1 9JN (01-837 7851) Latest edition August 1984.
Price: £4.95

*Zoning in on Enterprise, a Businessman's Guide to the Enter-
prise Zones*, by David Rodrigues and Peter Bruinvels, published
by Kogan Page, 120 Pentonville Road, London N1 9JN (01-837
7851) 1982. Price: £11.95

BUSINESS AND THE LAW

Everyone is affected in some way or another by the law, and ignorance does not form the basis of a satisfactory defence. Businesses are also subject to specific laws, and a particular responsibility rests on those who own or manage them. Although an indication of some of the main legal implications is given here, there is no substitute for specific professional advice.

A lawyer will probably know the way in which your particular business will be affected by the laws mentioned here and other laws. In the area of taxation an accountant can earn his fee several times over. Other organisations and professionals who can advise you are listed at the end of each sub-section. Most of the organisations in the first section of this book will be able to give you some guidance in this field.

This section identifies and outlines some ninety of the services or publications that can help you get a better understanding of business and the law. These include a number of relatively inexpensive advisory services. One, for example, will provide, for as little as £18 per annum, on-the-spot advice, back-up research and information, as well as insurance cover to provide professional accounting or legal advice to defend yourself if you are prosecuted under one of the many relevant business laws.

Five comprehensive books that cover most of the field are listed below. Start with *Law for the Small Business*, that should meet most needs.

Commercial Law, by R. M. Goode, August 1982, published by Penguin, 536 King's Road, London sw10 (01-351 2393) Price: £14.95

The Consumer, Society and the Law, by Gordon Borne and Aubrey L. Diamond, fourth edition, 1981, published by Penguin, 536 King's Road, London sw10 (01-351 2393) Price: £3.50

Know Your Law, by Greville Janner, 1984, published by Business Books Ltd, 25 Highbury Crescent, London n5 1rx (01-387 2811) First in a series of four books

Law for the Small Business, The Daily Telegraph Guide, by Patricia Clayton. Moving into its fourth edition, it covers the whole field well. Price: £4.50

Principles of Business Law, by Brian Ball and Frank Rose, published by Sweet and Maxwell, 11 New Fetter Lane, London EC4 (01-583 9855) A rather more technical 550 pages. Price: £9.85

CHOOSING THE FORM OF THE BUSINESS

At the outset of your business venture you will have to decide what legal form your business will take. There are four main forms that a business can take, with a number of variations on two of these. The form that you choose will depend on a number of factors: commercial needs, financial risk and your tax position. All play an important part. The tax position is looked at in more detail later, but a summary of the main pros and cons is set out on page 267.

Sole Trader   If you have the facilities, cash and customers, you can start trading under your own name immediately. Unless you intend to register for VAT, there are no rules about the records you have to keep. There is no requirement for an external audit, or for financial information on your business to be filed at Companies House. You would be prudent to keep good books and to get professional advice, as you will have to declare your income to the Inland Revenue.

Without good records you will lose in any dispute over tax. You are personally liable for the debts of your business, and in the event of your business failing your personal possessions can be sold to meet the debts.

A sole trader does not have access to equity capital, which has the attraction of being risk-free to the business. He must rely on loans from banks or individuals and any other non-equity source of finance.

Partnership   There are very few restrictions to setting up in business with another person (or persons) in partnership. Many partnerships are entered into without legal formalities and sometimes without the parties themselves being aware that they have entered a partnership.

All that is needed is for two or more people to agree to carry on a business together intending to share the profits. The law will then recognise the existence of a partnership.

Most of the points raised when considering sole tradership

264

apply to partnerships. All the partners are personally liable for the debts of the partnership, even if those debts were incurred by one partner's mismanagement or dishonesty without the other partner's knowledge.Even death may not release a partner from his obligations, and in some circumstances his estate can remain liable.Unless you take 'public' leave of your partnership by notifying your business contacts, and advertising retirement in *The London Gazette*, you will remain liable indefinitely. So it is vital before entering a partnership to be absolutely sure of your partner and to take legal advice in drawing up a partnership contract.

The contract should cover the following points.

Profit Sharing, Responsibilities and Duration This should specify how profit and losses are to be shared, and who is to carry out which tasks. It should also set limits on partner's monthy drawings, and on how long the partnership itself is to last (either a specific period of years or indefinitely, with a cancellation period of, say, three months).

Voting Rights and Policy Decisions Unless otherwise stated, all the partners have equal voting rights. It is advisable to get a definition of what is a policy or voting decision, and how such decisions are to be made. You must also decide how to expel or admit a new partner.

Time off Every partner is entitled to his share of the profits even when ill or on holiday. You will need some guidelines on the length and frequency of holidays, and on what to do if someone is absent for a long period for any other reason.

Withdrawing Capital You have to decide how each partner's share of the capital of the business will be valued in the event of either partner leaving or the partnership being dissolved.

Acountancy Procedure You do not have either to file accounts or to have accounts audited. However, it may be prudent to agree a satisfactory standard of accounting and have a firm of accountants to carry out that work. Sleeping partners may well insist on it.

Sleeping Partners A partner who has put up capital but does not intend to take an active part in running the business can protect himself against risk by having his partnership registered as a limited partnership.

Limited Company The main distinction between a limited company and either of the two forms of business already discussed is that it has a legal identity of its own separate from the people who own it. This means that, in the event of liquidation, creditors' claims are restricted to the assets of the company. The shareholders are not liable as individuals for the business debts beyond the paid-up value of their shares. This applies even if the shareholders are working directors, unless the company has been trading fraudulently.

Other advantages include the freedom to raise capital by selling shares and certain tax advantages.

The disadvantages include the legal requirement for the company's accounts to be audited by a chartered or certified accountant, and for certain records of the business trading activities to be filed annually at Companies House.

In practice, the ability to limit liability is severely restricted by the requirements of potential lenders. They often insist on personal guarantees from directors when small, new or troubled companies look for loans or credits. The personal guarantee usually takes the form of a charge on the family house. Since the Boland Case, in 1980, unless a wife has specifically agreed to a charge on the house, by signing a Deed of Postponement, then no lender can take possession in the case of default.

A limited company can be formed by two shareholders, one of whom must be a director. A company secretary must also be appointed, who can be a shareholder, director, or an outside person such as an accountant.

The company can be bought 'off the shelf' from a registration agent, then adapted to suit your own purposes. This will involve changing the name, shareholders and articles of association.

Alternatively, you can form your own company, using your solicitor or accountant.

Co-operative   There is an alternative form of business for people whose primary concern is to create a democratic work environment, sharing profits and control. If you want to control or substantially influence your own destiny, and make as large a capital gain out of your life's work as possible, then a co-operative is not for you.

The membership of the co-operative is the legal body that controls the business, and members must work in the business. Each member has one vote, and the co-operative must be registered under the Industrial and Provident Societies Act, 1965, with the Chief Registrar of Friendly Societies. (See also pages 90–100.)

Forms of business: pros and cons

Form	Advantages	Disadvantages
Sole trader	Start trading immediately; Minimum formalities; No set-up costs; No audit fees; No public disclosure of trading information; Pay Schedule 'D' Tax; Profits or losses in one trade can be set off against profits or losses in any other area; Past PAYE can be clawed back to help with trading losses.	Unlimited personal liability for trading debts; No access to equity capital; Low status public image; When you die, so does the business.
Partnership	No audit required, though your partner may insist on one; No public disclosure of trading information; Pay Schedule 'D' tax.	Unlimited personal liability for your own and your partners' trading debts (except sleeping partners); Partnership contracts can be complex and costly to prepare; Limited access to equity capital; Death of a partner usually causes partnership to be dissolved.
Limited company	Shareholders' liabilities restricted to nominal value of shares; It is possible to raise equity capital; High status public image; If income is substantial, corporation tax for small business is lower than equivalent income-tax rate; The business has a life of its own and continues with or without the founder.	Directors are on PAYE; Audit required; Trading information must be disclosed; Suppliers, landlords and banks will probably insist on personal guarantees from directors (except for government loan guarantee scheme); You cannot start trading until you have a certificate of incorporation.

Useful Organisations and publications

Accountancy bodies are listed, together with their services, on page 256.

Organisations

The Chief Registrar of Friendly Societies, 15–17 Great Marlborough Street, London w1v 2az (01-437 9992)

The Companies Registration Office, Crown Way, Maindy, Cardiff cf43 (0222 388588) and for Scotland: 102 George Street, Edinburgh eh2 (031-225 5774) Both provide information and guidance on registering a limited company

The Law Society, 113 Chancery Lane, London wc2 (01-242 1222). Their Legal Aid Department publishes booklets which give the name, address and telephone number of solicitors in each area, indicating their area(s) of specialisation, e.g. consumer law, landlord–tenant problems, employment or business problems generally, including tax and insolvency. They are available at libraries or Citizens' Advice Bureau, and are solely concerned with solicitors willing to undertake legal aid work.

Alternatively the society will simply give you the names of some firms of solicitors in your area.

Publications

How to Form a Private Company, by Alec Just, 29th ed. published by Jordans, Jordan House, 47 Brunswick Place, London n1 (01-253 3030) Price £3.25

Solicitors Regional Directory from the Law Society, 1st ed. 1984. Lists solicitors with details of their specialities, region by region.

THE BUSINESS NAME

The main consideration in choosing a business name is its commercial usefulness. You want one that will let people know as much about your business, its products and services as possible. Since 26 February 1982, when the provisions of the Companies Act, 1981 came into effect, there have been some new rules that could influence your choice of name.

Firstly, anyone wanting to use a 'controlled' name will have to get permission. There are some 80 or 90 controlled names that include words such as 'International', 'Bank' and 'Royal' This is simply to prevent a business implying that it is something that it is not.

Secondly, all businesses that intend to trade under names

other than those of their owner(s) must state who does own
the business and how the owner can be contacted. So, if you are
a sole trader or partnership and you only use surnames with
or without forenames or initials, you are not affected.
Companies are also not affected if they simply use their full
corporate name.

If any name other than the 'true' name is to be used, then
you must disclose the name of the owner(s) and an address in
the UK to which business documents can be sent. This information has to be shown on all business letters, on orders for goods
and services, invoices and receipts, and statements and
demands for business debts. Also, a copy has to be displayed
prominently on all business premise. The purpose of the Act is
simply to make it easier to 'see' who you are doing business
with.

Useful Organisations and Publications

Department of Trade, Guidance Notes Section, 55 City Road,
London EC1Y 1BB, produce two useful free publications, notes
for guidance on *Disclosure of Business Ownership* and *Control
of Business Names*.

Jordan's Business Information Service, Jordan House,
Brunswick Place, London N1 6EE (01-253 3030) Under the 1982
Company Rules, the onus is on you to object within twelve
months to someone else using your business name. For around
£30 per annum, Jordans will alert you if anyone tries to register
a company using your trading name.

PROTECTING YOUR IDEAS

Patent law can give you temporary protection for technological
inventions. The registration of a design can protect the appearance or shape of a commercial product; copyright protects
literary, artistic or musical creations and, more recently,
computer programmes; trade marks protect symbols, logos and
pictures.

The period of the protection which these laws can give vary
from five years, for the initial registration of the design, to
fifty years after your death, for the copyright on an 'artistic'
work. The level and scope of protection varies considerably,
and is in the process of change. A flurry of activity in the late
seventies set UK patent law on a course to harmonise it with
EEC law. So, for example, it is now possible with a single patent
application made in the UK to secure a whole series of protec-

tions throughout Europe. The Patent Co-operation Treaty will eventually extend that protection to the USA, USSR and Japan.

In practice, however, defending 'intellectual' property is an expensive and complex process for a new or small business.

Patent Protection This covers inventions which are 'truly' novel and are capable of industrial application. Scientific or mathematical theories and mental processes are included in the long lists of unpatentable items. Ideas that may encourage offensive, immoral or antisocial behaviour are also excluded.

Obviously, it is important to establish first whether or not your idea is really new. With 20 million or so registered patents it is possible that the idea belongs to someone else, even if it is not being used. A search of patents granted and applied for will give you some idea of the activity in your area of interest. This can be done by studying abstracts of published specifications. These are classified under 400 main headings, with 6000 'catch' words to guide you. You can get details of the classification key free of charge from the Patent Office. You can then either subscribe to a weekly service that selects and supplies patent specifications under the classification that interests you, or you can carry out a search yourself at the Science Reference Library. Otherwise, you could get a Patent Agent both to investigate your claim and look after your interests.

If the patent is good, then you may be able to sell a 'licence' to manufacture under that patent, or even sell the patent rights. This may not be as profitable as setting up a business to exploit the patent yourself, but that task may be beyond your means anyway. It would be unwise to discuss your patent in any detail with any other person until you have either registered it or got him to sign a non-disclosure agreement. This will prevent him from making use of your idea, if you do not reach an agreement with him.

Registering Designs The shape, design or decorative features of a commercial product may be protectable by registering the design. The laws exclude any shape or appearance which is dictated solely by the production function. Thus, in order to be registerable, a design must be new or original, never published before or, if already known, never applied to the type of product you have in mind.

Unlike patent searches, which you can do yourself, as a design application you have to entrust this work to the officials at the Design Registry.

Copyright The copyright laws protect you from the unlicensed copying of 'original' creative works. Some skill and judgement are required to qualify a work for protection, but the 'originality' itself may be of quite a low order.

The categories protected by copyright include literary works (including not just the obvious, but such items as rules for games, catalogues, advertising copy, etc); dramatic and musical works; artistic works, including maps, graphs, photographs; films, TVs and radio programmes, records, tapes and so on.

While the work remains unpublished no legal steps need to be taken to protect it. Once it is published, all you need do is to add a copyright line to each copy of the work. This must take the form © BARBARA UPCHURCH 1984. If you want to record the date on which a work was completed this can be registered for a fee with The Registrar, Stationers Hall. It is a fairly unusual thing to do, only important if you expect an action for infringement.

It is generally illegal to reproduce copyright work, but less than a substantial part may be used without infringement. The use of the word 'substantial' is more likely to mean important rather than large, though it is up to the courts to interpret.

Trade Marks A trade mark is a symbol by which the goods of a particular manufacturer, merchant or trader can be identified by customers. This can take the form of a word, a signature, a monogram, a picture or logo – or any combination of these. If you have been using an unregistered trade mark so extensively that it is clearly associated in your customers' mind with your brand or product, then you may have acquired a 'reputation' in that mark, which gives you rights under common law.

Otherwise the process of registration is similar to that of patents. First a search must be carried out either in person or having a Trade Mark Agent to act for you. Then, using forms from the Trade Marks Registry, you can apply for registration. Once your application has been accepted by the registry it is advertised in a weekly journal, *The Trade Marks Journal.* If this raises no objections the mark is officially registered. Once your mark is registered you have the right to bring an 'infringement' action if anyone else uses your trade mark. The courts also recognise that a trade mark acts as a protection to your customers. When they ask for a branded product by its trade mark, they can be confident of getting your product and not a 'pirate' product.

Organisations

The British Technology Group, 101 Newington Causeway, London SE1 6BU (01-403 6666) Publicity Department. They can help you with the exploitation and development of your invention. They have financial, technological and commercial resources and expertise.

The Chartered Institute of Patent Agents, Staple Inn Buildings, High Holborn, London WC1V 7PZ (01-405 9450) They can put you in contact with a Patent Agent in your area, and advise on the subject generally.

The Design Council, 28 Haymarket, London SW1 4DG (01-839 8000)

The Design Registry, Room 1124A, 11th Floor, State House, High Holborn, London WC1R 4TP For textiles: The Design Registry, Baskerville House, Browncross Street, New Bailey Street, Salford M3 5PU. Free pamphlet from either office of the Design Registry, *Protection of Industrial Designs*, June 1981, 17 pages. (There are Design Agents, but no register as such, although either a Patent Agent or a Trade Mark Agent will be able to act for you.)

Institute of Information Scientists, Harvest House, 62 London Road, Reading RG1 5AS (0734 861345) Formed in 1978, it represents the interests of searchers, and has a register of searchers who will carry out literature searches in the patent field.

The Institute of Inventors, 19 Fosse Way, Ealing, London W13 0BZ (01-998 3540)

The Institute of Patentees and Inventors, Staple Inn Buildings, 335 High Holborn, London WC1V 7PZ (01-242 7812) The Institute looks after the interest of patent holders and inventors. They can provide useful advice and guidance on almost every aspect of 'intellectual' property. (More information on this society on page 149.)

The Institute of Trade Mark Agents, 69 Cannon Street, London EC4N 5AB (01-833 0875) The institute can put you in contact with a trade mark agent in your area, and advise you on the subject generally.

Legal Protection Group, 30 High Street, Sutton, Surrey (01-661 1491) Can provide insurance at Lloyds, to cover some of the cost of fighting a patent infringer. The worst infringers of small inventors ideas are international companies who bank on the little man being too poor to embark on a costly legal action, so this £250,000 (approx) a year insurance policy could be worthwhile.

The Patent Office, 25 Southampton Buildings, London WC2A

1AY (01-405 8721) Open to the public 10.00–16.00, Monday to Friday. They produce free pamphlets. *Basic Facts* is a simple introduction for inventors and gives a brief rundown on what patents are, how they are obtained and the kind of protection they give. *Introducing Patents* – a guide for inventors is aimed at inventors who need more detailed information. It should help them to decide whether to patent, and if so, whether to apply for a national patent or to try one of the international routes. Some idea of the costs and the various pitfalls that can occur are given. *How to prepare a UK Patent Application* is only for those who have decided to apply for a patent without professional help, at least in the initial stages, but is not intended as a substitute for the services of a patent agent. This booklet is only available on personal request from the Patent Office.

The Registrar, Stationers Hall, Ludgate Hill, London EC4M 7DD (01-248 9279) Accepts and advises on the registration of copyrights.

The Register of Trademarks, State House, Rm 1302, 13th Floor, Red Lion Street, Holborn, London WC1 (01-403 8721) Open 10.00 to 16.00. Monday to Friday. Accepts and advises on the registration of trade marks. Free pamphlet, *Applying for a Trademark*, April 1980, 24 pages.

The Science Reference Library, 25 Southampton Buildings, London WC2A 1AY (01-405 8721) The Library houses all patent details, and is open from 9.30 to 20.00, Monday to Friday, and on Saturday from 10.00 to 13.00. More details of this library are given in the section on specialist libraries (page 185).

Provincial Patent Libraries:
Belfast, Central Library, Royal Avenue, Belfast BT1 1EA (0232 43233)
Birmingham, Patent Department, Paradise Circus, Birmingham B3 3HQ (021-235 4537/8)
Glasgow, Mitchell Library, Science & Technology Department, North Street, Glasgow G3 7DN (041-221 7030)
Leeds, Central Library, Calverley Street, Leeds LS1 3AB (0532 462006)
Liverpool, Patent Library, Science & Technology Library, William Brown Street, Liverpool L3 8EW (051-207 2147)
Manchester, Patent Library, Central Library, St Peter's Square, Manchester M2 5PD (061-236 9422)
Newcastle-upon-Tyne, c/o Business & Technology Library, Central Library, Newcastle, PO Box MC NE99 1MC (0632 610691 ext 38 or 44)
Sheffield, Commerce and Technology Library, Surrey Street, Sheffield S1 1XZ (0742 734742)

Apart from UK, European, PCT and US specifications, the holdings of these libraries are varied. It is wise to check whether their holdings cover your requirements before going to the library.

Publications

The Inventors Information Guide, by T. S. Eisenschitz and J. Phillips, Fernsway Publications, 5 Crane Grove, London N7 A very useful 90 pages covering the whole field – lots of useful addresses too. Price: £2.95

Patents, Trade Marks, Copyright & Industrial Designs, by T. A. Blanco White and Robin Jacob, in the Concise College Texts Series, published by Sweet and Maxwell, 11 New Fetter Lane, London EC4 (01-583 9855). Price: £5.50

A Practical Introduction to Copyright, by Gavin McFarlane, January 1982, published by McGraw-Hill Book Co. (UK) Ltd, Shoppenhangers Road, Maidenhead, Berkshire SL6 2QL (0628 23431) In July 1981 the UK Government published a Green Paper on copyright for public discussion. It is based on the recommendations of the Copyright Committee of 1977, and, if it is finally accepted, radical changes in the law are likely. The book represents, clearly and simply, the effect of today's laws and the probable effect of the new provisions. The existing Copyright Act of 1956 with all its later amendments, plus the salient points of the Green Paper, are included. Price: £15.95

See also section on Financial and Advisory Services for Technology, and 'Training to use Patents' in the Other Small Business Courses section (pages 145 and 331).

PREMISES

Buying or leasing a business premises entails a number of important and often complex laws affecting your decisions. To some extent these laws go beyond the scope of the physical premises, into areas such as opening hours and health and safety. (See also Property Services, pages 70–4.)

Planning Permission   An important first step is to make sure that the premises you have in mind can be used for what you want to do. There are nearly a score of different 'use classes', and each property should have a certificate showing which has been approved. The classes include retail, offices, light industrial, general industrial, warehousing and various special classes.

Certain changes of class do not need planning permission – for example, from general industrial to light industrial. Also, changes of use within a class – say, from one type of shop to another – may not need planning permission.

In November 1980 a circular was issued to local authorities

by the Department of the Environment. The circular stated, amongst other things that if a business premises was put to a 'non-conforming' use, that was not in itself sufficient reason for taking enforcement action or refusing planning permission. Permission should only be refused where the business would cause a nuisance or a safety or health hazard.

Once you have taken on a premises, then the responsibilities for 'conforming' fall on your shoulders, so take advice.

Building Regulations Even if you have planning permission, you will still have to conform to building regulations. These apply to the materials, structure and building methods used, in either making or altering the premises. So if you plan any alterations you may need a special approval.

The Lease Before taking on a lease, look carefully at the factors below.

Restrictions If you are taking on a leasehold property, then you must find out if there are any restrictions in the lease on the use of the property. Often shop leases have restrictions protecting neighbouring businesses. The lease will often stipulate that the landlords cannot 'unreasonably' withhold consent to a change in use. He may, however, insist on the premises being returned in its original shape before you leave.

Repairs Most leases require the tenant to take on either internal repairing liability or full repairing leases. Resist the latter if at all possible, particularly if the property is old. If you have to accept a full repairing lease, then it is *essential* to get a Schedule of Condition. This is an accurate record of the condition of the premises when you take it over. It is carried out by your own and the landlord's surveyor. It is one expense you may be tempted to forgo – don't.

Rent Reviews However long (or short) your lease is, it is likely that a rent review clause allowing rent reviews every three to seven years will be included. Look very carefully at the formulas used to calculate future rents.

Security of Tenure The Landlord and Tenant Act, 1954, protects occupiers of business premises. When your lease ends you can stay on at the same rent until the steps laid down in the Act are taken. These steps are fairly precise, and you would be well advised to read the Act and take legal advice.

You will get plenty of warning, as the landlord must give you six months' notice in writing, even if you pay rent weekly. The landlord cannot just ask you to leave. There are a number of statutory grounds for re-possession. The two main types of grounds are, Firstly, that you are an unsatisfactory tenant, an allegation you can put to the test in court; or secondly, that the landlord wants the premises for other purposes. In that case you must be offered alternative suitable premises. These are obviously matters for negotiation, and you should take advice as soon as possible.

Health and Safety at Work   Whatever legal form your business takes (if you are a sole trader for instance, or a limited company) you will be responsible for the working conditions of all your premises. Your responsibility extends to people who work on those premises, to visitors and to the public. If you have more than five employees, you will have to prepare a statement of policy on health, and let everyone who is working for you know what that policy is. You may also be required to keep records of such events as the testing of fire alarms and accidents.

The main laws concerned are the Health and Safety at Work Act (1974), the Offices, Shops and Railway Premises Act (1963), and the Factories Act (1961). Employers' liability is based on the common law, and your responsibilities can be extensive. A catalogue listing more than 2000 relevant publications covering health and safety legislation is available from HMSO.

The Acts cover, among other matters, fire precautions and certificates; general cleanliness and hygiene; means of access and escape; machine and equipment safety; work-space; temperature; noise; welfare; catering arrangements; security of employees' property; toilet and washing facilities; protective clothing; the appointment of safety representatives and committees; and minimum insurance cover.

Special Trades   Restaurants and all places serving food, hotels, pubs, off-licences, employment agencies, nursing agencies, pet shops and kennels, mini cabs, taxis, betting shops, auction sale rooms, cinemas and hairdressers are among the special trades that have separate additional regulations or licensing requirements.

Your local authority Planning Department will be able to advise you of the regulations that apply specifically to your trade. It would be as well to confirm the position whatever you planned to do. They can also tell you if any local by-laws are in force which could affect you.

Opening Hours   Sunday trading and opening hours may be the subject of local restrictions. Once again, your local authority Planning Department will be able to advise you whether or not special local rules apply.

276

Advertising Signs There are some restrictions on the size and form that the name or advertising hoarding or your premises can take. A look around the neighbourhood will give you an idea of what is acceptable. If in doubt, or if you are going to spend a lot of money, take advice.

Organisations

British Institute of Interior Design, Lenton Lodge, Wollaton Hall Drive, Wollaton, Nottingham (0602 221255)

The Building Centre 26 Store Street, London WC1E 7BT (01-637 1022) This has the most extensive library and information service on the whole building field, including building regulations and sources of professional advice. Their free information service (01-637 8361) will provide answers to almost any building problem.

Regional centres are at the addresses below:

The Building Centre, Stonebridge House, Colston Avenue, The Centre, Bristol BS1 4TW (0272 22953)

Northern Counties Building Information Centre, c/o NFBTE, Green Lane, Durham DH1 3JY (0385 62611)

The Building Centre, 3/4 Claremont Terrace, Glasgow G3 7PF (041-332 7399)

The Building Centre, 113/115 Portland Street, Manchester M1 6FB (061-236 9802)

The Building Materials Information Service, 22 Broadway, Peterborough PE1 1RU (0733 314239)

The Building Research Establishment, Bucknalls Lane, Garston, Watford WD2 7JR; or Scottish Laboratory, Department of Environment, Kelvin Road, East Kilbride, Glasgow

CoSIRA, see also CoSIRA (page 17), who have advisers who can help with both building regulations and planning permission.

Design Selection Service, The Design Council, 28 The Haymarket, London SW1Y 4SU (01-839 8000) They offer a service to people looking for a designer to deal with the inside of a premises.

The Environmental Health Department will be able to advise you on particular problems related to using premises for serving or producing food or drink.

The Federation of Master Builders, 33 John Street, London WC1N 2BB (01-242 7583)

Health and Safety Executive, 1 Long Lane, London SE1 4PG (01-407 8911) Apart from supplying pamphlets and reference on the various regulations, they can put you in contact with the nearest of their 21 area office information services. In each of these offices there are groups of Inspectors specialising in the specific local industries and their problems.

Incorporated Association of Architects and Surveyors, Jubilee House, Billing Brook Road, Weston Favell, Northants (0604 404121)

Local authorities Each has a Planning Department, which can give information and opinions on planning applications and other matters relating to your premises; a Building Control Department, covering building regulations; an Environmental Health Department, covering health and safety at work; and an Industrial Liaison Department, giving general advice to encourage industrial development.

Rating Surveyors Association, c/o Montague, Evans & Son, Awdry House, 11 Kingsway, London WC2 (01-240 2444)

Rating and Valuation Association, 115 Ebury Street, London SW1 9QT (01-730 7258/7250/7359)

Royal Institute of British Architects, 66 Portland Place, London W1N 4AD (01-580 5533) They have a clients advisory service in London and nine provincial centres. They can deal with all types of enquiry by phone, letter, or even a personal call. The Advisory Service direct line is 01-323 0687.

Royal Institute of Chartered Surveyors, 12 Great George Street, London SW1P 3AD (01-222 7000)

Royal Town Planning Institute, 26 Portland Place, London W1N 4BE (01-636 9107) A contentious or complex planning application may need the services of a planning consultant – perhaps from this institute. They produce a list of consultant firms throughout the UK. Otherwise, 'local knowledge' is the best source of a good surveyor or an architect who will be able to manage most planning and building regulation matters for you.

Publications

Land Law, by W. Swinfen Green and N. Henderson, in the Concise College Text series, published by Sweet and Maxwell, 11 New Fetter Lane, London EC4 (01-583 9855) Fourth edition 1980. Price: £8.00

Selwyn's Law of Health and Safety at Work, Butterworths Bookshop, 9–12 Bell Yard, Temple Bar, London WC2 (01-405 6900) Price: £7.95

Planning Directory and Development Guide, contains information on planning in central government in the UK, planning consultants, and organisations concerned with or related to the planning process. The information on local government, which forms the bulk of the book, includes names and addresses of chief officers in charge of planning, the names and functions of key planning staff and a summary of the development opportunities existing in each authority area, plus a list of publications relating to planning in the area. Available from Ambit Publications Ltd, 6A College Green, Glos GL1 2LY

TRADING LAWS

Once you start trading, whatever the legal form of your business, you will have certain obligations to your customers. These are contained in a number of legal acts and some of these are described below.

Sale of Goods Act, 1979 This Act states that the seller has three obligations. Firstly, the goods sold must be of merchantable quality – that is, reasonably fit for their normal purpose. Secondly, those goods must also be fit for any particular purpose made known to the seller. This makes you responsible for your advice, if, for example your customer asks you whether or not a product will perform a particular job. Thirdly, the goods sold must be as described. This would include the colour or size of the goods concerned.

The Food and Drugs Act, 1955 This Act makes it a criminal offence to sell unfit food; to describe food falsely; or to mislead people about its nature, substance or quality. This regulation covers food wherever it is sold, manufactured, packed, processed or stored for sale.

Prices Act, 1974 The Prices Act enables the Government to require prices to be displayed and to control how they are displayed. This requires restaurants, pubs, cafe and petrol stations to display their prices.

Trade Descriptions Acts, 1968 and 1972 The Acts make it a criminal offence for a trader to describe his goods falsely. These acts cover such areas as declared car mileage on second-hand cars and statement of the country of manufacture on jeans.

Unsolicited Goods and Services Act, 1971 The Act makes it an offence to send goods without a customer's order, in the hope that they will then buy them.

Weights and Measures Acts, 1963 and 1979 The Acts make

it an offence not to mark the quantity (weight, volume or, in a few cases, the number) on the containers of most packaged grocery items and many other items.

Unfair Contract Terms Act, 1977 The Act prevents firms from escaping their responsibilities by using 'exclusion clauses' or disclaimers, such as statements saying 'articles left at owners' risk'. The onus is on the trader to prove that his exclusions are fair and reasonable in the circumstances. The notice itself is not enough.

Organisations

Advertising Standards Authority, 2–16 Torrington Place, London WC1E 7HN (01-580 5555) Will put you right on your legal responsibilities if you advertise your goods for sale.

Environmental Health Departments of the local authority will be able to provide advice on all matters to do with food, drink and hygiene.

Office of Fair Trading, Fields House, Breams Building, London EC4A 1PR (01-242 2858) The office provides useful booklets on most aspects of trading law from the consumer's point of view. Their booklet *Fair Deal* provides a very good brief summary of the main laws affecting traders. It is 68 pages long and costs 95p.

The Small Claims Procedure is a useful low cost way to collect money owed to you. Small debts of up to around £500 can be sued for with the minimum of formalities. All County Courts keep a stock of an invaluable book, Small Claims in the County Court, written in layman's language. A companion volume, Enforcing Judgements in the County Court is also available.

Trading Standards Department of the local authority can also give you advice on acceptable trading behaviour.

Publications
Consumer Law For the Small Business, by Patricia Clayton, published in 1983 by Kogan Page Ltd, 120 Pentonville Road, London N1 (01-837 7851) Covers: Trade Descriptions Acts, Supply of Goods and Services, Hath and Safety, Cash and Credit, Quality and Quantity, Unfair Trading and Codes of Practice. Price: £5.95

A Guide to Successful Debt Collecting, by Andrew Theunissen, published in 1983 by Jordan & Son Ltd, 15 Pembroke Road, PO Box 260, Bristol BS99 7DX (0272 732861) Topics covered include: Checking the credit-worthiness of customers, and methods of collecting overdue accounts; Examples of letters and court forms; How to issue proceedings avoiding errors debtors can use to their advantage; Which court to use; When to involve a solicitor; How to conduct a hearing before the registrar; Ways of enforcing a judgement; The new County Court Rules; Addresses of registries, etc; Check-list of steps and actions. Price: £4.00

Hotel and Catering Law, by Davis Field, in the Concise College Texts series, published in 1982 by Sweet & Maxwell. Price £5.65

How to Collect the Money That Is Owed to You, by Mel Lewis, published by McGraw-Hill Book Co. (UK) Ltd, Shoppenhangers Road, Maidenhead, Berks SL6 2QL (0628 23431) 1982. Written for managers in small-to-medium sized businesses, it contains a wealth of ideas for getting payment. It also has a guide to credit insurance and factoring, examples of contracts invoiced and collection letters, lists of useful organisations and addresses and a guide to telephone collection techniques. Price: £9.50

Legal Aspects of Marketing, by John Livermore, 4th edition 1984, published by William Heinemann Ltd, 10 Upper Grosvenor Street, London W1X 9PA Price: £10.95

Managing Your Business, a Complete Guide, published by Stoddart & Co., Bakers Farm, Stapleton, Nr Presteigne, Powys LD8 2LS (0544 260098) Is a loose-leaf and regularly updated publication, covering most aspects of running a business. It has useful sections on law related to sale of products and services.

Product Liability, by Dewis, Hutchins and Madge, published by William Heinemann Ltd, 10 Upper Grosvenor Street, London W1X 9PA (01-493 4141) Price: £11.50

Sale of Goods and Consumer Credit, by A. P. Dobson, in the Concise College Texts series, published by Sweet and Maxwell, 11 New Fetter Lane, London EC4 (01-583 9855) New edition July 1984

EMPLOYING PEOPLE

Apart from the problems of finding the right people to work in your business, and making sure that the conditions under which they will have to work are satisfactory, you may have other responsibilities. Examples are given below.

Terms of Employment Within thirteen weeks of starting to work for you, you have to give people a written set of terms of employment. These terms will cover pay, holidays, sick pay and overtime commitments and pay.

Notice of Lay-offs Once an employee has worked for you for over four weeks, they are entitled to at least one week's notice of dismissal. They are also entitled to guaranteed pay up to five days in any three months if you decide to either lay them off or to put them on short time.

Discrimination You cannot discriminate against anyone on colour or racial grounds. The same protection applies to married people. If you employ five people, including part-timers, then you cannot discriminate against them or against any applicant for a job, on the grounds of their sex. There are further laws and protections covering, amongst other considerations, pregnancy, disabled people, minimum wages, union recognition, discipline and wrongful dismissal.

You may find it useful to join an organisation such as the Institute of Personnel Management or the Industrial Society, who can give you timely and cost-effective advice in this field. Such organisations keep absolutely up to date with all the many changes in this field of legislation, a task beyond the resources of most small firms with other, more pressing problems.

Useful Organisations
Advisory, Conciliation and Arbitration Service (ACAS), 11–12 St James Square, London SW1Y 4LA (01-214 6000) Although you mainly hear of ACAS in big public disputes between unions and their management, a large part of their work is concerned with preventing disputes and dispensing information. Nearly a quarter of their 12,500+ (p.a) advisory visits are to firms with fewer than 50 employees.

They offer advice on recruitment and selection, payment systems and incentive schemes, manpower planning, communications and consultations, collective bargaining and so on.

They also produce free advisory booklets on job evaluation, introduction to payment systems, personnel records, labour turn-over, absence, recruitment and selection and introduction of new employees. Their Regional Offices are at:

Northern Region, Westgate House, Westgate Road, Newcastle-upon-Tyne NE1 1TJ (0632 612191) Cumbria, Tyne and Wear, Cleveland, Northumberland and Durham

Yorkshire and Humberside Region, Commerce House, St Alban's Place, Leeds LS2 8HH (0532 431371) North Yorkshire, South Yorkshire, Humberside and West Yorkshire

London Region, Clifton House, 83–117 Euston Road, London NW1 2RB (01-388 5100)

South-east Region, Clifton House, 83–117 Euston Road, London NW1 2RB (01-388 5100) Cambridgeshire, Norfolk, Suffolk, Oxfordshire, Buckinghamshire, Bedfordshire, Hertfordshire, Essex, Berkshie, Surrey, Kent, Hampshire (except Ringwood), Isle of Wight, East Sussex, West Sussex

South-west Region, 16 Park Place, Clifton, Bristol BS8 1JP (0272 211921) Gloucestershire, Avon, Wiltshire, Cornwall, Devon, Somerset, Dorset, Ringwood

Midlands Region, Alpha Tower, Suffolk Street, Queensway, Birmingham B1 1TZ (021-643 9911) Northamptonshire (except Corby), Shropshire, Staffordshire (except Burton-on-Trent), West Midlands, Hereford and Worcester, Warwickshire

North-west Region, Boulton House, 17–21 Chorlton Street, Manchester M1 3HY (061-228 3222) Lancashire, Cheshire, High Peak District of Derbyshire, Greater Manchester

Midlands Region, Nottingham Office, 66–72 Houndsgate, Nottingham NG1 6BA (0602 415450) Derbyshire (except High Peak District), Nottinghamshire, Leicestershire, Corby, Lincolnshire, Burton-on-Trent

Merseyside Office, Cressington House, 249 St Mary's Road, Garston, Liverpool L19 0NF (051-427 8881)

Scotland, Franborough House, 123–157 Bothwell Street, Glasgow G2 7JR (041-204 2677)

Wales, Phase 1, Ty-Glas Road, Llanishen, Cardiff CF4 5PH (0222 762636)

Employees' Protection Insurance Services Ltd, 30 High Street, Sutton, Surrey SM1 1NF (01-661 1491) They also under-take commercial legal proceedings insurance, provide legal fees for the protection of patents, copyright, registered designs and trade marks, and in respect of 'passing off' actions.

Industrial Participation Association, 85 Tooley Street, London SE1 2QZ (01-407 90833 or 01-403 6018) The association is concerned with bringing all parties in industry together in a common effort to promote employee participation in a practical and realistic way.

The Industrial Society, Peter Runge House, 3 Carlton House Terrace, London SW1Y 5DG (01-839 4300) The society campaigns for the involvement of people at work and argues that increased involvement means greater efficiency and productivity.

Annual membership costs £105 for companies with up to 250 employees, and this gives access to an extensive range of serv-ices and publications.

Their Information and Personnel Advisory Services depart-ment on ext 249/237 will answer enquiries from members on any subject in the field of personnel management and industrial relations. Most enquiries are dealt with the same day, though complicated questions that have to be referred to their legal advisers or the medical advisory panel may take about ten days. Of particular interest to small business is the Personnel Advisory Service, which can, in effect, provide you with all the services of a professional personnel manager, from recruitment to redundancy. The fees for this service are about £1800 per annum.

Institute of Personnel Management, IPM House, 35 Camp Road, Wimbledon sw19 4uw (01-946 9100) The institute has 20,000 individual members, and has extended its service to businesses through its Company Service Plan. The cost of membership for a company employing up to seventy-five people would be £80.00 per annum, an entrance fee of £17.25 plus VAT. This would give access to the institute's library, publications, conferences and seminars, and, more importantly, it would allow use of the Information and Advisory Service. This service is staffed by a small team of multi-disciplines specialists, including a legal adviser, who is a barrister at law. They can answer or find answers to, most problems in this field.

Enquiries can be made by letter, telephone or a personal visit between 09.00 and 17.00 daily, Monday to Friday.

Interestingly enough, of the 800 or so enquiries they handle each month, pay and conditions of employment account for half, followed by employment law, employee relations and then training.

Job Centres As well as providing you with employees, your local Job Centre can also advise you on most aspects of employment law, or at any rate introduce you to other local organisations which can help.

See also National Federation of Self Employed and Small Business; and Alliance of Small Firms and Self Employed People (pages 76 and 80).

Publications

An A–Z of Employment and Safety Law, by Peter Chandler, published by Kogan Page Ltd, 120 Pentonville Road, London N1 (01-837 7851) 528 pages, hardback. Covers all aspects of current employment and health safety law. Price: £16.95

Contract, by F. R. Davies, in the Concise College Texts series, published by Sweet and Maxwell, 11 New Fetter Lane, London EC4 (01-583 9855) Price: £4.25

Employing People, Guidance for Those Setting Up in Business for the First Time, is a free booklet, from the Department of Industry, Small Firms Service. Your local office can be reached on Freephone 2444.

Janner's Guide to the Law on Sick Pay and Absenteeism, by Greville Janner QC, MP, published by Business Books, Hutchinson House, 17–21 Conway Street, London W1P 6JD A comprehensive and definitive work bringing together all the details of this complex area. Price: £9.95

Labour Law, by C. D. Drake, published in the Concise College Texts series by Sweet and Maxwell, 11 New Fetter Lane, London EC4 (01-583 9855) It is a sort of A-level crammer which covers all the ground and case law illustrations. Price: £7.50

The Law on Unfair Dismissal, Guidance for Small Firms, by Joan Henderson, Free from Job Centres, Employment Offices, Unemployment Benefit Offices and Department of Industry Small Firms Centres.

The Statutory Sick Pay Wall Chart, available from Dilloway and Son, Highcroft, Gunhouse Lane, Stroud, Glos GL5 2BD (04536 3387) Designed to help small companies to set up their own system to operate the rules embodied in the Social Security Departments Employers Guide to SSP. Sickness and Absence Forms £2.95 per hundred. Assessment and Calculation forms £3.95 per hundred. Price: £10.00 + VAT

INSURANCE

Insurance forms a guarantee against loss. You must weigh up to what extent your business assets are exposed to risk and what effect such events could have on the business if they occurred. Insurance is an overhead, producing no benefit until a calamity occurs. It is therefore a commercial decision as to how much to carry, and it is a temptation to minimise cover. You must carry some cover, either by employment law, or as an obligation imposed by a mortgager.

You will have to establish your needs by discussing your business plans with an insurance broker. Make sure you know exactly what insurance you are buying; and, as insurance is a competitive business, get at least three quotations before making up your mind.

Employer's Liability   You must carry at least £2 million cover to meet your legal liabilities for death or bodily injury incurred by any employee during the course of business. In practice, this cover is usually unlimited, with the premiums directly related to your wage bill.

Personal Accident Employer's liability only covers those accidents in which the employer is held to be legally responsible. You may feel a moral responsibility to extend that cover to anyone carrying out an especially hazardous task. You may also have to cover your own financial security, particularly if the business depends on your being fit.

Public Liability This protects employers against legal liability for death or injury to a third party on their property. These events can occur through defects in Your premises, negligent acts by your employees or from liabilities arising from the product that you market.

Professional Liability Solicitors, accountants and management and computer consultants are obvious examples. Anyone involved in giving professional advice should consider their possible liability arising from wrongful advice and negligence to their client.

Business Premises, Plant and Equipment obviously need cover. There are, however, a number of ways of covering them. 'Reinstatement' provides for full replacement cost, whilst 'indemnity' meets only the current market value of your asset, which means taking depreciation off first. There are other things to consider too. Removal of debris, architect's fee, employees' effects and (potentially the most expensive of all) local authorities sometimes insist that replacement buildings must meet much higher standards than the ones they replace.

Stock From raw materials through to finished goods stock is as exposed as your buildings and plant in the event of fire or another hazard. Since 1982 theft from commercial property has exceeded £50 million.

Consequential Loss Meeting the replacement costs of buildings, plant, equipment and stock will not compensate you for the loss of business and profit arising out of a fire or other disaster. Your overheads, employees' wages, etc, may have to continue during the period of interruption. You may incur expenses such as getting sub-contracted work done.

Insurance for consequential loss is intended to restore your business's finance to the position it was in if the interruption had not occurred.

Goods in Transit Until your goods reach your customer and he accepts them, they are still at your risk. You may need to protect yourself from loss or damage in transit.

Commercial Vehicle Policy   Although you may have adequate private use cover for your present vehicle, this is unlikely to be satisfactory once you start to use the vehicle for business purposes. That and any other vehicles used in the business should be covered by a commercial use policy.

Fidelity Guarantee and Other Thefts   Once in business you can expect threats from within and without. A Fidelity Guarantee can be taken to protect you from fraud or dishonesty on the part of key employees. Normal theft cover can be taken to protect your business premises and its contents.

Useful Organisations
These organisations will be able to put you in contact with either a broker or an insurance company that can help you to assess your needs and level of cover.

British Insurance Association Aldermary House, 10–15 Queen Street, London EC4P 4JD (01-248 4477)

British Insurance Brokers Association, Fountain House, 130 Fenchurch Street, London EC3M 5DJ (01-623 9043) BIBA brokers will take a detailed look at a business, see what risks it is running, and put together a package of policies from different Insurers to meet exactly the needs of a client.

Credit Insurance Association Ltd, 1 Portsoken Street, London E1 8DF (01-480 4000)

Insurance Brokers Registration Council, 15 St Helens Place, London EC3A 6DS (01-588 4387)

Legal Protection Group, 31–35 St Nicolas Way, Sutton SE1 1JB (01-661 1491) Specialises in 'Legal Fees' Insurance covering such fields as Unfair Dismissal, Sale and Purchase Indemnity and other consumer and employee related legal areas.

National Association of Trade Protection Societies, 4 and 6 New Street, Leicester LE1 5NB (0533 531951)

NATIONAL INSURANCE, PAYE, TAX, VAT AND PENSIONS

This is one field where good professional advice at the outset will more than pay for itself. Although considerable publicity is given to the 'Black Economy', there are also many people paying more tax than they need. However, you will get the best out of your professional adviser if you understand the basics yourself.

Tax   The tax that you have to pay will depend on the legal form of the business you decide on. As a sole trader or partner you will pay tax under Schedule 'D', Case I or II. If you choose a limited company, then the company will pay corporation tax and the directors will be on Schedule 'E', under the PAYE scheme.

The difference in net tax paid by a sole trader or a company can be very significant, and there are many other factors to take into account. For example, a sole trader can offset any trading losses against other income. Company losses are locked into the company. In the event of losses, a sole trader can even claw back past taxes paid – for example from PAYE in his last job. A company cannot do this.

There is also a difference in when the tax is due. As the director of a company, you pay as you earn. A sole trader or partner can pay tax up to nearly two years after earning the income, depending on his accounting year. For new businesses there are still more factors to consider and some variations on the normal rules. (See page 267 for other pros and cons.)

This is not an area in which to take uninformed guesses.

National Insurance Contributions   Once again, the legal form of your business will determine what you pay. A sole trader or partner is self-employed and pays contributions in class 2, which is a weekly sum, and in class 4, based on annual profits. A company director pays as an employee, and his company pays as an employer. So it is quite possible for a small company to pay up to four times the National Insurance contributions that it would have paid, had it been operated as a sole trader or partnership.

As a rule of thumb, if you do not expect to make more than £10,000 per annum profit, you would be better off not trading as a company. But the level of contributions are not the only consideration. For example, the 'employee' director has better benefits out of the National Insurance than the 'self-employed' sole trader.

Pay-As-You-Earn (PAYE)   Either as an 'employee' director, or in any other form of enterprise employing people, you will be responsible for maintaining the PAYE system. This will involve you in deducting the appropriate tax from your employees' pay and sending it to the Collector of Taxes. If you do not, then you; and not the employee, will be liable for the uncollected tax.

VAT (Value Added Tax)   Whatever the legal form of your business, if your turn-over exceeds £6000 in any calendar quarter, or if it exceeds £18,000 in the last four calendar quarters, then you must register for VAT. This has to be done by notifying your local VAT office, within twenty-one days of the end of the quarter in question. VAT is normally charged at 15%, but some areas are zero-rated and some are exempt. There are also some special rules on exports and imports. Before you reach this level of turn-over would be prudent to become better informed. (VAT thresholds are usually revised in the Budget.)

Pensions   Once you are working for yourself, you will have to make your own pension provision (and perhaps provision, for those working for you). Fortunately for people in profitable self-employment, there are now a large number of highly tax-efficient pension schemes. By selecting the right scheme you can get tax relief at your highest income-tax rate, and so get the Inland Revenue to contribute up to three-quarters of your pension. In addition, it is possible eventually to receive the benefit from the pension plan partly as a lump sum free of all capital-gains tax on the profits made on your contributions over the years; and partly as a pension which will be treated as earned income and so not be subject to the investment income surcharge.

It is a complex but potentially very rewarding investment, with a considerable difference in performance by the different pension plans. For example, over the period 1970–1980, the best-performing pension 'annuity' turned £500 per annum into an accumulated cash sum of £9480 and the worst only £5309.

You can pay up to $17\frac{1}{2}\%$* of your net earnings into an approved pension scheme, so once again good professional advice is a must.

It is also possible, under certain circumstances to use the funds in a self-adminstered pension fund to finance investments in your own business.

The Pension Mortgage is a package that will pay off the mortgage, win full tax relief, and provide at least a small pension into the bargain. It may not even cost any more. Building Societies who offer pension mortgages include: Alliance, Anglia, Cheltenham and Gloucester, Halifax, Leicester and Woolwich.

Employee Buy Outs   Employees who borrow money to buy out their company can, under some circumstances, get tax relief on loan interest.

---

*This has been increased to 20% for those born between 1916 and 1933, and there are also small increases for those born between 1912 and 1915.

Profit Sharing   Companies can give tax free shares to employees each year up to the value of £5000, or 10% of their earnings, whichever is the lower.

Organisations

Association of Consulting Actuaries, 7 Rolls Building, Fetter Lane, London EC4A 1NL (01-831 7130)

Company Pensions Information Centre, 7 Old Park Lane, London W1Y 3LJ (01-409 1933) Publish a free booklet *What Pension Terms Mean*, explaining the 200 or so commonly used words and phrases.

National Association of Pension Funds, Sunley House, Bedford Park, Croydon CR0 0XF (01-681 2017)

Professional Advisers, see page 256 for accountants and page 287 for insurance.

Society of Pension Consultants, Ludgate House, Ludgate Circus, London EC4A 2AB (01-353 1688)

The Tax Payers Society, Room 22, 1st Floor, Wheatsheaf House, 4 Carmelite Street, London EC4Y 0JA (01-583 6020) Business and professional membership costs £35.00 p.a. and the Society provides these services for members:

1   Free advice on any point of law or practice concerning Income Tax, Corporation Tax, Capital Gains Tax and Capital Transfer Tax. The complexities of these taxes make this service of inestimable value.

2   (a)   A news letter which is sent from time to time to keep members informed on tax affairs.

   (b)   Booklets published by the Society on current tax subjects.

3   The views of the Society's members are, when appropriate, brought up in Parliament. In particular, an annual letter from the Society is addressed to the Chancellor of the Exchequer prior to the Budget, putting forward suggested tax changes in line with the needs of members.

Trade and Professional Organisations, including those independent business associations given in Section 2, can often point you towards help in this field.

Publications

Business Start-Up-Package, from the Alliance of Small Firms, 42 Vine Road, East Molesey, Surrey KT8 9LF (01-979 2293) Book II in this five-part series is on tax and National Insurance, twelve pages. Gives you a few useful clues. The others cover law generally and book-keeping and banking. They also run an information and consultancy reference service for members. See also National Federation of Self Employed and Small Business, which also runs an information service in this field (page 80). Price: £1.25 each or £6.25 for 5

Check Your Tax, by J. D. Finnigan, FCA and G. M. Kitchen, FCA, published by W. Foulsham & Co. (0753 26769) 1984/85 edition. Covers personal tax well, but has only a small section on the self-employed. Price: £1.30

Employer's Guide to PAYE, leaflet P7

Employer's Guide to National Insurance Contributions, leaflet NP15

Grundy's Tax Havens, edited by Milton Grundy, The Bodley Head Ltd, 9 Bow Street, London W1X 3RA (01-379 6637) Gives details on a score of tax havens from the Bahamas to Switzerland.

Guide to Running a Small Business, The Guardian Book, edited by Clive Woodcock, published by Kogan Page Ltd, 120 Pentonville Road, London N1 (01-837 7851) Chapter 7 has nearly fifty pages of very useful advice in the taxation field. Price: £5.95

A Guide to the Taxation of Companies, by Mavis Moullin and John Sergent, published by McGraw-Hill Book Co. (UK) Ltd, Shoppenhangers Road, Maidenhead, Berks SL6 2QL (0628 23431) Latest edition February 1982. A very authoritative and comprehensive book concentrating on the tax affairs of the 'average company'. Really for the professional, but if you are technically inclined it may help. Price: £39.95

Hambro Tax Guide, published by Macdonald General Books, Paulton House, 8 Shepherds Walk, London N1, is produced each year and has extensive special sections on income from business and professions, partnerships, companies, VAT and a useful section on tax-saving hints. This should be available in most book shops. Price: £8.00

Key to Corporation Tax, by Taxation Publishing Co. Ltd, 98 Park Street, London W1Y 4BR (01-629 7888) 1983 edition. Technical but thorough. Price: £9.00

Managing Tax in your Business, by Robert Walters, Published by Business Books, Hutchinson House, 17–21 Conway Street, London W1P 6JD (01-387 2811) Well illustrated and plenty of worked examples. Price: £14.95 Provides answers to these questions:

- How are businesses and partnerships taxed?
- What reliefs are available?
- When is tax payable?
- What is a capital gain?
- How are dividends treated?
- What is Development Land Tax?
- Do I have to pay if I get planning permission?
- What is a Capital Transfer?
- What is Value Added?
- How do I transfer Assets and Shares?
- What are the pitfalls of converting to a Company?
- Do I have to make a loss, to get tax relief from losses?

National Insurance Guide for the Self Employed, leaflet N1, from the Department of Health and Social Security.

Peat Marwick Mitchell & Co., 1 Puddle Dock, Blackfriars, London EC4V 3PD Free tax booklet from the Librarian.

Pensions for the Self Employed, by Mark Daniel, published by the *Sunday Telegraph*, 135 Fleet Street, London EC4P 4BL (01-353 4242) First edition 1981. A very readable, comprehensive, yet concise guide to the subject. Price: £1.75

Self Employed Pensions, by the Financial Times Business Publishing Ltd, Fifth edition, March 1982. This is the only source of detailed comparative information on pensions for the self-employed. The book analyses nearly 100 schemes, explains different types of pension plans available, and summarises the tax position. It also shows how each pension scheme has performed and makes projections on likely future results. Price: £12.50

Starting in Business, is a free pamphlet issued by the Board of Inland Revenue, and is available from your local tax inspectorate. It provides a simple and basic introduction to most aspects of tax, PAYE, National Insurance and VAT.

Tax Havens and their uses, March 1983. The attractions, and pitfalls of tax havens as a counter to the ever growing burden of taxation are examined in this comprehensive study of the individual havens available both to corporations and individuals. The Economist Intelligence Unit Limited, Subscription Department (FT), 27 St James's Place, London SW1A 1NT (01-493 6711) Price: £30.00

Tax and Insurance News Letter, published by Stonehart Publications, 13 Golden Square, London W1 (01-637 4383) Monthly, by subscription only; covers topical and highly relevant business tax and insurance problems. It will keep you up to date between budgets.

Tolley's Corporation Tax (annual) from Tolley Publishing Co., 102/104 High Street, Croydon, Surrey CRO 1ND (01-686 0115) 1983/84 edition. A very authoritative guide, concerned only with business taxation. Price: £8.75

Tolley's Value Added Tax, from Tolley Publishing Co. (address as above) 1984 edition – a new series, as yet unnamed and unpriced.

Value Added Tax, Scope and Coverage and *The General Guide* are two free publications from HM Customs & Excise local VAT offices.

101 Ways of Saving Tax, published by the *Sunday Telegraph*, 135 Fleet Street, London EC4P 4BL (01-353 4242) Thirty-four apply directly to a business, and they are very readable and clear guidelines. This is no substitute for Hambro's or Tolley's. Price: £2.50

'Which' Tax Saving Guide, produced each year, concentrates on personal tax.

SECTION 8

TRAINING FOR BUSINESS

There are now many opportunities for education and training, at every level, in the business and management field. No formal academic qualifications are required for most of the courses and costs are generally modest. In certain cases, those taking some of the longer courses may be eligible for grants.

The bulk of the activities are concentrated in universities and colleges throughout the whole of the UK. However, there are a growing number of opportunities for the less mobile to take up some form of home study in the business field in general, and small business opportunities in particular.

COURSES AT COLLEGES AND OTHER INSTITUTIONS

Nearly three hundred Institutions are offering courses in the new and small business field. This is greater than a doubling in provision over the past two years. Our survey has divided the courses on offer into the following main categories.

Short Courses, that is up to 2 weeks, for people considering starting up a business. These are usually of one or two days' duration, and cost around £15 to £25 per day. They concentrate on giving an introduction on how to start your own business. The courses as well as providing lectures, give an opportunity for those who have recently started up in business to talk about their experiences. The demand for these courses is very high. Various estimates suggest that upwards of 10,000 people attend such courses in the South East alone during 1983/1984. This certainly forms the most cost effective method of finding out very quickly a lot about what is going on in the 'new and small business world'. These courses are frequently run at weekends and sometimes on evenings during the week.

Longer Courses   Following on from the introductory, one or two day courses, a number of colleges run programmes lasting up to sixteen weeks. In the main, the longer courses are sponsored by the Manpower Services Commissions,* Training Division. Their courses, called either New Enterprise Programmes or Small Business Courses, are run at business schools in universities and polytechnics throughout the country.

Such courses very often consist of 3 to 4 weeks of classroom content, covering all the main aspects of running a small business. This is complemented by up to 10 further weeks, with business school staff working with the 'entrepreneurs' on the mechanics of starting up their own business. This can involve detailed work on preparing a business plan, raising finance, finding premises, applying for grants or aid, or marketing and market research. During this period the student entrepreneur can be given an allowance of around £40 per week, together with some subsistence allowance, and a grant for market research.

These schemes have been extremely successful, and the MSC is extending their provision.

There are other longer courses, on a part-time or linked weekend basis. The former may be one or two evenings each week over 10 weeks or more covering a specific topi , such as book-keeping or marketing.

The linked weekends tend to cover the whole field of starting up a business, with individual project work carried out between weekends. In this way participants can bring their problems back to the business school staff and get their advice and help.

Topic Courses   These are usually run over a few days or weeks, for those already in business. They cover topics such as: Financial Management, Marketing, Book-keeping, Exporting, Computers, employing people and Law. Also after the budget some colleges hold tax update courses.

Provision on Existing Courses   Many courses in colleges are modular or in discrete sections, with, say, a few weeks of one topic given in a fairly concentrated form. The subject may be marketing, finance, computer systems or business law. Although these courses are not aimed specifically at people running small businesses, the subject matter is certainly appropriate. Some colleges encourage people to join in parts of an existing full-time course, so in effect you join a class for a few weeks and learn the topic of particular interest to you.

*Addresses at end of section.

Scholarships and Bursaries   A limited number of awards for full-time postgraduate courses leading to higher degrees (e.g. Master of Business Administration) and diplomas are made available by the Economic and Social Research Council, Postgraduate Training Division, 1 Temple Avenue, London EC47 0BD (01-953 5252).

Alternatively you could contact your nearest college and see what they have to offer. The situation is constantly changing, and many innovations in education for small business are being introduced.

Future Trends   New colleges and courses are coming on stream all the time. As well as using this directory, try your local college or education department and see what they have on offer. Two other organisations that keep abreast of developments are:

The UK Small Business Management Education Association, c/o The London Business School, Sussex Place, Regents Park, London NW1 4SA (01-262 5050) *Contact: Miss Sue Loan*
The Scottish Association for Small Business Education, 22 Great King Street, Edinburgh EH3 6QH (031-557 4555) *Contact: George B. Preston*

Manpower Services Commission   Training Division offices at the following locations will be able to advise you on dates and courses in their areas:

Head Office: Moorfoot, Sheffield S1 4PQ (0742 753275)
Office for Scotland: 9 St Andrew Square, Edinburgh EH2 2QX (031-225 8500)
London: Selkirk House, 166 High Holborn, London WC1V 6PF (01-836 1213)
Midlands: Alpha Tower, Suffolk Street, Queensway, Birmingham B1 1UR (021-632 4144)
Northern: Broadacre House, Market Street, Newcastle-upon-Tyne NE1 6HH (0632 326181)
North West: Washington House, The Capital Centre, New Bailey Street, Manchester M3 5ER (061-833 0251)
South East: Telford House, Hamilton Close, Basingstoke RG21 2UZ (0256 29266)
South West: 4th floor, The Pithay, Bristol BS1 2NQ (0272 291071)
Wales: 4th floor, Companies House, Crown Way, Maindy, Cardiff CF4 3UT (0222 388588)
Yorkshire & Humberside: Jubilee House, 33–41 Park Place, Leeds LS1 2RL (0532 446299)

WHERE TO FIND A COURSE

The results of our 1984 survey of the small business education provisions are set out below. As well as showing the nature of the course run and the person to contact, you can see if the programme is run fulltime(F) or Part-time(P). In the case of topic courses the legend corresponds to the initials of the subject covered. So Financial Management is (F), Marketing is (M), Book-keeping is (B), Exporting is (E), Computers is (C), employing people is (P), Law is (L) and any other courses are (●).

We have also identified where advice and consultancy are available, and research activities are underway.

Business Club is the name often given to the regular meetings of small business people for discussions or seminars. These are often hosted by colleges and we have shown those that do. Finally, we have listed whether or not the college has a full time commitment to the small business field. Very often the task of teaching in this field is divided up amongst people with other important and time consuming commitments.

The British Institute of Management also run a major information advisory service on management education throughout the country. This includes information on starting up or running a small business. BIM, Management House, Parker Street, London WC2B 5PT (01-405 3456)

ENGLAND

	Short Courses-start up	Long Courses-start up	Topic Courses	Prov. on Exist. Courses	Advice, Info. & Counsell	Consultancy Service	Research Activity	Business Club	Special Unit
Acton Technical College, Dept of Business & General Studies, Millhill Road, Acton, London W3 8UX (01-993 2344) *Contact: B. V. Marshall*	P							●	
Accrington & Rossendale College, Business & Management Studies, Sandy Lane, Accrington, Lancashire BB5 2AW (0254 35334) *Contact: Mr J. J. Harrison*	P	P	F M B C P	●	●	●	●		
Airedale & Wharfedale College of Further Education, Small Business Unit, Calverley Street, Horsforth, Leeds LS18 4RQ (0532 581723 ext 37) *Contact: David Hardy, Trevor Ducker*	P	P F	F M B C P		●	●		●	●
University of Aston in Birmingham, Management Centre, Nelson Building, Gosta Green, Birmingham BH 7DN (021-359 3011) *Contact: Miss J. Skinner*	F P	F P	F M C P L	●	●	●			
Banbridge Technical College, Castlewellan Road, Banbridge BT32 4AY						●			
Basingstoke Technical College, Worting Road, Basingstoke, Hampshire RG21 1TN (0256 54141) *Contact: B. T. Gurden, Head of Dept; M. Walton, Senior Lecturer I/C Management Short Courses*	F P	P	F M B E C P L	●	●	●		●	
University of Bath, Claverton Down, Bath BA2 7AY (0225 61244) *Contact: N. K. Crawford*			●				●	●	
Boxtowe College of Further Education, Business Studies Department, High Road, Chilwell, Beeston, Nottingham (0602 228161) *Contact: Mr Gerry Gardner*			P						

298

	Short Courses-start up	Long Courses-start up	Topic Courses	Prov. on Exist. Courses	Advice, Info. & Counsell	Consultancy Service	Research Activity	Business Club	Special Unit
University of Birmingham, PO Box 363, Birmingham B15 2TT (021-472 1301 ext 3480) *Contact: Mr N. J. Kavanagh, Dept of Industrial Economics & Business Studies*	P	F		•	•		•	•	
Blackburn College of Technology & Design, Dept of Management & Professional Studies, Neilden Street, Blackburn BB2 1LH (0254 55144) *Contact: R. Walne, A. Jones*		F P	F B C P	•	•	•	•	•	•
Blackpool College of Further & Higher Education, Faculty of Business Food & Management, Ashfield Road, Blackpool FY2 0HB (0253 52352) *Contact: P. Lavelle*	P F	P F	F M B E C P L		•	•			
Bolton Institute of Higher Education, Management & Business Studies Department, Deane Road, Bolton BL3 5AB (0204 28851 ext 225) *Contact: Dr A. Kitson*	F P	F P	F M B C P L		•	•	•		
Bournemouth & Poole College of Further Education, North Road, Parkstone, Poole, Dorset BH14 0LS (0202 747600) *Contact: B. H. Sutton*			P						
Bradford & Ilkley Community College, Management & Language, Gt Horton Road, Bradford, BD7 1AY (0274 75311) *Contact: P. Noble*	P	P	F M B C L	•	•	•			
Bradford University Management Centre, Heaton Mount, Bradford, W Yorks BD9 4JU (0274 42299 ext 262) *Contact: Dr A. E. Peacock*			F M C P	•					
Brighton Polytechnic, Business Studies Dept, Lewes Road, Mithras House, Moulsecoomb, Brighton (0273 693 655) *Contact: Mr Barry Lee Scherer*	P F		P	•	•		•		

	Short Courses-start up	Long Courses-start up	Topic Courses	Prov. on Exist. Courses	Advice, Info. & Counsell	Consultancy Service	Research Activity	Business Club	Special Unit
Brighton Technical College, Pelham St, Brighton BN1 4FA (0273 685971) *Contact: T. J. Garnell, Small Bus. Unit*	P		F M B C P L	●	●	●			
Bristol Polytechnic, Coldharbour Lane, Frenchay, Bristol BS16 1QY (0272 656261) *Contact: Mr John Howdle*			F B C L			●	●		
University of Bristol, Extra-Mural Studies, 32 Tyndall's Park Road, Bristol BS8 1HR (0272 24161 ext 657) *Contact: P. T. Gray*	F P	F	F B P		●		●		
Brooklands School of Management, Brooklands Technical College, Heath Road, Weybridge, Surrey KT13 8TT (3300 ext 280) *Contact: Mr M. Tredgett, Mr R. Lambert*					●				
Brunel University, Brunel Management Programme, Uxbridge, Mddx UB8 3PH (0895 56461) *Contact: Keith Alsop*			F M C P		●	●			
Brunel University, Continuing Education, Uxbridge, Middlesex (0895 37188) *Contact: Prof. Jean Miller*	F P	F P	F M B E C P L	●	●	●	●		
Buckinghamshire College of Higher Education, Dept of Man, Queen Alexandra Road, High Wycombe, Bucks HP11 2JZ (0494 22141) *Contact: W. Anson*	P	F	F M E C P L	●	●	●	●	●	●
Burnley College of Arts & Technology, Shorey Bank, off Ormerod Road, Burnley (0282 36111) *Contact: Mr E. Beswick*	F	P	F M B C P L		●	●		●	●
Burton-upon-Trent Technical College, Lichfield Street, Burton-upon-Trent, Staffs DE14 3RL (0283 45401) *Contact: T. G. Edwards*	P	P	F M B C P L	●	●	●		●	

	Short Courses-start up	Long Courses-start up	Topic Courses	Prov. on Exist. Courses	Advice, Info. & Counsell	Consultancy Service	Research Activity	Business Club	Special Unit
Bury Metropolitan College of Further Education, Business Studies, Management Unit, Bank House, Blackburn Street, Radcliffe, M26 9WQ (061-723 2480) *Contact: David H. Draper*	F P	F P	F M B C P L		•	•			•
Canterbury College of Technology, New Dover Road, Canterbury, Kent CT1 3AJ (0227 66081) *Contact: Neil D. Stein*			P		•				
Carlisle Technical College, Business & Secretarial Dept, Victoria Place, Carlisle CA1 1HS (0228 24464)	P	F	F M B C P L	•	•	•			
Cassio College, Retail Distribution & Services, Langley Road, Watford, Herts WD1 3RH (92 40311 ext 47) *Contact: K. G. Forrow, D. Sparkes*	P F	P F	F M B E C P L		•	•	•	•	
The Polytechnic of Central London, School of Management Studies, 35 Marylebone Road, London NW1 5LS (01-486 5811 ext 225) *Contact: Prof John Stanworth, Director of Small Business Unit*	P	F		•	•	•	•	•	•
Chelmer Institute of Higher Education, Victoria Road, South Chelmsford, Essex CM1 1NH (0245 350388) *Contact: R. W. McLarty, Small Business Centre*	F P	F P	F M B E C P L		•	•	•	•	•
Chichester College of Technology, Westgate Fields, Chichester, West Sussex PO19 1SB (0243 786321 ext 263) *Contact: Mr D. W. Evans, Mr J. Bettell, Management & Business Studies*	P		F M B C P L		•				
City & East London College, General Education & Applied Social Studies, Bunhill Row, London EC1 8LQ (01-628 0864) *Contact: Richard Chaloner*		F P			•	•	•		•

	Short Courses-start up	Long Courses-start up	Topic Courses	Prov. on Exist. Courses	Advice, Info. & Counsell	Consultancy Service	Research Activity	Business Club	Special Unit
City of London Polytechnic, Short Course Unit, 84 Moorgate, London EC2M 6SQ (01-283 1030) *Contact: Rosemary Royds, Short Courses Co-ordinator; John Collins, Business Liaison Officer*	F P		F M B C P L	●	●	●			●
The City University Business School, Post Experience Courses Unit, Frobisher Crescent, Barbican, London EC2Y 8HB (01-920 0111) *Contact: Mrs B. Henniker, Marketing Manager*			●						
Clarendon College of Further Education, Pelham Avenue, Nottingham NG5 1AL (06027 08373) *Contact: John Taylor*	P	F P	●		●	●			●
Coalville Technical College, Business & Management Dept, Bridge Road, Coalville, Leicester LE6 2QR (0530 36136)		P	F B C P	●					
Colchester Institute, Sheepen Road, Colchester, Essex (0206 70271) *Contact: Deryck Roberts*						●			
Cornwall College of Further & Higher Education, Faculty of Management, Business & Professional Studies, Redruth, Cornwall, TR15 3RD (0209 712911) *Contact: W. A. N. Sully, Course Director, Small Business Courses; N. Jopling, Head of Centre*	P F	P F	F M B C P L	●	●		●	●	
CoSIRA, Information Section, 141 Castle Street, Salisbury, Wilts SP1 3TP (0722 336255) *Contact: Marilyn D. Jarvis*	P		F M E C P	●	●	●	●	●	
Coventry (Lanchester) Polytechnic, Business Management Centre, Faculty of Business, Priory Street, Coventry CV1 5FB (0203 24166 ext 7718) *Contact: Mr R. D. F. Morris*		P	F M B C P L						

	Short Courses-start up	Long Courses-start up	Topic Courses	Prov. on Exist. Courses	Advice, Info. & Counsell	Consultancy Service	Research Activity	Business Club	Special Unit
Cranfield Institute of Technology, Cranfield, Bedford MK43 0AL (0234 750941) *Contact: Professor Paul Burns*	F		•		•	•			•
Crewe & Alsager College of Higher Education, Business & Management Studies, Crewe Road, Crewe, Cheshire CW1 1DU (0270 583661 ext 41) *Contact: Ronald A. Fisher*	P F	P F	F M B E C P L		•	•	•	•	•
Cricklade College, Charlton Road, Andover, Hants SP10 1EJ (0264 63311) *Contact: Mr G. A. Horner, Mr R. Reeves*		P	F B		•	•			
Darlington College of Technology, Management & Business Studies, Cleveland Avenue, Darlington, Co. Durham DL3 7BB (0325 467651) *Contact: J. D. Rosser*	F		F M B C P L	•	•	•			
College for the Distributive Trades, Management Studies, 30 Leicester Square, London WC2H 7LE (01-839 1547) *Contact: Norman E. Richmond*	F P	F P	F M B E C P L	•	•	•			
Doncaster Metropolitan Institute of Higher Education, Dept of Management Studies, Barnsley Road, Scawsby, Doncaster DN5 7UD (0302 783421) *Contact: Chris Pike*	F P	F P	F M B C P L	•	•	•		•	
Dorset Institute of Higher Education, Dept of Management Studies, Wallisdown, Poole, Dorset BH12 5BB (0202 52411) *Contact: Mr J. Carter, Management, Mrs J. Nagle, Secretary*		P	F M C P L	•	•	•	•	•	•
Dudley College of Technology, Dept of Business & Management Studies, The Broadway, Dudley, West Midlands DY1 4AS (0384 53585) *Contact: G. K. Morgan*		F	F M C	•	•	•		•	•

	Short Courses-start up	Long Courses-start up	Topic Courses	Prov. on Exist. Courses	Advice, Info. & Counsell	Consultancy Service	Research Activity	Business Club	Special Unit
Durham University Business School, Small Business Centre, Mill Hill Lane, Durham DH1 3LB (0385 41919) *Contact: Professor A. A. Gibb, Director, Small Business Studies*	P	F	E C		●	●	●	●	●
Ealing College of Higher Education, School of Business & Management, St Mary's Road, Ealing, London W5 5RF (01-579 4111) *Contact: R. Johnson*	F P		F M B C P L	●	●	●	●		
College of Further Education, St Anne's Road, Eastbourne BN21 2HS (0323 644711) *Contact: Ted Platt*	P		B C	●					
East Devon College, Business Studies Dept, Tiverton, Devon EX16 6SH (0884 254247) *Contact: Mr David G. Anderson, Miss P. Webber, Business & Secretarial Dept*				●					
East Herts College, Turnford, Broxbourne, Herts EN10 6AF (66451) *Contact: Mr W. Jones, Head of Adult Education Dept*				●					
English Multi-national Business School, 8 Connaught Road, Eastbourne, East Sussex BN21 4PY (0323 35073) *Contact: P. A. Goodman*						●			
European School of Management Studies, 12 Merton Street, Oxford OX1 4JH (0865 724545) *Contact: K. Starling, Mr S. Prodano*	P					●	●		
Exeter University, Extra-mural Studies, St Luke's, Heavitree Road, Exeter EX1 2LU (0392 74425) *Contact: Prof. Daveney*			F C						

	Short Courses-start up	Long Courses-start up	Topic Courses	Prov. on Exist. Courses	Advice, Info. & Counsell.	Consultancy Service	Research Activity	Business Club	Special Unit
Fielden House Productivity Centre Ltd, 856 Wilmslow Road, Didsbury, Manchester M20 8RY (061-445 2426) *Contact: R. Roocroft*	F P		F M / B C / P L	•	•			•	
Gloucestershire College of Arts & Technology, Oxstalls Lane, Gloucester (0452 25559 ext ?) *Contact: C. S. C. Bennett, Management Business Studies*	F P	F	F M / B C / P L	•	•	•		•	
Great Yarmouth College of Further Education, Southtown, Great Yarmouth NR31 0ED (0493 55261 day, 667175 evening) *Contact: Philip Gunn*	F P	•	F M / B C / P	•	•			•	
Grimsby College of Technology, Management & Business Studies Dept, Nuns Corner, Grimsby, South Humberside DN34 5BQ (0472 79292) *Contact: B. B. Green (ext 266) or N. Burns (ext 297)*					•				
Groby Community College, Ratby Road, Groby LE6 0GE (0533 879921) *Contact: Dr Graham Platts*					•				
Hackney College, Dept of Business Studies, Ayrsome Road, London N16 0RH (01-249 7221) *Contact: M. Marshal*	P								
Hall Green Technical College, Business Studies & General Education, Cole Bank Road, Hall Green, Birmingham B28 8ES (021-778 2311) *Contact: E. G. Owen*	P	P	F M / B E / C L	•	•	•			
Halton College, Business & General Education, Kingsway, Widnes, Cheshire (051-423 1391) *Contact: Mr S. C. Pickett*	P					•			
Handsworth Technical College, Business Studies & Clothing Trades, Small Business Unit, Soho Road, Handsworth, Birmingham B21 9DP (021-551 6031 ext 241)		F	F M / B E / C L	•				•	•

Contact: Masood Rizva, Courses Co-
ordinator

Hartlepool College of Further Education, Stockton Street, Hartlepool, Cleveland TS26 ODP (0429 75453)
Contact: Colin Doram

Hatfield Polytechnic, Business & Social Science, Balls Park, Hertford, Herts (0992 58451 ext 242)
Contact: T. J. Baldwin

Henley College of Further Education, Engineering, Edgwick, Henley College Section, Cross Road, Coventry
Contact: G. C. Mason, Lecturer, Topshop

Henley, The Management College, External Affairs, Greenlands, Henley on Thames, Oxon RG9 3AU (049 166 454)
Contact: Ms Nina Read, Director

Highbury College of Technology, Dept of Management Studies, Cosham, Portsmouth, PO6 2SA (0705 383131)
Contact: D. B. Wright, Head of Dept

Highlands College, PO Box 142, St Saviour, Jersey, Channel Islands (0534 71065 ext 313)
Contact: Mrs G. Renouf

Hotel & Catering Industry Training Board, PO Box 18, Ramsey House, Central Square, Wembley, Middlesex HA9 7AP (01-902 5316) Small Business Information Servce

Huddersfield Polytechnic, Management & Administrative Studies Dept, Queensgate, Huddersfield HD1 3DH (0484 22288)
Contact: Mr J. L. Thompson

Organisation	Short Courses-start up	Long Courses-start up	Topic Courses	Prov. on Exist. Courses	Advice. Info. & Counsell	Consultancy Service	Research Activity	Business Club	Special Unit
Hartlepool College of Further Education	F		F M / B C / P L	•	•		•		
Hatfield Polytechnic	F	P	F M / B C / P L	•	•	•	•	•	•
Henley College of Further Education						•			
Henley, The Management College			F M / P	•	•	•	•		
Highbury College of Technology	•		F C	•	•	•	•		
Highlands College	P	P		•	•			•	
Hotel & Catering Industry Training Board	P	P	F M / C P	•	•				•
Huddersfield Polytechnic	F			•	•	•	•	•	

	Short Courses-start up	Long Courses-start up	Topic Courses	Prov. on Exist. Courses	Advice, Info. & Counsell	Consultancy Service	Research Activity	Business Club	Special Unit
Humberside College, Higher Education, Cottingham Road, Hull HU6 7RT (0432 41451) *Contact: Mr M. Hird, A. McFarlane, Business & Industrial Studies*	F	F	M E C	•	•	•	•		•
Huntingdon Technical College, Small Business Service, Business, Professional & Management Department, California Road, Huntingdon, Camb (0480 52346) *Contact: Mrs Sheila May, Small Business Service, Mr D. R. Gibbons, Head of Dept*					•				
Imperial College of Science & Technology, Dept of Management Science, Exhibition Road, London SW7 2BX (01-589 5111 ext 2802) *Contact: Anne Benjamin, Assistant Director, Ray Tomkins*				•	•	•			
Isle of Wight College of Arts & Technology, Newport, Isle of Wight PO30 5TA (0983 526631) *Contact: John Lucas*	P	P	F M B E C P L	•	•	•	•		
Kendal College of Further Education, Business & General Education, Milnthorpe Road, Kendal, Cumbria LA9 5AY (0539 24313) *Contact: Alan Hart, Alec Speakman*		•	F B C		•				
Kidderminster College of Further Education, Science & Industrial Studies, Hoo Road, Kidderminster, Worcs DY10 1LX (0562 66311) *Contact: P. Ingham, Head of Dept, J. C. Moyle, Senior Lecturer*	F P		F M B C	•	•		•	•	
Kingston Polytechnic, Kingston Regional Management Centre, Gipsy Hill Centre, Kingston Hill, Kingston upon Thames, Surrey KT2 7LB (01-546 2181 ext 365 Ansafone) *Contact: Dr C. R. Priestley, Industrial Liaison Officer*	P	F	M E	•					

	Short Courses-start up	Long Courses-start up	Topic Courses	Prov. on Exist. Courses	Advice, Info. & Counsell	Consultancy Service	Research Activity	Business Club	Special Unit
University of Lancaster, Dept of Economics, Gillow House, Lancaster (0524 65201 ext 4227) *Contact: R. W. Daniels*				•	•	•	•	•	
Lancastrian School of Management, Short Course Unit, 8 East Cliff, Preston PR1 3JN (0772 262076) *Contact: C. W. Cunliffe*	F P	F P	F M / B E / C P / L	•	•	•	•		•
Leeds Polytechnic, Business School, 5 Queen's Square, Leeds LV2 8AY (0532 439726) *Contact: M. R. Robertson, L. S. Wood*	F P	F	F M / B E / C P / L	•	•	•	•	•	
Leek College, Dept of Business Studies, Stockwell Street, Leek, Staffs ST1 4DP (0538 382506) *Contact: D. A. Jagger*		P	F M / B E / C P / L	•	•	•	•		
Leicester Polytechnic (East Midlands Regional Management Centre) PO Box 143, Leicester LE1 9BH (0533 551551 ext 2600) *Contact: John T. Charlton*	F P	F P	F M / B E / C P / L	•	•	•	•		•
Leicester Business Advice Centre, 30 New Walk, Leicester LE1 6TF (0533 554464) *Contact: Mrs G. Grenfell*	P		F M / B P / L		•	•	•	•	•
Leigh College, Business & Professional Studies, Railway Road, Leigh, Lancs WN7 4AH (0942 608811) *Contact: N. Pemberton, R. Stockwell*	F	F P	F M / B C / P L		•	•		•	•
Lewes Technical College, Business Education Dept, Mountfield Road, Lewes, East Sussex (079 16 6121) *Contact: J. D. Breeze, Head of Dept; John Hudson, Senior Lecturer*		P	F M / B C / P L	•					
Lincoln College of Technology, Business & Management Studies, Cathedral Street, Lincoln LN2 5HQ (0522 30641 ext 252) *Contact: Roy Sanderson, Head of Small Business Unit*	P F	F	F M / B E / C P / L	•	•	•			•

	Short Courses-start up	Long Courses-start up	Topic Courses	Prov. on Exist. Courses	Advice, Info. & Counsell	Consultancy Service	Research Activity	Business Club	Special Unit
University of Liverpool, Dept of Economics & Business Studies, Eleanor Rathbone Building, Liverpool L69 3BX (051-709 6022 ext 2187) *Contact: Peter Stoney*				•	•	•			
London Business School, Institute of Small Business Management, Sussex Place, Regent's Park, London MW1 4JA (01-262 5050) *Contact: Dr Stuart Slatter*			F			•		•	
Loughborough University, Management Studies, Ashby Road, Loughborough, Leicestershire LE11 3TU (0509 263171) *Contact: C. McEvoy, G. Gregory*				•	•	•			
Luton College of Higher Education, Dept of Management & Organisational Studies, Putteridge Bury, Hitchin Road, Luton, Beds LU2 8LE (0582 34111 ext 731) *Contact: R. Wooding*	P		F M C P L	•	•	•			
Central Manchester College, St John's Centre, Lower Hardman Street, Manchester M3 3FP (061-831 7091 ext 24) *Contact: W. F. Smith, Head of Dept*	P		F M B E C P L	•	•		•		
Central Manchester College, Industry & Commerce Dept, (Openshaw Centre), Whitworth Street, Openshaw, Manchester 11 (061-223 8282) *Contact: P. C. Earl, R. J. Emery, J. Edwards*	F P	F P	F M B E C P L	•	•	•		•	•
The College of Management, Dunchurch, Rugby, Warwicks CV22 6QW (0788 810656) *Contact: Miss F. Edwards, Customer Liaison*	F P	F	F M B E C P		•	•	•		
College of Marketing, Moor Hall, Cookham, Berks (06285 24922) *Contact: J. Milward*	F		M E C		•	•			

	Short Courses-start up	Long Courses-start up	Topic Courses	Prov. on Exist. Courses	Advice, Info. & Counsell	Consultancy Service	Research Activity	Business Club	Special Unit
Macclesfield College of Further Education, Business & European Studies, Park Lane, Macclesfield SK11 8LF *Contact: D. J. Brightmore*	P	P	F M B E C P L	•				•	
Manchester University, Manchester Business School, New Enterprise Centre, Booth Street West, Manchester M15 6PB (061-273 8228 ext 322) *Contact: David Watkins, Director*			F P	•	•	•	•	•	•
Merseyside Training Education & Enterprise Ltd, 6 Salisbury Street, Liverpool L3 8DR (051-207 2281) *Contact: either Enterprise Dept or Training Dept*	P	P	F M B C	•	•			•	•
Middlesex Polytechnic, Business School Dept, The Burroughs, Hendon, Middlesex NW4 4BT (01-202 6545) *Contact: The Dean*					•	•			
Mid-Gloucestershire Technical College, Business Studies & Management, Stratford Road, Stroud, Gloucs GL5 4AH (04536 3424) *Contact: A. Harrison, Head of Department*	P		F B C P	•	•	•			
Mid-Kent College of Higher & Further Education, Maidstone Road, Horsted, Chatham, Kent ME5 9UQ (Medway 44265) *Contact: Dr C. M. Fletcher, Director Business Advisory Centre*					•	•	•		•
Mid-Kent College of Higher & Further Education, Dept of Business Studies, Oakwood Park, Tonbridge Road, Maidstone, Kent ME16 8AQ (Maidstone 56531) *Contact: Mr N. M. Brisk*	P	F	M B C	•	•	•	•		

	Short Courses-start up	Long Courses-start up	Topic Courses	Prov. on Exist. Courses	Advice, Info. & Counsell	Consultancy Service	Research Activity	Business Club	Special Unit
Nene College, Management Centre, Moulton Park, Northampton, NN2 7AL (0604 719531) *Contact: Dr Salvard*	F	F	F M B E C P L	•	•	•			
Newbury College, Management Training Unit, Oxford Road, Newbury, Berkshire RG13 1PQ (0635 42824) *Contact: G. Wood*					•				
Newcastle-upon-Tyne Polytechnic, Small Business Unit, Manor House, Coach Lane Campus, Coach Lane, Newcastle-upon-Tyne NE7 7XA (0632 664878/326002) *Contact: G. R. L. Parkinson, N. U. Middlemas*	P	F		•	•	•		•	•
North Cheshire College, Business Management & TV Studies, Winwick Road, Warrington, Cheshire (0925 37311) *Contact: A. Conrad, P. Taylor, P. O'Byrne*	F	P	F M B E C P L		•	•	•	•	
North East Derbyshire College of Further Education, Dept of Community Studies, Rectory Road, Clowne, Chesterfield, Derbys S43 4BQ (0246 810332) *Contact: F. Marsh, Head of Department*	P		B P						
North East London Polytechnic, Business Studies Dept, Langbridge Road, Dagenham, Essex RM8 2AS *Contact: Mr Rusi Edulji, Terry Goodwin*					•				
The Polytechnic of North London, Dept of Business, 2–16 Eden Grove, London N7 8DB (01-607 2789) *Contact: Head of Dept*				•	•	•	•	•	•
North Nottinghamshire College of Further Education, Carlton Road, Worksop S81 7HP (0909 473581) *Contact: J. G. Wilson, Head of Dept*	P	P	F M B C	•	•	•	•	•	

Institution	Short Courses-start up	Long Courses-start up	Topic Courses	Prov. on Exist. Courses	Advice, Info. & Counsell	Consultancy Service	Research Activity	Business Club	Special Unit
North Staffordshire Polytechnic, West Midlands Regional Management Centre, College Road, Stoke-on-Trent ST4 2DE (0782 412143) *Contact: Mrs J. E. Sutherland*	F P	F P	F M B E C P L	●	●	●	●	●	●
North West Kent College of Technology, Miskin Road, Dartford DA1 2LU (32 25471/3) *Contact: Dr T. Seddon*					●				
NWRMC, North West Regional Management Centre, Woodlands Centre, Southport Road, Chorley, Lancs PR7 1QR (02572 66942) *Contact: N. P. Maynard*	F P	F P	●	●	●	●		●	
North Tyneside College of Further Education, Business Studies Department, Embleton Avenue, Walsend, Tyne and Wear NE28 9NL (063 262 4081) *Contact: Mr Norman Moore*	F P		F B C	●	●				
Northumberland Technical College, College Road, Ashington, Northumberland (0670 55551) *Contact: Norman Ostle, Business Studies*		P			●		●		
Norwich City College of Further & Higher Education, Management Centre, Ivory House, All Saints Green, Norwich NR1 3NB (0603 28619) *Contact: Rad Spassitch*	P	P	F M B E C P L	●	●	●	●	●	
Nottingham University, Small Firms Unit, Dept of Economics, University Park, Nottingham NG7 2RD (0602 56101) *Contact: Dr M. R. Binks*						●	●		●
Oldham College of Technology, Business & Management Dept, Rochdale Road, Oldham (061-624 5214) *Contact: Mr M. Beaumont, Mr D. McKeown, Mr B. Kay*	P	P F	C M	●	●	●	●	●	

	Short Courses-start up	Long Courses-start up	Topic Courses	Prov. on Exist. Courses	Advice, Info. & Counsell	Consultancy Service	Research Activity	Business Club	Special Unit
Open University, see Distance Learning (page 330)	P								
Oxford Centre for Management Studies, Kennington, Oxford OX1 5NY (0865 735422)				•					
Oxford Polytechnic, Management & Business Studies Dept, Lady Spencer Churchill College, Wheatley, Oxon OX9 1HX (0865 64777) *Contact: P. J. Reynier*	F		F C	•	•	•		•	
Park Lane College of Further Education, Park Lane, Leeds LS3 1AA (0532 443011) *Contact: Paul Stanilands*	P	F P	F M B E C P L						
Peterborough Technical College, High Trees Management Centre, Park Crescent, Peterborough PE1 4DZ (0733 67366 ext 155) *Contact: P. Gardner, C. Saunders*	F P	F P	F M B E C P L	•	•	•		•	
Plymouth Business School, Plymouth Polytechnic, Drake Circus, Plymouth, Devon PL4 8AA (0752 264655) *Contact: D. Blackler*	F P	F P	F M B L	•	•	•	•	•	•
Portsmouth College of Art & Design & Further Education, Winston Churchill Avenue, Portsmouth PO1 2DJ (0705 826435) *Contact: Mel Parker, R. Clunes, Business Studies*	P	P	F M B C P	•	•	•		•	•
Portsmouth Polytechnic, Portsmouth Management Centre, 141 High Street, Portsmouth PO1 2HY (0705 812611) *Contact: Ted Fenner, Keith Kirkland*		F	F M B E C P L				•		•
Preston Polytechnic, Corporation Street, Preston, Lancs PR1 2TQ (0772 22141) *Contact: J. M. Kidd, N. R. Hall*		P F	B	•	•	•	•		
Redhill Technical College, Dept of Business Studies & Languages, Gatton Point, Redhill, Surrey RH1 2JX (0737 72611)	P	P	F M B C P L						

Contact: R. Fitton, Head of Dept; Mr W. Spear (Deputy Head of Dept)

	Short Courses-start up	Long Courses-start up	Topic Courses	Prov. on Exist. Courses	Advice, Info. & Counsell	Consultancy Service	Research Activity	Business Club	Special Unit
Rockingham College of Further Education, Business & Commercial Dept, West Street, Wath-Upon-Dearne, Rotherham, Sth Yorks s63 6PX (0709 874310) *Contact: Don Davison*		•	B	•	•				
Rother Valley College of Further Education, Business & General Studies, Doe Quarry Lane, Dinnington, Sheffield s31 7NH (0742 568681) *Contact: L. Wickham, K. Furnell*	P	P	F M B E C P L	•	•	•			
St Helens College of Technology, School of Management Studies, Water Street, St Helens, Merseyside WA10 1PZ (0744 33766 ext 277) *Contact: Mr G. T. Brown, Mr J. A. Wright*	F	F	F M C P L	•	•		•		
Salford University, Dept of Business & Administration, Salford, Lancs M5 4WT (061-736 5843 ext 7319) *Contact: W. E. Roberts*						•	•		
University of Sheffield, Business Studies, Sheffield s10 2TN (0742 78555 ext 6799) *Contact: Dr Everett M. Jacobs*			F M B C P	•	•	•	•		•
Sheffield Polytechnic, Dept Economics & Business Studies, Pond Street, Sheffield s1 1WB (0742 20911) *Contact: Colin Gilligan*			F M E C P L	•	•		•		
Shirecliffe College, Management and Computer Studies, Shirecliffe Road, Sheffield s5 8XZ (0742 78301) *Contact: R. W. Stringer, J. L. Bull*	F P	F	F M B C P	•	•		•	•	
Slough College of Higher Education, Management Centre, Management Training Division, Slough, Berks SL1 1YG *Contact: Head of Division*	F		F C P L						

314

	Short Courses-start up	Long Courses-start up	Topic Courses	Prov. on Exist. Courses	Advice, Info. & Counsell	Consultancy Service	Research Activity	Business Club	Special Unit
Small Business Advisory Service, Croxley House, 14 Lloyd Street, Manchester M2 5ND (061-833 9828) *Contact: Cathy McCarten, John Jackson*	F P	F	F M B E C P L	●	●	●		●	●
The South Down College, Dept of Business Studies, College Road, Purbrook Way, Havant, Hants PO7 8AA *Contact: R. P. Jones*			P B E	●					
South Kent College of Technology, Dept of Business Studies, Ashford Branch, Jemmett Road, Ashford TN23 2RJ (0233 24513) *Contact: John Holloway*			P F M B E C P L	●	●	●	●	●	
South Warwickshire College of Further Education, The Willows North, Stratford upon Avon CV37 0QR (0789 66245) *Contact: John Furnival*	P F		F M B C P L	●	●		●		
South West London College, Management Studies, Abbotswood Road, Streatham, London SW16 1AN (01-677 8141) *Contact: P. J. Ayling*			P M C	●	●	●			
Southampton College of Higher Education, East Park Terrace, Southampton SO9 4WW (0703 29381 ext 55) *Contact: Sue Williams, Mr K. N. Cook*					●				
The University of Southampton, Dept of Accounting & Management Economics, Southampton SO9 5NH (0703 559122 ext 2553) *Contact: M. J. Page*					●				
States of Guernsey College of Further Education, Route des Coutanchez, St Peter Port, Guernsey, Channel Islands (0481 27121) *Contact: M. J. Vance*			P FM BC P	●	●	●		●	

	Short Courses-start up	Long Courses-start up	Topic Courses	Prov. on Exist. Courses	Advice, Info. & Counsel	Consultancy Service	Research Activity	Business Club	Special Unit
Stockport College of Technology, Wellington Road South, Stockport, Cheshire SK1 3UQ (061-480 7331) *Contact: Mr Bennett, Mrs Abbot*	P F	P	F M B C P L	•	•		•		•
Stocksbridge College of Further Education, Business & General Studies, Holehouse Lane, Stocksbridge, Sheffield S30 5DF (0742 392621) *Contact: D. G. Griffiths, R. K. Williams*		F P	F M B C P L	•	•	•			•
The Suffolk College of Higher & Further Education, Rope Walk, Ipswich IP4 1LT (0473 55885 ext 209) *Contact: Mr N. Hogg, Professional & Management Studies*	P	P	F M B C E P L	•	•	•	•		
Sunderland Polytechnic, Dept of Business Management, Small Business Centre, 1–4 Thornhill Park, Sunderland, Tyne & Wear SR2 7JZ (0783 41231 ext 23) *Contact: Mr Al Halborg, Mr Bob Joyce*	F P	F P	F M E		•	•	•	•	•
University of Surrey, Research Park Office, Guildford, Surrey GU7 1QQ (0483 571281) *Contact: Dr Malcolm Parry*			•		•	•		•	
University of Surrey, Bureau of Industrial External Liaison, Guildford GU2 5XH (0483 571281 ext 505) *Contact: J. P. Moore*			F M E C P L		•	•	•		
Thames Polytechnic, Dept of Business Administration, Riverside House, Beresford Street, London SE18 6BU (01-854 2030) *Contact: Ms J. Severn, Mr P. Saunders*	P	F	F M B E C P L		•	•	•	•	
Telford College of Arts & Technology, Business & Management Studies, Haybridge Road, Wellington, Telford, Shropshire TE1 1NP (0942 55511 ext 41) *Contact: Gerald H. Wallis, Miss J. Bradley*	F P	F P	F M B C P L		•	•	•	•	

	Short Courses-start up	Long Courses-start up	Topic Courses	Prov. on Exist. Courses	Advice, Info. & Counsell	Consultancy Service	Research Activity	Business Club	Special Unit
Thurrock Technical College, Management & Business Studies, Woodview, Grays, Essex (Grays Thurrock 71621) *Contact: Mr Howard Hollow, Tutor for Small Business Development*	P	P	F M B E C P L		•	•	•	•	
Tile College of Further Education, Small Business Centre, Tile Hill Lane, Coventry (0203 461444) *Contact: D. C. Ferris*	F P	F P	F M B E C P L		•	•		•	•
Totnes Business Development Centre, 1 Fore Street, Totnes (0803 864200) *Contact: Richard Jacobs*					•	•	•	•	•
Trent Polytechnic, Small Business Centre, Burton Street, Nottingham NG1 4BU (0602 418248) *Contact: Judy Barson*		F	F M C P	•	•	•	•	•	
URBED/Urban and Economic Development Group, Kirkaldy's, 99 Southwark Street, London SE1 0JF (01-928 9515) *Contact: Janette Bowman*	F P	F	F M		•	•	•	•	
Wakefield District College, Management & Business Studies, Whitwood Centre, Four Lane Ends, Whitwood, Castleford, W Yorks (0977 554571 ext 69) *Contact: Roger Thornton, Ernest Barrow*		P	F M B E C P	•	•	•		•	
Waltham Forest, Dept of Business Administration, Forest Road, London E17 4JB (01-527 2311) *Contact: C. Faulkner, A. McGinley*		P	B C L	•	•				
University of Warwick, School of Industry & Business Studies, Coventry CV4 7AL (0203 465291 & 24022) *Contact: Jenny Blake*	P	F	•		•	•	•	•	•

	Short Courses-start up	Long Courses-start up	Topic Courses	Prov. on Exist. Courses	Advice, Info. & Counsell	Consultancy Service	Research Activity	Business Club	Special Unit
Watford College, Dept Management Studies, Hempstead Road, Watford, Herts WD2 7HT (92 41211 ext 37) *Contact: K. F. Young, Head of Dept*			F M C P	•	•				
Wellingborough Technical College, Church Street, Wellingborough NN8 4PD (0933 224165)	P	P	F M B C P L	•	•	•			
West Bromwich College of Commerce & Technology, Small Business Unit, Wood Green, Wednesbury, West Midlands (021-471 2081) *Contact: P. T. Wilson, Jim Haliburton*					•			•	
West Cumbria College, Park Lane, Workington, Cumbria CA14 3RW (0900 64331) *Contact: Mr A. L. Watters, Dept of Business & Management Studies*			C P						
West Nottinghamshire College of Further Education, Business Studies & Management Dept, Derby Road, Mansfield, Nottinghamshire NG18 5BH (0623 27191) *Contact: Mr P. W. Usher, Kevin Hodgson*	F		B C	•	•	•	•		
West Oxfordshire Technical College, (WOTC) Hollaway Road, Witney, Oxon OX8 7EE (0993 3464) *Contact: R. Evans, Business Studies Lecturer*	P		F M B C P L	•	•	•			
West Suffolk College of Further Education, Out Risbygate, Bury St Edmunds, Suffolk (0284 701301) *Contact: Mrs Wendy Payne*					•				
Wigan College of Technology, The Management Centre, Ashfield House, Wigan Road, Standish WN6 0EQ (0257 424659) *Contact: J. M. Swift, Mr H. Beeley*	F P		F M B E C P L	•	•	•	•	•	•

	Short Courses-start up	Long Courses-start up	Topic Courses	Prov. on Exist. Courses	Advice, Info. & Counsell	Consultancy Service	Research Activity	Business Club	Special Unit
Wirral Metropolitan College, Business and Management Studies Dept, Carlett Park, Eastham, Wirral, Merseyside L62 0AY (051-327 4331) *Contact: D. B. Mitchell*		P	F M B C P L	•	•	•			
Worthing College of Technology, Dept of Business Studies, Littlehampton Road, Goring By Sea, Worthing, West Sussex BN12 6NV (0903 64424 ext 15) *Contact: Derek Haynes (Small Firms Unit)*	P	P	F M B E C P L	•	•	•	•	•	•
Wye College, Ashford, Kent TN25 5AH (0233 812401 ext 277) *Contact: J. A. H. Nicholson, Business Ventures Workshop*	F				•	•	•		
Yorkshire & Humberside Regional Management Centre, Small Business Development Unit, Management House, 32 Collegiate Crescent, Sheffield S10 2BJ (0742 667051) *Contact: Dr P. Prynne*	F P	F P	F M B C P		•	•	•	•	•
SCOTLAND									
Aberdeen University, Dept of Chemistry, Aberdeen AB9 2UE (0224 40241 ext 5658) *Contact: Dr Lesley Glasser*					•	•			
Angus Technical College, Keptie Road, Arbroath DD11 3EA (0241 72056) *Contact: Ms G. MacMillan, Head of Division, Mr A. Welsh, Senior Lecturer*	F P		F B C P L		•	•	•		
Bell College of Technology, Almada Street, Hamilton, Lanarkshire ML3 0JB (0698 283100) *Contact: Mr George Cantley*	F P	F P	F M B C P		•	•	•	•	•
Cardonald College of Further Education, 690 Mosspark Drive, Glasgow G52 3AY (041-883 6151) *Contact: Mr D. S. Baillie*		P	M B C P L		•				

	Short Courses-start up	Long Courses-start up	Topic Courses	Prov. on Exist. Courses	Advice, Info. & Counsell	Consultancy Service	Research Activity	Business Club	Special Unit
Clydebank College, Kilbowie Road, Clydebank G81 2AA (041-952 7771) *Contact: Mr D. Bathie*	P		F M / C P	●	●	●	●		
College of Commerce, 30 Constitution Road, Dundee DD3 6TB *Contact: Mr J. K. Pringle*	P		B		●				
Deans Community High School, Livingston, Scotland EH54 8PS (0506 31972) *Contact: John Thompson*					●				
Dumfries & Galloway College of Technology, Heath Hall, Dumfries DG1 3QZ (0387 61261) *Contact: Mr W. A. Brydson*	P	P	F B / C P / L	●	●	●		●	
Duncan of Jordanstone College of Art, Room 6016, 13 Perth Road, Dundee (0382 23261) *Contact: Mr Sultan Kermally*	P		F P / L	●					
Dundee College of Commerce, 30 Constitution Road, Dundee DD3 6TB (0382 29151) *Contact: J. Pringle*	P		B		●				
Dundee College of Technology, Bell Street, Dundee DD1 1HG (0382 23291 ext 397) *Contact: J. R. A. Hughes, Accountancy & Economics*	F P	F	F M / B E / C P / L	●	●	●	●	●	
Dundee University, Dept of Chemistry, Carnelly Building, Dundee DD1 4HN (0382 23181 ext 286) *Contact: Dr Tony Nechvatal*	F				●				
Edinburgh College of Art, Interior Design Department, Laurieston Place, Edinburgh EH3 9DF (031-229 9311) *Contact: Margaret Campbell*	P				●	●			
University of Edinburgh, Dept of Business Studies, William Robertson Building, 50 George Square, Edinburgh EH8 9IY (031-667 1011 ext 6438) *Contact: Ewan S. Gowrie, Lecturer in Marketing*	F		M P	●	●	●			

Institution	Short Courses-start up	Long Courses-start up	Topic Courses	Prov. on Exist. Courses	Advice, Info. & Counsell	Consultancy Service	Research Activity	Business Club	Special Unit
Falkirk College of Technology, Grangemouth Road, Falkirk FK2 9AD (0324 24981) Contact: Mr J. K. McNab, Mr T. C. Otten, Dept of Commerce Business Studies	P	F P	F M C P L B E	•	•	•			
Glasgow College of Technology, Dept of Management Studies, Cowcaddens Road, Glasgow G4 0BA (041-332 7090 ext 257) Contact: Mr Dick Weaver	F P	F P	F M E C P	•	•	•	•	•	
Glasgow School of Art, Head of Design, 167 Renfrew Street, Glasgow G3 6RQ (041-332 9797 ext 259) Contact: Mr Dugald Cameron					•				
University of Glasgow, 25 Bute Gardens, Glasgow G12 8RT (041-339 8855) Contact: Mr David Weir, Mr John L. Lewis, Management Studies Dept	P	F	C		•	•	•		
Glenrothes & Buckhaven Technical College, Stenton Road, Glenrothes South KY6 2RA (0592 772233) Contact: I. S. Ovens, A. Murphy, S. McKinstry	P F	P F	F M B E C P L	•	•	•		•	•
The Henderson Technical College, Commercial Road, Hawick TD9 7BW (0450 74191) Contact: Mr Robert McDonald	P F	F	F M B C P L	•	•	•			
Heriot-Watt University, Business Organisation Dept, Mountbatten Buildings, 31 Grassmarket, Edinburgh EH1 (031-225 8432) Contact: Mr Parker Nicol	P		M L		•	•	•		
Inverness Technical College, Longman Road, Inverness IV1 1SA (0463 236681) Contact: John Hunter, Business Studies	F	F	F M B L	•	•			•	

	Short Courses-start up	Long Courses-start up	Topic Courses	Prov. on Exist. Courses	Advice, Info. & Counsell	Consultancy Service	Research Activity	Business Club	Special Unit
Kirkcaldy College of Technology, St Brycedale Avenue, Kirkcaldy, Fife KY1 1EX (059 2268591) *Contact: Mr A. G. Gill, Head of Dept; Mr A. Blair, Senior Lecturer*			F M B E C P L	•	•	•		•	
Moray House College of Education, Holyrood Road, Edinburgh EH8 8AQ (031-556 8455) *Contact: Mr S. Chalmers*					•				
Napier College Management Centre, Colinton Road, Edinburgh EH10 5DT (031-447 7070) *Contact: Mr D. Stobie*			F M E C P	•	•	•		•	
Paisley College of Technology, Small Business Centre, High Street, Paisley PA1 2BE (041-887 1241 ext 354) *Contact: Dr Alan Leyshon*	F P	F P	F M C P	•	•	•	•		•
Perth College of Further Education, Brahan Estate, Crieff Road, Perth PH1 2NX (Perth 27044 ext 36, 37) *Contact: Mr G. T. Norwell, Business Studies*	P	P		•					
Queen Margaret College, Clerwood Terrace, Edinburgh EH12 8TS (031-339 8111) *Contact: Mr J. Blyth Wilson, Head of Dept of Management, Mr R. Shirley*		F	F M B P		•	•			•
The Queen's College, 1 Park Drive, Glasgow G3 6LP (041-334 8141) *Contact: Dr G. Richardson, Dr C. Williams, (Research Project)*					•	•	•	•	
Reid Kerr College, Renfrew Road, Paisley PA3 4DR (041-889 4225/7) *Contact: Mr G. Anderson*							•		
Robert Gordon's Institute of Technology, School of Business Management Studies, Block 'C', Hilton Place Aberdeen AB9 1FA (0224 42211) *Contact: H. A. B. Harper*	P		F M B C P L	•	•	•	•		•

St Andrews University, Economics Management Department, North Haugh, St Andrews KY16 9AL (0334 76161 ext 546)
Contact: Dr P. McKiernan

Scottish College of Textiles, Dept of Management Studies, Netherdale, Galashiels, Selkirkshire (0896 3351)
Contact: Mr D. Blyth

University of Stirling, Stirling FK9 4LA (0786 3171)
Contact: Prof. T. Cannon, Jack Denny, Bob Hale

Strathclyde Business School, 130 Rotten-row, Glasgow G4 0GE (041-552 7141)
Contact: Prof. N. Hood, Mr C. S. Greensted

James Watt College, Dept of Industrial Studies, Finnart Street, Greenock, Renfrewshire PA16 8HF (0475 24433)
Contact: W. J. W. Stoddart, Senior Lecturer

West Lothian College, Dept of Business Studies, Marjoribanks Street, Bathgate, West Lothian (0506 634300)
Contact: J. Lornie

NORTHERN IRELAND

Industrial Training Services, 47 Malone Road, Belfast 7, N. Ireland (0232 681444)
Contact: Peter Gay

Lisburn Technical College, 39 Castle Street, Lisburn, Co Antrim, Northern Ireland BT27 4SU (08462 4326)
Contact: R. W. McCahon, HOD, Commerce, Catering & Home Economics

Institution	Short Courses-start up	Long Courses-start up	Topic Courses	Prov. on Exist. Courses	Advice, Info. & Counsell	Consultancy Service	Research Activity	Business Club	Special Unit
St Andrews University		F	F M B C P L	●	●	●	●	●	●
Scottish College of Textiles	F P	F P	F M B E C P L		●	●			
University of Stirling	F P	F P	F M B E P		●	●	●	●	●
Strathclyde Business School	F P	F P	F M E C P L	●	●	●			
James Watt College	F P	F P	F M B E C P L	●	●	●	●		
West Lothian College		F P	F M B C	●	●	●			
Industrial Training Services	F	F	M		●	●	●		
Lisburn Technical College		P	B C	●					

	Short Courses-start up	Long Courses-start up	Topic Courses	Prov. on Exist. Courses	Advice, Info. & Counsell	Consultancy Service	Research Activity	Business Club	Special Unit
Ulster Polytechnic, Dept of Marketing & Business Policy, Shore Road, Newtonabbey, Co Antrim, Northern Ireland (0231 65131 ext 2303) *Contact: Mr Ken E. O'Neill, Faculty of Business & Management (ext 2630)*	F P	F B C L	M E P	•	•	•	•	•	•
Newcastle College of Further Education, Dept of Vocational Studies, Donard Street, Newcastle, Co Down BT33 0AP (03967 22451) *Contact: Mr Attridge or Mr Brown*	P	F	F B P M C L	•	•	•			•
Western Education & Library Board Technical College, Omagh, Co Tyrone, Northern Ireland BT79 7AH (Omagh 45433/4) *Contact: J. J. Devlin, Head of Dept of Business & Secretarial Studies*						•			
Southern Education and Library Board, Department of Business Studies, 3 Charlemont Place, Armagh (0861 523811)						•			
The New University of Ulster, Department of Continuing Education, Londonderry, N. Ireland (0504 65621) See Co-operatives, page 99				•					
Queen's University, Business Studies Department, Belfast (0232 245233 ext 3242) *Contact: Mr David A. Fleming*						•	•	•	

REPUBLIC OF IRELAND

	Short Courses-start up	Long Courses-start up	Topic Courses	Prov. on Exist. Courses	Advice, Info. & Counsell	Consultancy Service	Research Activity	Business Club	Special Unit
University College Dublin, The Enterprise Centre, Faculty of Commerce, Belfield, Dublin 4 (01-693 244) *Contact: Dr John A. Murray, Dr F. W. Roche*	P		•	•	•	•	•		•

WALES

	Short Courses-start up	Long Courses-start up	Topic Courses	Prov. on Exist. Courses	Advice, Info. & Counsell	Consultancy Service	Research Activity	Business Club	Special Unit
Aberdare College of Further Education, Cwmdare Rd, Aberdare, Mid Glamorgan (0685 873405) *Contact: Mr W. B. Owen*	F P	F P	F B C	●					
Aberystwyth College of Further Education, Llanbadarn Fawr, Aberystwyth SY23 3BP (0970 4511) *Contact: Mr E. Evans*					●				
Ammanford Technical College, Ammanford, Dyfed SA18 3TA (0269 2712) *Contact: Mr I. Jones*					●				
Barry College of Further Education, Barry, South Glamorgan (0446 733251) *Contact: Miss B. C. Perring*	P		M C						
Brecon College of Further Education, Penlan, Brecon LD3 9SA (0874 5252) *Contact: Mr J. Fletcher*					●				
Bridgend College of Technology, Cowbridge Road, Bridgend, Mid Glam CF31 3DF (0656 55588) *Contact: T. H. Pugh*	P								
Cardigan College of Further Education, Cardigan, Dyfed SA43 1AB (0239 2032) *Contact: Mr J. Jones*			B C L	●	●	●			
Carmarthen Technical College, Carmarthen, Dyfed SA31 2NH (0267 4151) *Contact: Mr W. G. Price*					●				
Coleg Meirionnydd, Barmouth Road, Dolgellau, Gwynedd LL40 2SW (0341 422 827) *Contact: Mr D. R. Owen*	P	P	C						

	Short Courses-start up	Long Courses-start up	Topic Courses	Prov. on Exist. Courses	Advice, Info. & Counsell	Consultancy Service	Research Activity	Business Club	Special Unit
Coleg Pencraig, Llangefni, Anglesey LL77 7HY (0248 4186) *Contact: Mr I. W. Hughes, Head of Business Studies*				•					
Cross Keys College, Gwent NP1 7ZA (Newport 270295) *Contact: Mr G. J. Neale, Head of Business Studies or P. McCarthy*	F P	P	F M C P L		•	•	•		•
Ebbw Vale Department of Business Studies, College Road, Ebbw Vale, Gwent NP3 6LE (302083/4) *Contact: T. Reid*		P	F B C P L		•	•			
Gorseinon College of Further Education, 52 & 58 Belgrave Road, Gorseinon, Nr Swansea, West Glam SA4 2RF (0792 892037) *Contact: L. F. Davies, Business Studies*	P F	P F	M B C L		•	•			
Gwent College of Higher Education, Allt-Yr-Yn Avenue, Newport, Gwent (0633 51525) *Contact: Mr M. Cromey-Hawke, Faculty of Management & Business Studies*	F P	F P	F M B C P	•	•	•	•	•	•
Gwynedd Technical College, Bangor, Gwynedd (0248 4186) *Contact: Mr J. B. Colwell, Head of Commerce*						•			
Llandrillo Technical College, Colwyn Bay, Clwyd LL28 4HZ (0248 46666 ext 293) *Contact: Mr J. R. Davies, Head of Business Studies*	P		F M B C P L		•				
Llanelli Technical College, Alban Road, Llanelli, Dyfed (05542 59165) *Contact: Mr R. M. Jones*						•			
Merthyr Tydfil Technical College, Ynysfach, Merthyr Tydfil CF48 1AR (0685 3663) *Contact: Ms S. Grant, Mr S. James, Business & General Studies*	P	P	F M B C P L		•	•	•		

	Short Courses-start up	Long Courses-start up	Topic Courses	Prov. on Exist. Courses	Advice, Info. & Counsell	Consultancy Service	Research Activity	Business Club	Special Unit
Montgomery College of Further Education, Llanidloes Road, Newtown, Powys (0686 27444) *Contact: Mr O. W. Tyres, Head of Commerce*				•					
Neath Technical College, Duryfelin Road, Neath (0639 58271) *Contact: Business Dept*			•						
North East Wales Institute of Higher Education, Management & Business Dept, Connah's Quay, Deeside, Clwyd CH5 4BR (0244 817531) *Contact: R. Wilson, D. Barnes*	F	F P	F M B C P L	•	•	•		•	
Pembrokeshire Technical College, Jury Lane, Kenton, Haverfordwest SA61 1TG (0437 5247) *Contact: Mr J. Barter-Davies, Head of Business Studies*	P	P	F B C P L	•	•				
Pontypool College, Blaendare Road, Pontypool, Gwent NP4 5YE (Newport 55141/3) *Contact: Mr G. Evans, Head of Commerce & Community Care*			B C L						
Pontypridd Technical College, Ynys Terrace, Rhydyfelin, Pontypridd (400121) *Contact: D. Herbert, Business Studies*	P	P	F M B E C P L	•	•				
Port Talbot College of Further Education, Beechwood Road, Port Talbot SA13 2AF (0639 882107) *Contact: Business Studies Department*					•				
Radnor College of Further Education, Llandrindod Wells, Powys (0597 2696) *Contact: Mr C. Hughes*					•				
Rhondda College of Further Education, Uwynypia, Tonypandy CF40 2TQ (0443 432187) *Contact: Mr N. E. Dawson-Jones, Head of Commerce and Business*									

	Short Courses-start up	Long Courses-start up	Topic Courses	Prov. on Exist. Courses	Advice, Info. & Counsel	Consultancy Service	Research Activity	Business Club	Special Unit
Rumney College, Friary Centre, The Friary, Cardiff (0222 27471) *Contact: A. Marrin, General Studies*				•	•				
South Glamorgan Institute of Higher Education, Western Avenue, Llandaff, Cardiff CF5 2YB (0222 561241) *Contact: Business & Liberal Studies*			F M B E C P L						
South Gwent College of Further Education, Nash Road, Newport, Gwent (0633 274861) *Contact: Mr G. R. Savey, Head of Business Studies*					•				
Polytechnic of Wales, Pontypridd, Mid Glamorgan CF37 1DL (0443 405133) *Contact: Eric Willis, Welsh Regional Management Centre*	F P	F P	F M B C P L	•	•	•	•	•	•
University of Wales, St David's University College, Geography Department, Lampeter, Dyfed SA48 7ED (0570 422351 ext 261, ext 246) *Contact: Dr D. A. Kirby, G. Finlayson*	P	F	F M B C		•	•	•		•
University College of Wales, Aberystwyth Dept of Agricultural Economics, Penglais, Aberystwyth SY23 3DD (0970 3111 ext 3305) *Contact: Professor M. Haines*				•	•	•			
West Glamorgan Institute of Higher Education, Mount Pleasant, Swansea SA1 63P (0792 201475/66376) *Contact: Mr D. Davidson, Dean of Faculty of Business Studies*	F P	F P	F M B E C P L	•	•	•	•		
Ystrad Mynach College of Further Education, Twyn Road, Ystrad Mynach, Hengoed, Mid Glamorgan CF8 7XR (812929) *Contact: W. H. Davies, G. A. Smith, Business Studies*	F P		B C L		•				

Other Small Business Courses

These institutions also run courses for new and small business:

Construction Industry Training Board, Bircham Newton, King's Lynn, Norfolk PE31 6RH (048-523 291) *Contact: D. J. Bishop.* They have recently introduced a three day residential programme for potential and existing proprietors of small firms. It covers; marketing, working with people, safety, estimating, planning and organising and financial management. Course fee £60.00. They also have a very comprehensive catalogue of training publications and audio-visual aids.

The Hotel and Catering Industry Training Board, PO Box 18, Ramsay House, Central Square, Wembley, Middlesex HA9 7AP (01-902 8865), run frequent short courses for people starting up in these industries. They also offer a small business service from regional centres around the country.

Pickup Professional, industrial and commercial updating, – this is a programme designed by the Department of Education and Science to encourage educational institutions to help businessmen and their employees to keep up with the latest technology and skills.

The Pickup scheme is operated in colleges, universities and polytechnics and can take any form – one-to-one tutorials, distance learning, small group work, and formal lectures.

Teaching can take place at an education centre, at the workplace or at home – and at different times of the day, week or year. For small firms the scheme can offer individual teaching or can bring together several businesses with the same or similar needs. Pickup provision can cover any facet of general business, or it can be tailored to the needs of a particular industry or employer.

Each course comprises four days full-time tuition for a group of 10 students, spread over a period of six weeks. Courses are not free – they have to cover their costs – and the DES says that owner/managers should expect to pay a realistic price for training. More details of courses and costs are available from the Pickup agents.

Where to go for a Pickup

As well as a national centre in London, the Pickup scheme is operated locally by regional agents. The contacts are:

National Pickup, Department of Education and Science, Elizabeth House, York Road, London SE1 7PH (01-928 9222 ext 3507) *Team Leaders: Richard Yelland and Marilyn Evans, general enquiries to Lesley Sambridge and Jenny Cox*

East Counties, Pickup Office, Cambridge College of Art and Technology, Collier Road, Cambridge CB1 2AJ (0223 63271) *Agent: Tony Winkless*

East Midlands, Pickup Office, Room 20, Spur F, Block 5, Government Buildings, Chalfont Drive, Nottingham (0602 298298) *Agent: Ronald Arnfield*

London and Thames valley, Pickup Office, Oxford Polytechnic, Headington, Oxford (0865 64777) *Agent: David Thomas*

North East and Cumbria, Pickup Office, Allendale, Newcastle-upon-Tyne Polytechnic, Coach Lane Campus, Newcastle-upon-Tyne N37 7XA (0632 666241) *Agent: Neil Ellidge*

North West, Pickup Office, Woodlands Centre, Southport Road, Chorley, Lancs TR7 1QR (02572 75474) *Agent: David Esther*

West Midlands, Pickup Office, University of Aston, Gosta Green, Birmingham B4 7ET (021-359 3611) *Agent: Peter Wilson*

Yorkshire and Humberside, Pickup Office, Yorkshire and Humberside Association for Further and Higher Education, Bowling Green Terrace, Leeds LS11 9SX (0532 438634) *Agent: John Geale*

South West, Pickup Office, Bristol Polytechnic, Coldharbour Lane, Frenchay, Bristol BS16 1QY (0272 656261) *Agent: Ray Hadfield*

DISTANCE LEARNING

There are now a number of home study kits and books that can help you learn the basics of running a business, if for one reason or another it is not possible for you to attend a college-based course. Home study kits include:

Association of British Correspondence Colleges, 6 Francis Grove, London SW19 4DT They keep a register of correspondence colleges and courses that they teach. Relevant subjects include; Accountancy, Book-keeping, Computer Appreciation, Cost Accountancy, Market Research, Marketing, Sales Management and Salesmanship.

Book-keeping, Accounting and Business Finance and Computing, a seven cassette and workbook system, each costing about £12.00. Launched in 1983 by Sussex Publications, Devizes, Wiltshire, SN10 1BR

Business Club is a BBC-TV series, that shows how other small businesses have faced and dealt with a range of problems. This gives a 'live' insight into the proprietors' thoughts as they face each problem and put solutions into effect. For details of transmissions of the Business Club series in 1984–5 write to Education Liaison, BBC, London W1A 1AA

The Open University has diversified into business and management courses through its Open Business School which was launched in October 1983 with 'The Effective Manager' and 'Personnel Selection and Interviewing'. 'Starting Up a Business' and 'Evaluating and Selecting a Business Computer System' are designed particularly for those in the small business sector where releasing a manager for training is not feasible. About 50 hours of study is required for each course, amounting to 5 hours per week over 3 months.

For further information apply to: Associate Student Central Office, Open University, Box 76, Milton Keynes MK7 6AN (0908 74066)

Running Your Own Business, a correspondence course launched in 1982. The programme covers starting off; setting up your business; selling; money matters and staff. It costs £113.00, and further details are available from ICS, Intertext House, Stewart's Road, London SW8 4UJ (01-622 9911)

The Scottish Business School has introduced a new (1984) MBA Masters Degree in Business Administration by Distance Learning Programme, participants work alone or in small groups at 'on campus' schools on a series of exercises. Students are issued with specially prepared materials including study guides, guided reading programmes and self assessment questionnaires. Students work at their own pace off campus attending the university only for a one week summer school and two weekend courses. The subjects covered in the MBA are of considerable use to potential entrepreneurs. Further details from Liz Sutherland, Strathclyde University, 130 Rottenrow, Glasgow G4 0GE

Henley open Management Education, Greenlands, Henley-on-Thames, Oxon RG9 3AU (049 166552). The Administrative Staff College has recently launched a series of distance learning programmes, complete with a 'hot line' to your tutor. Subjects covered include: Accounting; Managing People; Information Management; Marketing; Production; and Business Strategy. The course pack includes video and audio cassettes as well as books, and fees start from £350.00

Training to use Patents, from Newcastle-upon-Tyne Polytechnic, Lipman Building, Sandyford Road, Newcastle-upon-Tyne NE1 8ST (0632 612181 ext 29) *Contact: J. Stephenson*

Nine separate packages using various media such as video cassettes, tape-slide and a students handbook. Covers everything from 'Inventing the Patent' to 'Computer Online Patent Retriever's systems.

Books and Journals

This is a selection of useful reading that will give you a good appreciation of the subject. Other, more specialist reading is given in other sections.

Black Business Enterprise in Britain by Peter Wilson, Runnymede Trust, 37a Gray's Inn Road, London WC1X 8PP A survey of Afro-Caribbean and Asian Business activity and opportunities. Price: £5.00

Choosing and Using Professional Advisers, by Paul Chaplin, Enterprise Books, P.O. Box 81, Hemel Hempstead, Herts HP1 1AA. Price £4.95.

Guide to Managing Your Own Business, available from MacMillans publishers, Basingstoke (0256 29242)

Croner's Reference Book for the Self-Employed and Small Business and *Croner's Reference Book for Employers*, Croner Publications Ltd, 16–50 Coombe Road, New Malden, Surrey KT3 4QL Price: £26.30 and £32.80 respectively, including 1st year's amendment.

The Daily Telegraph Guide – Working for Yourself, published by Kogan Page Ltd, 120 Pentonville Road, London N1 9JN (01-278 3393) (paperback) Price: £5.95 (including p&p)

The Dictionary of Business Biography, to be published in 5 volumes at six monthly intervals starting in January 1984. Contains over 1000 biographies and should prove to be a valuable reference source for students of entrepreneurship. For more details contact: Mary Allan, Butterworth & Co. Ltd, 88 Kingsway, London WC2

European Small Business Journal, Amber Publications Ltd, 6 Bank Square, Wilmslow, Cheshire SK9 1AN. Published quarterly it provides a forum for views and research in the small business sector. Single copies £13, annual subscription £48.00

Going Solo (1981 edition) by William Perry and Derek Jones. BBC Publications. Price: £1.95

The Guardian Guide to Running a Small Business (Third edition 1983) Edited by Clive Woodcock, published by Kogan Page Ltd, 120 Pentonville Road, London N1 9JN (01-278 3393) Price: £4.95 (including p&p)

In Business Now, published by the Department of Industry from Eleventh Floor, Millbank Tower, Millbank, London SW1P 4QU (01-211 6088) (launched in October 1983)

London Business School Small Business Bibliography, published in 1983 from Alan Armstrong and Associates, The Busi-

ness Bookshop, 72 Park Road, London NW1 4SH (01-723 3902)
The first edition published in 1980 had 2600 entries, this one
has nearly 4400, which speaks volumes for the 'activity' in this
field. Price: £67.00 (including p&p)

The Practice of Entrepreneurship, by Meredith, Nelson & Neck,
published in 1982 by the ILO, 96/98 Marsham Street, London
SW1P 4LY The first third of the books' 196 pages are devoted to
analysing the personal characteristics of entrepreneurs, and as
such provide enlightening reading. Price: £5.70

Small Business Confidential, a subscription magazine published
by Stonehart Publications Ltd, 57/61 Mortimer Street, London
W1N 7TD (01-637 4383) (launched in August 1983)

Small Business Digest, published by the National Westminster
Bank plc, Small Business Section, 3rd Floor, 116 Fenchurch
Street, London EC3M 5AM

Starting a Business by Richard Hargreaves, published in 1983
by Heinemann, 10 Upper Grosvenor Street, London W1X 9PA
A good checklist approach to starting up, including some
detailed information on eight different types of venture. Price:
£9.95

Starting Your Own Business, a free publication (1984) from the
Small Firms Division of Department of Industry, Ashdown
House, 123 Victoria Street, London SW1E 6RB

Your Business, a monthly magazine for Enterprise from; 60
Kingley Street, London W1R 5LH (01-437 5678) Available from
most newsagents (launched September 1983) Price: 80p

Books on Specific Trades or Industries
Buying A Shop by A. S. & J. Price, published in October 1983
by Kogan Page Limited, 120 Pentonville Road, London N1 (01-
278 3393) Price: £2.95 paperback

Catering From Home, by Christine Brady, published in 1980 by
Pelham Books, 44 Bedford Square, London WC1 (01-323 3200)
Price: £4.50

Doing Bed and Breakfast, by Vollacott and Christmas, published in 1982 by David and Charles, 33 Baker Street, London
(01-486 6959) Price: £4.95

Innkeeping, from the Brewers Society, 42 Portman Square,
London W1. Price £4.95. (They also run short courses in
pubmanship.)

Managing and Marketing a Small Holding, by Michael Allaby,
published in 1979 by David and Charles, 33 Baker Street,
London (01-486 6959) Price: £6.95

The Retail Handbook: a practical guide to running a successful small retail business, by Ann Foster & Bill Thomas, published in 1981 by McGraw-Hill Book Co., Maidenhead, Berks SL6 2QL (0628 23431) Price: £7.50

Running Your Own series, being published throughout 1984 and 1985 by Kogan Page Ltd, 120 Pentonville Road, London N1 9JN (01-278 3393) Titles will include:
Running Your Own Wine Bar, Running Your Own Driving School, Running Your Own Small Hotel, Running Your Own Restaurant, Running Your Own Catering Business, Running Your Own Antiques Business, Running Your Own Photographic Business, Running Your Own Boarding Kennels
All the authors have been actively involved in the business written about. New titles will be added, so it is worth asking for your topic. Price: £4.95

Running Your Own Electronics, TV Servicing, or Electrical Business; a tuition programme by ICS, Dept N268, 160 Stewarts Road, London SW8 4UJ (01-622 9911)

Running Your Own Restaurant, by R. H. Johnson, published in 1982 (2nd edition) by Hutchinson Education, Hutchinson House, 17–21 Conway Street, London W1P 6JD Price: £5.95

Sewing and Knitting from Home, by Christine Brady, published in 1981 by Pelham Books, 44 Bedford Square, London WC1 (01-323 3200) Price: £4.95

Small Beginnings, by Alan Bollard, published by Intermediate Technology Publications, 9 King Street, London WC2E 8HN in 1984 Explains in some detail the opportunities for new small ventures in the following industries: The Brewing Industry, The Printing Industry, The Brick Industry, The Wool Textile Industry, Plastic and other Recycling Industries, small repair and service garages, small scale cheese production. Price: £12.50

Starting Up Your Own Business in the Hotel and Catering Industry: A self help guide, from the Hotel and Catering Industry Training Board, PO Box 18, Ramsay House, Central Square, Wembley, Middx HA9 7AP (01-902 8865) Published in 1982

Successful Salon Management, by Roger Cliffe-Thomson, published in 1982 by MacMillan Publishers, Houndmills, Basingstoke RG21 2XF (0256 29242) Price: £6.95

Your Own Dress Agency or Nearly New Shop, by Julian Maynard, published by Malcolm Stewart Books (London) High Street, Hornsey, London N8 7TS (01-349 2045) Price: £4.50

THE NATIONAL TRAINING INDEX

The National Training Index, founded in 1968, provides comprehensive information and advice on business training courses, correspondence courses, training films and training packages. The Index provides:

- Detailed information (dates, duration, location, cost and syllabus summaries) on more than 12,000 business courses in the UK;
- Comprehensive listings of in-company training schemes, course organisers, correspondence courses, training films and packages;
- a thorough but easy-to-use classification system which lists all courses and other training aids under 124 different subject headings;
- a Quarterly information up-date and newsletter;
- A unique and confidential assessment of the quality of courses and training films listed in the Index, based on constant reports (more than 10,000 a year) sent in by members;
- The Lecturers' Index maintains cards on 9,600 lecturers who have spoken at training courses, external and internal, during the past decade. Advice can also be given to members planning to run their own in-company training programmes on suitable external speakers.
- The Conference Location Guide maintains files on hotels and conference centres with facilities for courses and conferences. Members who let them know the location, size and audiovisual requirements of any external course planned, will be supplied promptly with the names and address of suitable venues.

Contact: Stuart Macnair, Manager, National Training Index, 7 Prince's Street, Hanover Square, London W1R 7RB (01-629 7262)

Membership costs, from 1st April 1984, £385 which is probably the cost of sending one person on one of the shorter courses in the Index.

The service may be an attractive proposition to a small company which is sending people on external courses for the first time, or considering running its first internal course.

YOUTH OPPORTUNITIES FOR SELF EMPLOYMENT

OPPORTUNITIES FOR YOUR PEOPLE TO START UP A BUSINESS

There is a growing recognition that young people have been neglected in the major initiatives intended to help people to get a business started. There are signs that a major push is underway, to redress this imbalance. As well as the 18 initiatives briefly described below, the Enterprise Allowance Scheme explained in Section 6 is of real use to young entrepreneurs.

Most of the small business courses listed in Section 8 are open to young people, and the Enterprise Agencies in Section 2 can also help.

Associated Resources, Job Change Project, c/o Birmingham Settlement, 318 Sumner Lane, Newtown, Birmingham B19 6RL (021-359 6596) A group of unemployed Executives who provide a free consultancy service to young entrepreneurs. Partly to keep their hand in, but helpful nevertheless.

Bootstrap Enterprises, 18 Ashwin Street, London E8 (01-249 7915) *Contact: Julie Connette* A scheme to help young unemployed people start a co-operative venture. Initially the business starts up with their help and advice. The aim then is that those people move on and new ones come in.

Brass Tacks, 298–300 Brixton Hill, London SW2 (01-674 8015) *Contact: Jill Mercer* Started off as a community enterprise programme providing on-the-job training for youngsters of 18+. Now turning its hand to helping young people start up on their own.

CRAC Publications, Hobsons Ltd, Bateman Street, Cambridge CB2 1LZ (0223 314640) *Your Own Business*. This book has been written for school leavers, trainees from MSC schemes, A-level leavers and graduates and designed as a 'starter' to give information, ideas, inside knowledge and know-how on organisation and planning of self-employment.

Included in the book are:
- Personal stories of successful – and unsuccessful – starters.
- Are you the type? – a quiz to test ideas and attitudes.
- The 'idea' – what every business needs.
- Market research.
- Getting the business on the road.
- Advertising.
- Money matters – how to prepare costs and estimates.
- Premises and equipment.
- Co-operatives and franchises.
- Using the professionals – eg: accountant, solicitor.
- Where next? – books, organisations to help, and addresses.

A4 48pp; illustrated paperback Price: £2.85

Education for Enterprise Network, c/o NICEC, Bateman Street, Cambridge CB2 1LZ (0223 354551) Founded in October 1982 to offer a training and information resource for those concerned with enabling young people to become self-sufficient and self-motivated. *Contact: Tony Watts*

Enterprise Scholarships, open to University or college students showing outstanding ability or insight into the area of business enterprise. The scholarships are to allow them to develop relevent knowledge and practical skills whilst at college. The grants would be worth about £850.00, and available from 1985. Details from: Professor Tom Cannon, Scottish Enterprise Foundation, University of Stirling, Stirling FK9 4LA (0786 3171)

Face, Workface, Market Place, Glastonbury, Somerset BA6 9HL (0458 33917) They offer training places to young people under the Manpower Services Commission's Youth Training Scheme. As well as providing the opportunity to learn a skill, they provide help to those who want to set up in business for themselves. This support and guidance can continue for up to three years after the training period has finished.

Graduate Enterprise Programme, An eighteen week programme to help recent graduates of universities and colleges, to set up their own businesses. An intensive foundation course, continuous counselling, a training allowance and a Market Research Grant, all combine to make this an unbeatable package for potential new entrepreneurs.

In England this is run at the Cranfield School of Management, Cranfield, Bedfordshire, MK 43 0AL (0234 750941) *Contact: Paul Burns and Colin Barrow*

In Scotland the contact is *Bob Hale* at the University of Stirling (0786 3171).

Graduate Extension Programme, University of Glasgow, 25 Bute Gardens, Glasgow G12 8RT (041-339 8855) *Contact: John Lewis* A programme to help unemployed graduates to develop small business skills. They work in a 'Consultancy' role in a small business for a couple of months, and are certainly better prepared to start their own firm after their experience. A training allowance is paid throughout. (Also at Durham University Business School, see page 304.)

Head Start is a joint Abbey National Industrial Society project which aims to encourage young people to try self-employment. Moreover, the Prince's Jubilee Trust has provided financial support and Capital Radio publicised the first stage of the scheme in the London area. The competition, aimed at the unemployed between the ages of 16 and 21, identified some 20 potential entrepreneurs interested in a wide range of ventures including computer maintenance, cake making, printing, painting and decorating and Caribbean catering. The scheme offers a counselling and advisory service in the skills essential to running a business; practical help and support during the first year of the businesses' operation, and Abbey National have also made available spare accommodation and equipment to the young entrepreneurs.

The experience of the businesses established under the scheme will be collated into a DIY kit to help other potential young business people and a manual will be prepared for circulation to the 16,000 Industrial Society members to provide a basis on which they might consider promoting such a scheme themselves.

Further information about the schemes can be obtained from the Industrial Society at Peter Runge House, 3 Carlton House Terrace, London SW1Y 5DG (01-839 4300)

Live Wire, National Extension College, 18 Brooklands Avenue, Cambridge (0223 316644) *Contact: Paul Moran* A scheme to help young people aged 16–24 to get their own business started. In 1984/85 it will be run in England and Wales, as a competition with the winners getting good three figure prizes, and everyone getting help and advice. The initiative comes from Shell UK, but it has many other supporters.

Make-it-yourself, c/o Inter Action Trust Ltd, 15 Wilkin Street, London NW5 3NX (01-267 9421) *Contact: Mike Jenn* Helps groups of young people from youth clubs to get together to make and sell such products as: garden furniture and calendars. A valuable training experience only.

National Youth Bureau, 17–23 Albion Street, Leicester LE1 6GD (0533 554775) 'Aim to act as a national resource centre for information, publication, training, research and development, and as a forum for association, discussion and joint action in the broad field of the social education of young people.'

Their youth opportunities section have produced some publications on how young people can start up a business, a co-operative, or become self-employed. They try to keep abreast of current events so are a useful organisation to contact.

New Enterprise Telford, Telford Development Corporation, Priorslee Hall, Telford, Shropshire TF2 9NT (0952 613131) *Contact: Col. Boxall* A small scheme that caters for 20 people aged between 16 and 18. As well as a training allowance, they get £500 worth of tools and materials to help get started. They are also encouraged to take specific training courses, if they need them. (Not at Telford).

Practical Action, Victoria Chambers, 16–20 Strutton Ground, London SW1P 2HP (01-222 3341/2) *Contact: Stuart Cobley, Liz Rhodes* Operate a number of youth initiatives. One of their latest, 'Youth Enterprise', plans to invest up to £2000 in financially viable business ideas, put forward by young people. The money could be either a loan or a grant. The scheme is on pilot in six areas, but should be national by the end of 1984. London, Tyne and Wear, Surrey, Cheshire, Nottinghamshire and Leicestershire are the pilot areas.

Prince's Trust, Drapers' Hall, London EC2N 2DQ (01-920 0861) The Trust has devised a package which sets out to help unemployed 16–25 year olds to set up their own enterprises. Grants of up to £500.00 can be given to buy equipment, and voluntary tutors can give business advice.

Royal Jubilee Trust, 8 Buckingham Street, London WC2 (01-930 9811) *Contact: Richard Shaw* The Trust operates a scheme to help youngsters raise money to start a business. It can also give grants of up to £1000 and can appoint people to help them set up.

Young Enterprise, Head Office, 221 New Road, Chatham, Kent ME4 4QA (0634 49907) Helps pupils get together to form a company as an extra curricular activity. Everything is small scale, the company can issue up to £130.00 worth of shares only. But all the trading activity is real. An extremely valuable training initiative.

Young Enterprise Fund, ASSET, 21 Green Street, Saltcoats, Ayrshire KA21 5HQ (0294 602515) *Contact: George Weir* They are pioneering low-cost loans for young starters in Scotland.

Youth Business Initiative – see Royal Jubilee Trust

STARTING UP OVERSEAS

Interest in going overseas to work has been widespread in the UK for a long time. A more recent activity has been for entrepreneurs to both 'emigrate' and set up a business.

The relaxation of exchange controls by the first Thatcher Government have played their part in making this a more viable option. And of course our membership of the EEC has made the environment in those countries less hostile.

The risks inherent in starting up a business in a completely new environment are clearly greater. But both the rewards and the incentives can be greater too. Many countries positively discriminate in favour of the in-coming entrepreneur, and have programmes of commercial and industrial support.

Most countries have a near equivalent to the Small Firms Service, and some have very familiar names.

The commercial attache at the UK embassy of the country you are interested in starting up in, may be able to help you. But the organisations listed in this section will be a source of direct help.

AUSTRALIA
Department of Industry & Commerce, First Assistant Secretary, Tertiary Industry Division, Commerce & Small Business, Edmund Barton Building, Kings Avenue, Barton, ACT 2600, Australia.

BELGIUM
For the Brussels Area:
Ministere de la Region bruxelloise, Rue Royale, 2–6, 1000 Bruxelles (02/513.41.10.) *Contact: M. L. Van Praet, Counsellor*

For the Flemish Area:
Vlaamse Executieve, Jozef II straat, 30, 1040 Brussel (02/218.12.10.) *Contact: M. K. Rogiers, Counsellor*

For the Walloon Area:
Ministere de l'Economie Walloone, Boulevard de l'Empereur, 11, 1000 Bruxelles (02/511.72.95.) *Contact: M. Destexhe, Counsellor*

CANADA
CDN Federation of Independent Businesses, 41 Young Street, Willowdale, Ontario, Canada M2P 2A6 *Contact: Judith McDonald*
CDN Federation of Independent Businesses, 1888 Brunswick Street, Halifax N.S., Canada *Contact: Peter O'Brien*

CDN Organisation of Small Businesses, 50 River Street, Toronto, Ontario, Canada M5A 3N9 *Contact: Geoffrey Hale*

N.S. Department of Development, 5151 George Street, Halifax N.S., Canada *Contact: John Chiasson*

Ontario Government, 900 Bay Street, Toronto, Ontario, Canada M7A 2E4 *Contact: D. O. Crawford*

Offices of Regional and Industrial Expansion:

Alberta: Department of Regional and Industrial Expansion, The Cornerpoint Building, Suite 505, 10179–105th Street, Edmonton, Alberta, Canada T5J 3S3

British Columbia: Regional & Industrial Expansion, Bentall Centre, Tower IV, Suite 1101, 1055 Dunsmuir Street, PO Box 49178, Vancouver, British Columbia, Canada V7X 1K8

Manitoba: Department of Regional & Industrial Expansion, 3 Lakeview Square, 4th Floor, 185 Carlton Street, PO Box 981, Winnipeg, Manitoba, Canada R3C 2V2

New Brunswick: Department of Regional & Industrial Expansion, Assumption Place, 770 Main Street, PO Box 1210, Moncton, New Brunswick, Canada E1C 8P9

Newfoundland: Department of Regional & Industrial Expansion, Parsons Building, 90 O'Leary Avenue, PO Box 8950, St John's, Newfoundland, Canada

Northern Territories: as for Saskatchewan

Nova Scotia: Department of Regional & Industrial Expansion, 1496 Lower Water Street, Halifax, Nova Scotia, Canada B2Y 4B9

Ontario: Department of Regional & Industrial Expansion, 1 First Canadian Place, Suite 4840, PO Box 98, Toronto, Ontario, Canada M5X 1B1

Prince Edward Island: Department of Regional & Industrial Expansion, Confederation Court, 134 Kent Street, Suite 400, PO Box 1115, Charlottetown, Prince Edward Island, Canada C1A 7M8

Quebec: Department of Regional & Industrial Expansion, Stock Exchange Tower, 800 Victoria Square, Room 3709, PO Box 247, Montreal, Quebec, Canada H4Z 1E8

Saskatchewan: Department of Regional & Industrial Expansion, Bessborough Tower, Suite 814, 601 Spadina Crescent East, Saskatoon, Saskatchewan, Canada S7K 3G8

Small Business Development Corporation N.S., 277 Pleasant Street, SU100, Dartmouth N.S., Canada 32Y 4B7 *Contact: Harold Clarke*

DENMARK

Ministry of Foreign Affairs Trade Department, Asiatisk Plads 2, DK-1448 Copenhagen K (01 920000)

FRANCE

Delegation a la Petite et Moyenne Industrie, Ministere de la Recherche et de l'Industrie, 13 rue de Bourgogne, 75700 Paris. ((1) 556.45.30 Telex: 203930) This department deals specifically with industrial as opposed to commercial firms.

For help in setting up businesses (e.g. in the retail trade) in rural areas, etc., enquirers may seek the assistance of their local

Chamber of Commerce and Industry, who will intervene on their behalf (especially as regards grants) with the: Direction du Commerce Interieur, 41 Quai Branly, 75007 Paris.

GERMANY
German Chamber of Industry and Commerce, 12/13 Suffolk Street, St James's, London SW1Y 5HG (01-930 7251) *Contact: Angelika Baumgarte*

GREECE
Ministry of National Economy, Department of Private Investment Promotion and Evaluation, Platia Syntagmatos, Athens (324 8556)
Hellenic Industrial Development Bank, 18 El. Venizecou Str., Athens 135, (323 7981)

HOLLAND
Institute of Small and Medium Businesses – Holland, Nettogen-doylean 49, Werden, Holland *Contact: T. G. Viarien*

ITALY
Confederazione Italiana, Piccola Industria, Via Colonna Antonine 52, 00186, Roma
Ministero Industria e Commercio, D. G. Produzione Industriale, Via Vittorio Veneto 33, 00100, Roma

LUXEMBOURG
Service de l'Industrie, (Ministere de l'Economie), 19–21 boulevard Royal Luxembourg (4794–231) *Contact: M. Claude Lanners, Chef de Service/Inspecteur Principal*

NETHERLANDS
Central Institute for Medium and Small sized Businesses, Dalste-indreef 9, 1112 XC Diemen, The Netherlands
Co-ordinating Foundation for maintaining Service-supply Centres for Small Businesses (same address as above)
Economic Institute for Medium and Small sized Businesses, Neuhuyskade 94, 2509 LR, The Hague, The Netherlands

REPUBLIC OF IRELAND
Department of Industry, Trade Commerce and Tourism, Kildare Street, Dublin 2 (0001-789411 Telex 24651)
Industrial Development Authority, Lansdowne House, Lansdowne Road, Dublin 4 (0001-686633 Telex 24525)
Shannon Development Co. Ltd, Shannon Town Centre, Co Clare (020-353-61-61555 Telex 26282)

NEW ZEALAND
Small Business Agency, Development Finance Centre, Cnr Feather-ston and Greystreets, Wellington, New Zealand (04-723-141)

SOUTH AFRICA
Small Business Development Corporation Ltd, National Board House, 94 Pritchard Street, PO Box 4300, Johannesburg 2000 (29-2677)
Small Business Information Centre South Africa, PO Box 1880, Potchefstroom, South Africa 2520 *Contact: William Conradie*

UNITED STATES OF AMERICA

Small Business Administration, 1441 L Street NW, Washington, D.C. 20416 (202-653-6565) *Contact: James C. Sanders, Administrator*
The fundamental purposes of the Small Business Administration, (SBA) are to aid, counsel, assist, and protect the interests of small business; ensure that small business concerns receive a fair portion of Government purchases, contracts and subcontracts, as well as of the sales of Government property; make loans to small business concerns, State and local development companies, and the victims of floods or other catastrophies, or of certain types of economic injury; and license, regulate, and make loans to small business investment companies.

TRAINING FOR BUSINESS OVERSEAS

These universities and colleges have a specific expertise in the Small Business field and may fulfil a similar service to their UK equivalents, listed in Section 8.

AUSTRALIA

James Cook University, Department of Commerce, James Cook University of North Queensland, Townsville, Australia, Q4811. (010-61-77-81-4425) *Contact: Miss J. E. Berryman, Mr A. M. Mirza, (010-61-77-81-4331)*

The University of Melbourne, Graduate School of Business Administration, Parkville, Victoria 3052, Australia *Contact: Prof. Bernard Barry*

The University of Newcastle, Department of Commerce, New South Wales 2305, Australia (010-61-49-685-741) *Contact: Prof. Alan J. Williams*

BELGIUM

Economic Council of East Flanders Small Business Department, Kouter 4, B-900 Gent, Belgium (010-32-91-2368-47) *Contact: Daniel De Steur*

Seminarie Voor Productiviteitsstudie En Onderzock, Ryksuniversiteit Gent, St Pieternieuurstraat 49, B9000 Gent, Belgium (010-32-91-256-353) *Contact: B. J. Verbrugge*

Solvay Business School, Avenue F. D. Roosevelt 50, C.P. 145, 1050 Brussels, Belgium (010-32-2-384-9602) *Contact: Jean-Claude Ettinger*

State University of Gent, Interfacultair Centrum Management, St Pietersnieuwstraat 49, B-9000 Gent, Belgium (010-32-91-256-353) *Contact: Prof. D. Deschoolmeester*

CANADA

B.C. Institute of Technology, 3700 Willingdon Avenue, Burnaby B.C., Canada v5G 3H2 *Contact: Randy Vandermark*

Queens School of Business, Kingston Ont., Canada K7L 3N6 *Contact: John McKirdy*

Saint Mary's University, Department of Management, Halifax, Nova Scotia B3M 3C3 *Contact: John Chamard*

University of Calgary, 2500 University Ave, Calgary Alta, Canada T2N 1N4 *Contact: P. M. Maher*
University of West Ontario, London Ont, Canada N6A 3K7 *Contact: Russell Knight*

DENMARK
Danish Employers' Confederation, Small Business Management School, Oster Alle 54, OK-8400 Ebeltroft, Denmark (06-344000) *Contact: Mr Ole M. Olsen*
Mr I. B. Ginge Hansen, Safirves 5, OK-3060 Espergaerde, Denmark
The Jutland Technological Institute, 135 Marselia Boulevard, 8000 Arhus C., Denmark (010-45-6-142-400) *Contact: Bjerremand Thorkild*

FINLAND
Finnish Institute of Leadership Training, Pohjoiskaari 34, 00200, Helsinki 20, Finland *Contact: Pirkko Tamminen*
Helsinki School of Economics, Small Business Management Programme, Runeberginkatu 14-16, 00100 Helsinki 10, Finland (43131) *Contact: Mr Eska Oksiala*
Helsinki School of Economics, Small Business Unit, Raatihuoneen-katu 13, SF 50100 Mikkeli 10, Finland (Mikkeli 368-952) *Contact: Mrs Ratia Partanen*

FRANCE
Groupe ecole superieure de commerce de Lyon, 23 av Guy de Collongue, B.P. 174 – 69132 Ecully Cedex, France (010-33-78-33-81-22) *Contact: Ali Garmilis*
INSEAD, Boulevard de Constance, 77305 Fontainebleau Cedex, France (422-48-27) *Contact: Mr Lister Vickery*

GERMANY
Centre for Technological Co-operation, Technical University of Berlin, Strasse des 17 Juni 135, D-1000 Berlin (West) 12

INDIA
Small Industry Extension Training Institute, Yousufguda, Hyder-abad 500 045, India

INDONESIA
Institute for Management Development, Mentene Kaya 9, Jakarta Pusat, Indonesia (375-309) *Contact: Mr Vincentius Winarto*

ISRAEL
Mount Carmel International Training Centre for Community Development, 12 David Pinsky Street, Haifa 31060, Israel

ITALY
ILO International Centre for Advanced Technical and Vocational Training, 201 Via Ventimiglia, 10127 Turnin, Italy
ISTUD – Institute Studi Direzionali, Corso Umberto 1, 67, 28049 Stresa, Italy *Contact: Mr Gabriele Impemba*
SDA Bocconi, Via Sarfatti 25, I 20136 Milano, Italy (010-39-02-958-1280) *Contact: Angelo Vergani*
Universita di Urbina, Facolta di Economia e Commercio, Passo Pale-stro 4, Genova, Italy (894139) *Contact: Miss Isabella Marchini*

MALAYSIA

MEDEC, Mara Institute of Technology, 14th Floor, Shah Alam, Selangar, Malaysia *Contact: Humam b. Haji Mohamed*

NETHERLANDS

Centre for Management and Industrial Development, Exchange Building, Coolsingel/Meent, Postbox 30042, 3001 DA Rotterdam, Netherlands

Research Institute for Management Science, PO Box 143, 2600 AC Delft, Netherlands

NORWAY

Norwegian Institute of Technology (STI), Small Business Management Training, PO Box 8116, Dep. Oslo 1, Norway *Contact: Otto Kaltenborn*

Oppland College, Small Business Management Centre, PO Box 1004, Skurva, N 2601 Lillehammer, Norway (062-55600)

Statens Teknologiske Institutt, PO Box 8116 Dep. N-Oslo 1, Norway *Contact: Otto Kaltenborn*

PHILIPPINES

University of the Philippines, Institute for Small Scale Industries, Quezon City, Philippines

SPAIN

Univeridad Autonoma De Madrid, Facultad De Ciencias Economicasy, Empresariales, Catno Blanco, Madrid 34, Spain *Contact: Emilio Ontiveros*

SOUTH AFRICA

Potchefstroom University, Potchefstroom, South Africa 2520 *Contact: Chris Conradie*

University of Natal, PO Box 375, Pietermartzburg, South Africa 3200 *Contact: Fiona Hake*

University of Orange Free State, Bloemfontein, South Africa 9301 *Contact: J. D. Nortje*

SWEDEN

Linkoping University, Department of Management and Economics, EKI, S-581 83 Linkoping, Sweden *Contact: Christer Alvehus*

Swedish Institute of Management, Stockholm School of Economics, PO Box 6501, S113 Stockholm, Sweden (08-235-820) *Contact: Mr Goran Odeen*

UMEA University, Department of Business Administration, S-901 87 UMEA, Sweden *Contact: Hakan Boter*

SWITZERLAND

University of Geneva, Department D'Economie Commerciale et Industrialles, 2 Rue de Candolle, Comin/Fac SES 1211 Geneve 4, Switzerland (20-93-33) *Contact: Dr Madeleine Conway*

UNITED STATES OF AMERICA

Baylor University, Waco TX, United States 76798 *Contact: Carlos Moore*

College of Lake County, 19351 West Washington Street, Grayslake, Illinois 60030 ((312) 223-6601) *Contact: James Paradiso*

Florida Atlantis University, Boca Raton Fl., United States 33441
Contact: Larry Klatt
Harvard Business School, Smaller Company Management
Programme, Soldiers Field, Boston MA 02163 (617-495-6450).
Kent State College of Business Administration, Kent OH, United
States 44242 *Contact: Leonard Konopa*
Kentucky State University, Frankfurt KY, United States *Contact:
Gus Ridgel*
Memphis State Fogelman College of Business/Economics,
Memphis TN, United States 38152 *Contact: Leonard Rosser*
PACE University, The Lubin Schools of Business, One Pace Plaza,
New York, N.Y. 10038 ((212) 285–3000) *Contact: Dr T. H. Bona-
parte, Dr L. Winner*
S.U.N.Y. At Albany, School of Business, Albany N.Y., United States
12222 *Contact: Thomas Dandridge*
San Diego State Mgt School of Business Administration, San
Diego Cal., United States *Contact: Oliver Galbraith*
University of Akron, Akron OH, United States 44325 *Contact: James
Dunlop*
University of D.C., 929 E Street N.W., Washington D.C., United
States 20004 *Contact: W. L. Crump*
University of Florida, 4164 N.W. 38th Street, Gainesville Fl, United
States 32606 *Contact: Robert Ramey*
University of Hawaii, Honolulu H.W., United States 96822 *Contact:
Ralph Hook, Jnr*
University of Montana, Missoula Mt, United States 59812 *Contact:
Richard Dailey*
University of North Alabama, Florence AL, United States 35630
Contact: William Stewart
University of Notre Dame, College of Business, South Bend, Indiana,
United States 46556 (219-239-5235) *Contact: Dr Sue Birley*
University of South Carolina, College of Business Administration,
Columbia S.C. United States 29208 *Contact: Richard Robinson*
University of Tulsa, Tulsa Okla, United States 74104 *Contact: Lyle
Trueblood*
Washburn University, 17th s College, Topeka K.S., United States
66621 *Contact: Ray Siehndel*
Wichita State Department of Market and Business Management,
Wichita Kan, United States 67208 *Contact: Charles Davis*

These may also be of use:

The Association of International Accountants Ltd, 2–10 St John's
Street, Bedford (0234-213577/8)
The Insider's Guide to Small Business Resources, by Gumpert and
Timmons, published in 1982 by Doubleday, Garden City, New
York. A guide to more or less everything in the American small
business word.

GLOSSARY OF KEY BUSINESS TERMS

This glossary gives a meaning to words that have either been used in the book (unless explained in the context of their use), or that you are likely to meet early on in your business life.

Access time Time between asking a computer for information, and the information being available.

Account(s) Usually annual financial records of a business.

Accrual An accounting concept that insists that income and expenses for the accounting period be included, whether for cash or credit.

Added value The difference between sales revenue and material costs. *See also* Value added.

Annual report *See* Audit.

Articles of association Usually a standard and comprehensive set of rules drawn up when a company is formed to show the purpose of the business.

Asset Something owned by the business which has a measurable cost.

Audit A process carried out by an accountant (auditor) on all companies each year, to check the accuracy of financial records. The auditor cannot be the company's own accountant. The result is the annual report.

Authorised capital The share capital of a company authorised by law. It does not have to be taken up. For example, a £1000 company need only 'issue' 2 £1 shares. It can issue a further 998 £1 shares without recourse to law. After that sum it has to ask the permission of its shareholders.

Balance sheet A statement of assets owned by a business and the way in which they are financed taken from both liabilities and owner's equity. This report does not indicate the market value of the business.

Bankruptcy Imposed by a court when someone cannot meet his bills. The bankrupt's property is managed by a court-appointed trustee, who must use it to pay off the creditors as fairly as possible.

Basic Beginners' All-purpose Symbolic Instruction Code. The most popular microcomputer language.

BIT A binary digit, usually represented by '0' or '1', or 'off' and 'on'.

Black economy Usually refers to businesses run by the self-employed who illegally avoid tax and National Insurance. There is therefore no official record, and they are collectively referred to as the Black Economy.

Blue chip In gambling, the high chips are usually blue. In business, this refers to high-status companies and their shares. They are usually large companies with a long successful trading history.

Book-keeping The recording of all business transactions in 'journals' in order to provide data for accounting reports.

Book value Usually the figure at which an asset appears in the accounts. This is not necessarily the market value.

Break-even-point The volume of production at which revenues exactly match costs. After this point profit is made.

Byte A sequence of eight 'bits', used to represent one character of information. A letter, digit, symbol or punctuation mark.

Capital It has several meanings, but unprefixed it usually means all the assets of the business.

Cash The 'money' assets of a business, which include both cash in hand and cash at the bank.

Cash flow The difference between total cash coming in and going out of a business over a period of time.

Computer programme Instructions telling a computer to carry out a specific task.

Cost of goods sold The cost of goods actually sold in any period. It excludes the cost of the goods left unsold, and all overheads except manufacturing.

Current asset Assets normally realised in cash or used up in operations during the year. It includes such items as debtors and stock.

Current liability A liability due for payment in one trading period, usually a year.

Debenture Long-term loan with specific terms on interest, capital repayment and security.

Depreciation A way of measuring the cost of using a fixed asset. A set portion of the asset's cost is treated as an expense each period of its working life.

Direct costs Expenses, such as labour and materials, which vary 'directly' according to the number of items manufactured. Also called variable costs.

Diskette A flexible disc used to store computer data, often called a 'floppy disc'.

Entrepreneur Someone who is skilled at finding new products, making and marketing them, and arranging finance.

Equity The owner's claims against the business, sometimes called the shareholder's funds. This appears as a liability because it belongs to the shareholders and not to the business itself. It is represented by the share capital plus the cumulative retained profits over the business's life. The reward for equity investment is usually a dividend paid on profits made.

Financial ratio The relationship between two money quantities, used to analyse business results.

Financial year A year's trading between dates agreed with the Inland Revenue. Not necessarily the fiscal year, which starts on 5 April.

Firmware Computer instructions stored in a read-only memory (*see* ROM).

Fixed assets Assets such as land, building, equipment, cars, etc., acquired for long-term use in the business and not for stock in trade. Initially recorded in the balance sheet at cost.

Fixed cost Expenses that do not vary directly with the number of items produced. For example, a car has certain fixed costs, such as tax and insurance, whether it is driven or not.

Floppy disc *See* Diskette.

Forecast A statement of what is likely to happen in the future, based on careful judgement and analysis.

Funds Financial resources, not necessarily cash.

Gearing The ratio of a business's borrowings to its equity. For example, 1:1 ratio would exist where a bank offered to match your investment £1 for £1.

Going concern Simply an accounting concept, it assumes in all financial reports that the business will continue to trade indefinitely into the future unless there is specific evidence to the contrary – i.e. it has declared an intention to liquidate. It is not an indication of the current state of health of the business.

Goodwill Value of the name, reputation or intangible assets of a business. It is recorded in the accounts only when it is purchased. Its nature makes it a contentious subject.

Gross Total before deductions. For example, gross profit is the difference between sales income and cost of goods sold. The selling and administrative expenses have yet to be deducted. Then it becomes the net profit.

Hardware The physical parts of a computer.

Income statement *See* Profit and loss account.

Insolvency A situation in which a person or business cannot meet the bills. Differs from bankruptcy, as the insolvent may have assets that can be realised to meet those bills.

Interface Electronic device that links computer hardware together. For example, a printer or VDU to the computer itself.

Know-how-agreement This is a promise to disclose information to a third party. If the disclosure is made for them to evaluate the usefulness of the know-how, the agreement is called a secrecy agreement. If the disclosure is made to allow commercial production, it is called a know-how licence.

Learning curve The improvement in the performance of a task as it is repeated and as more is learned about it.

Liabilities The claims against a business, such as loans and equity.

Liquidation It is the legal process of closing down a business and selling off its assets to meet outstanding debts.

Loan capital Finance lent to a business for a specific period of time at either a fixed or varied rate of interest. This interest must be paid irrespective of the performance of the business.

Marginal cost The extra cost incurred in making one more unit of production.

Marketing mix The combination of methods used by a business to market its products. For example, it can vary its price; the type and quantity of advertising; the distribution channels can be altered; finally, the product itself can either be enhanced or reduced in quality.

Market segment A group of buyers who can be identified as being especially interested in a particular variant of the product. For example, a cheap day return ticket for a train is a variant of a rail fare, especially attractive to people who do not have to get to their destination early perhaps to work.

Market share The ratio of a firm's sales of a product, in a specified market, during a period, to the total sales of that product in the same period in the same market.

Microcomputer A small computer using a microprocessor as its central processing unit.

Microfiche A sheet of photographic film on which a number of microcopy images have been recorded. You need a special viewer to look at the recorded information, which is very efficiently stored.

Microprocessor Electronic circuitry etched onto a silicon chip that can be used to manipulate information.

Modem A device that allows computers (and ancillary equipment) to communicate over telephone wires. The portable version is called an accoustic coupler.

Non-disclosure agreement An agreement which allows you to reveal secret commercial information – for example, about an invention – to a third party, and which prevents them from making use of that information without your agreement.

Opportunity cost The value of a course of action open to you but not taken. For example, keeping cash in an ordinary share account at a building society will attract about 2% less interest than a five-year-term share at the same society. So the opportunity cost of choosing not to tie up your money is 2%

Overhead This is an expense which cannot be conveniently associated with a unit of production. Administration or selling expenses are usually overheads.

Overtrading Expanding sales and production without enough financial resources – in particular, working capital. The first signs are usually cashflow problems.

Piggy-backing Usually associated with firms that market other firms' products as well as their own, but the term can be used to describe any 'free riding' activity.

Profit The excess of sales revenue over sales cost and expenses during an accounting period. It does not necessarily mean an increase in cash.

Profit and loss account A statement of sales, costs, expenses and profit (or loss) over an accounting period monthly, quarterly or annually. Also known as the income statement.

RAM Random-access Memory is the space used for storing computer data as programs. It can be changed as new programs or data are called up.

Reserves The name given to the accumulated and undistributed profits of the business. They belong to the ordinary shareholders. They are not necessarily available in cash, but are usually tied up in other business assets.

Revenue Usually from sales. Revenue is recognised in accounting terms when goods have been dispatched (or services rendered) and the invoice sent. This means that revenue pounds are not necessarily cash pounds. A source of much confusion and frequent cash-flow problems.

ROM Read-only memory.

Schedule 'D' Cases I and II are the Inland Revenue rules that govern tax allowances for self-employed people.

Schedule 'E' Allowances for employed people.

Seasonality A regular event, usually one that causes sales to increase or decrease in an annual cycle. For example, the weather caused by the seasons or events associated with the seasons: Christmas, spring sales, summer holidays, etc.

Secured creditor Someone lending money to a business whose debt is secured by linking a default in its repayment to a fixed asset, such as a freehold building.

Share capital The capital of the business subscribed for by the owners or shareholders (*see* Equity).

Software A computer term usually associated with programs and related documentation.

Strategy A general method of policy for achieving specified objectives. It describes the essential resources and their amounts, which are to be committed to achieving those objectives (*see* Tactics).

Synergy A co-operative or combined activity which is more effective or valuable than the sum of their independent activities.

Tactics The method by which resources allocated to a strategic objective are used.

True and fair An accounting concept that states that the business financial reports have been prepared using generally accepted accounting principles.

Turn key Usually refers to a client-commissioned system, accepted only when you can 'turn on a key' and are satisfied with the results, or output.

Value In accounting it has several meanings. For example, the 'value' of a fixed asset is its cost less its cumulative depreciation. A current asset, such as stock, is usually valued at cost or market value, whichever is the lower.

Value added The difference between sales revenue that a firm gets from selling its products (or services), and the cost to it of the materials used in making those products.

Variable cost *See* Direct cost.

Variance The difference between actual performance and the forecast (or budget or standard).

Working capital Current assets less current liabilities, which represents the capital used in the day-to-day running of the business.

Working life The economically useful life of a fixed asset. Not necessarily its whole life. For example, technological development may render it obsolete very quickly.

Work in progress Goods in the process of being produced, which are valued at the lower of manufacturing costs or market value.

INDICES

ENTERPRISE AGENCY SPONSORS

ENGLAND

Abbeycraft Furniture
Forest Enterprise
Agency Trust (Feat)

Abbey Life Assurance Co
Southampton Enterprise
Agency

ABC Engraving
Bury Enterprise Centre

Accrington Package & Storage Co
Hyndburn Enterprise
Trust

Act (UK)
Dudley Business
Venture

Action Resource Centre
Islington Small Business
Counselling Service
Tameside Venture Trust

Adams Foods
Burton Enterprise
Agency

Addison Hudson
Darlington & SW
Durham Business
Venture

AD Print
Gloucestershire
Enterprise Agency

Advantage Services (London)
Brent Business Venture
Ltd

Adwise
Gloucestershire
Enterprise Agency

K & S Ainsworth
Rossendale Enterprise
Trust

Aiton & Co
Derby & Derbyshire
Business Venture

Aklo Chemie UK Ltd
Metra 'Business Help'

Albany International
Bury Enterprise Centre

Alexandra Towing Co
Business in Liverpool

Allders of Croydon
Croydon Business
Venture Ltd

Allerdale District Council
Moss Bay Enterprise
Trust (Mobet)

Allmand Smith
Macclesfield Business
Venture

Allsorp Sellars
Dudley Business
Venture

Alton Chamber of Commerce
Fast Hampshire Enterprise Agency Ltd

Ames Crosta Babcock
Metra 'Business Help'
Rochdale

Amp of GB
Harrow Enterpise
Agency

Amoco Fabrics
Derwentside Industrial
evelopment Agency

Amoco Fabrics
Derwentside Industrial
Development Agency

Amway (UK)
Milton Keynes Business
Venture

Andrea Jewels Ltd
Hastings Business
Venture

Anglian Registered Management Centre
Newham Business
Advice & Consultancy
Service

Anglia TV
(Neat)
Norwich Enterprise
Agency Trust

Appleby Slag Co
Sohbac, Brigg

Arbuthnot Factors Ltd
Hastings Business
Venture

John Arden Marketing
Bury Enterprise Centre

E J Arnold & Son
Leeds Business Venture

Armitage & Norton
Hyndburn Enterprise
Trust
Calderdale Small Business Advice Centre
Leeds Business Venture

Rossendale Enterprise
Trust Ltd

Arthur Andersen & Co
Business in Liverpool
Leeds Business Venture
Watford Enterprise
Agency
Gloucestershire
Enterprise Agency
Dudley Business
Venture

**Arthur Young
McClelland Moores**
Derwentside Industrial
Development Agency
Entep Trust Ltd
Business in Liverpool
Manchester Business
Venture
Business in Oldham
Birmingham Venture
Dudley Business Venture
Nottinghamshire
Business Venture

**Ashford Borough
Council**
Enterprise Ashford

Ashford Trades Council
Enterprise Ashford

Associated Container
Southampton
Enterprise Agency

Associated Fresh Foods
Hyndburn Enterprise
Trust

Astley Baldwin
Blackburn & District
Enterprise Trust

**Atlantic Container Line
Services**
Southampton
Enterprise Agency

Axe Machine Tools
Milton Keynes Business
Venture

Babcock Construction
Medway Enterprise
Agency

Bacofoil Limited
Newham Business
Advice & Consultancy
Service

Bacup Shoe Co
Rossendale Enterprise
Trust

Bain Dawes
Leeds Business Venture
Leicestershire Business
Venture
Aid to Bristol Enterprise
(ABE)

Baker Perkins
Peterborough
Enterprise Programme

**J & W Baldwin
(Holdings)**
Vale Royal Small Firms

Balfour Beatty
Croydon Business
Venture
Derwentside Industrial
Development Agency

Ball & Percival
Southport Enterprise

Bally Group
Norwich Enterprise
Agency Trust (Neat)

Bampton Brothers
Swindon Enterprise
Trust

Bank of England
Business in Liverpool
Birmingham Venture

**Bank of England
Printing Works**
Forest Enterprise Agency
Trust

Barclays Bank
Cleveland Enterprise
Agency
Derwentside Industrial
Development Agency
Darlington & S W
Durham Business
Venture
Hartlepool Enterprise
Agency Ltd
Furness Business
Initiative
Blackburn & District
Enterprise Trust
Bury Enterprise Centre

Hyndburn Enterprise
Trust
Business for Lancaster
Business in Liverpool
Ltd
Macclesfield Business
Venture
Business in Oldham
Wyre Business Agency
Calderdale Small Busi-
ness Advice Centre
Leeds Business Venture
Rotherham Enterprise
Agency
Sheffield Business
Venture
Sohbac, Brigg
Vale of York Small Busi-
ness Association
Birmingham Venture
Burton Enterprise
Agency
Dudley Business
Venture
Business Initiative,
Stoke/Staffs
Warwickshire Enter-
prise Agency
Derby & Derbyshire
Business Venture
Leicestershire Business
Venture
Nottinghamshire Busi-
ness Venture
Colchester Business
Enterprise Agency
Great Yarmouth Busi-
ness Advisory Service
Harlow Enterprise
Agency
Newham Business
Advice & Consultancy
Service
Ipsenta, Ipswich
Forest Enterprise
Agency Trust
Lowestoft Enterprise
Trust
Beds & Chiltern Enter-
prise Agency (Becenta)
Maldon Branch of
Colechester (BEA)
Milton Keynes Business
Venture

Norwich Enterprise
Agency Trust (Neat)
Peterborough Enterprise
Programme
Fens Business Enter-
prise Trust
Blackwater Valley
Enterprise Trust
Basingtoke & Andover
Enterprise Trust
East Hampshire Enter-
prise Agency Ltd
Isle of Wight Enterprise
Trust Ltd
Maidstone Enterprise
Agency
Medway Enterprise
Agency
Portsmouth Area
Enterprise
Southampton Enterprise
Agency
Aid to Bristol Enterprise
(ABE)
Gloucestershire Enter-
prise Agency
New Work Trust Co Ltd
Swindon Enterprise
Trust
Brent Business Venture
Ltd
Harrow Enterprise
Agency
London Enterprise
Agency (Lenta)
Tower Hamlets Centre
for Small Business Ltd
Enterprise North
Wolverhampton Enter-
prise Ltd
Merton Enterprise
Agency
Hammersmith &
Fulham Business
Research Ltd
Metra 'Business Help'
Rossendale Enterprise
Trust Ltd
Hastings Business
Ventures

Barlow & Associates
Derby & Derbyshire
Business Venture

**Barnsley Metropolitan
Borough Council**
Barnsley Enterprise
Centre

**Barrow in Furness
Borough Council**
Furness Business
Initiative

Barwick Group
Fens Business Enter-
prise Trust

**Basingstoke & Dean
Borough**
Basingstoke & Andover
Enterprise Centre

Bass Brewing
Business Link, Runcorn
Sheffield Business
Venture (Bass North)
Vale of York Small Busi-
ness Association (Bass
North)
Burton Enterprise
Agency
East Hampshire Enter-
prise Agency Ltd

Bass Mitchells & Butler
Birmingham Venture

BAT Industry (UK)
Business in Liverpool
Southampton Enterprise
Agency
New Work Trust Co Ltd

**BAT Industry Small
Business**
Portsmouth Area
Enterprise

Batchelors Foods
Sheffield Business
Venture

Baxi Boilers Ltd
Small Industries Group,
Somerset

Beatson Clark & Co
Rotherham Enterprise
Agency

Beaver Fell Russel
Southport Enterprise
Trust

**Bedfordshire County
Council**
Beds & Chiltern Enter-
prise Agency (Becenta)

Bee Mouldings
Bury Enterprise Centre

Beehive Workshops
Bury Enterprise Centre

Bell-Fruit International
Nottinghamshire Busi-
ness Venture

Bell Watson
Sohbac, Brigg

Bemrose Corporation
Derby & Derbyshire
Business Venture

Berry Bros
Milton Keynes Business
Venture

Dennis Berry & Co
Berkshire Enterprise
Agency

Bestik Permeko Ltd
Leicestershire Business
Venture

BICC
Tameside Venture
Trust

J Biddy & Sons
Business for Lancaster

Binder Hamlyn
Manchester Business
Venture

Birmid Qualcast
Derby & Derbyshire
Business Venture

**Birmingham Chamber
of Commerce**
Sandwell Enterprise

Birmingham Post & Mail
Birmingham Venture

Birds (Derby)
Derby & Derbyshire
Business Venture

Birds Eye Walls
Great Yarmouth Busi-
ness Advisory Service
Gloucestershire Enter-
prise Agency

William Birch & Son
Vale of York Small
Business Association

Bishop of Norwood
Lowestoft Enterprise
Trust

Bitmac
Sohbac, Brigg

BJT Print Services
Warwickshire Enterprise Agency

Blackburn Borough Council
Blackburn & District
Enterprise Trust

Blackburn & District Chamber of Commerce
Blackburn & District
Enterprise Trust

Blackburn Cord Co
Blackburn & District
Enterprise Trust

Blackley Box Co
Bury Enterprise Centre

Blackshaw Sykes & Morris
Bolton Business
Venture

Blackwell Grange Moat House
Darlington & S W
Durham Business
Venture

Charles H Blatchford & Sons
Basingstoke & Andover
Enterprise Centre

Blue Circle Cement
Sohbac, Brigg

Blue Circle Industries
Gravesham Industrial
Enterprise Agency

Blythe Colours
Business Initiatives,
Stoke/Staffs

William Blythe & Co
Hyndburn Enterprise
Trust

BMW
Berkshire Enterprise
Agency

BOCM Silcock
Basingstoke & Andover
Enterprise Centre

Boddingtons
Manchester Business
Venture

Bonfield Hirst Turner
Leicestershire Business
Venture

Bordon Businesses Group
East Hampshire Enterprise Agency Ltd

BOS Shipping
Sohbac, Brigg

BOC
Manchester Business
Venture

Bolton Metropolitan Borough Council
Bolton Business
Venture

Boots
Nottinghamshire Bus
Venture

Booth & Co
Leeds Busines Venture

Boothferry Borough Council
Sohbac, Brigg

Boulton & Paul
Maldon Branch of
Colchester BEA
Norwich Enterprise
Agency Trust (Neat)

Bovis Construction
Leicestershire Business
Venture
Gloucestershire Enterprise Agency

Bowater Scott Group
Gravesham Industrial
Enterprise Agency

Bowaters
Stevenage Initiative

W Bowker & Co
Blackburn & District
Enterprise Trust

Boyden Data Ltd
Croydon Business
Venture

BP
Lambeth Industrial
Enterprises
Harlow Enterprise
Agency
Medway Enterprise
Agency
London Enterprise
Agency (Lenta)
Tower Hamlets Centre
for Small Business
Small Industries Group,
Somerset
Lambeth Business
Advisory Service

W Bradley Trimmer
East Hampshire Enterprise Agency Ltd

Braintree District Council
Bees Enterprise Office

Brake Bros
Enterprise Ashford

Breckland District Council
Norwich Enterprise
Agency Trust

Brent Area Health Authority
Park Royal Enterprise
Trust

Brent Chamber of Commerce
Brent Business Venture
Ltd

Brickhouse Dudley PLC
Dudley Business
Venture

Bridge Insurance
Manchester Business
Venture

John Bright
Metra 'Business Help'

Bristol Cham of Comm, Ind & Shipping
Aid to Bristol Enterprise (ABC)

Bristol City Council
New Work Trust Co Ltd
Aid to Bristol
Enterprises

Bristol Composite Materials Engineering
Aid to Bristol Enterprise (ABE)

Bristol Corporation
Aid to Bristol Enterprise (ABE)

Britannia Building Society
Business Initiatives, Stoke/Staffs

British Aerospace
Business in Oldham
Stevenage Initiative

British Aerospace Aircraft/Dynamics
Aid to Bristol Enterprise (ABE)

British Cellophane
Furness Business Initiative
Small Industries Group, Somerset

British Hovercraft Corp
Isle of Wight Enterprise Trust

British Institute of Management
Shropshire Enterprise Trust

British Leyland
Wolverhampton Enterprise Ltd

British Mathews
Forest Enterprise Agency Trust (Feat)

British Millerain
Rossendale Enterprise Trust Ltd

BPCC
Watford Enterprise Agency Ltd

British Rail Engineering
Bolton Business Venture
Derby & Derbyshire Business Venture

British Rail
Vale of York Small Business Association

British Steel Industry
Cleveland Enterprise Agency
Derwentside Industry Development Agency
Hartlepool Enterprise Agency
Moss Bay Enterprise Trust
Rotherham Enterprise Agency
Sohbac, Brigg
Dudley Business Venture
Sheffield Business Venture

British Shoe Corporation
Leicestershire Business Venture

BSR (UK)
Dudley Business Venture

British Sugar Co
Vale of York Small Business Association
Peterborough Enterprise Programme

British Telecom
Colchester Business Enterprise Agency
Ipswich Enterprise Trust (Ipsenta)
Swindon Enterprise Trust
Croydon Business Venture Ltd
Business Initiatives, Carlisle
Dudley Business Venture
Rossendale Enterprise Trust
Hastings Business Venture

British Syphon Industry
Sheffield Business Venture

British United Shoe Machinery Co
Leicestershire Business Venture

Broadbents
Sefton Enterprise Trust

Broadland District Council
Norwich Enterprise Agency Trust (Neat)

Jas Broadley
Hyndburn Enterprise Trust

Brooke Bond Oxo
Croydon Business Venture Ltd

Nigel Brooks
East Hampshire Enterprise Agency Ltd

Broseley Estates
Wyre Business Agency

Brown Engineering
Forest Enterprise Agency Trust (Feat)

Brown Brothers
Swindon Enterprise Trust

Brown & Murphy
Furness Business Initiative

Brunning Advertising & Marketing (Liverpool)
Business in Liverpool

Brunnings
Manchester Business Venture

Bryand Construction
Birmingham Venture

BTP Tioxide
Hartlepool Enterprise Agency

Bunker & Tomalin
Watford Enterprise Agency

BUPA
Harrow Enterprise Agency

Burall Bros Ltd
Fens Business Enterprise Trust

Burley & Geach
East Hampshire Enterprise Agency Ltd

Burton & District Chamber of Commerce
Burton Enterprise Agency

Burmah Oil Company
Swindon Enterprise
Trust

Burrows & Day
Enterprise Ashford

Buss Farm Fresh Foods
Hastings Business
Ventures

**Bury Chamber of
Commerce**
Bury Enterprise Centre

Burton Group
Leeds Business Venture

**Bury Metropolitan
Borough Council**
Bury Enterprise Centre

Bury Cooper Whitehead
Bury Enterprise Centre

Bury Times Group
Bury Enterprise Centre

J Butterworth (BACUP)
Rossendale Enterprise
Trust

**Calderdale Metropolitan
Borough Council**
Calderdale Small Business Advice Centre

**Calderdale Innovation
Centre**
Caldis

Cadbury
New Work Trust Co Ltd
Shropshire Enterprise
Trust

Calligen Focus
Hyndburn Enterprise
Trust

Patricia Calway & Co
Rossendale Enterprise
Trust Ltd

**Cambridgeshire County
Council**
Fens Bus Enterprise
Trust

J W Cameron & Co
Hartlepool Enterprise
Agency

Cannon Assurance
Brent Business Venture

Canon (UK)
Croydon Business
Venture

Caparo Industries PLC
Dudley Business
Venture

Carborundum
Hyndburn Enterprise
Trust

**Careless Oil
Explorations**
East Hampshire Enterprise Agency Ltd

Carleton Real Estate
Business for Lancaster

Carlisle City Council
Business Initiatives,
Carlisle

**Carlisle Chamber of
Trade**
Business Initiatives,
Carlisle

C & I Supplies
East Hampshrie Enterprise Agency

**Carnon Consolidated
Tin Mines**
West Cornwall Enterprise Trust Ltd

Carpets International
Calderdale Small Business Advice Centre

Carreras Rothmans
Darlington & S W
Durham Business
Venture

Carr's Flour Mills
Business Initiatives,
Carlisle

F R Cass
Bury Enterprise Centre

Case
Watford Enterprise
Agency

Cassio College
Watford Enterprise
Agency

Castle Kitchens
Wyre Business Agency

Catalin
Forest Enterprise
Agency Trust

Cavaghan & Gray
Business Initiatives,
Carlisle

**Central Electricity
Generating Board**
Business for Lancaster
Colchester & Maldon
Business Enterprise
Agency

Central Independent TV
Derby & Derbyshire
Business Venture

Century Oils
Business Initiatives,
Stoke/Staffs

Chadwicks
Bury Enterprise Centre

Chancel Construction
Wolverhampton Enterprise Ltd

Charrington & Co Ltd
Newham Business
Advice & Consultancy
Service

**Charter Consolidated
Services**
Enterprise Ashford

**Cheltenham Borough
Council**
Gloucestershire Enterprise Agency

**Cheshire County
Council**
Business in Liverpool
Macclesfield Business
Venture
Vale Royal Small Firms
Ltd
Warrington Business
Promotion Bureau
Business Link, Runcorn

**Cheshire County
Newspapers**
Vale Royal Small Firms
Ltd

**Chesterfield Borough
Council**
Chesterfield ARC

Chrisp & Wilson (NE)
Darlington & S W
Durham Business
Venture

Chubb
Wolverhampton Enter-
prise Ltd

Churches
Swim/Swap Enterprise
Centre

Ciba-Geigy
Macclesfield Business
Venture

Citibank
London Enterprise
Agency (Lenta)

**E A Clare & Son
(Locksmiths)**
Croydon Business
Venture Ltd

Clarke Securities
Burton Enterprise
Agency

**Clarkson Puckle (West
Midlands)**
Dudley Business
Venture

Claxton & Garland
Vale of York Small
Business Association

Cleanaway
Enteprise Trust Ltd,
Wirral

**Cleethorpes Borough
Council**
Great Grimsby Small
Firms Advisory Bureau

Clement Keys & Co
Dudley Business
Venture

**Cleveland County
Council**
Cleveland Enterprise
Agency
Hartlepool Enterprise
Agency

Clifford Dairies
Berkshire Enterprise
Agency

Clugson Holdings
Sohbac, Brigg

Cobble Blackburn
Blackburn & District
Enterprise Trust

**Coca-Cola Export
Corporation**
Milton Keynes Business
Venture

Coin Controls
Business in Oldham

**Colchester Building
Society**
Colchester Business
Enterprise Agency

Colchester Council
Colchester Business
Enterprise Agency

**Colchester & District
Chamber of Trade
and Commerce**
Colchester Business
Enterprise Agency

Colman of Norwich
Norwich Enterprise
Agency Trust (Neat)

**Commission for New
Towns**
Harlow Enterprise
Agency

Compair Industrial
Ipsenta, Ipswich

**Compair Mining &
Construction**
West Cornwall Enter-
prise Trust Ltd

Compass Caravans
Derwentside Industrial
Development Agency

**Computing Devices Co
Ltd**
Hastings Business
Ventures

Condor Ltd
Burton Enterprise
Agency

**Confederation of Ship
building & Engineering
Workers**
Coventry Business
Centre Ltd

Connells Commercial
Milton Keynes Business
Venture

Consett Industries
Derwentside Industrial
Development Agency

Contraplan
Warwickshire Enter-
prise Agency

Co-op Bank
Manchester Business
Venture
Mid Cornwall Indus-
tries Group
Newham Business
Advice & Consultancy
Service

Co-op Retail Services
Mid Cornwall Industries
Group

**Cooper Basden &
Adamson**
Business for Lancaster

Coopers & Lybrand
Derwentside Industrial
Development Agency

**Copeland District
Council**
Moss Bay Enterprise
Trust (Mobet)

Corah
Leicestershire Business
Venture

R Corben & Son
Maidstone Enterprise
Agency

Corby District Council
Corby Business
Advisory Bureau

**Corby New Town
Commission**
Corby Business Advisory
Bureau

**Cornwall County
Council**
West Cornwall Enter-
prise Trust

CoSIRA
Northumberland
Business Centre
Shropshire Employment
Promotion Association

Wm Coulthard & Co Ltd
Business Initiatives,
Carlisle

361

County Glass
Vale Royal Small Firms

Courage Breweries
Berkshire Enterprise
Agency

Courage Eastern
Maidstone Enterprise
Agency

Courage Western
New Work Trust Co Ltd

Courtaulds
Manchester Business
Venture
Business in Oldham
Derby & Derbyshire
Business Venture

CPC (UK)
Manchester Business
Venture

Coventry City Council
Coventry Business
Centre

**Coventry Chamber of
Commerce and
Industry**
Coventry Business
Centre

**Cranfield Institute of
Technology**
Milton Keynes Business
Venture

R Cressey & Sons
Macclesfield Business
Venture

Crosse & Blackwell Ltd
Newham Business
Advice and Consultancy
Service

**Croydon Chamber of
Commerce & Industry**
Croydon Business
Venture Ltd

Croydon Motor Traders
Croydon Business
Venture Ltd

CRS
Sohbac, Brigg

Crown Paints
Blackburn & District
Enterprise Trust

Cubitt & West
East Hampshire Enter-
prise Agency Ltd

Michael Cull Ltd
Bolton Business
Venture

**Cumbria County
Council**
Furness Business
Initiative
Business Initiatives,
Carlisle
Moss Bay Enterprise
Trust (Mobet)

**Cumbrian Newspaper
Group**
Business Initiatives,
Carlisle

Cummins Eng Co
Darlington & SW
Durham Business
Venture

Cupal
Blackburn & District
Enterprise Trust

Cyril Moss Arkwright
Bolton Business
Venture

C L Dain & Co
Burton Enterprise
Agency

Danks of Netherton
Dudley Business
Venture

Darchem
Darlington & SW
Durham Business
Venture

**Darling, Heslop &
Forster**
Darlington & SW
Durham Business
Venture

**Darlington Borough
Council**
Darlington & SW
Durham Business
Venture

Dataview
Colchester Business
Enterprise Agency

Davis Estates
Isle of Wight Enterprise
Trust Ltd

Dawbarns
Fens Business Enter-
prise Trust

DEB Ltd
Derby & Derbyshire
Business Venture

Debenhams
Croydon Business
Venture Ltd
Southport Enterprise
Trust

Deloitte Haskins & Sells
Derwentside Industrial
Development Agency
Business in Liverpool
Leeds Business Venture
Nottinghamshire
Business Venture
Berkshire Enterprise
Agency
Southampton
Enterprise Agency
Croydon Business
Venture Ltd
Rossendale Enterprise
Trust

Delta Electrical Access
Business in Oldham

**Department of
Environment**
Tyne & Wear Enterprise
Trust Ltd
Wigan New Enterprise
New Work Trust Co Ltd
Brixton United
Small Industries Group,
Somerset
Corby Business Advice
Bureau
Action Research Centre
Fashion Centre Ltd,
London
Wandsworth Business
Research Centre
Lambeth Industrial
Enterprises

**Department of
Trade & Industry**
Business Initiatives,
Carlisle

362

Wigan New Enterprise
Sohbac, Brigg
Warwickshire Enter-
prise Agency
Maldon Branch of
Colchester, BEA
New Work Trust Co Ltd
Bolton Business
Ventures Ltd
Enterprise North
North Devon Enterprise
Group

Dept of Industry Small Firms Service
Northumberland
Business Centre

Derby Building Society
Derby & Derbyshire
Business Venture

Derby City Council
Derby & Derbyshire
Business Venture

Derby & Derbyshire Chamber of Commerce
Derby & Derbyshire
Business Venture

Derwentside District Council
Derwentside Industrial
Development Agency

Derwentside Industrial Group
Derwentside Industrial
Development Agency

Development Commission
East Hampshire Enter-
prise Agency Ltd
Small Industries Group,
Somerset
Mendip & Wansdyke
Local Enterprise Group

Devenish Redruth Brewery
West Cornwall Enter-
prise Trust Ltd

North Devon District Council
North Devon Enterprise
Group

Allen Dick Engineering
Business for Lancaster

Dickinson Robinson Group
Aid to Bristol Enter-
prise (ABC)

Dimplex Heating
Southampton Engi-
neering Agency

**District Society of Char-
tered Accountants**
Wolverhampton Enter-
prise Ltd

H M Dockyard, Chatham
Medway Enterprise
Agency

H M Dockyard
Portsmouth Area
Enterprise

Robert M Douglas Holdings
Birmingham Venture

John Dowler & Sons
East Hampshire Enter-
prise Agency Ltd

Dove Group
Croydon Business
Venture Ltd

Dowty Boulton Page
Wolverhampton
Enterprise Ltd

Dowty Group
Gloucestershire
Enterprise Agency

DTI
Wyre Business Agency

Dudley Metropolitan Borough Council
Dudley Business
Venture

Dudley Chamber of Industry & Commerce
Dudley Business
Venture

Thomas Dudley
Dudley Business
Venture

Dunham Bush (Manufacturing)
Portsmouth Area
Enterprise

Dunlop Ltd
Leicestershire Business
Venture

Du Pont
Stevenage Initiative

Durham University Business School
Enterprise North

Durnford Ford
Hastings Business
Venture

Dyer & Overton
Hastings Business
Venture

Eagle Star Group
Gloucestershire
Enterprise Agency
Harrow Enterprise Agency

East Anglian Ind. Relations Service
Great Yarmouth Busi-
ness Advice Service

East Anglian Daily Times Co
Ipswich Enterprise
Trust (Ipsenta)

Eastbourne Mutual
Hastings Business
Ventures

Eastern Counties Newspapers
Norwich Enterprise
Agency Trust (Neat)

East Devon District Council
East Devon Small Indu-
stries Group

East Hampshire Post
East Hampshire Enter-
prise Agency Ltd

East Hants District Council
East Hampshire Enter-
prise Agency Ltd

East Hampshire District Council
Portsmouth Area
Enterprise

East Midlands Allied Press
Peterborough
Enterprise Programme

East Sussex County Councils
Hastings Business Venture

Eaton
Darlington & SW Durham Business Venture

Ecclesiastical Insurance
Gloucestershire Enterprise Agency

F Edmondson Estates
Business for Lancaster

N & M Edwards
Macclesfield Business Venture

Elkan Electronics
Bury Enterprise Centre

Elddis Transport
Derwentside Industrial Development Agency

Electrolux
Beds & Chiltern Enterprise Agency (Becenta)

F W Elliott Ltd
Hastings Business Venture

Emerson Electrics
Swindon Enterprise Trust

English China Clays
Mid Cornwall Industries Group
Restormel Local Enterprise Trust Ltd

English Industrial Estates
Hartlepool Enterprise Agency
Northumberland Business Centre

Enterprise North
Northumberland Business Centre
Tyne & Wear Enterprise Trust Ltd

Entwistle Green & Duckworth
Hundburn Enterprise Trust

Epping Forest Dist. Council
Forest Enterprise Agency Trust (Feat)

Erewash Borough Council
Derby & Derbyshire Business Venture

Ernst & Whinney
Birmingham Venture
Beds & Chiltern Enterprise Agency (Becenta)

Essex County Newspapers
Colchester Business Enterprise Agency

Esso Petroleum Co
Birmingham Venture

Esso Chemical
Southampton Enterprise Agency
Macclesfield Business Venture

Essex Water Co
Maldon Branch of Colchester, BEA

European Social Fund
Tyne & Wear Enterprise Trust Ltd
Wigan New Enterprise
New Work Trust Co Ltd

Europ Assistance
Croydon Business Venture Ltd

Europrint
Swindon Enterprise Trust

Estee Lauder Cosmetics
East Hampshire Enterprise Agency Ltd

Everards Brewery
Leicestershire Business Venture

Everett Collins & Loosley
Milton Keynes Business Venture

Ever Ready (GB)
Derwentside Industrial Development Agency

Exclusive Cleaning Services
Milton Keynes Business Venture

Expanded Metal
Hartlepool Enterprise Agency

Express Lift Co
Input, Northampton

Express & Star
Wolverhampton Enterprise Ltd
Dudley Business Venture

Falconer Partnership
Gloucestershire Enterprise Agency

Falmouth Shiprepair
West Cornwall Enterprise Trust Ltd

Fareham Borough Council
Portsmouth Area Enterprise

Farnham Castle Newspapers
East Hampshire Enterprise Agency Ltd

Ferranti
Manchester Business Venture

Ferranti Computer Systems
Business in Oldham

Fine Art Developments
Burton Enterprise Agency

Fine Fare
Lowestoft Enterprise Trust

Finn-Kelcey & Chapman
Enterprise Ashford

Fisons-Pharmaceutical Division
Leicestershire Business Venture

Flitwick Oil Company
Beds & Chiltern Enterprise Agency (Becenta)

Flymo
Darlington & SW Durham Business Venture

Ford & Western (SW)
Gloucestershire
Enterprise Agency

Ford & Weston
Derby & Derbyshire
Business Venture

Forest of Dean District Council
Gloucestershire
Enterprise Agency

Thomas Forman & Sons
Nottinghamshire
Business Venture

Foster Bros Clothing Co
Warwickshire
Enterprise Agency

Foundation Communications
Warwickshire
Enterprise Agency

Foundations for Alternatives
Small Industries Group,
Somerset

Foundation Gatsby
Small Industries Group,
Somerset

FPT Industries
Portsmouth Area
Enterprise

Freeman & Rich
Blackburn & District
Enterprise Trust

French Kier Holdings
Forest Enterprise
Agency Trust (Feat)

Furness Building Society
Furness Business
Initiative

Gabriel Securities
Stevenage Initiatives

Gallacher Tobacco
Camden Enterprise

George Gale & Co
East Hampshire Enterprise Agency Ltd

Galliford
Warwickshire
Enterprise Agency

Gammon & Smith
East Hampshire Enterprise Agency Ltd

H Garnett & Co
Rotherham Enterprise
Agency

Gates Group
Forest Enterprise
Agency Trust (Feat)

GEC
Cleveland Enterprise
Agency
Darlington & S W
Durham Business
Venture
Hartlepool Enterprise
Agency
Warwickshire
Enterprise Agency
Leicestershire Business
Venture

GEC/Wembley
Brent Business Venture

GEC/AEI Cables
Gravesham Industrial
Enterprise Agency

Geedings of Ashford
Enterprise Ashford

Gerrard Neale Fennemore
Milton Keynes Business
Venture

Gibbings & Thornborrow
Business Initiatives,
Carlisle

Gillingham Borough Council
Medway Enterprise
Agency

GKN Fasteners
Birmingham Venture
Dudley Business
Venture

GKN Sankey
Shropshire Enterprise
Trust

Glanford Borough Council
Sohbac, Brigg

Glaxo Operations
Darlington & SW
Durham Business
Venture

Gloucester City Council
Gloucestershire
Enterprise Agency

Gloucestershire County Council
Gloucestershire
Enterprise Agency

Glynwed Group
Shropshire Enterprise
Trust

Godwins
Blackwater Valley
Enterprise Trust

Godwins (North) Ltd
Rossendale Enterprise
Trust

Good News Marketing Consultancy
Great Yarmouth Business Advisory Service

Goole & District Chamber of Commerce & Shipping
Sohbac, Brigg

Gosport Borough Council
Portsmouth Area
Enterprise

GPO Doncaster
Sohbac, Brigg

Gravesham Borough Council
Gravesham Industrial
Enterprise Agency

Great Grimsby Borough Council
Great Grimsby Small
Firms Advice Bureau

George Green Co
Dudley Business
Venture

Great Yarmouth Borough Council
Yarmouth Business
Advisory Service

Great Yarmouth Chamber of Commerce
Great Yarmouth Business Advisory Service

Great Yarmouth College of Further Education
Great Yarmouth Business Advisory Service

Greenbank Engineering
Blackburn & District Enterprise Trust

Greenwood & Coope
Rossendale Enterprise Trust

Grimshaw & Townsend
Hyndburn Enterprise Trust

Grosvenor Estates & Commercial Development
Business Link, Runcorn

Gruber Levinson Franks & Co
Manchester Business Venture

Guardian Royal Exchange Group
Ipswich Enterprise Trust (Ipsenta)

Guest Keen & Nettlefolds PLC
Birmingham Venture

Guest Shaw
Manchester Business Venture

Arthur Guinness & Son & Co
Brent Business Venture Ltd

Guinness Wharf
Sohbac, Brigg

Gulf Oil
Gloucestershire Enterprise Agency

Halberts
Dudley Business Venture

Sir W Halcrow & Partners
Swindon Enterprise Trust

Halifax Building Society
Calderdale Small Business Advice Centre

Hall Brothers (Whitefield)
Bury Enterprise Centre

Mathew Hall Engineering
Camden Enterprise

Halton Borough Council
Business Link, Runcorn

Hambros Life Assurance
Swindon Enterprise Trust

Hamilton & Co (London)
Harrow Enterprise Agency

Hampshire County Council
Blackwater Valley Enterprise Trust
Southampton Enterprise Agency

Hands
Hartlepool Enterprise Agency

Hards Toys
Watford Enterprise Agency Ltd

Henry Hargreaves
Bury Enterprise Centre

Harlow Council
Harlow Enterprise Agency

Harlow Chamber of Trade
Harlow Enterprise Agency

Harlow Chemical/Revertex
Harlow Enterprise Agency

Harrison & Pitt
Business for Lancaster

Great Harrow Chamber of Commerce
Harrow Enterprise Agency

Governors of Harrow School
Harrow Enterprise Agency

Hart District Council
Blackwater Valley Enterprise Trust
Basingstoke & Andover Enterprise Centre

Hartlepool Borough Council
Hartlepool Enterprise Agency

Hartlepool Small Business Club
Hartlepool Enterprise Agency

Hartmann Fibre
Great Yarmouth Business Advisory Service

Harvey Ingram
Leicestershire Business Venture

Harveys of Bristol
Aid to Bristol Enterprise (ABE)

Harvey Plating
Darlington & SW Durham Business Venture

Hastings Borough Council
Hastings Business Venture

Havant Borough Council
Portsmouth Area Enterprise

Hawkins & Co
Milton Keynes Business Venture

E & B Haworth & Nuttall
Hyndburn Enterprise Trust

Head Wrightson Stampings
Hartlepool Enterprise Agency

Heald & Nickinson
Milton Keynes Business Venture

Heaton Motors
Derwentside Industrial Development Agency

Hedges & Butler Ltd
Newham Business
Advice & Consultancy
Service

**Hedley Greentree
Partnership**
Portsmouth Area
Enterprise

Heeley Mouldings
Dudley Business
Venture

H J Heinz
Brent Business Venture
Ltd

**Hereford & Worcester
County Council**
Kidderminster College of
Further Education

W Hermanns & Son
Sohbac, Brigg

Higgs & Sons
Dudley Business
Venture

T R Highton Ltd
Southport Enterprise
Ltd

Higsons Brewery
Business in Liverpool

Hill Samuel & Co Ltd
Rossendale Enterprise
Trust Ltd

Hill & Smith
Dudley Business
Venture

**Robert Hitchins
Builders**
Gloucestershire
Enterprise Agency

Hodgson & Angus
Derwentside Industrial
Development Agency

Hoechst (UK)
Calderdale Small Business Advice Centre

W Holland & Son
Rossendale Enterprise
Trust Ltd

J Hollingsworth Ltd
Hastings Business
Venture

**John Holt & Co
(Liverpool)**
Business in Liverpool

**Holt & Longworth
(Solicitors)**
Rossendale Enterprise
Trust Ltd

William Hood & Co
Macclesfield Business
Venture

A E Hook & Co
Isle of Wight Enterprise
Trust Ltd

Houchin Engineering
Enterprise Ashford

Howard & Hargreaves
Rossendale Enterprise
Trust Ltd

Howson Algraphy Ltd
Leeds Business Venture

HTH Peck Holdings
Leicestershire Business
Venture

Hull City Council
Action Research Centre,
Hull

**Humberside County
Council**
Sohbac, Brigg
Action Research Centre,
Hull

**Hyndburn Borough
Council**
Hyndburn Borough
Council

**Hyson Green
Development Tenants'
Association & Action
Research Centre**
Hyson Green Workshops Ltd

IBM
Warwickshire
Enterprise Agency
Basingstoke & Andover
Enterprise Centre
Portsmouth Area
Enterprise
Southampton Enterprise
Agency
Small Industries Group,
Somerset

London Enterprise
Agency (Lenta)

H Ibbotson
Blackburn & District
Enterprise Trust

ICFC
Business in Liverpool
Leicestershire Business
Venture
Norwich Enterprise
Agency Trust (Neat)
Berkshire Enterprise
Agency
London Enterprise
Agency (Lenta)

ICI
Cleveland Enterprise
Agency
Blackburn & District
Enterprise Trust
Business for Lancaster
Macclesfield Business
Venture
Business in Oldham
Vale Royal Small Firms
(ICI Mond. Division)
Business Link, Runcorn
Wyre Business Agency
Vale of York Small
Business Association
Stevenage Initiatives
Maidstone Enterprise
Agency (Plant Protection
Division)
Tameside Venture Trust

ICL
Manchester Business
Venture

IMA
Manchester Business
Venture

Impact News Services
Hastings Business
Ventures

Imperial Group
Aid to Bristol Enterprise (ABE)

Imperial Tobacco
Swindon Enterprise
Trust

**Ind Coope (Burton)
Brewery**
Burton Enterprise
Agency

Industry & Trade Fairs Ltd
Birmingham Venture

Industrial Trading & Marketing Systems
Derwentside Industrial Development Agency

Intel Corporation (UK)
Swindon Enterprise Trust

Intercraft
Manchester Business Venture

Interdec
Milton Keynes Business Venture

Intermediate Technology
Small Industries Group

International Distillers & Vintners
Harlow Enterprise Agency

Ipswich Borough Council
Ipswich Enterprise Trust (Ipsenta)

Ipswich Port Authority
Ipswich Enterprise Trust (Ipsenta)

Ipswich & Suffolk Chamber of Commerce and Shipping
Ipswich Enterprise Trust (Ipsenta)

Island Builders
Isle of Wight Enterprise Trust Ltd

Island Link
Isle of Wight Enterprise Trust Ltd

Isle of Wight County Council
Isle of Wight Enterprise Trust Ltd

ITS Rubber
East Hampshire Enterprise Agency Ltd

Iveco (UK)
Vale Royal Small Firms

Jardine Glanville (UK)
Croydon Business Venture Ltd

Jarrold & Sons
Norwich Enterprise Agency Trust (Neat)

Jeffrey Trading
Macclesfield Business Venture

J Jellinek
Sohbac, Brigg

Robert Jenkins & Co
Rotherham Enterprise Agency

H & R Johnson Tiles
Business Initiatives, Stoke/Staffs

Johnson & Johnson
Berkshire Enterprise Agency

Johnson Matthey Metals
Brent Business Venture

Johnston & Wright
Business Initiatives, Carlisle

W Johnston & Partners
Business Initiatives, Carlisle

Johnson Wax
Blackwater Valley Enterprise Trust

Robert Jordan & Partners
Macclesfield Business Venture

Josolyne & Co
Macclesfield Business Venture

Josolyne & Co
Macclesfield Business Venture

Kalamazoo
Birmingham Business Venture

Kangol Magnet
Business Initiatives, Carlisle

Karrymore International
Hyndburn Enterprise Trust

T W Kempton
Leicestershire Business Venture

Kenross Containers
Rossendale Enterprise Trust

Kenroy Dispersions
Rossendale Enterprise Trust

Kent County Council
Gravesham Industrial Enterprise Agency
Maidstone Enterprise Agency
Enterprise Ashford
SWIM/SWAP Enterprise Centre

Kenyons
Blackburn & District Enterprise Trust

Kershaw Press Services
Business in Liverpool

Keytor
Business Initiatives, Carlisle

Kimberly-Clark
Maidstone Enterprise Agency

King Sumners & Partners
East Hampshire Enterprise Agency Ltd

King's College School, Wimbledon
Merton Enterprise Agency

Kingswood District Council
New Work Trust Co Ltd

Edmund Kirby & Sons
Business in Liverpool

Kirklees & Wakefield Chamber of Commerce
Kirklees & Wakefield Venture Trust

Kirklees & Wakefield District Council
Kirklees & Wakefield Venture Trust

Kirkstall Forge Engineering Co
Leeds Business Venture

Knights of St Columbia
Business Initiatives,
Carlisle

Kodak
Harrow Enterprise
Agency

**Ladbroke Mercury
Hotel**
Warwickshire
Enterprise Agency

Ladbroke Group
Brent Business Venture
Ltd

**Lady Margaret Hall
Settlement**
Lambeth Industrial
Enterprises

**John Laing
Construction**
Manchester Business
Venture

**Lakeland Pennine
Group**
Furness Business
Initiative

**South Lakeland District
Council**
Furness Business
Initiatives

**Lancashire & Cheshire
County Newspapers
Limited**
Macclesfield Business
Venture

Lancaster City Council
Business for Lancaster
Enterprise Lancaster

Lancaster Glass Fibre
Business for Lancaster

Lancaster Guardian
Business for Lancaster

**Lancastria (Gt)
Co-operative Society**
Business for Lancaster

LCP Holdings
Dudley Business
Venture

George H Lee
Business in Liverpool

Lee, Shaw Millsum
Dudley Business
Venture

**Leech Peirson Evans
& Co**
Warwickshire
Enterprise Agency

**Leeds Chamber of
Commerce**
Leeds Business Venture

Leeds City Council
LCVS Enterprises

**Leeds Council for
Voluntary Service**
LCVS Enterprises

**Legal and General
Group**
Croydon Business
Venture Ltd
London Enterprise
Agency (Lenta)
Milton Keynes Business
Venture
Small Industries Group,
Somerset
Warwickshire
Enterprise Agency

**Leicestershire Building
Society**
Leicestershire Business
Venture

**Leicestershire City
Council**
Leicestershire Business
Venture

Leicester Polytechnic
Business Advice Centre

Leigh & Sillavan
Macclesfield Business
Venture

W & L Leigh
Bolton Business
Venture

**Letchworth Garden City
Corporation**
Letchworth Enterprise

Levi Strauss
Brent Business Venture
Ltd

Lewis's
Business in Liverpool
Leeds Business Venture

Light Fabrication
Derwentside Industrial
Development Agency

Lightnin Mixers
Macclesfield Business
Venture

Eli Lilley & Co
Basingstoke & Andover
Enterprise Centre

Lillieshall Co PLC
Shropshire Enterprise
Trust

Linford Holdings
Milton Keynes Business
Venture

Link 51
Shropshire Enterprise
Trust

Linthorpe Insurance
Cleveland Enterprise
Agency

**Littlewoods
Organisation**
Business in Liverpool

**Liverpool Daily Post
& Echo**
Business in Liverpool

Lloyds Bank
Hastings Business
Venture
Cleveland Enterprise
Agency
Derwentside Industrial
Development Agency
Hartlepool Enterprise
Agency
Furness Business
Initiatives
Blackburn & District
Enterprise Trust
Business Initiatives,
Carlisle
Entep Trust Limited
Hyndburn Enterprise
Trust
Business for Lancaster
Business in Liverpool
Manchester Business
Venture
Business in Oldham
Vale Royal Small Firms
Warrington Business
Promotion Bureau
Newham Business
Advice & Consultancy
Service
Wigan New Enterprises

Calderdale Small Business Advice Centre
Rotherham Enterprise Agency
Sheffield Business Venture
Vale of York Small Business Association
Birmingham Venture
Burton Enterprise Agency
Business Initiatives, Stoke/Staffs
Shropshire Enterprise Trust
Warwickshire Enterprise Agency
Derby & Derbyshire Business Venture
Nottinghamshire Business Venture
Colchester Business Enterprise Agency
Great Yarmouth Business Advisory Service
Ipsenta, Ipswich
Forest Enterprise Trust (Feat)
Lowestoft Enterprise Trust
Beds & Chiltern Enterprise Agency (Becenta)
Milton Keynes Business Venture
Norwich Enterprise Agency Trust (Neat)
Peterborough Enterprise Programme
Stevenage Initiatives
Fens Business Enterprise Trust
Enterprise Ashford
Basingstoke & Andover Enterprise Centre
East Hampshire Enterprise Agency Ltd
Isle of Wight Enterprise Trust Ltd
Medway Enterprise Agency
Portsmouth Area Enterprise
Southampton Enterprise Agency
Small Industries Group, Somerset
Aid to Bristol Enterprise

(ABE)
Swindon Enterprise Trust
West Cornwall Enterprise Trust
Brent Business Venture
Croydon Business Venture Ltd
Blackwater Valley Enterprise Trust
Dudley Business Venture
Harlow Enterprise Agency
Macclesfield Business Venture
Wolverhampton Enterprise Limited
Southport Enterprises Trust
Merton Enterprise Agency

Corporation of Lloyds
Medway Enterprise Agency

Lloyds of London Press
Colchester Business Venture Agency

Local Authorities
Park Royal Enterprise Trust

Local Panels of Businessmen
Enterprise North

Local Companies
East Devon Small Industries Group
South Hams Small Industries Group
Park Royal Enterprise Trust
Northamptonshire Enterprise Agency

Local Retail Employers
SWIM/SWAP Enterprise Centre
Brixton United

Local Industry
Kirklees & Wakefield Venture Trust

Local Employers
SWIM/SWAP Enterprise Centre

Local Residents Association
Park Royal Enterprise Trust

Loders & Nucoline Limited
Newham Business Advice & Consultancy Service

London Borough of Camden
Camden Enterprise

London Borough of Croydon
Croydon Business Venture Ltd

London Borough of Hackney
Hackney Business Promotion Service
The Fashion Centre

London Borough of Hammersmith & Fulham
Hammersmith & Fulham Business Research Ltd

London Borough of Harrow
Harrow Enterprise Agency

London Borough of Islington
Islington Small Business Counselling

London Borough of Lambeth
Brixton United
Lambeth Business Advisory Service
Lambeth Industrial Enterprise

London Borough of Merton
Merton Enterprise Agency

London Borough of Tower Hamlets
Tower Hamlets Centre for Small Businesses Ltd

London Borough of Wandsworth
Wandsworth Enterprise Development Agency
Wandsworth Business Resource Service

London Brick
Peterborough Enterprise Programme

London Enterprise Agency
Hammersmith & Fulham Business Research Ltd
Lambeth Business Advisory Service
Tower Hamlets Centre for Small Businesses Ltd
Wandsworth Business Resource Service
Lambeth Industrial Enterprise

London & Essex Guardian Newspapers
Forest Enterprise Trust (Feat)

Longmans
Harlow Enterprise Agency

Lords of Rossendale
Rossendale Enterprise Trust

Loughton College of Further Education

Lovenwell Blake & Co
Great Yarmouth Business Advisory Service

Lowden Noall
Furness Business Initiative

Lowndes Lambert Group
Swindon Enterprise Trust
Rossendale Enterprise Trust Ltd

Lowestoft College of Further Education
Lowestoft Enterprise Trust

Lucas Industries
Birmingham Venture

Lumatic Limited
Hastings Business Ventures

Luton Borough Council
Beds & Chiltern Enterprise Agency (Becenta)

McGlashan, Sweby Cowan
Brent Business Venture Ltd

Mac Intyre Hudson
Milton Keynes Business Venture

Mackarness & Lunt
East Hampshire Enterprise Agency Ltd

McKiernan Group
Hyndburn Enterprise Trust

Macmillan R B
Derby & Derbyshire Business Venture

Donald Macpherson
Bury Enterprise Centre

Macclesfield District Council
Macclesfield Business Venture

Magnet & Southern
Darlington & SW Durham Business Venture

Maidstone Borough Council
Maidstone Enterprise Agency

Maidstone Chamber of Trade
Maidstone Enterprise Agency

The Mail, Hartlepool
Hartlepool Enterprise Agency

Maldon District Council
Maldon Branch of Colchester BEA

Greater Manchester County Council
Greater Manchester Economic Development Corporation Ltd

Greater Manchester Economic Development Corporation
Bury Enterprise Centre

Manchester Evening News
Manchester Business Venture

Manners & Harrison
Hartlepool Enterprise Agency

Manpower Services Commission
Vale Royal Small Firms
Warrington Business Promotion Bureau
Wigan New Enterprise
SWIM/SWAP Enterprise Centre
New Work Trust Co Ltd
Small Industries Group, Somerset
Southport Enterprise Trust
Small Business Centre, University of Aston
Merton Enterprise Agency

R Mansell
Croydon Business Venture Ltd

Mansfield Brewery
Nottinghamshire Business Venture

Marconi
Milton Keynes Business Venture

Marconi/Avionics
Medway Enterprise Agency

Marconi/Space & Defence Systems
Portsmouth Area Enterprise

Marcus Hazelwood & Co
Gloucestershire Enterprise Agency

Mardon Packaging (International)
Aid to Bristol Enterprise (ABE)

371

Marks & Clerk
Manchester Business
Venture

Mark & Moody
Dudley Business
Venture

Marks & Spencer
Hastings Business
Venture
Camden Enterprise
Cleveland Enterprise
Agency
Darlington & SW
Durham Business
Venture
Hartlepool Enterprise
Agency
Furness Business
Initiative
Blackburn & District
Enterprise Trust
Bolton Business Venture
Bury Enterprise Centre
Business Initiatives,
Carlisle
Hyndburn Enterprise
Trust
Business for Lancaster
Business in Liverpool
Macclesfield Business
Venture
Manchester Business
Venture
Calderdale Small Busi-
ness Advice Centre
Rotherham Enterprise
Agency
Sheffield Business
Venture
Sohbac, Brigg
Vale of York Small Busi-
ness Association
Burton Enterprise
Agency
Warwickshire
Enterprise Agency
Derby & Derbyshire
Business Venture
Leicestershire Business
Venture
Nottinghamshire
Business Enterprise
Agency
Harlow Enterprise
Agency

Ipsenta, Ipswich
Milton Keynes Business
Venture
Norwich Enterprise
Agency Trust (Neat)
Peterborough Enterprise
Programme
Isle of Wight Enterprise
Programme
Isle of Wight Enterprise
Agency
Enterprise Ashford
Basingstoke & Andover
Enterprise Centre
Portsmouth Area
Enterprise
Aid to Bristol Enterprise
(ABE)
Gloucestershire
Enterprise Agency
Swindon Enterprise
Trust
West Cornwall Enter-
prise Trust Ltd
Brent Business Venture
Ltd
Croydon Business
Venture Ltd
Harrow Enterprise
Agency
London Enterprise
Agency (Lenta)
Dudley Business
Venture
Wolverhampton
Enterprise Ltd

Marley
Maidstone Enterprise
Agency

**Marmaduke Pilling &
Sons**
Calderdale Small Busi-
ness Advice Centre

Marshall Sons & Co
Sohbac, Brigg

**Marston, Thompson &
Evershed**
Burton Enterprise
Agency

Harry Mason & Son
Bolton Business
Venture

Mathey Print Products
Business Initiatives,
Stoke/Staffs

May & Baker
Forest Enterprise
Agency Trust (Feat)

**Maydella
Manufacturing**
Manchester Business
Venture

Mears (Civil Engineers)
Swindon Enterprise
Trust

Mechanical Services
Bolton Business
Venture

Medens Trust
Isle of Wight Enterprise
Trust Ltd

**Medway & Gillingham
Chamber of Commerce**
Medway Enterprise
Agency

Mellor Bellamy
Fens Business Enter-
prise Trust

**Mellors (Confectioners)
Ltd**
Southport Enterprise
Trust

Meon Travel
East Hampshire Enter-
prise Agency Ltd

E Merck
East Hampshire Enter-
prise Agency Ltd

Meridan Group
Nottinghamshire
Business Venture

**Merseyside Chamber of
Commerce**
Business in Liverpool
Community of St Helens
Trust

Metal Box
Leicestershire Business
Venture

Metro Vending
Bury Enterprise Agency

Michelin Tyres
Business Initiatives,
Stoke/Staffs

Micro Focus
Swindon Enterprise Trust

Middlesbrough Borough Council
Middlesbrough Council Enterprise Centre

Midland Bank
Cleveland Enterprise Agency
Derwentside Industrial Development Agency
Hartlepool Enterprise Agency
Hyndburn Enterprise Trust
Business for Lancaster
Business in Liverpool
Business in Liverpool
Business in Oldham
Warrington Business Promotion Bureau
Rotherham Enterprise Agency

Sheffield Business Venture
Sohbac, Brigg
Vale of York Small Business Association
Birmingham Venture
Business Initiatives, Stoke/Staffs
Warwickshire Enterprise Trust
Derby & Derbyshire Business Venture
Leicestershire Business Venture
Nottinghamshire Business Venture
Great Yarmouth Business Advisory Service
Forest Enterprise Agency Trust (Feat)
Lowestoft Enterprise Trust
Beds & Chiltern Enterprise Agency (Becenta)
Maldon Branch of Colchester BEA
Norwich Enterprise Agency Trust (Neat)
Peterborough Enterprise Programme
Watford Enterprise Agency

Basingstoke & Andover Enterprise Centre
East Hampshire Enterprise Agency Ltd
Isle of Wight Enterprise Trust Ltd
Medway Enterprise Agency
Portsmouth Area Enterprise
Southampton Enterprise Agency
Aid to Bristol Enterprise
Gloucestershire Enterprise Agency
Swindon Enterprise Trust
London Enterprise Agency (Lenta)
Dudley Business Venture
Leeds Business Venture
Hammersmith & Fulham Business Research Ltd
Southport Enterprise Trust
Camden Enterprise
Hastings Business Venture

Midland Poultry Holdings
Shropshire Enterprise Trust

Midshires Building Society
Business in Liverpool

J Miller & Sons (Builders)
East Hampshire Enterprise Agency Ltd

R F Miller & Co
Furness Business Initiatives

Milliken Industrials
Bury Enterprise Agency

Borough of Milton Keynes
Milton Keynes Business Venture

Milton Keynes Development Corporation
Milton Keynes Business Venture

Milton Keynes & District Chamber of Commerce
Milton Keynes Business Venture

Minolta (UK)
Milton Keynes Business Venture

Mitchell & Wright (Printers) Ltd
Southport Enterprise Trust

Andry Montgomery Limited
Birmingham Venture

Moore Young & Co
Fens Business Enterprise Trust

Roy Moore
Wyre Business Agency

Morecambe Press
Business for Lancaster

H W Morley & Sons
Isle of Wight Enterprise Trust Ltd

Keith Morton
Derwentside Industrial Development Agency

Robert Morton DG
Burton Enterprise Agency

Mott Hay & Anderson
Croydon Business Venture Ltd

Mowlem Industrial
Derwentside Industrial Development Agency

A & J Mucklow (Inv) Ltd
Dudley Business Venture

Muirhead
Croydon Business Venture Ltd

Mullard
Blackburn & District Enterprise Trust

Multi Arc (Europe) Ltd
Derwentside Industrial Development Agency

Nabisco Brands Limited
Berkshire Enterprise
Agency

Nairn Coated Products
Business for Lancaster

National Coal Board
Derwentside Industrial
Development Agency
Rotherham Enterprise
Agency
Vale of York Small Business
Association
Leicestershire Business
Venture

National Cash Register
Moss Bay Enterprise
Trust (Mobet)

National Girobank
Furness Business
Initiative
Business Initiatives,
Carlisle
Business in Liverpool
Manchester Business
Venture
Business Link, Runcorn
Wigan New Enterprise
Moss Bay Enterprise
Trust (Mobet)
Metra 'Business Help'
Rossendale Enterprise
Trust
Southport Enterprise
Trust

**National Federation of
Self-employed Small
Businesses**
Gloucestershire
Enterprise Agency

**National Institute of
Agricultural
Engineering,
Silsoe**
Beds & Chiltern Enterprise Agency (Becenta)

**National Westminster
Bank**
Cleveland Enterprise
Agency
Derwentside Industrial
Development Agency
Darlington & S W
Durham Business
Venture

Hartlepool Enterprise
Agency Ltd
Furness Business
Initiative
Blackburn & District
Enterprise Trust
Bolton Business Venture
Business Initiatives,
Carlisle
Entep Trust Limited
Hyndburn Enterprise
Trust
Business for Lancaster
Business in Liverpool
Macclesfield Business
Venture
Manchester Business
Venture
Business in Oldham
Rossendale Enterprise
Trust
Vale Royal Small Firms
Warrington Business
Promotion Bureau
Moss Bay Enterprise
Trust (Mobet)
Wyre Business Agency
Calderdale Small Business Advice Centre
Leeds Business Venture
Rotherham Enterprise
Agency
Sheffield Business
Venture
Sohbac, Brigg
Vale of York Small Business Association
Birmingham Venture
Burton Enterprise
Agency
Business Initiatives,
Stoke/Staffs
Shropshire Enterprise
Trust
Walsall Small Firms
Advice Unit
Warwickshire
Enteprise Trust
Derby & Derbyshire
Business Venture
Leicestershire Business
Venture
Nottinghamshire
Business Venture
Colchester Business
Enterprise Agency

Great Yarmouth Business Advisory Service
Harlow Enterprise
Agency
Ipsenta, Ipswich
Forest Enterprise
Agency Trust (Feat)
Milton Keynes Business
Venture
Norwich Enterprise
Agency Trust (Neat)
Peterborough Enterprise
Programme
Stevenage Initiative
Watford Enterprise
Agency .
Fens Business Enterprise Trust
Blackwater Enterprise
Trust
Enterprise Ashford
Basingstoke & Andover
Enterprise Centre
East Hampshire Enterprise Agency Ltd
Isle of Wight Enterprise
Trust Ltd
Maidstone Enterprise
Agency
Medway Enterprise
Agency
Portsmouth Area
Enterprise
Southampton Enterprise
Agency
Aid to Bristol Enterprise
(ABE)
Swindon Enterprise
Trust
Brent Business Venture
Ltd
Croydon Business
Venture Ltd
Harrow Enterprise
Agency
Lambeth Business
Advisory Service
Small Industries Group,
Somerset
Dudley Business
Venture
Metra 'Business Help'
Camden Enterprise
Merton Enterprise
Agency
Hastings Business
Venture

Newham Business
Advice & Consultancy
Service

**Nationwide Building
Society**
Swindon Enterprise
Trust

Nei Pelcom Services
Business for Lancaster

Nei Ape Lee Howl Ltd
Dudley Business
Venture

Nestle Company
Croydon Business
Venture Ltd

**Borough of Newcastle
Under Lyme**
Business Initiatives,
Stoke/Staffs

Newcastle Breweries
Derwentside Industries
Development Agency

Newmans Slippers
Blackburn & District
Enterprise Trust

Newtime Foods
Hastings Business
Venture

Neville Russell
Dudley Business
Venture

Noble Lowndes
Rossendale Enterprise
Trust Ltd

Norfolk County Council
Norwich Enterprise
Agency Trust

**Norman Jones Sons &
Rigby**
Southport Enterprise

Normanby Estate Co
Sohbac, Brigg

**Northants County
Council**
Input, Northants

**Northants Chamber of
Commerce and
Industry**
Input, Northampton
Northamptonshire
Enterprise Agency Ltd

**Northamptonshire
County Council**
Corby Business Advisory
Bureau
Northamptonshire
Enterprise Agency

**Northampton
Development
Corporation**
Input, Northampton
Northamptonshire
Enterprise Agency Ltd

**North Beds. Borough
Council**
Beds & Chiltern Enter-
prise Agency (Becenta)

North Eastern BRS
Cleveland Enterprise
Agency

**North of England
Newspapers**
Darlington & SW
Durham Business
Venture

**Northumberland
County Council**
Northumberland
Business Centre

**Northumbria Tourist
Board**
Northumberland
Business Centre

**North Wales
Newspapers**
Shropshire Enterprise
Trust

**N Warwicks Borough
Council**
Warwickshire
Enterprise Agency

**North West Electricity
Board**
Business for Lancaster

**North York County
Council**
Vale of York Small Busi
ness Association

Norweb
Bolton Business
Venture
Business Initiatives,
Carlisle

Norwich City Council
Norwich Enterprise
Agency Trust (Neat)

**Norwich Industrial
Mission**
Norwich Enterprise
Agency Trust (Neat)

**Norwich & Norfolk
Chamber of
Commerce and
Industry**
Norwich Enterprise
Agency Trust (Neat)

**Norwich Union
Insurance Group**
Norwich Enterprise
Agency Trust (Neat)

**Nottingham Building
Society**
Nottinghamshire
Business Venture

**Nottinghamshire
Chamber of
Commerce and
Industry**
Nottinghamshire
Business Venture

**Nottingham City
Council**
Hyson Green
Workshops

**Nuneaton & Bedworth
Borough Council**
Warwickshire
Enterprise Agency

**Ocean Transport &
Trading**
Business in Liverpool

Associated Octel Co
Entep Trust Wirral

Offley Bros
Entep Trust, Wirral

Ogdens
Business in Liverpool
Leeds Business Venture

Oldham Brewery
Business in Oldham

**Oldham & District
Chamber of
Commerce**
Business in Oldham

Oldham Metropolitan Borough Council
Business in Oldham

George Oliver (Footwear) Ltd
Leicestershire Business Venture

Oysten Industries Investments
Rossendale Enterprise Trust Ltd

Ozalids (UK)
Forest Enterprise Agency Trust (Feat)

Pall Europe
Portsmouth Area Enterprise

Pannell Kerr Foster
Sheffield Business Venture
Great Yarmouth Business Advisory Service

Park Royal Enterprise Trust
Brent Business Venture

Park Yarns
Rossendale Enterprise Trust Ltd

F J Parsons Westminster Press
Hastings Business Venture

Paton & Baldwins
Darlington & SW Durham Business Venture

Pauls & Whites
Ipsenta, Ipswich

Paxman Diesels
Colchester Business Enterprise Agency

Pearl Assurance
Camden Enterprise
Peterborough Enterprise Programme

Peat Marwick Mitchell
Cleveland Enterprise Agency
Darlington & SW Durham Business Venture
Business in Liverpool

Leeds Business Venture
Sheffield Business Venture
Business Initiatives, Stoke/Staffs
Derby & Derbyshire Business Venture
Leicestershire Business Venture
Milton Keynes Business Venture
Dudley Business Venture
Ipswich Enterprise Trust (Ipsenta)

Pedigree Petfoods
Leicestershire Business Venture

Peel Holdings
Bury Enterprise Agency

Penryn Granite
West Cornwall Enterprise Trust Ltd

Performance Plastics
Rossendale Enterprise Trust

Persimmon Homes
Vale of York Small Business Association

Peterborough City Council
Peterborough Enterprise Programme

Peterborough Development Corporation
Peterborough Enterprise Programme

Petersfield Chamber of Trade
East Hampshire Enterprise Agency

PFD (Carlisle) Ltd
Business Initiatives, Carlisle

PHH Services
Swindon Enterprise Trust

Phillips-Hitex
Bury Enterprise Agency

Phillips Electronics
Croydon Business Venture Ltd

Philip Lait & Co
Forest Enterprise Agency Trust (Feat)

Phoenix Brewery Co Ltd
Hastings Business Venture

T F Pierce & Co
Hyndburn Enterprise Trust

Pike Textiles Display Ltd
Fens Business Enterprise Trust

Pilkington Bros
Community of St Helen Trust

Pinset & Co
Dudley Business Venture

Pirelli
Burton Enterprise Agency
Southampton Enterprise Agency

Plan-It Welding
Hyndburn Enterprise Trust

Plantpak
Maldon Branch of Colchester, BEA

John Player & Sons
Ipswich Enterprise Trust (Ipsenta)
Nottinghamshire Business Venture

Plessey Telecommunications
Business in Liverpool

Plessey Office Systems
Nottingham Business Venture

Plessey Radar
Isle of Wight Enterprise Trust Ltd

Plessey Company
Portsmouth Area Enterprise

Pneu-o-Plant
West Cornwall Enterprise Trust Ltd

Pollock, Webb & Gall
Great Yarmouth Business Advisory Service

Pork Farms
Leicestershire Business Venture

Porter Mathews Marsden
Blackburn & District Enterprise Trust

Port of Falmouth Chamber of Comm
West Cornwall Enterprise Trust Ltd

Portsmouth Building Society
Portsmouth Area Enterprise

Portsmouth City Council
Portsmouth Area Enterprise

Portsmouth Polytechnic
East Hampshire Enterprise Agency Ltd

Post Office
Business Initiatives, Carlisle
Rossendale Enterprise Trust

Potterton International
Warwickshire Enterprise Agency

Premier Footwear
Wyre Business Agency

WM Press Construction
Darlington & SW Durham Business Venture

Price Waterhouse
Dudley Business Venture
Leeds Business Venture

Priestley Footwear
Hyndburn Enterprise Trust

Printed Forms Equipment
Forest Enterprise Agency Trust (Feat)

Provincial Insurance
Furness Business Initiative
Bolton Business Venture
Business Initiatives, Carlisle
Moss Bay Enterprise Trust (Mobet)

Prudential Assurance
Camden Enterprise

Pye/Phillips
Lowestoft Enterprise Trust

Racal
Berkshire Enterprise Agency

Radio City (Sound of Merseyside)
Business in Liverpool

Ramsden Developments
Furness Business Initiatives

Rank Organisation
West Cornwall Enterprise Trust Ltd

Rank Xerox
Gloucestershire Enterprise Agency
New Work Trust Co Ltd

REA Publicity (West)
Gloucestershire Enterprise Agency

Readfearn National Glass
Vale of York Small Business Association

Readson
Manchester Business Venture

Reckitt Toiletry Products
Derby & Derbyshire Business Venture

Red Funnel
Isle of Wight Enterprise Trust Ltd

Reed Corrugated Cases
Hartlepool Enterprise Agency

Reed Group
Maidstone Enterprise Agency

Reedecor
Gloucestershire Enterprise Agency

Reed (Lydebrook Site)
Gloucestershire Enterprise Agency

Reeds Paper & Board (UK)
Gravesham Industries Enterprise Agency

Refuge Assurance Co
Manchester Business Venture

Reliance Hosiery
Calderdale Small Business Advice Centre

Reynolds Johnson & Green
Watford Enterprise Agency

RHM Foods
Hartlepool Enterprise Agency

Rice-Jones & Smiths
Calderdale Small Business Advice Centre

Richardson Bros
Dudley Business Venture

Riker Laboratories
Leicestershire Business Venture

Roba (UK) Limited
Harlow Enterprise Agency

F Roberts & Sons
Vale Royal Small Firms

Rochdale Metropolitan Borough Council
Metropolitan Enterprise Trust, Rochdale Area (Metra)

Rochester upon Medway City Council
Medway Enterprise Agency

Rohan Developments
Vale of York Small Business Association

Rolls Royce Motors
Aid to Bristol Enterprise (ABE)
Shropshire Enterprise Trust

Ronix Computers
Dudley Business Venture

Ronwood Greetings
Bury Enterprise Agency

Rope Holdings
Basingstoke & Andover Enterprise Centre

Rotary Club of Loughton
Forest Enterprise Agency Trust (Feat)

Rotary Club of Watford
Forest Enterprise Agency Trust (Feat)

Rotherham Metropolitan Borough Council
Rotherham Enterprise Agency

Rotherham Chamber of Commerce
Rotherham Enterprise Agency

Roussel Laboratories
Swindon Enterprise Trust

R Rowley & Co
Leicestershire Business Venture

Rowley Regis Building Society
Dudley Business Venture

Rowntree Mackintosh
Calderdale Small Business Advice Centre
Norwich Enterprise Agency Trust (Neat)
Vale of York Small Business Association

Roy Manufacturing Co Ltd
Tower Hamlets Centre for Small Businesses

Royal Borough of Kensington & Chelsea
Resource Centre

Royal Brierley Crystal
Dudley Business Venture

Royal Doulton
Business Initiatives, Stoke/Staffs

Royal Insurance (UK)
Entep Trust, Wirral
Business in Liverpool
Derby & Derbyshire Business Venture
Leeds Business Venture
Beds & Chiltern Enterprise Agency (Becenta)

Royal London Mutual Insurance Society
Colchester Business Enterprises Agency

Royal York Hotel
Vale of York Small Business Association

Rugby Borough Council
Warwickshire Enterprise Agency

Rumenco
Burton Enterprise Agency

Rushmoor Borough Council
Blackwater Valley Enterprise Trust

Rushton, Ibbotson & Clay (Solicitors)
Blackburn & District Enterprise Trust

Rydale District Council
Vale of York Small Business Association

Sadler & Son (Ipswich)
Ipswich Enterprise Trust (Ipsenta)

J Sainsbury
Basingstoke & Andover Enterprise Centre
Vale of York Small Business Association

Samuelson Film Service
Brent Business Venture Ltd

Metropolitan Borough of Sandwell
Sandwell Enterprise

Savacentre
Berkshire Enterprise Agency

SCAPA Group
Blackburn & District Enterprise Trust

Scicon
Milton Keynes Business Venture

SCS Business Systems
Croydon Business Venture Ltd

Scunthorpe Borough Council
Industrial Development & Enterprise Agency

Scunthorpe Glanford & Gainsborough Chamber of Commerce
Sohbac, Brigg

Securicor Ltd
Croydon Business Venture Ltd

James Seddon (UK)
Manchester Business Venture

Seddon Atkinson
Business in Oldham

Sedgemoor District Council
Small Industrial Group, Somerset

Sedgwick
Norwich Enterprise Agency Trust (Neat)

Sefton Newspapers Ltd
Southport Enterprise Ltd

Selby District Council
Vale of York Small Business Association

Selective Cleaning Services
Bury Enterprise Agency

Senior Service
Metra 'Business Help'

Sentry Holdings (UK)
Milton Keynes Business Venture

Seton
Business in Oldham

Sheffield Chamber of Commerce
Sheffield Business Venture

Shell (UK)
Cleveland Enterprise Agency
Entep Trust Ltd
Macclesfield Business Venture
Birmingham Venture
Lowestoft Enterprise Trust
Isle of Wight Enterprise Trust Ltd
Small Industries Group, Somerset
West Cornwall Enterprise Trust Ltd
London Enterprise Agency (Lenta)
Hastings Business Ventures

Shepherd Construction
Darlington & SW Durham Business Venture
Vale of York Small Business Association

William A Shepherd
Manchester Business Venture

Sherfield Investments
Basingstoke & Andover Enterprise Centre

Shorrock Securities
Blackburn & District Enterprise Trust

J Shipston & Sons
Nottinghamshire Business Venture

Shipway Communications Limited
Dudley Business Venture

Shrewsbury & Wem. Brewery
Shropshire Enterprise Trust

Shropshire County Council
Shropshire Enterprise Trust

Shropshire Star Newspapers
Shropshire Enterprise Trust

Silkolene
Derby & Derbyshire Business Venture

Silver Paint Lacquer
Leeds Business Venture

Silver-Reed
Wolverhampton Enterprise Ltd

Silverthorne Gillott
Dudley Business Venture

Simon Engineering
Dudley Business Venture

Simpson Curtis & Co
Leeds Business Venture

Singleton Birch
Sohbac, Brigg

G F Singleton & Co
Blackburn & District Enterprise Trust

Sketchley
Leicestershire Business Venture

SKF
Beds & Chiltern Enterprise Agency (Becenta)

The Small Back Room
Business Initiatives, Stoke/Staffs

Herman Smith
Dudley Business Venture

John Smith's Tadcaster Brewery
Vale of York Small Business Association

Smith & Graham
Hartlepool Enterprise Agency

Smith Industries
Basingstoke & Andover Enterprise Centre

W H Smith & Son
Swindon Enterprise Trust
Croydon Business Venture Ltd

W H Smith Do-it-All Limited
Dudley Business Venture

Snamprogretti
Basingstoke & Andover Enterprise Centre

Somerset County Council
Small Industries Group, Somerset

Sony Broadcast
Basingstoke & Andover Enterprise Centre

Southampton Chamber of Commerce
Southampton Enterprise Agency

Southampton City Council
Southampton Enterprise Agency

South Bedfordshire District Council
Beds & Chiltern Enterprise Agency (Becenta)

South Hampshire District Council
South Hampshire Small Industries Group

Southern Bulk Traffic Services
East Hampshire Enterprise Agency Ltd

Southern Electricity Board
Basingstoke & Andover Enterprise Centre

South East Electricity Board
Croydon Business Venture Ltd

South East Hampshire Chamber of Commerce
Portsmouth Area Enterprise

Southern Gas
Southampton
Enterprise Agency

South East Gas
Croydon Business
Venture Ltd

South Norfolk District Council
Norwich Enterprise
Agency Trust (Neat)

Southport Council
Sefton Enterprise Trust

South Yorks County Council
Rotherham Enterprise
Agency
Sheffield Business
Venture

Spencers Estate Agents
Leicestershire Business
Venture

Henry Spencer & Sons
Sohbac, Brigg

H R Spencer
Isle of Wight Enterprise
Trust Ltd

Spicer & Pegler
Dudley Business
Venture

Square D
Swindon Enterprise
Trust

Staffordshire County Council
Staffordshire
Development
Association

Staffordshire District Council
Burton Enterprise
Agency

Staffordshire Moorland District Council
Business Initiative,
Stoke/Staffs

Stag Furniture Holdings
Nottinghamshire
Business Venture

Stancliffe Todd & Hodgson
Cleveland Enterprise
Agency

Standard Telephone & Cables
Southampton
Enterprise Agency

St Helens Metropolitan Borough Council
Community of St Helens
Trust

St Quentin
Leeds Business Venture

Standen Homes
Nottingham Business
Venture

STC Component Group
Great Yarmouth Business Advisory Service
Harlow Enterprise
Agency

Stead & Simpson
Leicestershire Business
Venture

Steetley Brick
Business Initiatives,
Stoke/Staffs

Steetley (MFG)
Hartlepool Enterprise
Agency

Stenner & Co
Great Yarmouth Business Advisory Service

Stephenson, Benton, Smith Partnership
Hartlepool Enterprise
Agency

Stevenage Borough Council
Stevenage Initiative

Stevenage Chamber of Trade
Stevenage Initiative

Stevenage Employers Group
Stevenage Initiative

Stirling Metals
Warwickshire
Enterprise Agency

City of Stoke on Trent
Business Initiatives,
Stoke/Staffs

Stoke/Staffs Chamber of Commerce
Business Initiatives,
Stoke/Staffs

Storeys Decorative Products
Business for Lancaster

Stratford on Avon District Council
Warwickshire
Enterprise Agency

Stroud District Council
Gloucestershire
Enterprise Agency

Sub Sea Surveys
Furness Business
Initiatives

Suffolk County Council
Ipswich Enterprise
Trust (Ipsenta)
Lowestoft Enterprise
Trust

Sun Alliance Insurance Group
Croydon Business
Venture Ltd
Shropshire Enterprise
Trust

Sun Life Assurance Society
Aid to Bristol Enterprise (ABE)

Sunderland Borough Council
New Enterprise
Advisory Service

Sunderland Polytechnic
Tyne & Wear Enterprise Trust Ltd

Superdrug Limited
Croydon Business
Venture Ltd

Surrey Health Borough Council
Blackwater Valley
Enterprise Trust

Swale Parish Council
Swim/Swap Enterprise
Centre

Swale Borough Council
Swim/Swap Enterprise
Centre

Swallows Hotels
Business Initiatives,
Carlisle

Thos Swain & Co Ltd
Derwentside Industrial
Development Agency

**Swindon Chamber of
Commerce**
Swindon Enterprise
Trust

Swindon College
Swindon Enterprise
Trust

**Swindon Training
Services**
Swindon Enterprise
Trust

Swindon TUC
Swindon Enterprise
Trust

Sybron Taylor
Stevenage Initiative

Systems Computers
Leeds Business Venture

**Tameside Metropolitan
District Council**
Tameside Venture Trust

Tarmac
Wolverhampton
Enterprise Ltd

TASC Drives
Lowestoft Enterprise
Trust

Tate & Lyle Refineries
Croydon Business
Venture Ltd
Newham Business
Advice & Consultancy
Service

**Tattersall (Fin.
Planning)**
Burton Enterprise
Agency

Taunton Cider
Small Industries Group

**G H Taylor (Waterfoot)
Ltd**
Rossendale Enterprise
Trust Ltd

John H Taylor
Derwentside Industrial
Development Agency

**Taylor Simpson &
Moseley**
Derby & Derbyshire
Business Venture

**TBA Industrial
Products**
Metropolitan Enterprise
Trust, Rochdale Area
(Metra)

TEC Equipment
Nottinghamshire
Business Venture

**Tees & Hartlepool Port
Authority**
Cleveland Enterprise
Agency

Teeside Polytechnic
Cleveland Enterprise
Agency

**Teeside Small Business
Club**
Cleveland Enterprise
Agency

Telford Bottling Co
Shropshire Enterprise
Trust

**Telford Development
Corporation**
Industrial Development
Unit
Shropshire Enterprise
Trust

**Telford & Shrop
Chamber of
Commerce**
Shropshire Enterprise
Trust

Joseph Terry & Sons
Vale of York Small
Business Association

Tesco
Harlow Enterprise
Agency
Isle of Wight Enterprise
Trust Ltd

**Test Valley Borough
Council**
Basingstoke & Andover
Enterprise Centre

Joshua Tetley & Son
Leeds Business Venture

**Tewkesbury Borough
Council**
Gloucestershire
Enterprise Agency

J S Textiles
Bury Enterprise Centre

Textured Jersey
Brent Business Venture
Ltd

Thames Television
Camden Enterprise
Harrow Enterprise
Agency

**Thamesdown Borough
Council**
Swindon Enterprise
Trust

Thomson McLintock
Derwentside Industrial
Development Agency
Norwich Enterprise
Agency Trust (Neat)
Shropshire Enterprise
Trust
Walsall Small Firms
Advice Unit

E Thomas & Co
West Cornwall Enter-
prise Trust Ltd

Thoma de la Rue & Co
Basingstoke & Andover
Enterprise Centre

Thorn EMI
Business in Oldham
(SBTG)
Birmingham Venture
Hyndburn Enterprise
Trust
Isle of Wight Enterprise
Trust Ltd

Thorn-Ericsson (MFG)
Sohbac, Brigg

Thornton Baker
Birmingham Business
Venture
Business for Lancaster
East Hampshire Enter-
prise Agency Ltd
Milton Keynes Business
Venture
Input, Northampton
Sheffield Business
Venture

Richard Threlfall
Bolton Business
Venture

D Thwaites & Co
Blackburn & District
Enterprise Trust

Tibbenham Advertising, Midlands
Nottinghamshire
Business Venture

Tipton & Coseley Building Society
Dudley Business Venture

Tollemache & Cobbold Breweries
Ipswich Enterprise
Trust (Ipsenta)

Tootal Group
Manchester Business
Venture

Torrington Company
Darlington & SW
Durham Business
Venture

Touche Ross & Co
Leicestershire Business
Venture

Town Centre Securities
Leeds Business Venture

Transportation Services
Southampton
Enterprise Agency

Trebor
Maidstone Enterprise
Agency

Treetops Hotel
Forest Enterprise
Agency Trust (Feat)

Tresises (Printers) Ltd
Burton Enterprise
Agency

J A Trickett (Insurance) Ltd
Rossendale Enterprise
Trust Ltd

Triumph International
Swindon Enterprise
Trust

Trustee Savings Bank
Shropshire Enterprise
Trust
Hartlepool Enterprise
Agency
Bury Enterprise Agency
Business for Lancaster
Vale Royal Small Firms
Wigan New Enterprise
Business Initiatives,
Stoke/Staffs
Derby & Derbyshire
Business Venture
Lowestoft Enterprise
Trust
Peterborough
Enterprise Programme
Basingstoke & Andover
Enterprise Centre
Bolton Business
Ventures

TUC
Tyne & Wear Enter-
prise Trust Ltd

Trade Councils
Swim/Swap Enterprise
Centre

Turriegraphic Limited
Basingstoke & Andover
Enterprise Centre

TVS
Hastings Business
Venture

Tyne & Wear Chamber of Commerce
Tyne & Wear Enter-
prise Trust

Tyne & Wear County Council
Tyne & Wear Enter-
prise Trust

UB (Foods)
Calderdale Small Busi-
ness Advice Centre

UBM Dibben
Isle of Wight Enterprise
Trust

Unicon Holdings
Rossendale Enterprise
Trust

Unilever
In Business, Wirral
Enterprise Ashford

Union Carbide (UK)
Swindon Enterprise
Trust

United Biscuits
Business Initiatives,
Carlisle
Business in Liverpool
Manchester Business
Venture
Rotherham Enterprise
Agency
Leicestershire Business
Venture
Brent Business Venture
Ltd
London Enterprise
Agency (Lenta)

University of Aston
Small Business Centre

University of East Anglia
Norwich Enterprise
Agency Trust (Neat)

University of Lancaster
Business for Lancaster
Enterprise Lancaster

Vauxhall Motors
Beds & Chiltern Enter-
prise Agency (Becenta)
Entep Trust, Wirral

L S Vail & Sons
Portsmouth Area
Enterprise

Vale Royal Council
Vale Royal Small Firms

Various Medium & Small Firms
Metropolitan Enterprise
Trust, Rochdale Area
(Metra)

Vectis Stone
Isle of Wight Enterprise
Trust Ltd

Vickers Shipbuilding & Engineering
Furness Business
Initiatives

Visionhire
Lowestoft Enterprise
Trust

Voluntary Organisations
Swim/Swap Enterprise Centre

Wade Potteries
Business Initiatives, Stoke/Staffs

Wake Smith & Co
Sheffield Business Venture

Walker Crisps
Leicestershire Business Venture

Walker Crosweller & Co
Gloucestershire Enterprise Agency

C Walker & Sons Limited
Blackburn & District Enterprise Trust

H Walker & Co
Rossendale Enterprise Trust Ltd

William Walkerdine
Derby & Derbyshire Business Venture

Walsall Chamber of Commerce
Walsall Small Firms Advice Unit

Walsall Metropolitan Borough Council
Walsall Small Firms Advice Unit

Walsall Trades Council
Walsall Small Firms Advice Unit

Walsall Trades Council
Walsall Small Firms Advice Unit

Waltons
Milton Keynes Business Venture

Warburtons
Bolton Business Venture

J B Ward
Hastings Business Venture

S H Ward & Co
Sheffield Business Venture

Wardell Publicity Bureau
Bury Enterprise Agency

Warrington Borough Council
Warrington Business Promotion Bureau

Thomas Warrington & Sons
Entep Trust, Wirral

Warrington & Runcorn New Town Development Corporation
Business Link, Runcorn
Warrington Business Promotion Bureau

F W Warwick & Sons
East Hampshire Enterprise Agency Ltd

Waterworth Rudd & Hare
Blackburn & District Enterprise Trust

Wates Limited
Croydon Business Venture Ltd

Watford Borough Council
Watford Enterprise Agency

Watkin Starbuck & Jones
Shropshire Enterprise Trust

Warwickshire County Council
Warwickshire Enterprise Agency

Warwickshire District Council
Warwickshire Enterprise Agency

Waveney District Council
Lowestoft Enterprise Trust

Weatherall Hollis & Gale
Leeds Business Venture

Samuel Webster & Sons
Calderdale Small Business Advice Centre

Wedgewood
Business Initiatives, Stoke/Staffs

Wellcome Foundation
London Enterprise Agency (Lenta)

Wembley Stadium
Brent Business Venture Ltd

West British Road Services
Aid to Bristol Enterprise (ABE)

West Lindsey District Council
Sohbac, Brigg

Westmain Insurance
Cleveland Enterprise Agency

West Midlands County Council
Dudley Business Venture

West Staff Bureau
Bury Enterprise Agency

J Wharton (Shipping)
Sohbac, Brigg

Whatman Reeve Angel
Maidstone Enterprise Agency

Whessoe
Darlington & SW Durham Business Venture

L Whitaker & Sons
Rossendale Enterprise Trust

Whitbread
Blackburn & District Enterprise Trust
Hyndburn Enterprise Trust
Sheffield Business Venture
Beds & Chiltern Enterprise Agency (Becenta)
Gloucestershire Enterprise Agency
Small Industries Group, Somerset
London Enterprise Agency (Lenta)

Whitbread/Wessex
Isle of Wight Enterprise
Trust Ltd
Portsmouth Area
Enterprise
Southampton Enterprise
Agency

Whitbread/Fremlins
Maidstone Enterprise
Agency
Enterprise Ashford

Whitecroft
Manchester Business
Venture

Whiteheads
East Hampshire Enter-
prise Agency Ltd

Whitman Laboratories
East Hampshire Enter-
prise Agency Ltd

Whiting & Partners
Fens Business Enter-
prise Trust

Whiting & Partners
Fens Business Enter-
prise Trust

Whitworth's Products
Fens Business Enter-
prise Trust

**Wigan College of
Technology**
Wigan New Enterprise

**Wigan Metropolitan
Borough Council**
Wigan New Enterprise

Wiggins Teape
Bury Enterprise Agency
Basingstoke & Andover
Enterprise Centre
Newham Business
Advice Consultancy
Service

Williams & Glyn's Bank
Darlington & SW
Durham Business
Venture
Manchester Business
Venture
Business in Oldham
Rotherham Enterprise
Agency
Sheffield Business
Venture

Vale of York Small
Business Association
Portsmouth Area
Enterprise

**Harold Williams,
Bennet & Partners**
Croydon Business
Venture Ltd

Wills Faber & Dumas
Ipswich Enterprise
Trust (Ipsenta)

Wilson & Garden
Bury Enterprise Agency

Wilson & Partners
Milton Keynes Business
Venture

Wiltshier Group
Darlington & SW
Durham Business
Venture

Wiltshire Newspapers
Swindon Enterprise
Trust

Wimpol
Swindon Enterprise
Trust

Wirral Borough Council
In Business Ltd, Wirral

**Wirral Chamber of
Commerce**
In Business Ltd, Wirral

Wolstenhome Rink
Bolton Business
Venture

**Wolverhampton
Chamber of
Commerce**
Wolverhampton
Enterprise Ltd

**Wolverhampton &
Dudley Breweries**
Dudley Business Venture

**Wolverhampton
Metropolitan District
Council**
Wolverhampton
Enterprise Ltd

**Wolverhampton Trades
Council**
Wolverhampton
Enterprise Ltd

Woodeaves
Business for Lancaster

Wood Mitchell & Co
Business Initiatives,
Stoke/Staffs

Woods of Colchester
Colchester Business
Enterprise Agency

**Woolwich Equitable
Building Society**
Croydon Business
Venture Ltd

Wrekin District Council
Shropshire Enterprise
Trust

Arthur Wren Sons & Co
Hastings Business
Venture

Wyko Group
Dudley Businss Venture

Wyre Borough Council
Wyre Business Agency

Wyvern Partnership
Swindon Enterprise
Trust

Yates & Jackson
Business for Lancaster

York City Council
Vale of York Small
Business Association

Yorkshire Bank
Hyndburn Enterprise
Trust
Leeds Business Venture
Sheffield Business
Venture
Vale of York Small Busi-
ness Assoc
Nottinghamshire
Business Venture
Dudley Business
Venture

**Yorkshire Electricity
Board**
Leeds Business Venture

**Yorkshire General Life
Assurance Co**
Vale of York Small Busi-
ness Association

Yorkshire & Humberside RMC
Sheffield Business Venture

Yorkshire Post Newspapers
leeds Business Venture

CM Yuill
Hartlepool Enterprise Agency

Zambia Engineering Services
Enterprise Ashford

Zurich Insurance Co
Portsmouth Area Enterprise

SCOTLAND

A C White, Silver Young & Cosh
Ayr Local Enterprise Research Trust

W Alexander (Coachbuilders)
Falkirk Enterprise Action Trust

Anderson Strathclyde
Motherwell Enterprise Trust

Anglo Overseas Transport Co
Falkirk Enterprise Action Trust

Ayr Chamber of Commerce
Ayr Local Enterprise Research Trust

Ayrshire Precision Engineering
Ayr Local Enterprise Research Trust

Bank of Scotland
Dundee Business Association
Glenrothes Enterprise Trust
Manchester Business Venture

Ballantyne & Copeland
Motherwell Enterprise Trust

Andrew Barclay & Sons
Kilmarnock Venture

Barr Construction
Ayr Locality Enterprise Research Trust

Robert Barr
Falkirk Enterprise Action Trust

W J Barr & Sons
Ayr Local Enterprise Research Trust

Barratt Scotland
Falkirk Enterprise Action Trust

Barratt Urban Renewal Scotland
Leith Enterprise Trust

Beckman Instruments
Glenrothes Enterprise Trust

Ben Line Steamers
Leith Enterprise Trust

Bett Bros
Glenrothes Enterprise Trust

Biggart Baillie & Gifford
Glasgow Opportunities

Borg Warner Chemicals
Falkirk Enterprise Action Trust

Boyd Jameson & Young, WS
Leith Enterprise Trust

BP
Falkirk Enterprise Action Trust
Glasgow Opportunities
Leith Enterprise Trust
Dundee Industrial Association

British Alcan
Falkirk Enterprise Action Group

British Leyland
Bathgate Area Support for Enterprise

British Steel Industries
Lanarkshire Industries Field Executive

Brown Brothers
Leith Enterprise Trust

Brown Ferguson
Falkirk Enterprise Action Trust

Butlins
Ayr Locality Enterprise Research Trust

Central Regional Council
Falkirk Enterprise Action Trust
Central Regional Council

Carter Geoghegan
Glenrothes Enterprise Trust

Christian Salvesen
Glenrothes Enterprise Trust
Leith Enterprise Trust

Clydesdale Bank
Glasgow Opportunities
Kilmarnock Venture

Clydesdale District Council
Lanarkshire Industries Field Executive

Coats Patons
Glasgow Opportunities

Jas. Craig
Ayr Locality Enterprise Research Trust

Craig & Rose
Leith Enterprise Trust

D S Crawford
Leith Enterprise Trust

385

Cunninghame District Council
Ardrossan, Saltcoats, Stevenston Enterprise Trust

Daniel Industries Ltd
Falkirk Enterprise Action Group

Deloitte Haskins & Sells
Event, Edinburgh

D B Projects
Falkirk Enterprise Action Trust

Digital
Ayr Locality Enterprise Research Trust

Douglas Engineering
Ayr Locality Enterprise Research Trust

W Duncan & Co
Ayr Locality Enterprise Research Trust

Edinburgh District Council
Leith Enterprise Trust

R C Ewart & Son
Leith Enterprise Trust

Falkirk Chamber of Commerce
Falkirk Enterprise Action Trust

Falkirk District Council
Falkirk Enterprise Action Trust

Farnbeck
Leith Enterprise Trust

Ferranti
Event, Edinburgh

Fife Fabrications
Glenrothes Enterprise Trust

Fife Secretarial Services
Glenrothes Enterprise Trust

Forth Studios
Glenrothes Enterprise Trust

Fraser & Co
Glenrothes Enterprise Trust

Garland & Roger
Leith Enterprise Trust

General Accident
Ayr Local Enterprise Research Trust
Glasgow Opportunities
Leith Enterprise Trust

General Instrument Microelectronics
Glenrothes Enterprise Trust

Glenrothes Development Corporation
Glenrothes Enterprise Trust

Glen Henderson Motors
Ayr Locality Enterprise Research Trust

Glynwed Group
Falkirk Enterprise Action Trust

Frank Graham Builders
Leith Enterprise Trust

Group 4 Securities
Leith Enterprises Trust

John Haig & Co Ltd
Glenrothes Enterprise Trust

D M Hall
Falkirk Enterprise Action Trust

Hamilton District Council
Lanarkshire Industrial Field Executive

J W Henderson
Ayr Locality Enterprise Research Trust

Higgs & Hill Properties
Falkirk Enterprise Action Trust

Highlands & Islands Development Board
Highland Craftpoint

Honeywell Control Systems
Motherwell Enterprise Trust

Howdens
Glasgow Opportunities

IBM
Glasgow Opportunities

ICI
Ardrossan, Saltcoats, Stevenston, Enterprise Trust
Falkirk Enterprise Action Trust

Ideas
Falkirk Enterprise Action Trust

Inglis Paul & Co Ltd
Falkirk Enterprise Action Trust

F Johnston Newspapers Group
Falkirk Enterprise Action Trust

J & F Johnston & Partners
Leith Enterprise Trust

Kilmarnock District
Kilmarnock Venture

Kwik-Fit (Euro) PLC
Event, Edinburgh

Kyle & Carrick District
Ayr Locality Enterprise Research Trust

Leith Chamber of Commerce
Leith Enterprise Trust

Long John International
Ayr Locality Enterprise Research Trust

Lothian Regional Council
Bathgate Area Support for Enterprise
Leith Enterprise Trust

Lowndes Lambert (UK) Ltd
Glenrothes Enterprise Trust

McDaid & Co
Motherwell Enterprise Trust

Macdonald & Muir
Leith Enterprise Trust

Mackay's of Leith
Leith Enterprise Trust

Marks & Spencer
Ayr Locality Enteprise
Research Trust
Falkirk Enterprise
Action Trust
Glasgow Opportunities
Kilmarnock Venture
Event, Edinburgh

R Mathieson & Sons
Falkirk Enterprise
Action Trust

John Menzies PLC
Event, Edinburgh

Miller Construction
Glenrothes Enterprise
Trust

Millers of Falkirk
Falkirk Enterprise
Action Trust

E E Minto Assoc
Falkirk Enterprise
Action Trust

**Monklands District
Council**
Lanarkshire Industries
Field Executive

Moorfield Enterprises
Ayr Locality Enterprise
Research Trust

Motherwell Bridge
Leith Enterprise Trust
Motherwell Enterprise
Trust

**Motherwell District
Council**
Lanarkshire Industries
Field Executive

William Muir
Leith Enterprises Trust

Bill Murray (Architects)
Leith Enterprise Trust

Neale House Properties
Glenrothes Enterprise
Trust

**Pagan Osborne & Grace,
WS**
Glenrothes Enterprise
Trust

**George Palmer & Sons
Stevedores Ltd**
Falkirk Enterprise
Action Trust

Peat Marwick Mitchell
Leith Enterprise Trust

PEC Barr (Printers)
Leith Enterprise Trust

Prestwick Circuits
Ayr Locality Enterprise
Research Trust

Radio Clyde
Glasgow Opportunities

Reed Stenhouse
Ayr Locality Enterprise
Research Trust

Royal Bank of Scotland
Kilmarnock Venture

Satchwell Sunvic
Motherwell Enterprise
Trust

Scoenfield Knitwear
Glenrothes Enterprise
Trust

Scott Oswald & Co
Falkirk Enterprise
Action Trust

**Scottish Agricultural
Ind.**
Leith Enterprise Trust

**Scottish Development
Agency**
Ardrossan, Saltcoats,
Stevenston Enterprise
Trust
Glasgow Opportunities
Ayr Locality Enterprise
Research Trust
Bathgate Area Support
for Enterprise
Falkirk Enterprise
Action Trust
Glenrothes Enterprise
Trust
Kilmarnock Venture
Highland Craftpoint
Lanarkshire Industries
Field Executive
Leith Enterprise Trust

**Scottish Express
International**
Ayr Locality Enterprise
Research Trust

Scottish Jig & Tool
Glenrothes Enterprise
Trust

Scot Met
Glasgow Opportunities

Scottish & Newcastie
Glasgow Opportunities
Event, Edinburgh
Motherwell Enterprise
Trust

**Scottish Provident
Institution**
Leith Enterprise Trust

Shell (UK)
Ardrossan, Saltcoats,
Stevenson Enterprise
Trust
Glasgow Opportunities

Thomas Smith & Sons
Ayr Locality Enterprise
Research Trust

Spring Hill
Glenrothes Enterprise
Trust

SSEB
Ayr Local Enterprise
Research Trust
Falkirk Enterprise Action
Trust

Stakis
Glasgow Opportunities

**Strathclyde Regional
Council**
Ardrossan, Saltcoats,
Stevenston Enterprise
Trust
Ayr Locality Enterprise
Research Trust
Kilmarnock Venture
Strathclyde Regional
Council Industrial Devel·
opment Unit
Lanarkshire Industries
Field Executive
Local Enterprise
Advisory Project

STV
Glasgow Opportunities

Robert Taylor
Falkirk Enterprise
Action Trust

Terex
Motherwell Enterprise
Trust

Tod Holdings
Leith Enterprise Trust

Trustee Savings Bank
Ayr Locality Enterprise
Research Trust
Glasgow Opportunities

Touche Ross
Glasgow Opportunities

Tullis Russell
Glenrothes Enterprise
Trust

United Biscuits
Glasgow Opportunities
Kilmarnock Venture
Event, Edinburgh

Viger McEvoy
Leith Enterprise Trust

John Walker & Sons
Kilmarnock Venture

Victoria Dairy
Ayr Locality Enterprise
Research Trust

Walker & Templeton
Kilmarnock Venture

Walker Timber
Leith Enterprise Trust

Wallacetown Engineering
Ayr Locality Enterprise
Research Trust

George Waterston & Son
Leith Enterprise Trust

Waverley Group
Leith Enterprise Trust

West Lothian District Council
Bathgate Area Support
for Enterprise

Wiggins Teape
Leith Enterprise Trust

WALES

Action Resource Centre
Merthyr Agency for the
Development of
Enterprise

AEUW
Deeside Enterprise
Trust Ltd
Llanelli Enterprise Co

Alyn & Deeside District Council
Deeside Enterprise
Trust Ltd

Laura Ashley PLC
Powys Self Help

Assoc. British Ports Authority
Cardiff & Vale
Enterprise
Newport Enterprise
Agency

Avon Inflatables
Llanelli Enterprise Co

W H Baker
Merthyr Tydfil Enter-
prise Co

Barclays Bank
Cardiff & Vale
Enterprise
Llanelli Enterprise Co
Merthyr Tydfil Enter-
prise Centre
Newport Enterprise
Agency
Pembrokeshire Business
Initiative

Baverstocks
Merthyr Tydfil Enter-
prise Centre

Berlei (UK) Ltd
Made, Merthyr Agency
for the Development of
Enterprise

Boskalis Westminster
Deeside Enterprise
Trust Ltd

British Alcan Sheet
Newport Enterprise
Agency

British Nuclear Fuels
Deeside Enterprise
Trust Limited

BP
Neath Partnership

British Steel Industry
Cardiff & Vale
Enterprise
Deeside Enterprise Trust
Ltd
Llanelli Enterprise Co
Newport Enterprise
Agency
Merthyr Tydfil Enter-
prise Centre

Buckleys Brewery
Llanelli Enterprise Co

Business in the Community
Merthyr Tydfil
Enterprise Centre
Pembrokeshire
Business Initiatives

Capital Trading (Coated Steels)
Cardiff & Vale
Enterprise

Cardiff Chamber of Commerce & Industry
Cardiff & Vale
Enterprise

Cardiff City Council
Cardiff & Vale
Enterprise

Celtic Press
Merthyr Tydfil Enter-
prise Centre

CEGB
Llanelli Enterprise Co
Newport Enterprise
Agency

Chester & N Wales Chamber of Commerce
Deeside Enterprise
Trust Ltd

Clwyd County Council
Deeside Enterprise
Trust Ltd

Community Projects Foundation
Newport Enterprise
Agency

Coopers & Lybrand
Cardiff & Vale
Enterprise

Courtaulds
Deeside Enterprise
Trust Ltd

Davis Lloyds
Newport Enterprise
Agency

Dee Bee Limited
Newport Enterprise
Agency

Deloitte Haskins & Sells
Cardiff & Vale
Enterprise
Cardiff & Vale Enterprise
Llanelli Enterprise Co
Glasgow Opportunities
Newport Enterprise
Agency

Delta Oilfield Cables
Llanelli Enterprise Co

Dyfed County Council
Antur Teifi
Llanelli Enterprise Co
Pembrokeshire Business
Initiatives

**Dyfed Sludge Disposal
Co**
Pembrokeshire Business
Initiatives

EGA
Deeside Enterprise
Trust Ltd

Esso Petroleum Co
Pembrokeshire
Business Initiatives

Evans & Williams
Pembrokeshire
Business Initiatives

Fibreglass
Deeside Enterprise
Trust
Newport Enterprise
Agency

Govan Davies Group
Pembrokeshire
Business Initiative

Gravells
Llanelli Enterprise Co

Green Bower Garages
Pembrokeshire
Business Initiatives

Hoover
Merthyr Tydfil
Enterprise Centre

Hydralift (Wales)
Pembrokeshire
Business Initiative

IMI Stanton
Newport Enterprise
Agency

**Iron & Steel Trades
Confederation**
Deeside Enterprise
Trust Ltd

Alfred S John & Co
Made, Merthyr Agency
for the Development of
Enterprise

JOP Construction
Pembrokeshire
Business Initiative

Legal & General
Cardiff & Vale
Enterprise

**Llanelli Borough
Council**
Llanelli Enterprise Co

Llanelli Radiators
Llanelli Enterprise Co

Lloyds Bank
Cardiff & Vale
Enterprise
Llanelli Enterprise Co
Merthyr Tydfil
Enterprise Centre
Newport Enterprise
Agency
Pembrokeshire
Business Initiative

David Lord-Phillips
Pembrokeshire
Business Initiative

**Manpower Services
Commission**
Industrial Resource
Centre

Mansel Davies & Son
Pembrokeshire
Business Initiative

Marks & Spencers
Cardiff & Vale
Enterprise
Llanelli Enterprise Co

Memory Lane Cakes
Cardiff & Vale
Enterprise

**Merthyr Tydfil Borough
Council**
Merthyr Tydfil
Enterprise Centre

Metal Box
Neath Partnership

**Mid-Glam County
Council**
Merthyr Tydfil
Enterprise Centre
Mid Glamorgan County
Council Industrial
Development and
Promotion Unit
Industrial Resource
Centre

Midland Bank
Cardiff & Vale
Enterprise
Llanelli Enterprise Co
Rossendale Enterprise
Trust
Powys Self Help

Monsanto
Newport Enterprise
Agency

**Montgomery District
Council**
Powys Self Help

National Coal Board
Llanelli Enterprise Co

National Farmers Union
Pembrokeshire
Business Initiative

**National Westminster
Bank**
Cardiff & Vale
Enterprise
Deeside Enterprise Trust
Ltd
Llanelli Enterprise Co
Merthyr Tydfil
Enterprise Centre
Newport Enterprise
Agency

Neath Borough Council
Neath Partnership

**Newport Borough
Council**
Newport Enterprise
Agency

**North Wales
Newspapers**
Deeside Enterprise Trust

Norwest Holt
Deeside Enterprise
Trust Ltd

Owens
 Llanelli Enterprise
 Company

Polytechnic of Wales
 Merthyr Tydfil
 Enterprise Centre

**Powell Duffryn
Quarries Ltd**
 Made, Merthyr Agency
 for the Development of
 Enterprise

Powys County Council
 Powys Self Help

Preseli District Council
 Pembrokeshire
 Business Initiative

**Pressed Steel Fisher/
ARG**
 Llanelli Enterprise Co

**Project Management
(Wales)
and Eurocast Interna-
tional Foundries**
 Cardiff & Vale
 Enterprise

Protern
 Cardiff & Vale
 Enterprise

Radnor District Council
 Powys Self Help

Redifussion
 Merthyr Tydfil
 Enterprise Centre

Riverlea Tractors
 Pembrokeshire
 Business Initiatives

Simbec Research Ltd
 Made, Merthyr Agency
 for the Development of
 Enterprise

**S E Wales Co-op
Development
Agency**
 Cardiff & Vale
 Enterprise

**South Glam County
 Council**
 Cardiff & Vale
 Enterprise Industrial
 Research Centre

**South Pembrokeshire
District Council**
 Pembrokeshire Business
 Initiative

South Wales Argus
 Newport Enterprise
 Agency

St David's Assemblies
 Pembrokeshire
 Business Initiative

**St John's Community
Programme Agency**
 Made, Merthyr Agency
 for the Development of
 Enterprise

Stephens & George
 Merthyr Tydfil
 Enterprise Centre

Swansea City Council
 Swansea Centre for
 Trade & Industry

Taylor Bros (Engineers)
 Newport Enterprise
 Agency

Taylor Woodrow
 Merthyr Tydfil
 Enterprise Centre

Texaco
 Llanelli Enterprise Co

TGWU
 Deeside Enterprise
 Trust Ltd

D G Thomas & Sons
 Pembrokeshire
 Business Initiative

Thomson International
 Neath Partnership

Triumph Bus Systems
 Merthyr Tydfil
 Enterprise Centre

Thyssen (GB)
 Llanelli Enterprise Co

**Vale of Glam Borough
Council**
 Cardiff & Vale
 Enterprise

Vine Chemicals (RTZ)
 Llanelli Enterprise Co

Vulcan Material Co
 Llanelli Enterprise Co

**Welsh Development
Agency**
 Deeside Enterprise
 Trust Limited
 Pembrokeshire
 Business Initiative
 Neath Development
 Partnership

Welsh Office
 Cardiff & Vale
 Enterprise
 Merthyr Tydfil
 Enterprise Co
 Newport Enterprise
 Agency
 Antur Teifi
 Industrial Resource
 Centre

Welsh Products
 Merthyr Tydfil
 Enterprise Co

Western Fuels
 Made, Merthyr Agency
 for the Development of
 Enterprise

**West Glam County
Council**
 Industrial Resource
 Centre

Whitbread Wales
 Cardiff & Vale
 Enterprise

NORTHERN
IRELAND

Bank of Ireland
 Action Resource Centre
 NW Ulster Enterprise
 Agency

Bass Ireland
 Action Resource Centre

Belfast City Council
 Belfast Development
 Agency

British Enkalon
Action Resource Centre

Carrickfergus Borough Council
Enterprise Carrickfergus

Dept of Economic Development
North Down Development Ltd

Fermanagh District Council
Fermanagh Enterprise Organisation

IBM
Action Resource Centre

ICI
Enterprise Carrickfergus

LEDU
Fermanagh Enterprise Organisation

Lisburn Borough Council
Lisburn Economic Development Organisation

Local Enterprise Development Unit
Enterprise Carrickfergus
Action Resource Centre
North Down Development Unit

North Down Borough Council
North Down Development Ltd

N I Voluntary Trust
Action Resource Centre
NW Ulster Enterprise Agency

Radio Rentals
Action Resource Centre

Joseph Rowntree Memorial
Action Resource Centre

Shell (UK)
Action Resource Centre

Standard Telephone Cables
Action Resource Centre

Ulster Bank
Action Resource Centre

GENERAL INDEX

Y